DATE DUE

			PRINTED IN U.S.A.

INTRODUCTION
to
INDEXING and ABSTRACTING

INTRODUCTION
to
INDEXING and ABSTRACTING
Second Edition

Donald B. Cleveland	Ana D. Cleveland
Professor School of Library and Information Sciences University of North Texas Denton, Texas	Associate Professor School of Library and Information Sciences University of North Texas Denton, Texas

1990
LIBRARIES UNLIMITED, INC.
Englewood, Colorado

LIBRARIES UNLIMITED, INC.
P.O. Box 3988
Englewood, CO 80155-3988

Library of Congress Cataloging-in-Publication Data

Cleveland, Donald B., 1935-
    Introduction to indexing and abstracting / Donald B. Cleveland,
Ana D. Cleveland. -- 2nd ed.
    xiii, 329 p. 17x25 cm.
    Includes bibliographical references.
    ISBN 0-87287-677-2
    1. Indexing. 2. Abstracting.   I. Cleveland, Ana D., 1943- .
II. Title.
Z695.9.C592 1990
025.3--dc20
                                         90-34493
                                             CIP

Dedication

This text is dedicated to Dr. William Goffman, professor, mentor, and friend. You have been a guiding light to us, both professionally and personally. Thanks for the quality of thinking that you demanded of us and, more importantly, for the friendship.

Table of Contents

Preface

This is a revised edition of an introductory text that has successfully provided guidance for both the student and the practitioner on the fundamentals of indexing and abstracting. The authors are grateful to the many instructors who have adopted this book as a textbook. Also, we appreciate the comments and suggestions we have received. We hope those suggestions are reflected in this revised version.

In this new edition, all chapters have been rewritten, with the exception of chapter X (an example of how to index and abstract a document), which received such praise from instructors, students, and critics in the first edition that we decided not to touch it.

Sections have been added on indexing for online services, computer-aided indexing, and the development of expert systems for indexing and abstracting. There are enlarged discussions on string indexing and career preparation and opportunities. More examples of indexes, abstracting services, and thesauri have been added, including almost sixty new illustrations of indexes, abstracts, and thesauri.

An extensive bibliography has been compiled that covers both recent and retrospective materials for several decades. The purpose of the bibliography is to provide a comprehensive, quality reading list that is both current and historical. Since this text is an introduction to the field, both recent references and classic papers serve a vital purpose. There is a substantial literature on the subject, and this new bibliography represents some of the best work done in the field over the years.

Related to the general bibliography are the suggested readings at the end of each chapter. The suggested readings do not necessarily reflect exact citations from the chapter text. Rather, the purpose of the reading list is to suggest items related to the discussions in each chapter. We hope readers will not limit their readings to the references included.

And, finally, the authors would like to express appreciation to librarian Jimmie Lyn Harris for the professional and courteous help she gave in obtaining material for this book.

I
Introduction

PURPOSE

Society's need for timely, well-constructed indexes, abstracts, digests, and reviews of the literature remains a critical concern. And the need for alert, well-trained indexers is critical as well.

Although online database searching has revolutionized the information retrieval field, finding a list of computer records in nanoseconds is not the key point. What *is* important is the information in those records, and the validity and completeness of that information still relies heavily on the expertise of human indexers and abstractors. Thus, the purpose of this text is to present the fundamentals of indexing and abstracting as a foundation for entry-level professional practice. This book is designed for use in an introductory course that includes a considerable amount of actual practice in indexing and abstracting in a supervised laboratory environment.

Although there is a growing body of research on the basic problems and theoretical concepts of indexing and abstracting, no formal theories exist, and these two professional activities remain much more an art than a science. The literature in the field represents a large and very valuable body of experiential knowledge based on empirical and practical reflections, resulting in a variety of ideas and viewpoints. The authors of this text have tried to represent the major viewpoints with an emphasis on what they perceive to be the general consensus of ideas among educators and practitioners in this key area of librarianship and information science.

This book is structured to introduce the neophyte indexer and abstractor progressively to the basic principles needed to take the first step toward becoming a professional in the field. The discussions begin with the basic concepts of information and its bibliographic control, then move through the methods of indexing and abstracting (with an emphasis on the how-to-do-it), and conclude with a section on the professional aspects of indexing and abstracting. Throughout this revised edition are references to the application of computers, since this is an integral part of our professional activity.

This book does not attempt to be a definitive and comprehensive coverage of the field of indexing and abstracting. Such a presumptuous coverage would be a multivolume work and would not serve as an introductory text.

1

RELATED BOOKS

Although indexing and abstracting can be traced back to the beginning of librarianship—they, in fact, have an interesting and admirable history—they have not been given as much attention as cataloging and classification. As a result, indexing and abstracting concepts and methodologies are not nearly as structured as cataloging, nor have as many books been written on the topic. It might be appropriate to mention briefly a few of the better-known, related titles to alert the student to their usefulness and to indicate how the present text complements these books.

A classic in indexing was published in 1878 by the newly formed Index Society of London. *What Is an Index?* was written by Henry Wheatley, who was the first secretary of the society. This book is historically important for several reasons: it describes the history of indexing and contains the ideas of early scholars on indexing; it lists rules for indexing, including compilation, formatting, and printing; and it contains an excellent compendium of early indexes.

More recently, in 1975 and 1976, Alan G. Brown published a two-volume, programmed text on subject analysis. Volume I was entitled *Introduction to Subject Indexing: A Programmed Text. Subject Analysis and Practical Classification*, and volume II was entitled: *Introduction to Subject Indexing: A Programmed Text. UDC and Chain Procedure in Subject Cataloguing*. Both volumes, while having the typical shortcomings of programmed texts, present clearly the basic concepts of subject analysis in a practical way. Although the volumes focus on application, they still manage to lay a theoretical foundation. These books are not directed toward indexing and abstracting *per se*, but their introduction to the problems of subject analysis and subject indexing is useful. They also have an index, which is rather unusual for a programmed text.

In 1975 Harold Borko and Charles Bernier coauthored *Abstracting Concepts and Methods*. This is a good, general approach to abstracting, with especially strong examples on the publication aspects of abstracting. It consists of three parts: (1) an introduction to what an abstract is, giving the neophyte an overview of uses, history, and a general description of criteria, standards, and instructions; (2) abstracting procedures, describing content of abstracts, format, editing and publishing; and (3) problems in management, automation, and personnel.

In 1978 Borko and Bernier coauthored a companion volume entitled *Indexing Concepts and Methods*. This is a well-written introduction to indexing, and it is also recommended. The primary drawback with this book is that it leaves an impression that indexing is concerned only with scientific literature.

In 1979 a book by G. Norman Knight appeared called *Indexing, the Art of: A Guide to the Indexing of Books and Periodicals*. The work of a real professional, its humanities tone complements the Borko and Bernier book.

Also in 1979, Eugene Garfield published *Citation Indexing—Its Theory and Application in Science, Technology and Humanities*. Although this book is written by the leading advocate and practitioner of citation indexing, its importance lies not so much in the discussion of citation indexing as in its extensive coverage of citation analysis. It particularly underscores the practical applications of citation analysis for managers and for makers of science policy.

Abstracting and Indexing by Jennifer E. Rowley is a brief, concise, introduction to indexing and abstracting. While it concentrates primarily on document analysis, it is useful in defining the basic terms and notions of the field.

A useful collection of writings, *Indexing Specialized Formats and Subjects*, was published by Hilda Feinberg in 1983. While the individual articles deal with specialized formats and subjects, the real strengths in this work are the excellent discussions of indexing in general, which are embedded in the various articles. Especially noteworthy are James D. Anderson's "Essential Decisions in Indexing Systems Design," Barbara E. Anderson's "Database Indexing," and David F. Mayhew's "Indexing the Biomedical Literature."

Finally, Timothy C. Craven, in 1986, published a needed specialty volume entitled *String Indexing*. The book leans toward general principles and features, but there are some very useful examples of actual string indexing systems.

Introduction to Indexing and Abstracting differs from other books on the topic by focusing on what indexers and abstractors do and how they go about it and by presenting principles and practice as one and the same thing. In the latter case, if theory and practice are radically different, then one or the other is wrong. As for focusing on what indexers and abstractors do, most of the recent titles in the field are full of valuable information. But it is unlikely that a student would finish any one of these books with a fundamental idea of how to actually index or abstract. The present text attempts to show as well as tell—a primary goal for any basic textbook. Chapter X is entirely an example of *one way* to index and abstract a document, and its purpose is to give confidence to the student by showing that this can be done in a procedural way.

HISTORICAL BACKGROUND

Indexing and abstracting were not "invented," but they evolved in a somewhat natural way. No doubt attempts to organize knowledge have a historical continuum that stretches as far back as the written record. Early on, scholars, businesspeople, government workers, religious officials, and other literate citizens recognized the need to organize the written records they were creating on a daily basis. From time to time these early people proposed systems of knowledge classification and document arrangement schemes and called upon many intellectual areas, such as philosophy, logic, psychology, and mathematics, to support their proposals.

Formal attempts at bibliographic management on a meaningful scale can be traced back at least as far as the scholar/bibliographers of the Alexandrian library founded by the Ptolemies some two centuries before Christ. These scholars understood that large books could give access problems, so they developed the custom of abstracting these books. In the third century B.C., Greek poet and scholar Callimachus made a list as a guide to information in the thousands of papyrus rolls in the Alexandrian library. In fact, it has turned out that many of the abstracts of classical times survived while the original source did not; thus the abstracts are often the only source the scholar has had.

During the same period, the practice of abstracting the plots of plays and inserting them before the script developed. These abstracts were called *hypotheses* in Greek, and they appeared at the beginning of each play (sometimes in verse) along with a list of characters.

Abstracts were not used for scholarly works alone. In the third century B.C., business records of all kinds were accompanied by abstracts of their contents. Again, modern scholars have found these early content guides to be paramount in reconstructing the everyday social and economic events of these early civilizations.

Early on, works of nonfiction began to have chapter heads or summaries, which, in a sense, were short-cuts or indexes to the content following. A good example of this was the Bible of early centuries. The familiar Bible indexes and concordances we know were to come much later. Indexing in its modern form did not evolve until the concept of alphabetizing was developed. According to Witty (1976), "although we have in Graeco-Roman times the use of alphabetic order and the employment of the capitulatio or placing of summaries at the beginning of certain non-fiction works, we do not ... have anything like an alphabetic index to a work before the Middle Ages." As a matter of fact, alphabetical indexing doesn't even show up in the Vatican archives before the fourteenth century.

There were exceptions, of course. Around 900 A.D. at least one encyclopedia was arranged in alphabetical order, but most such works had a classified arrangement. Even after true indexes began to develop, they were usually quite lengthy and in a rather crude form. Early Latin indexes were almost always arranged by simply grouping entries under the letters but with no particular order within the letters. This practice didn't fade away completely until the seventeenth century.

In the late twelfth century and afterwards, there came a new interest in scholarship and with it a natural need of scholars for indexes. The universities of Europe began to emerge as strong social institutions with a vigorous interest in law, theology, and, later, natural science. One of the characteristics of these institutions was the development of debate as a technique for intellectual discourse. With this, of course, came a need to find and refer to written authority; thus, a need for alphabetical indexing arose quite naturally.

The indexes of the fourteenth century were extremely simple in their makeup and were not particularly easy to read. The texts of works themselves were usually done with care, but the indexes left something to be desired. Although the alphabetic listing of chapter headings and theses represented some progress, it would seem that our own concept of indexing lay some distance in the future. If we examine incunabula, we are forced to conclude that indexing was still not a very common practice, even after the invention of printing had made the notion of an index much more feasible and practical. In the front of the work was the index, taken verbatim from the text and sometimes not entered under what would seem to be the proper keyword. Chief among the forms of annotation developed by the time of the invention of printing were annotation of manuscripts, library catalogs, and bibliographies.

Early books frequently contained blank pages at the beginning and end and had quite wide margins. On these blank spaces readers wrote or noted the subjects of importance contained in the volume so that they could readily find those subjects again. Lawyers, for example, filled in the back blank pages with extensive alphabetical lists of those statutes in which they were principally interested. Clerics used the blank pages in their Bibles to write in references to scriptures.

So indexes are at least as old as published writing and have existed in virtually every language. The early indexes were limited to personal names or were indexes to the occurrence of words in the text indexed; that is, they were concordances rather than topical subject indexes. They evolved from monographic indexes, through cumulative indexes, and finally to collective indexes. Until the eighteenth century, indexes to books were prepared primarily by their authors, but that century saw the advent of the professional indexer. Thereafter, indexes to books and to periodicals became fairly common, but it was not until the nineteenth century that attempts were made to compile indexes to cover entire fields of knowledge, including, of course, the journal literature.

Scholarly journals had been an important influence in society for several centuries. In fact, such journals played a primary role in the emergence of modern science. In the middle of the seventeenth century scientists sought ways to rapidly disseminate reports on their work. At first, these journals were primarily news media and brief abstracts and reviews, rather than journals that reported primary research. Gradually, the journals began to publish original papers. Probably these early works were papers that had been presented at professional meetings, but soon papers were being written directly for publication in the journals. With the rapid growth of journals, subject access became necessary.

Subject indexes to books and journals are found more frequently beginning with eighteenth-century literature, but the choice of terms, and even the order of entries in the index, remained haphazard for a long time. It was not until the late nineteenth century, with the development of taxonomy in library work and documentation, that subject indexing became not only widespread but also more systematic. The human instinct to make a guide to information has always been very strong, with guides to individual books starting early. Chapter headings are as old as books themselves, and content lists were introduced early. The need for indexes came to the fore once the English Bible was made available to ordinary people. Then, the printing machinery in the nineteenth century increased the need for indexes. At this time the initiative for compiling serviceable indexes seems to have passed to the United States, where the next important developments took place. Instead of an index to one periodical for one year, W. F. Poole put into practice the idea of a single publication indexing numerous issues of many periodicals.

H. W. Wilson started *Readers' Guide to Periodical Literature* in 1900, which was especially notable for the emphasis it placed on subject access and good cross-references. Here each article in a periodical was indexed under its author and its specific subject. There were numerous cross-references to link up each subject with related subjects and with aspects of itself.

Librarians did not become truly involved in periodical indexes until the need for such indexes was taken up at the first meeting of the American Library Association (ALA) in 1876. This discussion led to a cooperative effort among libraries, which resulted in the publication of the *Index to Periodical Literature* in 1882.

Also, at the end of the nineteenth century, indexing had a major boost when scholars began to express the need for improved bibliographic access to their literature. In 1892 Paul Otlet and Henri La Fontaine founded the International Institute of Bibliography to address, among other things, the problem of specific access to recorded knowledge. Historically, subject access had been predominately through classification schemes, and users complained that such systems provided generic access (e.g., groups of books on a subject) but not specific information or data. Title-word indexing was proposed, which eventually led to modern keyword and free-text indexing.

Parallel with the development of the learned journal was the development of the abstract journal. In January 1665 the first published abstract journal was issued, called the *Journal des Scavans*. Approximately half of each page was devoted to a single item, usually a new book, along with details of its author, title, and place of publication. With such a journal in hand, scholars could feel they had a chance to keep up to date with intellectual developments. We had begun to do something to make information in written records more accessible, either by arranging the important features in a known order, or by condensing long documents into convenient abstracts or epitomes.

By the 1700s other abstracting journals began to appear. For example, in 1703 the German abstract journal *Monatsextracte* started publication in Leipzig. During the eighteenth century this type of publication was begun in England and France as well. Many of these were similar to the *Journal des Scavans* in format and purpose. They served as a basic method of intellectual exchange among the diverse and scattered peoples of Europe.

The abstract journal began to proliferate in the nineteenth century, with a trend toward the development of specialized publications. Already the growth of the primary journal had people concerned about the so-called information explosion. In the *American Eclectic* for September 1841, a German writer protested against the increasing number of scientific periodicals in Germany:

> Of medical journals, there are forty-three in Germany. It must be granted that different modes of practice require different periodicals ... but forty-three journals are an astonishing number. What physician who practices daily can read them all, and to what physician who does not practice can they be useful?

This common problem of the scholar led to the growth and development of the abstract journal in the nineteenth century.

Meanwhile, book indexing continued to improve. Skill in indexing increased with the experience gained over the years. Until the twentieth century, the most widely used subject index consisted of a list of terms with no subdivisions or with subdivisions in a simple hierarchical structure of two or three levels (main heading and modifier or main heading, subheading, and modifier), with the terms or phrases at each level usually arranged in alphabetical order. The presence of an index in a book was generally taken for granted, its absence generally ignored, its quality rarely the subject of comment by publishers, critics, or readers. Indexing was done, if at all, by any available personnel, often clerks without training or skill.

A change in the attitude of publishers, librarians, and information users came about as a result of the "information explosion" during and immediately following World War II. Suddenly the dramatic increase in the amount of information being processed and disseminated, coupled with the dramatic decrease in the time allowed for processing and disseminating the information, caused a vast concentration of effort and attention to be given to the humble practice of indexing. Techniques were developed for indexing more quickly, consistently, and thoroughly. Machines were used to produce, sort, and search index cards, and even to create entire indexes. Systems were created for printing and distributing indexes faster and more widely.

In the 1950s computers had entered the indexing and abstracting arena and efforts were begun to evaluate indexing using quantitative methods. Hans Peter Luhn of IBM introduced a mechanized form of derived title-words indexing schemes where ambiguity could be reduced by showing terms in the context of their occurrence. These indexes were called KWIC indexes. About the same time, serious testing of the effectiveness of indexing techniques began, and the profession became a battleground for competing philosophies, methods, and techniques for indexing.

The emerging field of information science attracted practitioners from disciplines where experimental, quantitative approaches are basic, and such techniques were applied to information retrieval processes, including indexing. Historically, the Cranfield Project is the most famous. There were two stages to this investigation, the first beginning in 1957 and the second beginning in 1963, both under the direction of C. W. Cleverdon. Although this project has sparked criticism, it is a landmark in indexing evaluation. The project made a comparison of four index languages using a large database and some 1,200 searching subjects. It was the first significant use of the recall and precision measures to evaluate the performance of indexing languages. One of the major values of the Cranfield Project was the development of techniques for the quantitative evaluation of indexing.

On October 4, 1957 the Russians sent up Sputnik and inaugurated the space age. Indirectly, this created a boon for indexing in the 1960s. Sputnik created a frantic concern over the technological abilities of the United States, commissions were appointed, and we went into a crash program to close the perceived technological gap between the United States and the Soviet Union.

Scientific and technological information was given a high priority and the interest in the problem on the part of the government and the scientific community reached an unprecedented level, bringing a flow of money for research and development. Many of the current ideas and applications in indexing, abstracting, and information retrieval in general have as an antecedent the groundwork laid in the 1960s.

In the twentieth century, indexing has outstripped the ideas of previous ages. We have progressed from indexes to individual works, through indexes to several volumes, to cooperative indexes on an international scale. There are at present international indexes to books and periodicals on international affairs, forestry, education, and many other subjects. Total world literature is far from being adequately indexed and abstracted. But we have come a long way.

DEFINITIONS

A final note: Most of the chapters in this text will introduce new terms, which represent the key topics in those particular chapters. Definitions play a vital role in the study of a new subject area, and readers must understand and remember these definitions to properly benefit from what follows. An extensive glossary of basic terms is included as an appendix, and it is suggested that after completing each chapter readers use the list and reexamine the formal definitions in light of the discussion.

SUGGESTED READINGS

Besterman, Theodore. *The Beginnings of Systematic Bibliography.* 2nd ed. London: Oxford University Press, 1936.

Borko, Harold, and Charles L. Bernier. *Abstracting Concepts and Methods.* New York: Academic Press, 1975.

_____. *Indexing Concepts and Methods.* New York: Academic Press, 1978.

Brown, Alan George. *Introduction to Subject Indexing: A Programmed Text. Volume I: Subject Analysis and Practical Classification.* London: Clive Bingley, 1975.

_____. *Introduction to Subject Indexing: A Programmed Text. Volume II: UDC and Chain Procedure in Subject Cataloguing.* London: Clive Bingley, 1976.

Craven, Timothy C. *String Indexing.* Orlando, Fla.: Academic Press, 1986.

Feinberg, Hilda, ed. *Indexing Specialized Formats and Subjects.* Metuchen, N.J.: Scarecrow Press, 1983.

Garfield, Eugene. *Citation Indexing—Its Theory and Application in Science, Technology, and Humanities.* New York: Wiley, 1979.

Jackson, E. B. "Indexing: A Review Essay." *Journal of Library History* 15 (1980): 320-25.

Knight, G. Norman. *Indexing, the Art of: A Guide to the Indexing of Books and Periodicals.* London: George Allen and Unwin, 1979.

Roberts, N. "The Prehistory of the Information Retrieval Thesaurus." *Journal of Documentation* 40 (1984): 271-85.

Rowley, Jennifer E. *Abstracting and Indexing.* 2nd ed. London: Bingley, 1988.

Wheatley, Henry. *What Is an Index? A Few Notes on Index and Indexers.* 2nd ed. London: Society of Indexers, 1879.

Witty, Francis J. "The Beginnings of Indexing and Abstracting: Some Notes toward a History of Indexing and Abstracting in Antiquity and the Middle Ages." *The Indexer* 8 (1973): 193-98.

II
The Nature of Information

INTRODUCTION

At the heart of all efforts in communication, information science, and librarianship is a natural phenomenon called information. This is the basic, theoretical concept that determines, or should determine, all operational processes from archives to communication satellites.

In a sense, information exists in a human mind only, because records are merely symbols that represent what has been previously input into that mind and subsequently processed. However, these organized symbols may be thought of as marvelous adjuncts to the human mind for storing and transmitting information. These symbols are external storage for the mind.

This chapter is a general overview of the nature of information and the role that indexing and abstracting play in the process of information transfer.

WHAT IS INFORMATION?

We are being told, rather frequently, that this is the age of information. Librarians are only one part of a large group of professionals who produce and disseminate information.

Information processing is an integral part of every activity that humans undertake, from passing genes to posterity, to telling a joke, to smelling a rose, to building a bridge. Humankind took a first giant leap forward by creating language and a second giant leap by devising a way to record thoughts so that information could be transferred over time and distance to fellow human beings.

What *is* information? Strictly speaking, like gravity or electricity, it cannot be absolutely described, explained, or understood; but its properties and effects can be observed, enabling us to improve our communication systems. A consensus of absolute definition is not particularly necessary for understanding and is not always a critical point, even in the hard sciences. What is gravity? Or electricity? There are formulas describing the *behavior* of electricity, and on this alone we have built elaborate applications such as television and computing machines. We may not be able to define electricity, but if we wet our fingers and stick them into an electric socket, then we will surely be able to describe the *properties* of electricity.

The story is told about Lord Kelvin, the famous nineteenth-century physicist, noted for his work in electricity and dynamos. He was being escorted on a group tour of a new, modern generating plant that was utilizing his revolutionary methods. The guide, not knowing who the scientist was, expounded on the marvels of the whirling dynamos, and rising to oratorical heights he proclaimed the wonders of electricity. When he paused, the famous physicist asked a simple question: "Yes, my good man, but just what *is* electricity?" In the long silence that followed, only the quiet hum of the generators could be heard.

It is likewise difficult to answer the question "What is information?" although we know it is an indispensable aspect of modern society. Every facet of our lives, both incidental and major, is related to information. From the moment we wake in the morning until we flip off the late, late show in the evening, we face hundreds of situations requiring information for guidance, or even survival. A simple information machine (a clock) awakes us in the morning. While we blunder through our first cup of coffee, we read the paper to see if the world is still in one piece. We listen to the radio for the weather to see if we will need an umbrella (information!). Some of us, as we eat our cereal, read the box to see how many kinds of carcinogens we may be ingesting. On the way out, we stuff the grocery list into our pocket — another information retrieval system. On the way to work a red light (which is an information device pure and simple) allows us to arrive without being hit by an eighteen-wheeler. And so on, throughout the day.

The Evolution of Mechanisms for Information Preservation and Transmittal

Information was the key to the socialization of humanity. The development of language was followed by writing. Think what a marvelous thing happened when humans learned to record their thoughts with marks on a stone so that others, not just their contemporaries but their descendants thousands of years later, could see and understand them. What we now take as ordinary is in reality very extraordinary.

As society evolved, so did formal mechanisms for information preservation and transmittal. Libraries, educational systems, societies of scholars and professionals all date back into antiquity, and all had as a primary objective to preserve and transmit information and knowledge from generation to generation. All of these mechanisms had a common approach: to gather information and store it in a warm and dry place until someone expressed a desire for a particular record, at which time the record of interest was retrieved. It is a simple but powerful idea.

For centuries the traditional library as we know it carried out this idea without serious difficulty, but in the 1940s we entered an age of information proliferation or, as some now say, information pollution, which put a critical strain on the traditional mechanisms. We developed into a society of specialists with everybody taking a little tidbit of knowledge, becoming an expert, and demanding in-depth analysis of the information recorded. General pointers to information stores were no longer sufficient. We were not satisfied to have millions of documents; we needed rapid, effective analysis of the informational contents of those documents. We became impatient with traditional library techniques.

Paralleling this shift in informational needs was a technological change. We developed microform technology, data communication devices, television, computing machines, and reproduction devices. The documentation movement spread to this country from Europe, and here it attempted to wed the new information technology with our traditional library approaches. Being a people susceptible to gadgetry, we lived for a while with an innocent dream, believing that all we needed was a readable microform device and larger, faster computers. Now we have very large and unbelievably fast computing machines, but we still have problems in information handling. In many instances we found that computers simply allowed us to make the same old mistakes at an incredible speed. Why? Because there are deep intellectual complexities involved that we are only beginning to understand and appreciate—problems concerning users and their *individual* needs, the realization that the relevance of a particular document is the judgment of a single individual, not a universal constant. It is no longer acceptable to build systems geared to a mythical "average" user who has never existed and never will. There are problems concerning indexing, classification, and searching techniques. How do scientists look for information? How do non-scientists search? Slowly, we are realizing that an information system is concerned with more than just documents and their contents—very much involved is human behavior.

A National Resource

For many centuries now most enlightened people have believed that the pen is mightier than the sword, but in our time we have come to realize that the preservation and transmittal of what the pen has written is a key to both power and progress. Increasingly information is being viewed as a new, basic resource. Politicians, business managers, college presidents, and even the person on the street talk about the need for information, and they often expend considerable amounts of time and resources in information gathering. Many of these people have little understanding of what information is or how it is transferred, but they recognize its importance. The secret of the advent of the information age lies in the accumulation of information, and technological advances have increased many times over our capacity to accumulate and process information.

Information and knowledge are two closely related concepts that are neither simple nor precise. Like information, the term *knowledge* is intuitively understood, but it is such a fundamental phenomenon that it lacks a precise definition. Determining what knowledge is and how it is communicated has troubled thinkers since the beginning of reflective inquiry. It is a concept, a state, a phenomenon that cannot be precisely defined or measured, but still it remains a focal point of intellectual concern.

This much we do know—knowledge, which is closely related to information, is a vast national resource. The so-called knowledge and information industry in the United States makes up a sizeable proportion of the gross national product and ranges across such enterprises as advertising, book and magazine publishing, computers, education, government activities, research, business, libraries, and radio and TV broadcasting, just to name a few.

Electronic computers ushered in the information age, and there appears to be no limit to the information revolution we are experiencing. Almost unnoticed we evolved from an industrial society to a white-collar society, a great part of which is engaged in creating, processing, and distributing information. According to John Naisbitt, in his popular book *Megatrends*:

> The real increase [in service jobs] has been in information occupations. In 1950, only about 17 percent of us worked in information jobs. Now more than 65 percent of us work with information as programmers, teachers, clerks, secretaries, accountants, stock brokers, managers, insurance people, bureaucrats, lawyers, bankers, and technicians. And many more workers hold information jobs within manufacturing companies. Most Americans spend their time creating, processing, or distributing information (Naisbitt 1984, 8-9).

Later Naisbitt points out that almost all professional workers are information workers—lawyers, teachers, engineers, computer programmers, systems analyst, doctors, architects, accountants, librarians, newspaper reporters, social workers, nurses, and clergy.

If capital was the strategic resource for an industrial society, then surely information is the strategic resource for an information society. Again quoting Naisbitt:

> The five most important things to remember about the shift from an industrial to an information society are:
>
> - The information society is an economic reality, not an intellectual abstraction.
>
> - Innovations in communications and computer technology will accelerate the pace of change by collapsing the *information float* [reducing the time lapse between sender and receiver in a communication process].
>
> - New information technologies will at first be applied to old industrial tasks, then, gradually give birth to new activities, processes, and products.
>
> - In this literacy-intensive society, when we need basic reading and writing skills more than ever before, our education system is turning out an increasingly inferior product.
>
> - The technology of the new information age is not absolute. It will succeed or fail according to the principle of high tech/high touch (Naisbitt 1984, 11).

Information is like any other economic resource: It costs money to produce it and people will pay money for it.

Much of the information generated by the knowledge industry, good or bad, will be preserved for posterity, and the burden of retrieval falls on the professional information handlers. Thus, adequate systems of indexing and abstracting become even more crucial.

The Information Cycle

One of the primary attributes of the information phenomenon, both in scientific and nonscientific activity, is the dependency factor. Information builds on previous information. Very few people have an absolutely original and totally creative thought. Information creation and distribution form a distinct, repetitive pattern known as the information cycle, illustrated in figure 1. Collection, bibliographic control, storage, and retrieval of an exponentially growing corpus of knowledge records become more critical as society becomes more dependent on information and demands more and more from its information systems.

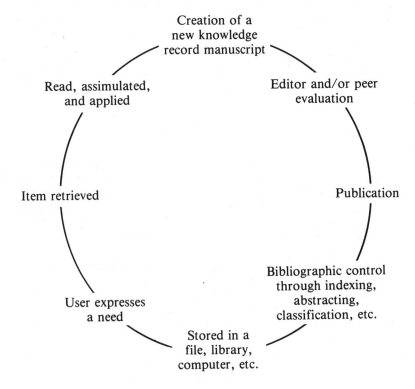

Fig. 1. The information cycle.

A glance at the illustration will show that the information specialist is directly involved in at least four of the eight activities, namely, in bibliographic control, storage, user queries, and the retrieval of the item. Of these four points we keep coming back to the one of bibliographic control. The increasingly critical question is: How do we efficiently and effectively get at the information being generated at an accelerating rate?

People who rely on information as a fundamental part of their professional activities have three basic levels of need. First, they need information related to the subject area in which they were trained. They need to know of advances and changes in their discipline, whether it be chemistry or accounting. Second, they need information related to their organization's particular goals and missions at a given point in time. Third, since they exist in a larger social and cultural circle, they need information that is not necessarily job-related.

Both formal and informal information systems exist (e.g., two scientists talking at a meeting would be an informal system), although we apparently know more about formal systems than about informal systems. The information cycle in figure 1 is a formal system. Highly simplified, the diagram does not reflect the fact that any information transfer is both a personal and an interpersonal event and therefore involves all the complexities of human behavior and social interaction.

The final observation of the information cycle is that it shows information in a constant state of change. Information is seldom, if ever, transferred exactly as it was originated. Even in a direct conversation between two individuals there is change in information as it is communicated.

The Structure of Information

According to Shannon and Weaver (1949), the transmittal of information can be studied on three different levels: (1) the technical, (2) the semantic, and (3) the influential (effectiveness). The first concerns the physical transfer of discrete symbols from sender to a receiver. That is, how accurate is the transference of the information? The second, the semantic level, deals with the meaning of the message. The third deals with reaction or results. How does the receiver react to the meaning conveyed?

A communication process is a sequence of events leading to a transmission of information from a source to a destination. The source and the destination can be either human beings or machines. This model should not imply that communication is a simple, linear process, since a communication process contains numerous subprocesses that regulate and adjust the basic process.

Professional librarianship has dealt very well with the first level, as is evidenced by the magnificent library collections we have in the world. The rich resources that are stored in our libraries are a tribute to a relatively unknown corps of librarians and others who have worked hard over a long period of time. They collected the records, stored them safely, and are eager for these resources to be used. Unfortunately, we have not been as successful on the other levels of information transmittal. On the semantical level, we have developed methods of classification, indexing, and subject cataloging, but very few professional librarians will concede that these techniques are sufficient. On the third level, we know almost nothing. How do people use information? When we give them a book or a journal article, what does it lead to? What do they want next, as a result of that particular item? If we could answer these questions we would be better able to plan our libraries and information systems for the demands of the future.

Another dimension in the information structure is the types of literature media, or the *forms* in which information is transferred from person to person. There are two general forms: primary information and secondary information. Primary information comes directly from the creator of the information, for example, from the author of a research article in a scientific journal or from the writer of a diary or autobiography. It should be noted that a "primary source" and "primary literature" might be the same thing. Items in the primary literature may also be primary sources. Secondary forms reflect further digestion, analysis, description, or synthesis, usually from an intermediary between the creator of the information and the user of the information. The following is an outline of the traditional forms the literature media have taken.

A. Conventional primary media
   1. The scholarly journal
   2. Alternatives to the journal
      a. Reprints
      b. Preprints
         (copies of papers prepared before presentation to a professional society, or in advance of publication, and sent to a selected group of interested people)
   3. Report literature
      (research that does not appear in scholarly journals before being distributed by some other means to interested users)
   4. Informal exchange groups
      (groups that distribute correspondence, newsletters, and manuscripts, sometimes through some sort of central agent)

B. Nonconventional primary media
   (e.g., audio tapes and disks, video tapes, microforms and magnetic forms)

C. Electronic and optional forms
   1. Cable
   2. Radio
   3. Television
   4. Videotext

D. Secondary media
   1. Standard reference books
   2. Bibliographies
   3. Reviews
   4. Indexing journals
   5. Abstracting journals

These forms of literature media have developed as people have sought to find ways to effectively give access to recorded knowledge. Each form is unique, has its own purpose, and presents special indexing problems.

RELATIONSHIP OF INDEXING, ABSTRACTING, AND SEARCHING

Indexing, abstracting, and searching do not exist independently but are inter-related to form the basis of an information retrieval system. Indexes and abstracts are meaningless unless they are used for searching. Conversely, searching without these content indicators puts the user back to the point of having to examine documents one by one. The relationship of these concepts is illustrated in figure 2.

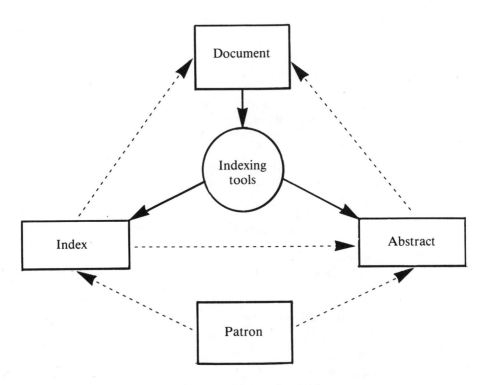

Fig. 2. Relationship of indexing, abstracting, and searching.

The broken lines indicate the path taken by the patron, who essentially works backwards on the indexing and abstracting path. Although not shown on the diagram, the patron may also use indexing tools (thesaurus or classification lists) to facilitate the use of the index. Notice the patron line from the index to the abstract. Abstracts are sometimes approached by an index, especially if the abstracts have a classified arrangement.

The nature of these relationships will be reflected in user satisfaction with the system. For example, users are generally concerned with how long it takes to get an information request filled. An unreasonably long delay will, in fact, discourage them from using a particular system, either computer-based or a printed manual index.

INDEXING VERSUS CLASSIFICATION

Classification is the systematic arrangement of entities into groups or categories according to established criteria. An index is a list of bibliographical information or citations to a body of literature, usually arranged in alphabetical order and based on some specified datum, such as author, subject, or keyword.

At first glance these definitions appear to describe two entirely different operations, but on closer examination it is apparent that there are some fundamental conceptual similarities. It would be useful to look briefly at the relationships between these two basic techniques of bibliographic control.

Classification seems to be a natural activity of the human mind. The entire spectrum of our thought processes relies on classification to organize the impressions that our brains receive through our senses. We immediately begin to try to understand a new bit of information by finding something it is similar to in our established framework of experience. Because classification shows relationships between basic units and between classes of units, we can relate to the new information we are processing.

Thus, it is quite natural that we turn to classification when we need to devise mechanisms for bibliographic control. The purpose of bibliographic control is to assist users in identifying that tiny part of an immense stored knowledge base that will serve their needs. Out of a million documents they can quickly and accurately identify the twenty or thirty that are needed. The best way to do this is to organize the documents so that they show their informational relationships and then direct the user to the cluster that is needed. This is the objective of both bibliographic classification and subject indexing; thus the two are conceptually similar. In fact, indexing is an act of classification. When we assign the index term "Cats" to a document, we place that document into a class of objects with the attributes of cats.

At the operational level there are some perceived differences between the two procedures. Cataloging and classification are viewed as being highly controlled and structured operations. Authority lists and rigid rules dictate exactly how information is to be organized. Also, classification usually allows only a few particular access points to the information. The problem, of course, is that it is impossible to organize all knowledge in the world into an ordered, perfectly structured pattern that is best for everybody. Generally, indexing systems give more flexibility.

Indexing systems may range from uncontrolled, uniterm systems all the way to systems with highly controlled vocabularies, where they finally diffuse into classification systems with rigid rules and generic relationships.

Vocabulary control for indexing systems will be discussed in a later chapter, but the point to be made here is that classification and indexing are conceptually very closely related.

FILES AND FILE SEARCHING

General Concepts

All the activities introduced up to this point are aimed at helping users find what they need in an information file. There is a close relationship between the way files are structured in an information retrieval system and the method of indexing. An indexer should therefore have an understanding of basic file construction.

A *file* is a collection of homogeneous records. That is, every record in the file has the same parts. A *record* is a single, basic unit of information. In turn, this unit may have subunits, called *fields*, which hold the same type of information in each record. For example, in a personnel *file*, units of information on employees would be described as *records*, each of which could be made up of four *fields* of subinformation, such as name, social security number, marital status, and number of children.

Records can be either variable in length or fixed. This means, for example, if the above record is variable, then the name field would be only as long as necessary to hold the name, and a name field might be of varying length. If the records are fixed, then the field would be the same length regardless of the length of the name in the particular record.

File structure was a concern of information handlers long before the invention of electronic computing machines. It was observed early that if you arranged information items physically and compiled a linear list of the items, you had only one way to retrieve information: in the way that the items were arranged. For example, if you arranged a shelf of books by author and listed the books that way, then you had no way to retrieve by title or subject. The solution was clever. Construct other lists of the items, arranged in different ways. These supplementary lists would point back to the basic order for retrieval purposes. In the above example, when a user would locate a title in the title list, the list would indicate who the author was and this would then allow the user to physically locate the book.

This basic, sequential order is called a *direct* file. It consists of an arranged sequence of the items or records in the file. The supplementary files are called *inverted* files.

Index terms are usually stored in an inverted file. Each record in the inverted file contains an index term and then the fields in the record indicate all the information items in the database that have been indexed with that term. A familiar example of an inverted subject file is the library subject catalog. A search under "Cats" will produce a sequence of entries describing all the cat books in the library.

Inverted files save searching time. A user could go through a direct file, item by item, until desired material is found, but this would be time consuming. If a file is searched in this manner, it is called a sequential search. Although a sequential search generally takes longer, the trade-off is that a sequential file saves space because it contains no duplication of information and does not require a supporting index file. If a file is to be processed record by record, then this is probably the best way to search. For example, a payroll file is processed from start to finish at a given point in time and a sequential search would be efficient. On the other hand, sequentially accessed files are generally difficult to update. The simple act of inserting a new record between existing ones requires moving a great many other records to make space for it.

Inverted files have the advantage of being fast when random searches are required. On the other hand, they take up space and must have some sort of index to lead from an access point to the record required.

In designing computer-based indexing files for information retrieval searching there are three basic considerations:

Information transfer speed of the medium. How fast can records be transferred from the storage device into the computer's internal working area? If it takes a relatively long time to make this transfer, the speed of the internal processing is wasted. When designing a searching file, this could be an important factor. For example, if the transfer is slow, the file should be designed to minimize the number of accesses the computer must make to the file and maximize the amount of data transferred per access.

Record arrangement. Some applications require only that all records be accessed sequentially while other applications require rapid access to particular, random records. For example, a monthly printout of new library acquisitions could be done by simply programming the computer to access the records one at a time in sequential order. However, a library circulation system needs to retrieve any record in the system directly and immediately. File design must take into account the particular application.

The amount of information to be stored. The volume of the file can affect its searching efficiency. Also, when a file is designed, thought must be given to the possibility of expansion when the workload is increased or the system is redesigned.

The Searching Procedure

Once the file has been designed, the searching procedure follows a standard pattern. A user poses a question or information need. The question, or "query," is translated into the same words or notations that are used to represent the document. In other words, the user's query is analyzed and then, in a sense, indexed so that the language of the user and of the knowledge record will coincide. A strategy or game plan is decided upon. Finally, the search is carried out, either manually or by computer (see figure 3).

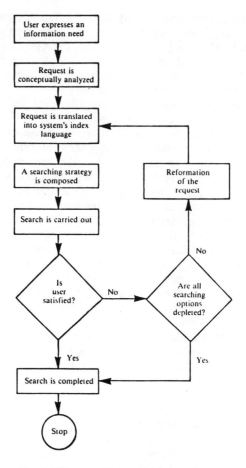

Fig. 3. The searching procedure

Boolean Searches

Most information systems utilize what is known as a Boolean search strategy. Boolean algebra is the formalization and algebrazation of logic. Of particular interest to the problems of information retrieval is the algebra of sets, which describes the inclusion or exclusion of elements from a defined class, aggregate, or collection of elements.

This mathematical model lends itself well to the procedures of information retrieval, since when users request information they create a class of subjects, e.g., *cats and dogs*. The searching procedure is then aimed at identifying informational units that fall into these classes. Boolean operators are used to create the exact class of information needed.

For example, when using the traditional card catalog, we are using a form of Boolean logic. If we need information dealing with *cats*, we flip through the cards until we either find such an entry or we don't. Sometimes, in a limited way, we try to combine terms and look for that combination in the catalog. The answer is yes or no; a binary decision is made. Of course in using the card catalog, we are constrained in that the combinations have already been made and we must discover what those combinations are. We may be temporarily diverted and directed to change our entry words. For example, we may see an entry such as: "For Cats, *see* Felines, domesticated." We now have a new term, and we search again on a yes or no basis. There are some fundamental weaknesses in this type of search and alternative approaches will be discussed in a later chapter, but for the present we must realize that this is the major searching model and it should be understood.

Most document systems are based on this matching of the terms in a document with the terms selected by the inquirer. From a mathematical point of view, Boolean algebra is a beautiful exercise in thought and a challenge to the aesthetic aspects of human inquiry. For the average, everyday librarian, it offers a technique that is both simple and practical.

With due regard to a man named Venn, an English logician who perfected visual diagrams to help represent sets and set relations, the following illustrations are offered. Let a rectangle represent the universe of knowledge:

KNOWLEDGE

Let circles show various subdivisions of knowledge:

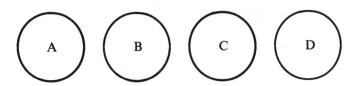

If we put the rectangle and three of the circles together we might have the following:

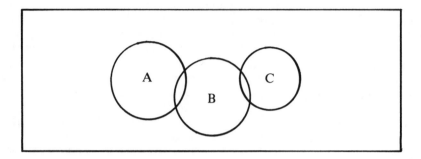

In the last diagram, *A* represents a certain proportion of knowledge, *B* represents another fraction, and *C* represents a smaller part. Why are they overlapping? Because knowledge is not simply divided into neat categories, as the first row of circles seems to show. When we deal with knowledge records we deal with overlap and interchange. If *A* is a paper about *cats*, *B* is a paper about *diseases*, and *C* is a paper about *medicines*, then "a drug to cure pneumonia in cats" will involve all three ideas. So the diagram shows where the papers overlap, thus giving an indication of common information. Paper *A*, although about cats primarily, has information about diseases. Paper *C* is basically about drugs, but since it also has information on diseases, it overlaps with *B* also. Thus, to identify a paper with two or more ideas we use Boolean combinations, and that leads us to three basic Boolean operations: logical sum, logical product, and logical differences.

Logical sum. A logical sum in a Boolean model means that we want any document that is related to any one of the topics under consideration. Suppose we are interested in drugs that will cure pneumonia in cats. In a logical sum Boolean search we would say, "Give me any document that deals with drugs. Or that deals with pneumonia. Or that deals with cats. Any of these or all." Such a broad, generalized request can be visualized as follows:

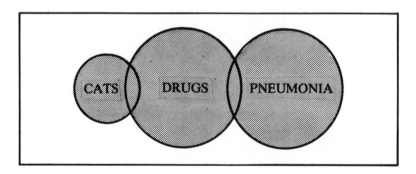

Logical Sum

Logical product. Suppose we want those documents that discuss cats, drugs, and pneumonia. In other words, we want each document to deal with all three concepts (cats *and* drugs *and* pneumonia).

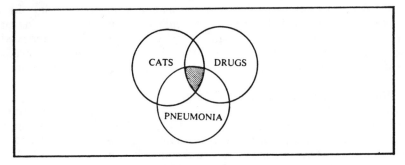

Logical Product

Logical differences. Suppose we want those documents that discuss cats but *not* drugs *nor* pneumonia. Then we have:

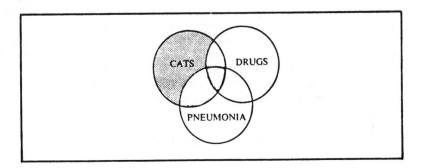

Logical Differences

Clearly, the indexing function extends itself to the searching stage. The query must also be indexed and the terms must be formed into a search plan using Boolean operators. Despite the mathematical accuracy of Boolean combinations, the wrong choice of query terms will lead to the retrieval of the wrong documents. The elements of any information system are not independent but interrelated. Indexing, vocabulary control, query formation, file structuring, and search strategies are both interrelated and interdependent.

Alternative Methods

The Boolean searching method is the most popular way to search information files, but it is not the only way. For example, when a citation index is used, retrieval is not achieved by using index terms and Boolean searching. In fact, index terms are not used. Relevant documents are found by identifying subsequent documents that cite a known document. We enter the citation index with a paper we know about and the index provides us with a list of documents published later on the same subject because those documents *cite* the document in hand.

William Goffman (1964, 1968) states that the notion of treating the searching procedure strictly as a matching procedure between index terms in a query and index terms in the documents in the file has at least two important defects. In the first case, a direct Boolean match requires the computer to know which documents have the index term and which do not. The necessity for this one-to-one matching affects the efficiency of the system. The second and more important weakness is that the direct Boolean search does not take into account the usefulness of a document in relation to what the user already knows at the time of the search. An ideal retrieval system will take into account the state of knowledge of the user. Goffman then suggests a method for doing this.

In other words, the Boolean procedure assumes no relationship between documents, but only a relationship between a specific query and *each* document in the file. Goffman proposes a method of clustering documents on the basis of their internal relatedness, independently of any particular search query. His contention is that if documents are interrelated in terms of content, they can be preclustered and a query can find a cluster all at once, without having to examine documents one by one. Several research projects have tested this concept with successful results. The abstracting and indexing exercise in chapter X will use a document that describes this method in more detail.

SUGGESTED READINGS

Brenner, Everett H., and Tefko Saracevic. *Indexing and Searching in Perspective.* 2nd ed. Philadelphia: National Federation of Abstracting and Information Services, 1985.

Cleveland, Donald, Ana D. Cleveland, and Olga B. Wise. "Less Than Full-Text Indexing Using a Non-Boolean Searching Model." *Journal of the American Society for Information Science* 35 (1984): 19-20.

Debons, Anthony. "Concept Formation." *Encyclopedia of Library and Information Science*, vol. 5. New York: Marcel Dekker, 1971, 586-92.

Goffman, William. "An Indirect Method of Information Retrieval." *Information Storage and Retrieval* 4, no. 4 (December 1968): 361-73.

_____. "On Relevance as a Measure." *Information Storage and Retrieval* 2 (February 1964): 201.

Levitain, Karen B. "Information Resources as 'Goods' in the Life Cycle of Information Production." *Journal of the American Society for Information Science* 33 (January 1982): 44-54.

Maron, M. E. "On Indexing, Retrieval and the Meaning of About." *Journal of the American Society for Information Science* 28 (January 1977): 38-43.

Naisbitt, John. *Megatrends.* New York: Warner Books, 1984.

National Academy of Sciences. Committee on Scientific and Technical Communication (SATCOM). *Scientific and Technical Communications: A Pressing National Problem and Recommendations for Its Solution.* Publication 1707. Washington, D.C.: National Academy of Sciences, 1969.

Radecki, Tadeusz. "Similarity Measures for Boolean Search Request Formulation." *Journal of the American Society for Information Science* 33 (January 1982): 8-17.

Shannon, Claude E., and Warren Weaver. *The Mathematical Theory of Communication.* Urbana: The University of Illinois, 1949.

Van Rijsbergen, C. J., D. J. Harper, and M. F. Porter. "Selection of Good Search Terms." *Information Processing and Management* 17 (1981): 77-91.

Vickery, B. C. "Analysis of Information." *Encyclopedia of Library and Information Science*, vol. 1. New York: Marcel Dekker, 1968, 355-84.

Wellisch, Hans H. "Some Vital Statistics in Abstracting and Indexing." *International Classification* 7 (November 1980): 135-39.

III

The Nature and Types of Indexes

INTRODUCTION

An index can be defined as an orderly guide to the intellectual content and physical location of knowledge records. Indexes systematically lead us to previously detected information whenever it is needed. An index is a pointer or guide and as such does not generally supply the desired information itself. Instead it employs a set of tags or descriptors, which earmark the source of information for which the user is searching. Each user is directed by the index device to the subjects and ideas expressed by the authors in the knowledge records.

The basic intellectual problem in constructing an index is to accurately represent a document, which may run into thousands of words, with a dozen or so index terms. These few index terms must be chosen in such a way that the essential meaning and objectives of the document can be conceptualized from these terms. An index is judged not only on the amount of time it saves in searching for information, but also on how well it reflects the subjects covered in the documents.

Indexes come in many different forms. Many are published and distributed on a national or international basis, while many others are localized in-house indexes, which are used to access local information stores. Indexes may be appended to primary journals, may be part of an abstract journal, may be separate journals, or may be part of a published classification scheme. They may be back-of-the-book indexes or they may be on cards, in microform or in computer-readable form. But all indexes have one common goal: to represent the content of a document in an orderly manner that will lead a user as directly and swiftly as possible to needed information.

This chapter will give an overview of the different types and levels of indexes. Example titles and illustrations are given, and the reader is urged to examine as many of the titles as possible to get a feeling for the nature and details of the many thousands of indexes that are available.

ARRANGEMENT OF INDEXES

Arrangement is a primary factor in defining the types of indexes that are available. Almost all standard indexes are either alphabetical or classified or a combination of the two.

Historically, the classified arrangement was predominant, but this is no longer true. However, some of the best of the modern indexes are, indeed, classified indexes. The strengths and weaknesses of these two major categories will be discussed in the remainder of this chapter, but at this point the obvious should be stated: arrangement is very closely related to file structure and searching. In terms of manual systems, the arrangement directly affects index users, because they cannot use the index if they do not understand its structure. If the index is computer-based, the arrangement affects users in an indirect way, because a poorly arranged computer file may compromise both the efficiency and the effectiveness of the search.

LEVELS OF INDEXING

All indexing has the common objective of guiding a user to the intellectual content and physical location of documents, but in terms of types and forms there are several levels or strata. And within these levels there are various kinds of indexes. The underlying philosophical base of all indexing is the same, but, in application, indexing forms, approaches, and uses vary widely. The categorization of indexes could be approached in several ways, but for our purposes it is convenient to look at the following levels first: word and name indexes, book indexes, periodical indexes, and information retrieval systems. Then, within these levels there are the following *types* of indexes: author indexes, alphabetical subject indexes, classified indexes, coordinate indexes, permuted title indexes, faceted indexes, string indexes, and citation indexes.

Word and Name Indexes

Knowledge records can be indexed solely on the basis of the actual words that make up the text. There is no synonymic substitution by an intermediary using an authority list of some type. Word and name indexes, which are sometimes called concordances, are indexes to the individual names and words that the author used, and in one sense most closely represent the information and ideas the author had in mind when creating the manuscript. These indexes are of value to users, particularly linguists, when the exact term or word within the context of the document will pinpoint the subject discussed and its location. There are limitations to the usefulness of these kinds of indexes, but in certain cases they perform a needed function. An obvious example is a Bible concordance.

Since such indexing is based on objectively determined criteria, that is to say, the words themselves can be quantitatively handled with a minimum amount of judgment on the part of the handler, the indexing can be done by people with very little training, or simply by machines, and therefore can be completed quickly and relatively inexpensively.

The main drawback with this type of index is that it complicates searching in several ways. Searching becomes more difficult and uncertain, since this type of index spreads similar entries over many synonymous terms, ignores misspellings, and confuses any general-specific term relationships that certainly exist in the implied indexing language being unconsciously used. Terms for entering the index list are confusing, and a user has to search from one to another to get all the possible approaches to the subject of interest and must second-guess the author as to what terms to use. Since one of the qualities of a good index is that it quickly focuses on those entry terms that express the needs of the users and connects the index language to their way of thinking, uncontrolled concordance-type indexes are time-consuming and place a burden on the searcher. The speed and economy achieved in creating such indexes are paid for by the user in time and effort. Even in a computer-controlled retrieval system, the user may have to query the system over and over because of the limitation of no vocabulary control. The computer simply allows the user to find the wrong things faster.

Two examples of indexes of this type that have worked well and have proven extremely useful are patent number and formula indexes. With these indexes the users begin the search with a patent number or, in the second case, the molecular formulas of chemical compounds. This saves a great deal of searching effort since it is easier than describing a patent or spelling out the name of a chemical compound. Example 1 shows the patent index from *Chemical Abstracts*.

Another useful type of name index is the corporate author index (see example 2). Sometimes the most obvious approach in an information search is by corporate author (e.g., a corporation, a foundation, or a university). The searcher may not remember individuals but might very well remember that the work was carried out by the Rockefeller Foundation.

Thus, word and name indexes have their place despite limitations. The following are some examples to look at:

Idioms and Phrases Index. Detroit: Gale Research, 1983.
This is a word index to *where* definitions or discussions of the idioms can be found.

Biography Index. New York: H. W. Wilson, 1947- . (See examples 3 and 4.)
Biographical information is one of the most heavily requested areas in reference work. This tool has a name alphabet and an index by professions and occupations. Large categories of professions, such as writers, are subdivided by country.

Ellison, John William. *Nelson's Complete Concordance of the Revised Standard Version Bible*. 2nd ed. New York: Thomas Nelson, 1985. (See example 5.)
This concordance, compiled under the supervision of John W. Ellison and prepared with the assistance of a computer, is comprehensive in its word coverage.

(Text continues on page 33.)

The Patent Index contains information on patent documents processed by Chemical Abstracts Service (CAS) during the current week. It replaces the *CA Numerical Patent Index* and the *CA Patent Concordance*. The Patent Index includes entries for all newly abstracted patent documents on an invention, cross-references to the first-abstracted document on an invention when more than one patent document describes that invention, and a listing at the first-abstracted document on a particular invention of all patent documents related to that invention. The primary ordering of entries is alphabetical by a two-character code for the country of issue. Under each country, the patent documents are listed in numerical order.

A patent family is a collection of patent documents concerned with a particular invention. A family member is considered equivalent to the first-abstracted document if the family member and the abstracted document contain only one priority number and that number is common to both documents. Family members containing multiple priority numbers, or a single priority number which is not in common with the first-abstracted document, may not be true equivalents and are designated as such by the term "Related". Family members containing no priority information, but which are found to describe the same invention found in other family members, are termed "Nonpriority". A family may contain more than one abstracted document depending on the various relationships among family members and the order in which such family members are processed at CAS. Family information is listed only at the first-abstracted document for a family. All new entries are highlighted by boldface type.

Domestically related documents are indicated by such terms as "Division", "Continuation-in-part", "Addition", "Reissue", etc. Those countries to which international and regional patent documents and reports are applicable are designated through the use of "Elected States", "Elected Regional States", "Designated States", or "Designated Regional States".

ILLUSTRATIVE KEY

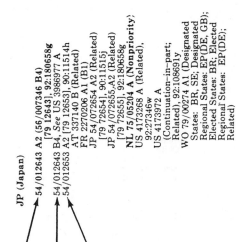

JP (Japan)

1 → 54/012643 A2 (56/007346 B4)
[79 12643], 92:180658g

2 → 54/012643 B4, *See* US 3986977 A

3 → 54/012653 A2 [79 12653], 90:11514h
AT 337140 B (Related)
FR 2270206 A1 (B1)
JP 54/072654 A2 (Related)
[79 72654], 90:11515j
JP 54/072655,A2 (Related)
[79 72655], 92:180658g
NL 75/05204 A (**Nonpriority**);
US 4173268 A (Related),
92:27346w
US 4173972 A
(Continuation-in-part;
Related), 92:108691y
WO 79/00274 A1 (Designated
States: BR, SE; Designated
Regional States: EP(DE, GB);
Elected States: BR; Elected
Regional States: EP(DE);
Related)

Example 1. *Chemical Abstracts* (patent index). (Reprinted with permission of Chemical Abstracts Service.)

<table>
<tr><td></td><td></td><td>Vol</td><td>Page</td></tr>
</table>

		Vol	Page
A			
A. & C. BLACK PLC (UNITED KINGDOM)	INTL		
A. AHLSTROM CORP. (FINLAND)	INTL	1	1395
A.A. IMPORTING CO., INC.	UOTC		481
A CORPORATE TRUST SERIES	B&F	3	10001
A CORPORATE TRUST, SERIES 1	B&F	3	10001
A.L. LABORATORIES, INC.	IND	1	2501
A-P-A TRANSPORT CORP.	TRANS		1660
A S ALFRED BENZON (DENMARK)	INTL	1	1339
A/S ATLANTICA (NORWAY)	INTL	2	2943
A/S BERGEHUS (NORWAY)	INTL	2	2943
A/S DAMPSKIBSSELSKABET SVENDBORG (DENMARK)	INTL	1	1339
A/S ELEKTRISK BUREAU (NORWAY)	INTL	2	2943
A/S FOLLUM FARIKKER (NORWAY)	INTL	2	2943
A/S HAFSLUND (NORWAY)	INTL	2	2944
A/S KONGSBERG VAPENFABRIKK (NORWAY)	INTL	2	2944
A/S NORCEM (NORWAY)	INTL	2	2944
A/S NORSK ELEKTRISK & BROWN BOVERI (NORWAY)	INTL	2	2945
A/S NORSK JERNVERK (NORWAY)	INTL	2	2958
A/S SYDVARANGER (NORWAY)	INTL	2	2945
A/S TH. WESSEL & VETT, MAGASIN DU NORD (DENMARK)	INTL	1	1339

Example 2. *Moody's Complete Corporate Index* (alphabetical corporate name index). (Reprinted with permission of Moody's Investors Service, Inc.)

A

Aarons, Lawrence, advertising executive
   Levine, H. Portfolio. il *Art Dir* 39[40]:65-71 My '88
Aaronson, Marc Arnold, d. 1987, astronomer
   Obituary
      Phys Today por 41:91-2 Jl '88
Aaseng, Nathan, author
   Something about the author, v51; facts and pictures
      about authors and illustrators of books for young
      people; edited by Anne Commire. Gale Res. 1988
      p1-3 bibl il pors
Abbey, Edward, 1927-1989, author
   Obituary
      N Y Times pD-19 Mr 15 '89
      Newsweek 113:76 Mr 27 '89
      Time 133:85 Mr 27 '89
Abbott, Jim, handicapped baseball player
   Callahan, T. Dreaming the big dreams. il por *Time*
      133:78 Mr 20 '89
Abboud, A. Robert, 1929-, banker
   Waddell, H. Why Abboud leaned against the wind. *ABA
      Bank J* 80:22 Je '88

Example 3. *Biography Index*, May 1989, p. 1 (main entry by name). (Copyright © 1989 by The H. W. Wilson Company. Material reproduced with permission of the publisher.)

A

Abolitionists
Peckham, Robert, 1785-1877
Ramsay, James, 1733-1789
Wilberforce, William, 1759-1833
Accountants
Bradshaw, Bill
Burmester, Robert W., d. 1989
Goldschmidt, Oswald, d. 1989
Graham, Alsy
Huband, Earnest A.
Macdonald, William A.
Mendelson, Charles L., d. 1989
Miller, Joseph K., d. 1988
Tunick, Stanley Block, 1900-1988
Worsley, Francis Edward
Acoustic engineers
Benade, Arthur H., 1925-1987
Acrobats
Petit, Philippe, 1949-
Actors and actresses
See also
Children as actors
Comedians
Entertainers
Pantomimists
Performance artists
Adler, Jacob P., 1855-1926
Alda, Alan
Alexander, Sir George, 1858-1918
Allen, Woody
Amis, Suzy
Andrews, Harry, 1911-1989
Archer, Anne
Attenborough, Richard
Bacall, Lauren
Bacon, Frank, 1864-1922
Bailey, Wes
Baldwin, Stephen
Ball, Lucille, 1911-
Bancroft, Sir Squire, 1841-1926
Barrows, Diana
Basquette, Lina
Beatty, Warren, 1937-
Belafonte-Harper, Shari
Berenson, Marisa, 1942-
Bergen, Candice
Berle, Milton

Coca, Imogene
Cole, Gary
Connery, Sean
Connor, Whitfield, 1916-1988
Cosby, Bill, 1937-
Cox, Courteney
Cronyn, Hume
Cruise, Tom
Cusack, John
Dafoe, Willem
Dalton, Timothy
Dawn, Hazel, d. 1988
De Niro, Robert, 1945?-
De Vito, Danny
Dean, James, 1931-1955
Dell, Gabriel, d. 1988
Dempsey, Patrick
Deneuve, Catherine
Depp, Johnny
Dern, Laura
Dobkin, Lawrence
Doohan, James
Douglas, Kirk, 1916-
Downey, Robert, Jr.
Drake, Jessica
Dukakis, Olympia
Duse, Eleonora, 1858-1924
Eastwood, Clint
Ebersole, Christine
Eldridge, Florence, 1901-1988
Evans, Maurice, 1901-1989
Farr, Florence, 1860-1917
Feldman, Corey
Field, Sally
Fishburne, Larry
Ford, Faith
Forest, Michael
Forrest, William, d. 1989
Fox, Michael J.
Freiwald, Tani
Frey, Leonard, 1938-1988
Gábor, Zsa Zsa
Gielgud, Sir John, 1904-
Gish, Lillian, 1896?-
Givens, Robin
Gleason, Jackie
Golino, Valeria
Goodman, John
Grant, Cary, 1904-1986
Griffith, Melanie

Example 4. *Biography Index*, May 1989, p. 117 (professions and occupations entry). (Copyright © 1989 by The H. W. Wilson Company. Material reproduced with permission of the publisher.)

AARON

"Is there not A., your brother, the	Ex 4.14
The LORD said to A., "Go into	4.27
And Moses told A. all the words of	4.28
Then Moses and A. went and gathered	4.29
And A. spoke all the words which	4.30
Afterward Moses and A. went to	5.01
"Moses and A., why do you take the	5.04
They met Moses and A., who were	5.20
But the LORD spoke to Moses and A.,	6.13
and she bore him A. and Moses,	6.20
A. took to wife Elisheba, the	6.23
These are the A. and Moses to whom	6.26
from Egypt, this Moses and this A.	6.27
and A. your brother shall be your	7.01
and A. your brother shall tell	7.02
And Moses and A. did so; they did	7.06
and A. eighty-three years old, when	7.07
And the LORD said to Moses and A.,	7.08
miracle,' then you shall say to A.,	7.09
So Moses and A. went to Pharaoh and	7.10
A. cast down his rod before Pharaoh	7.10
"Say to A., 'Take your rod and	7.19
Moses and A. did as the LORD	7.20
"Say to A., 'Stretch out your hand	8.05
So A. stretched out his hand over	8.06
Then Pharaoh called Moses and A.,	8.08
So Moses and A. went out from	8.12
"Say to A., 'Stretch out your rod	8.16
A. stretched out his hand with his	8.17
Then Pharaoh called Moses and A.,	8.25
And the LORD said to Moses and A.,	9.08
sent, and called Moses and A.,	9.27
So Moses and A. went in to Pharaoh,	10.03
So Moses and A. were brought back	10.08
called Moses and A. in haste,	10.16
Moses and A. did all these wonders	11.10
to Moses and A. in the land of	12.01
commanded Moses and A., so they did.	12.28
And he summoned Moses and A. by night,	12.31
And the LORD said to Moses and A.,	12.43
commanded Moses and A., so they did.	12.50

and when A. sets up the lamps in	30.08
A. shall make atonement upon its	30.10
with which A. and his sons shall	30.19
And you shall anoint A. and his sons,	30.30
garments for A. the priest and the	31.10
gathered themselves together to A.,	32.01
And A. said to them, "Take off the	32.02
their ears, and brought them to A.	32.03
When A. saw this, he built an altar	32.05
and A. made proclamation and said,	32.05
And Moses said to A., "What did	32.21
And A. said, "Let not the anger of	32.22
loose (for A. had let them break	32.25
they made the calf which A. made.	32.35
And when A. and all the people of	34.30
and A. and all the leaders of the	34.31
holy garments for A. the priest,	35.19
Ithamar the son of A. the priest.	38.21
they made the holy garments for A.;	39.01
fine linen, for A. and his sons,	39.27
holy garments for A. the priest,	39.41
Then you shall bring A. and his	40.12
and put upon A. the holy garments,	40.13
with which Moses and A. and his	40.31
and the sons of A. the priest shall	Lev 1.07
shall be for A. and his sons;	2.03
shall be for A. and his sons;	2.10
and the sons of A. shall throw its	3.13
"Command A. and his sons, saying,	6.09
The sons of A. shall offer it	6.14
And the rest of it A. and his sons	6.16
the children of A. may eat of it,	6.18
offering which A. and his sons	6.20
"Say to A. and his sons, This is the	6.25
shall be for all the sons of A.,	7.10
shall be for A. and his sons.	7.31
the sons of A. who offers the	7.33
given them to A. the priest and to	7.34
the portion of A. and of his sons	7.35
"Take A. and his sons with him, and	8.02
And Moses brought A. and his sons,	8.06
and A. and his sons laid their	8.14

Example 5. *Nelson's Complete Concordance of the Revised Standard Version Bible.* (Reproduced by permission.)

Book Indexes

Book indexes make up a large category of indexes. In fact, when the word *index* is mentioned, most people think of a book index, regardless of their sophistication in using libraries and library tools. The reading public is quite familiar with book indexes, which are lists of words, generally alphabetical, at the back of a book giving a page location of the subject or name associated with each word. Just as indexes to library collections make it unnecessary for a user to read all the million or so documents in a library to find a few useful ones, the book index pinpoints information so that the reader will not have to read, or reread, the entire book. Once again, the index is not a substitute for the information in the book but a pointer to the information included.

The lack of indexes, or the inclusion of poorly constructed ones, is a sore point with librarians, authors, and astute scholars — and, in all fairness, to a small group of editors and publishers. It remains an unexplainable mystery to this minority why the importance of indexes in books cannot be understood. Except perhaps with fiction, there is no such thing as a good book that has a poor index or none at all. Any book that ever serves as a reference in any sense of the word (and what book does not, except light fiction?) should have a quality index to make its information quickly and completely available. A good book is not to be read and forgotten but reread and used. Unfortunately, too many books, in every field, are published with poor indexes or no indexes at all. Such books are incomplete and are similar to books published with blank pages where text or illustrations were supposed to be or with upside-down pages. Readers are handicapped and penalized and have, in a sense, been cheated. It is like reading a mystery novel in which the solution is left out — one comes away unsatisfied.

Several examples come to mind that explain the nature of the problem.

In case one, a person is reading a book on the Civil War. Early in the book there is a discussion of Ulysses S. Grant's early military experience. Later on in the book the author keeps referring to "a result of his early experience." The reader wants to refer back, but without an index he must flip backwards until he finds the passage, if indeed he is able to.

In case two, the reader returns to the book later to look up some information but cannot do so easily because the book has no index. This general book cannot serve as a reference source because of the lack of an index.

In case three, the Civil War book stands on a library shelf. A browsing reader has been led to this general area and is pulling down potential books for his research. He may examine tables of contents, but he knows this is an inadequate source of information. Because he has no way of knowing the full nature of the Civil War book (since it has no index), he rejects it.

Of course, the definition of a good book index is not a simple matter. Indexes can be simple or complex; they can be basically subject indicators or mainly names and places. A certain type index can be perfectly adequate for one type of book but totally inadequate for another. A book index is molded to the book, and its quality is judged in relation to that particular book.

To elaborate a moment — basic texts and other school books, popular works in the arts and sciences, and other such works can usually survive with quite simple indexes. These indexes are characterized by a relatively small list of generic terms with few cross-references or subdivisions. A travel book will have an index heavily filled with place names, historical events, hotels, and recreational areas.

Biographies will be somewhat similar, with a heavy emphasis on place names, historical events, and people. Scholarly books, on the other hand, will generally need complete, complex indexes that bring out relationships and abstract ideas, as well as data.

Although there are many examples of good book indexes, the reader could do no better than to examine the indexes of several editions of the *Encyclopaedia Britannica*, especially the *Micropaedia* of the fifteenth edition.

Periodical Indexes

Periodical indexes are a somewhat different breed. It is generally recognized that one of the factors in the rise and spectacular growth of science over the last four centuries has been its development of a highly effective communication system. The information cycle described earlier is not a supplementary by-the-way in the scientific method, but an essential link. Since scientific "truth" rests on a consensus of peers, a scientific advance does not exist until it is communicated.

A vital key—perhaps the most vital—to the science communication process as it now exists is the periodical. The periodical is an amazing innovation and should be given a great deal of credit for the rapid advancement of science. The periodical is where primary research is reported, and where, in fact, most information found in books originally appeared. Most of the citations in books are to periodicals, and despite the large number of books published, only a small part of the vast periodical information is ever assimilated into monograph form.

It follows from this that the role of a periodical index is critical—not just to science, of course, but to all disciplines. These indexes are vital to the workers who must find information effectively and who must be assured of adequate coverage.

The first periodical appeared in the mid-1600s. After a slow start, periodical publishing began to grow at an exponential rate, and since 1750 the number of new scholarly periodicals has increased tenfold each fifty years. As early as the 1840s scholars were protesting the growth and explosion of information in terms of the difficulty of keeping up. With journals they now had a relatively fast way to spread ideas and new discoveries by writing brief reports and essays that would reach a maximum audience of peers. Personal letters gave way to the mass production concept of the periodical—a sensational idea that was rather quickly incorporated into the scholarly world. As the periodical literature grew, it became apparent that an effective means of bibliographic control and subject access was needed. A natural result was the periodical index to the contents of the periodicals.

Periodical indexes are based on the same principles and have the same general objectives as book indexes, but because their scope is broader, they present a number of unique problems. For example, preparing a book index is a well-defined operation, with a beginning and an end. It focuses in most cases on a general topic, and it can usually be prepared entirely by one person. On the other hand, periodical indexes are open-ended projects, usually done by a number of people, covering perhaps years, with shifts in subject emphasis and indexing objectives. Consistency, a vital key to quality indexing, becomes a paramount challenge. Each issue of a periodical may deal with unrelated topics by several different authors, written in different styles, and aimed at different users. The periodical index must bring order out of this divergency. Like book indexes, the periodical index is determined by the type of periodicals—their depth, structure, and readers. What are their subjects? Who reads them? How do the users approach their subject contents?

A variety of technical niceties must be considered in the preparation of periodical indexes. For example, the location indicator has to be exact and complete, giving volume and date, since the periodical of interest may be spread over many years, with many volumes and issue numbers. Decisions have to be made about what information indicators will be included. Should the advertisements be indexed? Times and vocabularies change, and so do the periodical indexes. Therein lies one of the fundamental problems.

There are two types of periodical indexes: (1) individual indexes to individual journals, and (2) broad indexes to a group of journals. In the first case, the publisher of the journal prepares an index, usually for a volume and at the end of a year's run of the journal. These indexes are prepared under the direction of the editor of the journal. The approach to this kind of indexing can range from a simple, uncontrolled vocabulary to a complex indexing system with a thesaurus. Sometimes permuted title indexes may be used. Although these indexes are important and certainly useful, the broad indexes to a group of journals, usually prepared by indexing services, play a bigger role. These services are discussed in chapter XII.

The following are examples of some familiar periodical indexes:

Readers' Guide to Periodical Literature. New York: H. W. Wilson, 1900- . (See example 6.)

This is an example of a well-known periodical index. It has a dictionary arrangement under author, subject, and sometimes title. Eugene Sheehy, editor of the tenth edition of *Guide to Reference Books* (Chicago: American Library Association, 1986), describes its special feature as

full dictionary cataloging of all articles ... (2) uniformity of entries, due to the fact that the work is done by a few professional indexers rather than by many voluntary collaborators; (3) use of catalog subject headings instead of catchword subjects; (4) full information in the references ...; (5) cumulative features which keep the indexing, in the second and third cumulated volumes, of some 597 composite books, thus forming an unofficial continuation of the *ALA Index ... to General Literature.* (p. 176)

Catholic Periodical and Literature Index. Haverford, Pa.: Catholic Library Association, 1967/68- . (See example 7.)

A cumulative author-subject index to selective Catholic periodicals, this is an example of a more narrow, specialized periodical index.

New York Times Index. New York: New York Times Co., 1913- . (See example 8.)

This is a good "role model" for newspaper indexes. The subject index is carefully constructed and it gives exact, specific information to date, page, and column. There are many cross-references to names and topics related to the area of interest.

7-ELEVEN STORES *See* Southland Corp.

A

AARP FEDERAL CREDIT UNION *See* American Association of Retired Persons. Federal Credit Union
ABBOTT, JIM
about
Angel on the ascent. B. Anderson. il por *Sports Illustrated* 70:27 Mr 13 '89
Dreaming the big dreams. T. Callahan. il por *Time* 133:78 Mr 20 '89
ABC *See* American Broadcasting Companies, Inc.
ABDULLAH ABD AL-HAMID LABID *See* Labid, Abdullah Abd al-Hamid
ABNORMALITIES
See also
Birth defects
Fetal alcohol syndrome
ABOLITIONISTS
Abolition revisited. J. N. Akers. il *Christianity Today* 33:13 Mr 3 '89
ABORTION
Laws and regulations
See also
United States. Supreme Court—Decisions—Abortion decisions
Letting the states set abortion policy. V. G. Rosenblum. *The Christian Century* 106:252-3 Mr 8 '89

Example 6. *Readers' Guide to Periodical Literature*, April 25, 1989, p. 1 (main entry). (Copyright © 1989 by The H. W. Wilson Company. Material reproduced with permission of the publisher.)

A

ABORIGINES, AUSTRALIAN
See AUSTRALIAN ABORIGINES.
ABORTION
DeMarco, Donald Thomas, 1937-. Abortion and compassion. SocJust 78:75-9+ My-Je'87
Freiling, Edward C. The position of modern science on the beginning of human life. SocJust 78:71-5 My-Je'87
Meehan, Mary. Activists plan sit-in strategy. Register 63:1+ My 17'87
Sheehan, Peter. Eclipse graphically depicts late-term abortion. OSV 76:4 My 31'87
Germany (West)
Schmitz, Philipp, S.J. Neue Akzente der Abtreibungsdebatte. Stimm Zeit 204:795-802 D'86
Laws and Legislation
Germany (West)
Schmitz, Philipp, S.J. Neue Akzente der Abtreibungsdebatte. Stimm Zeit 204:795-802 D'86
United States
Craven, Erma Clardy. [Craven on abortion & the black community]; interview by Goldkamp, Dick. Register 63:1+ My 10'87
Guarino, Jean. The voice behind The silent scream: Dr. Bernard Nathanson. il St Anth 94:35-9 My'87
McClory, Robert Joseph, 1932-. Pro-life network puts fetus fragments on display. Nat Cath Rep 23:6 My 22'87
ABSOLUTION (CANON LAW)
Mazanares, Julio. De absolutione sacramentali generali in casu gravis necessitatis considerationes. Periodica 76:121-59 (no.1, 1987)

Example 7. *Catholic Periodical Literature Index* (main entry).

AMERICAN BRANDS INC
Shares of American Brands rise $10.125, to $67.75, on speculation that unsolicited bid is in offing; speculation centers on Unilever NV, which is reportedly planning bid of at least $90 a share (M), D 24,I,35:3
Stock of American Brands Inc rises in heavy trading amid rumors that Unilever or another company is considering a takeover attempt (S), D 28,IV,3:4
AMERICAN BROADCASTING COS INC (ABC).
See also
Television, D 22,23
Television — Brian Boitano: Canvas of Ice (TV Program), D 19
Television — Burning Questions (TV Program), D 29
Television — Fine Romance, A (TV Program), D 27
Television — Thirtysomething (TV Program), D 20
AMERICAN CONTINENTAL CORP. See also
Banks and Banking, D 23
Lincoln Savings & Loan Assn, D 21
AMERICAN CYANAMID CO
American Cyanamid Co sells its remaining dye business to BASF Corp (S), D 28,IV,4:3
AMERICAN EXPRESS CO. See also
Automobiles, D 20
Travel and Vacations, D 25
AMERICAN FEDERATION OF LABOR-CONGRESS OF INDUSTRIAL ORGANIZATIONS.
See also
Labor, D 25
United States Politics and Government, D 25
AMERICAN INTERNATIONAL GROUP INC. See also
Belco Inc, D 17,20
AMERICAN INTERNATIONAL INDUSTRIES. See also
Poisoning and Poisons, D 17
AMERICAN MUSEUM OF NATURAL HISTORY (NYC). See also
Kwanza (Celebration), D 28
AMERICAN NATIONS. See
Latin America
AMERICAN PETROFINA INC
American Petrofina Inc appoints Ronald W Haddock president and chief executive; photo (M), D 20,IV,5:5
AMERICAN REPERTORY THEATER. See also
Theater — Serpent Woman, The (Play), D 30
AMERICAN SAVINGS & LOAN ASSN
Banks and Banking, D 29
Mario Antoci to become chairman and chief executive of American Savings and Loan Association after its acquisition by Robert M Bass Group is completed; Bass Group has agreed to inject $550 million into American Savings in exchange for financial aid from Federal Home Loan Bank Board of more than $2 billion; William Popejoy, current chief executive of American Savings, will remain a director and join a Bass affiliate as a principal (M), D 19,IV, 1:1

Respiration and Respirators
Transplants
ANDERSON, BONNIE S. See also
Book Reviews — History of Their Own, A (Book), D 18
ANDERSON, JACK. See also
Book Reviews — Control (Book), D 18
ANDERSON, MARTHA
Profile of Martha Pryor Anderson, black actress celebrating 99th birthday; photo (M), D 21,III,16:3
ANDERSON, ROBERT. See also
Timken Co, D 23
ANDERSON, WARREN M (SEN). See also
New York State — Finances — Budgets and Budgeting, D 23
New York State — Politics and Government, D 21
ANDOVER BANCORP
Andover Bancorp, a bank holding company, and its subsidiary, Andover Savings Bank promotes Robert M Henderson to new post of chairman and chief executive; both concerns also promote his son, Robert A Henderson, to executive vice president; James E McCobb Jr, chief financial officer of Andover Bancorp, adds the posts of president and chief operating officer; Joseph F Casey, controller of the bank, adds title of treasurer (S), D 23,IV,6:5
ANDREWS, JAMES. See also
Track and Field, D 16
ANDREWS AIR FORCE BASE (MD). See also
Airlines and Airplanes, D 25
ANDRUS, CECIL (GOV). See also
Atomic Weapons, D 17
ANDRUS PLANETARIUM. See also
Space, D 25
ANDRY, THOMAS (POLICE OFFICER). See also
Murders and Attempted Murders, D 21
ANGELO, RICHARD. See also
Murders and Attempted Murders, D 20,23
ANGELOZ, EDUARDO. See also
Argentina, D 16
ANGLE, JOHN C. See also
Guardian Life Insurance Co, D 23
ANGLICAN CHURCHES. See also
Christmas, D 26
South Africa, Republic of, D 26
Craig R Whitney travel article on viewing stained glass and other wonders of York Minster in England; photos; map (M), D 18,V,12:1

ANGOLA
Chester A Crocker, Assistant Secretary of State for African Affairs,is given credit by all sides as driving force behind negotiations that led to agreement that promises independence for Namibia and withdrawal of all Cuban troops from neighboring Angola; they say accord would not have been possible without Crocker's personal mediation; Crocker comments on his eight-year effort to achieve settlement; photo (M), D 18,I,28:1

Example 8. *New York Times Index.* (Copyright © 1988 by the New York Times Company. Reprinted with permission.)

Information Retrieval System Indexes

Information retrieval may be defined as the selective, systematic recall of logically stored information. In its generic sense it does not necessarily involve technology, but general usage implies machines. A traditional library, by any definition, is an information retrieval system. So is a telephone book. But current usage implies technology, especially electronic computing machines. The rise of our present era of the information age paralleled the rise of information technology and the development of information retrieval as a distinctive discipline.

For an information retrieval system to carry out the information process, at least six distinct functions are required: (1) the acquisition of the necessary and appropriate documents, (2) the preparation and representation of the content of those documents, (3) the coding of the content indicators for ease of manipulation, (4) the organized storage of those documents and their indicators in separate files, (5) the development of operational search strategies, and (6) the physical dissemination of the retrieval results. At the center of this system is the procedure that identifies and represents the content of the collection to the user; in most cases this is an index (see figure 4).

Most of the work in information retrieval, both theoretical and practical, has centered on indexing in one way or another. One of the ambiguous occurrences in the information science field was the entrance of experts from various subject areas. On the positive side was the desperate need of the library profession for the objective, disciplined thinking of mathematicians, philosophers, engineers, and computer technicians. On the other hand, these thinkers wasted a lot of time reinventing the wheel. For example, they went through a long, painful process of "discovering" that controlled vocabulary is important. Librarians have known this for centuries, although they called it an authority list.

The sole purpose of any index is retrieval, and we judge an information retrieval system ultimately on how well the index works. Since in computer-based systems much of the subjective, intuitive searching that we value in a "good reference librarian" is lost, we must compensate by having superior indexes. If we still want to allow intuition and human experience to be a part of the search itself, we must build it into the indexing system.

As an example, suppose we have only a computer-based system and we want to know how many eggs were laid in Iowa in 1989. Agricultural databases will probably be tried first. As inexperienced searchers, this seems to be the logical thing to do. Unfortunately, the computer will do only what we direct it to do. It has no intuition.

On the other hand, experienced reference librarians will "know" that *Statistical Abstracts* has an immediate answer, and they can probably pull down the handy paperback more quickly than they can log onto the computer.

If we intend to design systems that will "know" how to pull down *Statistical Abstracts*, then it all lies in a sophisticated indexing system.

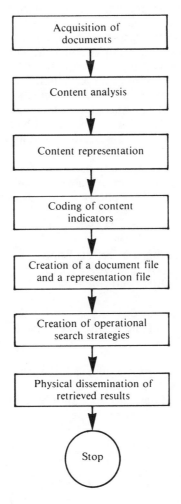

Fig. 4. Functions of an information
retrieval system

TYPES OF INDEXES

Author Indexes

Indexes whose entry points are people, organizations, corporate authors, government agencies, universities, and the like, are called author indexes. Users are guided to titles of documents by way of authors. Author indexes are not the most common type of indexes, but the author approach to information is not a rarity. The most obvious use is when someone is interested in a particular, known item and uses the index to see if the item is available. However, authors can also be used as an indirect subject approach. Workers in a discipline are generally well aware of the leading writers in a field and will often approach the literature from the avenue of these known authors. Cleveland (1976) has shown that in certain kinds of retrieval systems authors are strong indicators of subject content in a cluster of documents. This quantitative study supports the intuitive feelings of the importance of authors as subject indicators.

To maintain consistency in author indexes, a number of decisions have to be made, such as the number of names to be allowed per entry when a document has multiple writers, the method of alphabetizing to be used for titles and prefixes, use of full name or initials, delineation of authors with common names, and so forth. Author indexes must be constructed under carefully established guidelines.

Indexing and abstracting tools have a primary arrangement (e.g., alphabetical by author, classified) but they may also have secondary indexes. In the examples in the rest of this chapter, some of these secondary indexes are shown in order to fully illustrate the tool. The following are examples of author indexes:

Book Review Digest. New York: H. W. Wilson, 1905- . (See examples 11 and 12.)
 This is a digest and index of selected book reviews from English and American periodicals. It is arranged alphabetically by author of book reviewed, and it has a subject and title index.

Book Review Index. Detroit: Gale, 1965- . (See examples 9 and 10.)
 This is an author listing along with abbreviated citations to reviews in several hundred publications.

Population Index Bibliography, 1969-1981. Princeton University Office of Population Research. Boston: G. K. Hall, 1984.
 This is an example of basically an author index, which provides bibliographic data and then refers the user to the abstract in a companion publication (*Population Index*).

(Text continues on page 45.)

47th Street Photo
    r   M Photo - v52 - N '88 - p55
100 Successful College Application Essays
    y   BL - v85 - D 15 '88 - p702
100 Words About Transportation (Illus. by Richard E Brown)
    c   ASBYP - v21 - Summer '88 - p23
101 Ways to Answer the Request "Would You Please Put Out That...Cigar!"
    Am - v159 - D 10 '88 - pR2
AAMC Curriculum Directory
    r   BL - v85 - D 1 '88 - p623
AAMC Directory of American Medical Education
    r   BL - v85 - D 1 '88 - p623
Aardema, Verna - *Rabbit Makes a Monkey of Lion (Illus. by Jerry Pinkney)*
    c   PW - v235 - Ja 13 '89 - p89
Aaron, David - *Agent of Influence*
    KR - v56 - D 1 '88 - p1688
AARP Pharmacy Service Prescription Drug Handbook
    r   R&R Bk N - v3 - Ag '88 - p28
Aarts, Jan - *Corpus Linguistics II*
    Compt & Hum - v22 - #3 '88 - p221
Aaseng, Nathan - *The Disease Fighters*
    y   SB - v24 - N '88 - p85
Dwight Gooden: Strikeout King
    y   J Read - v32 - D '88 - p281
The Inventors: Nobel Prizes in Chemistry, Physics, and Medicine
    y   SB - v24 - N '88 - p86
Abbatiello, Judy - *Telecommunications and Data Communications Factbook*
    r   JQ - v65 - Summer '88 - p542
Abbey, Edward - *The Fool's Progress*
    LATBR - N 20 '88 - p3
    LJ - v113 - N 1 '88 - p105
    NYTBR - v93 - D 18 '88 - p22
    Time - v132 - N 28 '88 - p98
    VV - v34 - Ja 31 '89 - p54
Good News
    Critiq - v29 - Summer '88 - p223
One Life at a Time, Please
    WAL - v23 - N '88 - p229

ABC's of the Human Body
    R&R Bk N - v3 - Ag '88 - p27
Abdullah, Taufik - *Islam and Society in Southeast Asia*
    Pac A - v61 - Summer '88 - p360
Abe, K - *Jazz Giants*
    Dbt - v56 - Ja '89 - p56
    NYTBR - v93 - D 18 '88 - p21
    Stereo - v53 - D '88 - p108
    Trib Bks - D 4 '88 - p3
Abel, B - *Best Cartoons of the World from Atlas Magazine*
    SS - v79 - S '88 - p225
Abel, Christopher - *Jose Marti: Revolutionary Democrat*
    AHR - v93 - O '88 - p1146
    HAHR - v68 - N '88 - p858
Abel, Darrel - *The Moral Picturesque*
    Choice - v26 - D '88 - p642
Abel, Richard L - *Lawyers in Society*
    Choice - v26 - D '88 - p707
The Legal Profession in England and Wales
    TLS - D 30 '88 - p1440
Abell-Seddon, Brian - *Museum Catalogues*
    LR - v37 - #3 '88 - p61
Abels, Richard P - *Lordship and Military Obligation in Anglo-Saxon England*
    Choice - v26 - Ja '89 - p850
Abhyankar, Shreeram S - *Enumerative Combinatorics of Young Tableaux*
    SciTech - v12 - Jl '88 - p6
Abir, Mordechai - *Saudi Arabia in the Oil Era*
    Perspec - v17 - Summer '88 - p123
ABMS Compendium of Certified Medical Specialists 1988-1989. Vols. 1-7
    r   BL - v85 - D 1 '88 - p621
    r   LJ - v113 - N 1 '88 - p46
Abney, Glenn - *The Politics of State and Local Administration*
    PAR - v48 - N '88 - p1005
Abolafia, Yossi - *A Fish for Mrs. Gardenia (Illus. by Yossi Abolafia)*
    c   CBRS - v17 - O '88 - p13
    c   SLJ - v35 - N '88 - p83
Aboud, Frances - *Children and Prejudice*

Example 9. *Book Review Index* (author entry). (Reprinted by permission of Gale Research, Inc.)

1 2 3 (Illus. by Elizabeth Tansley) — *Tansley, Elizabeth*

2 Corinthians — *Martin, Ralph P*

2 Young 2 Go 4 Boys — *Lewis, Linda*

3rd September 1939 — *Gordon, Sheila*

VI Congress of the International Organization for Septuagint and Cognate Studies — *International Organization for Septuagint and Cognate Studies (6th: 1986: Jerusalem)*

14 Vicious Valentines — *Greenberg, Rosalind M*

20-Minute Menus — *Burros, Marian*

20 Under 30 — *Spark, Debra*

20 Under 35 — *Straus, Peter*

20th Century French Photography — *De Gouvion Saint-Cyr, Agnes*

24 Blacksmithing Projects — *Blandford, Percy W*

33 Poems — *Lax, Robert*

36 Children (Illus. by Robert G Jackson) — *Kohl, Herbert*

47th Street Photo

50 — *Corman, Avery*

The 60s Reader — *Haskins, James*

90 Years and 535 Miles — *Humphrey, Robert R*

100 Grams of Uranium Equal 290 Tons of Coal — *Robinson, Mark A*

100 Successful College Application Essays

100 Words About Transportation (Illus. by Richard E Brown)

100 Years of Lynchings — *Ginzberg, Ralph*

101 Experiments for the Young Scientist — *Prochnow, Dave*

101 Questions and Answers About Pets and People — *Squire, Ann*

101 Software Packages to Use in Your Library — *Dewey, Patrick R*

101 Ways to Answer the Request "Would You Please Put Out That...Cigar!"

175 Science Experiments to Amuse and Amaze Your Friends (Illus. by Kuo K Chen) — *Walpole, Brenda*

Example 10. *Book Review Index* (title entry). (Reprinted by permission of Gale Research, Inc.)

A

AAHA *See* American Association of Homes for the Aging

ABATE, YOHANNIS Ethiopia. See Wubneh, M.

AGANBEGÌÀN, ABEL GEZEVICH. The economic challenge of perestroika; [by] Abel Aganbegyan; edited by Michael Barratt Brown; introduced by Alec Nove; translated by Pauline M. Tiffen. 248p $18.95 1988 Indiana Univ. Press
  338.947 1. Soviet Union—Economic policy
  ISBN 0-253-32093-3   LC 88-3000
  Engl. title: The challenge, economics of perestroika

"Aganbegyan, member of the presidium of the Academy of Sciences of the USSR and chief economic adviser to Mikhail Gorbachev, presents his thoughts on the problems of the economic performance of the Soviet economy and the need for economic restructuring." (Choice) Index.

———

"The book is a companion piece to Gorbachev's book Perestroika [BRD 1988]. . . . Given the pattern of reforms he recommends, [the author's] proposal is not a return to Lenin's NEP (New Economy Policy), but seems to be more tinkering with the system. The book contains two short appendixes, one on the use of input-output analysis and a second on mathematical analysis of resource utilization. There is an index, but no bibliography or footnotes. Despite these limitations, the book will be of interest to undergraduate and graduate students of Soviet society."
  Choice 26:186 S '88. R.A. Battis (280w)

"The Aganbegyan prescriptions centre almost entirely on the existence of just one market, that for customers. The idea of a market economy without capitalism means, according to Mr. Aganbegyan, excluding markets in any of the building blocks of an economy—land, labour (no bidding for labour by raising wages, no unemployment) and capital. In the jargon, 'no factor markets'. This is supposed to be a coherent scheme: some markets good, others bad. It is not. . . . Nothing in Mr. Aganbegyan's book does more than tinker with the old design."
  Economist 307:97 Ap 23 '88 (800w)

Example 11. *Book Review Digest*, April 1989, p. 1 (main entry). (Copyright © 1989 by The H. W. Wilson Company. Material reproduced with permission of the publisher.)

A

A.I.D.S. (Disease) *See* AIDS (Disease)
Abdullah, King of Jordan, 1882-1951
   Shlaim, A. Collusion across the Jordan
Abolitionists
                       Juvenile literature
   Hamilton, V. Anthony Burns
Abortion
   Goldstein, R. D. Mother-love and abortion
   Hursthouse, R. Beginning lives
Abuse of the elderly *See* Elderly abuse
Accidents
   Holinger, P. C. Violent deaths in the United States
Acid rain
   Mello, R. A. Last stand of the red spruce
Acquired immune deficiency syndrome *See* AIDS (Disease)
Administration *See* Management
Adolescent mothers
   Vinovskis, M. An "epidemic" of adolescent pregnancy?
Adolescent pregnancy *See* Pregnancy, Adolescent
Adolescents *See* Youth
Adult education
        See also
           Continuing education
   Freire, P. Literacy
Adults and children *See* Children and adults
Advertising
   Jay, R. The trade card in nineteenth-century America
The Aeneid. Williams, R. D.
Africa
                       Antiquities
   Connah, G. African civilization
                       Civilization
   Connah, G. African civilization
                       History
   Darby, P. Three faces of imperialism
Africa, South *See* South Africa
African civilization. Connah, G.
African folk music *See* Folk music—Africa
Afro-Americans *See* Blacks
Aged *See* Elderly
Agonistic poetry. Fitzgerald, W.

Example 12. *Book Review Digest*, April 1989, p. 117 (subject and title entry). (Copyright © 1989 by The H. W. Wilson Company. Material reproduced with permission of the publisher.)

Alphabetical Subject Indexes

The term *alphabetical index* covers a number of different kinds of indexes, some of which are discussed below. The arranging of an index in alphabetical order is the most common method, since it is more convenient and follows a pattern familiar to us, but it is not the only method that can be used. The index may follow a classified arrangement or be both alphabetical and classified at the same time. Generally, any classified arrangement will need an alphabetical approach as a supplement, either separate or built in, to make it efficient to use.

An alphabetical index is based on the orderly principles of letters of the alphabet and is used for the arrangement of subject headings, cross-references, and qualifying terms, as well as main headings. All entry items are in one alphabetical order, including subject terms, author names, and place names. Even chemical formulas are placed in order by alphanumerical arrangement.

Of course, a decision of the order must be made. For example, we might say that symbols come first, then numbers, and, finally, letters. An example of such an order would be:

?

\#

32

106

A

AB

Zebra

One of the strong points of an alphabetical index is that it follows an order familiar to us. It is an order that we encounter every day when we use a telephone book or look up a word in our desk dictionary. To utilize such an arrangement we need few rules or explanations, since this is an order we began to understand in kindergarten. In fact, we are so attuned to this approach that we can often cut searching time by flipping to the point of the alphabet we need, with a minimum of scanning.

This may appear to be a simple, straightforward way to arrange an index, but it should be pointed out that alphabetizing is by no means an easy and absolutely deterministic procedure. We learned early that *ABC ... WXYZ* is a socially acceptable way—indeed, society's only way—to arrange letters if they are in order, but what they didn't teach us in kindergarten is what to do when a dollar sign or a number is thrown in. When alphabetizing words, do we order by words as units, or letter by letter? Does "Cats—Tigers" come before or after "Cats, Tigers"?

Clearly, the arrangement of the alphabet is arbitrary, but the concept of order in the alphabet has been a very useful idea for many centuries. In fact, it is a major example of how humans brought organization to their growing corpus of recorded knowledge.

The major drawbacks with the alphabetical arrangement are the problems of synonymity and scattering of entries. If we want information on house cats, do we look under "House cats," "Cats," or "Feline, domesticated"? Scattering means that subcategories of a subject are not drawn together under the generic term but are dispersed throughout the list. The technique used to overcome this, of course, is frequent cross-reference from the "wrong" terms to the preferred term, but now searchers are slowed by their choice of a "wrong" term, and the size and complexity of the index have grown.

It was not a simple matter to convert conventional human filing rules to computer filing rules. A human can make a judgment about filing M', Mc, and Mac in the proper place or in filing 12b in the *T*'s, but it requires some allowances to program a computer to follow the idiosyncrasies of the ALA filing rules.

The problem is that computers are coded to follow an *exact* numeric sequence. Such computer codes are based on standard systems that have been established by users and manufacturers of computers. For example, the American Standard Code for Information Interchange (ASCII) is one such code. Numbers, letters, and special characters are arranged in order, and numeric binary values are then associated with the numbers, letters, or special characters. The following is an example of the ASCII code:

Character	ASCII Code
0	0011 0000
1	0011 0001
2	0011 0010
A	0100 0001
B	0100 0010
a	0110 0001
b	0110 0010
c	0110 0011
{	0111 1011
$	0010 0100
%	0010 0110
&	0010 0111

It should be clear by now that the computer would make no allowances for "12b" and the character string would not be filed with the *T*'s. The different versions of *Mac* would be scattered. Also, numbers would always be filed before letters.

The basic way to overcome this rigid filing by the computer is to program sorting key routines. These routines instruct the computer to make filing decisions as closely as possible to the human filing rules.

Finally, it should be noted that some compromises had to be made with conventional rules to allow effective computer utilization.

As just suggested, there are two basic approaches to alphabetizing—letter by letter and word by word. Letter by letter is a rather mechanistic way of simply ignoring the blanks between words, visualizing a string of letters, and then ordering these separate strings. In word-by-word alphabetizing, all the items starting with one word are ordered before the items with a second word are considered. Punctuation is utilized to link similar things together. If numbers are involved, the general rule is that nothing comes before something; that is, numeric value is the determining factor. Sometimes, however, numbers are dealt with as though they were spelled out, the same way abbreviations are frequently handled. Contrary to public opinion, alphabetization is not a straightforward process; elaborate rules have been developed to standardize these procedures.

The following are examples of alphabetical subject indexes, with some examples of secondary indexes:

Applied Science and Technology Index. New York: H. W. Wilson, vol. 46- , 1958- . (See examples 13 and 14.)
This index is a good example of an alphabetically arranged subject index with a limited amount of secondary breakdown into subheadings.

Current Technology Index. Phoenix: Oryx Press, 1981- . (See examples 15 and 16.)
This is an example of a detailed subject index, arranged alphabetically, with good cross-references.

American Statistics Index. A Comprehensive Guide and Index to the Statistical Publications of the U.S. Government. Washington, D.C.: Congressional Information Service, 1973- . (See examples 17 and 18.)
The subjects and names index contains references to subjects, to corporate authors, and to individual authors of articles and publications. The categories index contains references to publication tables and to groups of tables that contain breakdowns of statistical data by state, by industry, by age, or by some other standard category.

Biological and Agricultural Index. New York: H. W. Wilson, 1964- . (See examples 19 and 20.)
This is a subject index in which all entries are arranged in one alphabet. The filing of the subject headings is alphabetical, word by word.

(Text continues on page 56.)

A

AAAS *See* American Association for the Advancement of Science

Abandoned buildings *See* Buildings, Abandoned

Abbreviations
Abbreviations come up short on meaning. *IEEE Spectr* 25:19 N '88

Aberration (Optics)
    See also
    Optics, Adaptive
Analytic optimisation for holographic optical elements. E. Hasman and A. A. Friesem. bibl diags *J Opt Soc Am A* 6:62-72 Ja '89
Design of null lens correctors for the testing of astronomical optics. J. M. Sasian. bibl diags *Opt Eng* 27:1051-6 D '88
Discussion of the optics of a new 3-D imaging system. L. Yang and others. bibl diags *Appl Opt* 27:4529-34 N 1 '88
Does the chromatic aberration of the eye vary with age? P. A. Howarth and others. bibl *J Opt Soc Am A* 5:2087-92 D '88
Holographic optical scanning elements with minimum aberrations. H. P. Herzig and R. Dandliker. bibl il diags *Appl Opt* 27:4739-46 N 15 '88
Interference of diffracted multiple wavefronts in the geometric shadow of the Fresnel region. P. V. Avizonis and others. bibl il diags *Appl Opt* 28:163-72 Ja 1 '89
Multifaceted laser beam integrators: general formulation and design concepts. F. M. Dickey and B. D. O'Neil. bibl diags *Opt Eng* 27:999-1007 N '88
On the fifth order aberration in a sextupole corrected probe forming system. Z. Shao. bibl diags *Rev Sci Instrum* 59:2429-37 N '88
Pseudoaxicon lenses. E. W. Marchand. *Appl Opt* 28:154-6 Ja 1 '89
Simple technique for designing teleconverters. I. Powell. diags *Appl Opt* 27:4183-6 O 15 '88
The triplet: an "embarrassment of riches". D. R. Shafer. bibl diags *Opt Eng* 27:1035-8 D '88
Underwater hologrammetry: aberrations in the real image of an underwater object when replayed in air. M. Kilpatrick and J. Watson. bibl diags *J Phys D* 21:1701-5 D 14 '88

Mathematical models
Aberrations in high aperture conventional and confocal imaging systems. C. J. Sheppard. bibl diags *Appl Opt* 27:4782-6 N 15 '88

Example 13. *Applied Science and Technology Index*, Vol. 77, No. 3, March 1989, p. 1 (main entry). (Copyright © 1989 by The H. W. Wilson Company. Material reproduced with permission of the publisher.)

BOOK REVIEWS

A

Accelerated processing of meat. 1987
    Food Technol 42:150-1 D '88. J. L. Secrist
Acidification of tropical countries.
    New Sci 120:59 N 5 '88. F. Pearce
Advances in command, control & communication systems.
1987
    J Phys E 21:1009 N '88. J. Bicknell
Aho, A. V. and others. The AWK programming language.
1988
    Computer 21:113-14 D '88. P. Hughes
Alexander, R. M. Elastic mechanisms in animal movement.
1988
    New Sci 120:54-5 N 19 '88. G. Vines
Alkaline igneous rocks. 1987
    Geology 16:1156 D '88. R. Batiza
Alkaloids. v6 1988
    Chem Ind no23:756-7 D 5 '88. J. R. Lewis
Allègre, C. J. The behavior of the earth. 1988
    Science 242:1451-2 D 9 '88. P. J. Wyllie
Allen, M. B. and others. Numerical modeling in science
and engineering. 1988
    J Appl Mech 55:996-7 D '88. W. K. Liu
Altman, L. K. Who goes first? 1985
    Am Sci 76:632 N/D '88. L. N. Magner
The American development of biology. 1988
    Science 242:1314-15 D 2 '88. D. J. Kevles
Amundsen, R. The Amundsen photographs. 1987
    Sci Am 259:120 D '88. P. Morrison and P. Morrison
Anderson, D. R. and others. Statistics. 1986
    Technometrics 30:461-2 N '88. A. Propst
Anderson, M. J. The American census. 1988
    Science 242:448-50 O 21 '88. R. V. Wells
Aneuploidy; pt A, Incidence and etiology. 1987
    Am Sci 77:80-1 Ja/F '89. C. G. Palmer
Angier, N. Natural obsessions. 1988
    Science 242:602-3 O 28 '88. H. Etzkowitz
Arctic and alpine mycology II. 1987
    Am Sci 77:85 Ja/F '89. R. D. Seppelt
Argvris, J. and Mlejnek, H.-P. Die methode der finiten
elemente, einführung in die dynamik; v3. 1988
    Comput Methods Appl Mech Eng 71:367-8 D '88.
    M. Frik
Arp, H. C. Quasars, redshifts, and controversies. 1987
    Phys Today 41:117-18 N '88. M. J. Rees

Example 14. *Applied Science and Technology Index*, Vol. 77, No. 3, March 1989, p. 783 (book review entries). (Copyright © 1989 by The H. W. Wilson Company. Material reproduced with permission of the publisher.)

AUTHOR INDEX

This index gives

(a) a direct reference to journal locations of works by given authors.

(b) the first word or phrase of the subject heading under which the article appears in the main C.T.I. subject index. Titles of articles may thus be traced through the main subject index.

Aalto, A. Wat. Pwr. Dam Constr., 33 (May 81) p.40-3 HYDROELECTRIC POWER

Aaras, A. Ergonomics, 23 (Aug 80) p.707-26 CABLES, ELECTRIC

Aartsen, M. Design (Jun 81) p.30-3 SOUND REPRODUCTION

Aartsen, M. Design (May 81) p.36-7 CAMERAS

Aastrup, S. J. Inst. Brew., 86 (Nov-Dec 80) p.277-83 MALT

Aatre, V.K. IEE Proc. F: Commun. Radar Signal Process., 128 (Apr 81) p.74-82 COMMUNICATIONS ENGINEERING, DIGITAL

Abate, A. Proc. Instn. Civ. Engrs. pt.2, 71 (Jun 81) p.395-406 BUILDINGS

Abbady, M.A. J. Chem. Technol. Biotechnol., 31 (Feb 81) p.111-14 3-(NITRODIPHENYLSULPHIDO)QUINAZOL-4-ONES

Abbas, I. J. Phys. D: Appl. Phys., 14 (14 Apr 81) p.649-60 GAS BREAKDOWN

Abbas, I. J. Phys. D: Appl. Phys., 14 (14 Apr 81) p.661-74 GAS BREAKDOWN

Abbas, K.B. Polymer, 22 (Jun 81) p.836-41 POLYCARBONATE RESINS

Abbas, T.K. J. Heat Recovery Syst., 1 no.3 (1981) p.181-203 HEAT PUMPS

Abbasy, M. J. Sci. Fd. Agric., 32 (Feb 81) p.166-74 SUNFLOWER SEED MEAL

Abbate, G. Opt. Laser Technol., 13 (Apr 81) p.97-8 REFRACTIVE INDEX—TEMPERATURE RELATIONSHIPS

Abraham, K.P. Metals Technol., 7 (Dec 80) p.483-7 STEEL—CHROMIUM—SILICON

Abraham, M. Electrochim. Acta, 26 (Oct 81) p.1397-1401 WATER: SOLUTIONS

Abrahams, M. Engng. Mater. Des., 25 (Jan 81) p.18-21 PLASTICS: ENGINEERING

Abrahams, R. Frozen Fds., 34 (Aug 81) p.10+ PASTA ALIMENTARE

Abrahamsson, P. Elect. Commun., 55 no.3 (1980) p.177-83 TELEPHONY: EXCHANGES

Abram, J. Biomaterials, 2 (Jul 81) p.185-6 BONE, SUBSTITUTE

Abuelma'atti, M.T. IEE Proc. G: Electron. Circuits Syst., 128 (Feb 81) p.32-4 COMMUNICATIONS ENGINEERING: AMPLIFIERS

Abuelma'atti, M.T. Int. J. Electron., 50 (Jan 81) p.55-60 SATELLITES, ARTIFICIAL

Abuelma'atti, M.T. Int. J. Electron., 51 (Jul 81) p.57-62 AMPLIFIERS, KLYSTRON

Abuelma'atti, M.T. Wireless Wld., 87 (Nov 81) p.79-80 FUNCTION GENERATORS, DIODE

Abu-Ghannam, B.J. J. Mech. Engng. Sci., 22 (Oct 80) p.213-28 AIRFLOW

Abu Hassan, M. Int. J. Control, 34 (Aug 81) p.371-81 ELECTRIC POWER SYSTEMS

Acerete, C. Electrochim. Acta, 26 (Aug 81) p.1041-5 ARABOASCORBIC

Example 15. *Current Technology Index* (author index). (Reprinted with permission.)

8mm FILM
 See
 Cinematography : Film, 8mm
16mm CAMERAS
 See
 Cinematography, Colour : Cameras, 16mm
16mm FILM
 See
 Cinematography : Film, 16mm
ABEL EQUATION
 See
 Plasmas : Spectroscopy : Abel equation
ABERDEEN
 See
 Petroleum : Drilling, Offshore : Supply bases : Aberdeen
 Transport : Aberdeen
ABRASION
 See
 Bearings, Rolling : Abrasion
 Fabrics : Abrasion
 Magnesium oxide : Crystals, Single, Doped : Lithium : Abrasion
 Metals : Abrasion
 Rubber : Abrasion
 Tape, Magnetic : Abrasion
ABRASIVE BELT GRINDING
 See
 Grinding, Abrasive belt
ABRASIVE BLASTED METALS
 See
 Metals, Abrasive blasted

A.B.S.
 Fatigue testing
 Rubber toughening of plastics. Pt.5: Fatigue damage mechanisms in a.b.s. and h.i.p.s. C.B. Bucknall & W.W. Stevens. *J. Mater. Sci.*, 15 (Dec 80) p.2950-8
 Products : Industrial design
 ABS proud to be a polymer. S. Braidwood. *Design* (Oct 81) p.38-41
ABSORBERS
 See
 Radar : Aerials : Absorbers
 Radar, H.F. : Aerials, Wire : Cross section : Reduction : Coatings : Absorbers
 Radar, V.H.F. : Aerials, Wire : Cross section : Reduction : Coatings : Absorbers
ABSORPTION
 See also
 Alkanolamines : Aqueous solutions : Carbon dioxide—Hydrogen sulphide absorption
 Calcium carbonate : Suspensions : Sulphur dioxide absorption
 Epoxy resin—Carbon fibres : Water absorption
 Ethanolamine : Carbon dioxide absorption
 Fabrics : Moisture absorption
 Films, Fluid, Non-Newtonian, Falling, Laminar : Gas absorption
 Flue gas : Sulphur dioxide absorption
 Furnaces : Fluidised beds, Coal fired : Sulphur dioxide absorption
 Germanium—Selenium, Amorphous : Defects : Studies : Light absorption

A.C. LOSSES
 See
 Cables, Electric, Superconducting : A.C. losses
 Magnets, Superconducting : Wires : Niobium—Titanium, Copper stabilised : A.C. losses
 Polythene : Insulating materials, Electrical : A.C. losses

A.C. MACHINES
 Reactive power : Matrices, Complex
 Im↓*GP N.N. Hancock. *Int. J. Elect. Engng. Educ.*, 18 (Jan 81) p.79-84
 Stators : Cores : Manufactures : Fixtures
 Designs for cost effective production [1980 Design Council GKN Tool Design Prizes] *Tooling*, 34 (Dec 80) p.5-7
 Jig and tool designers' Know-how takes GKN's prizes. *Metalwrkg. Prod.*, 125 (Jan 81) p.59+

A.C. MOTORS
 See
 Electric motors, A.C.
 Pumps : Electric motors, A.C.
 Pumps, Vertical : Electric motors, A.C.
ACCELERATED TESTING
 See
 Coal : Slurries : Pipelines : Steel : Erosion : Testing, Accelerated
 Dental materials : Wear : Testing, Accelerated
 Paint : Weathering : Testing, Accelerated
 Power stations : Boilers : Superheaters : Tubes :

Example 16. *Current Technology Index* (subject index). (Reprinted with permission.)

BY FOREIGN COUNTRY

Agriculture and Food

Africa (sub-Saharan) food emergency aid mgmt of AID, and PL 480 appropriations by country, 1984-86, evaluation rpt, 9916–11.11

Africa (West) intraregional agricultural trade, by commodity and country, 1970-85, 1528–252

Africa food supply and indicators of need, by country, 1966-84, 1528–249

Agricultural Statistics, 1986, annual rpt, 1004–1

Bean (dried) prices by State, and foreign and US production, use, stocks, and trade, weekly rpt, 1311–17

Bean (dried) production and prices by State, exports and foreign production by country, and USDA food aid purchases, by bean type, 1981-86, annual rpt, 1311–18

Casein imports of US by country, and Australia and New Zealand industry and export subsidies, 1970s-85,, 1528–254

Cocoa and cocoa products foreign and US production, prices, and trade, FAS semiannual circular, 1925–9

Coffee production, trade and quotas, and use, by country, with US and intl prices, FAS periodic circular, 1925–5

Corn and soybeans exports related to indicators of demand, by country, model

Exports (agricultural) competitiveness impacts of technological devs, with background data, 1960s-85 and projected to 2000, 26358–162

Exports (agricultural) of US, impacts of foreign agricultural and trade policy, with data by commodity and country, 1986, annual rpt, 1924–8

Exports (agricultural) program funding, agreements, sales, and trade assn contributions, by commodity and country, FY74-85, hearing, 21168–34

Exports and imports (agricultural) of US, by commodity and country, bimonthly rpt with articles, 1522–1

Exports and imports (agricultural) of US, by detailed commodity and country, 1986, annual rpt, 1524–8

Exports and imports (agricultural) of US, by detailed commodity and country, 1986, semiannual rpt, 1522–4

Exports and imports (agricultural) of US, outlook and current situation, quarterly rpt, 1542–4

Exports of grains, oilseed products, hides, skins, and cotton, by country, weekly rpt, 1922–3

Famine economic impacts, and deaths by country, various periods 1941-85, 1528–247

Example 17. *American Statistics Index* (index by categories). (Copyright 1987, Congressional Information Service, Inc. Published by permission.)

This index contains references to subjects, to corporate authors, and to individual authors.

References to individual items within a tabular breakdown (e.g. data about a particular State in a table that is broken down State-by-State) have been included only on a very selective basis. For complete references to information of this kind, please use the Index by Categories.

For information on how to make best use of both indexes, please consult the User Guide.

Abandoned property
Arson incidents by whether structure occupied, property value, and arrest rate, by property type, 1986, annual rpt, 6224–2.1
Fires, casualties, and property loss, by structure type and circumstances, 1983, annual rpt, 9434–4

Abilene, Tex.
Housing vacancy rates for single and multifamily units and mobile homes, by city and ZIP code, 1987, annual MSA rpt, 9304–19.3
see also under By City and By SMSA or MSA in the "Index by Categories"

Abnormalities
see Birth defects

Abortion
Cancer (cervical) incidence, by sexual history, and reproductive and other characteristics, 1982-84, local area studies, article, 4472–1.736
Deaths related to pregnancy, by race, age, and location, 1983, US Vital Statistics annual rpt, 4144–2.1

Teenage births and other pregnancy outcome by race and age of mother, and prevention and aid programs and funding, by State, 1960s-85, 21968–38
Teenage births and other pregnancy outcome, rates by State, 1980, hearings, 21788–170
Youth and children, social, economic, and demographic characteristics, and govt programs, 1950s-87, 21968–26

Abrasive materials
Employment, earnings, and hours, by SIC 1- to 4-digit industry, monthly 1983-Feb 1987, annual rpt, 6744–4
Exports and imports of US, and ratio to domestic production, by SIC-based 2- to 7-digit commodity, 1977-82, annual rpt, 2424–3
Exports of US, detailed commodities by country, monthly rpt, 2422–3
Exports of US, detailed Schedule B commodities with countries of destination, 1986, annual rpt, 2424–9
Exports of US, detailed Schedule E commodities by mode of transport, world area, and country, 1986, annual rpts, 2424–5
Freight (waterborne domestic and foreign) by commodity, traffic, and passengers, by port and waterway, 1985, annual rpt, 3754–3
Imports of US, detailed Schedule A commodities by country, monthly rpt, 2422–2
Imports of US, detailed Schedule A commodities by mode of transport, world area, and country, 1986, annual rpts, 2424–2

Example 18. *American Statistics Index* (subjects and names index). (Copyright 1987, Congressional Information Service, Inc. Published by permission.)

A

A.B.A. checklist. 2nd ed. 1982
  Auk 100:767-8 Jl '83. W. Hoffman
Abasiekong, E. M. Integrated rural development in the
  Third World. 1982
  Am J Agric Econ 65:834-5 N '83. R. D. Robbins
Abdel-Wahab, M. F. Schistosomiasis in Egypt. 1982
  Q Rev Biol 58:298 Je '83. D. Heyneman
Acid precipitation, effects on ecological systems
  J Appl Ecol 20:688 Ag '83. K. A. Brown
  J Ecol 71:1024-5 N '83. R. A. Skeffington
  J Environ Qual 12:158 Ja-Mr '83. D. F. Grigal
  Soil Sci 136:193-4 S '83. A. W. McIntosh
Acoustic communication in birds; v1-2
  Anim Behav 32:312 F '84. P. K. McGregor
Acta XVII Congressus Internationalis Ornithologici. 1980
  Auk 100:524-5 Ap '83. G. E. Woolfenden
Acute diarrhea
  Am J Clin Nutr 39:346 F '84. F. Lifshitz
  J Am Diet Assoc 84:376 Mr '84. L. J. Boyne
Adams, F. G. and Behrman, J. R. Commodity exports
  and economic development. 1982
  Can J Agric Econ 31:268 Jl '83. A. Schmitz
Addicott, F. T. Abscission
  Q Rev Biol 58:438 S '83. P. W. Morgan
The Adipocyte and obesity
  Am J Clin Nutr 39:644-5 Ap '84. S. K. Fried
Advanced views in primate biology. 1982
  Q Rev Biol 58:272 Je '83. T. I. Grand
Advances in biochemical psychopharmacology. 1982
  Q Rev Biol 58:300-1 Je '83. M. Fink
Advances in botanical research; v9
  Ann Bot 52:434-5 S '83. J. Chapman
  Phytochemistry 22 no8:1842 '83. J. R. Lenton

Example 19. *Biological and Agricultural Index*,
August 1983-July 1984, p. 2219 (book reviews).
(Copyright © 1984 by The H. W. Wilson Company. Material reproduced with permission of the
publisher.)

A

A-rest
Influence of ancymidol and light intensity on growth and flowering of Easter lily. E. J. Williams and A. J. Lewis. bibl il *Can J Plant Sci* 63:955-8 O '83
A23187 *See* Ionophores
AAEA *See* American Agricultural Economics Association
AAV (Viruses) *See* Adeno-associated viruses and infections
ABA *See* Abscisic acid
Abalones
Digalactosyldiacylglycerols isolated from a brown alga as effective phagostimulants for a young abalone. K. Sakata and K. Ina. bibl il *Agric Biol Chem* 47:2957-60 D '83
Estimation of abalone mortality rates with growth analysis. D. A. Fournier and P. A. Breen. bibl il *Trans Am Fish Soc* 112:403-11 My '83
Abattoir surveys *See* Veterinary disease surveys
Abatus cordatus
Reproductive cycle of the brooding echinoid Abatus cordatus (Echinodermata) in Kerguelen (Antarctic Ocean): changes in the organ indices, biochemical composition and caloric content of the gonads. P. Magniez. bibl il map *Mar Biol* 74:55-64 My '83
Abdomen
    See also
    Peritoneum

Abscesses
Diagnosis—Horses
Chyloabdomen and ultrasonographic detection of an intra-abdominal abscess in a foal. J. R. Hanselaer and T. G. Nyland. bibl il *J Am Vet Med Assoc* 183:1465-7 D 15 '83

Horses
Abdominal abscess associated with Parascaris equorum infection in a foal. J. A. DiPietro and others. bibl *J Am Vet Med Assoc* 182:991-2 My 1 '83
Diseases
    See also
    Peritonitis

Cattle
Congenital mesothelioma: cause of distended abdomen in a calf. B. C. Anderson and others. il *Vet Med Small Anim Clin* 79:395+ Mr '84

Diagnosis—Horses
Complications of abdominocentesis in the horse. E. P. Tulleners. *J Am Vet Med Assoc* 182:232-4 F 1 '83

Diagnosis—Pets
Diagnostic abdominal paracentesis techniques: clinical evaluation in 129 dogs and cats. D. T. Crowe, Jr. bibl il *J Am Anim Hosp Assoc* 20:223-30 Mr/Ap '84

Horses
    See also
    Colic in horses
Foreign bodies
Cats
What is your diagnosis? [abdominal mass outside the intestinal lumen and subluxation of T12-13] il *J Am Vet Med Assoc* 184:1291-2 My 15 '84
Innervation
Crustaceans
The organization of flexion-evoking interneurons in the abdominal nerve cord of the crayfish, Procambarus clarkii. J. L. Larimer and J. Jellies. bibl il *J Exp Zool* 226:341-51 Je '83

Example 20. *Biological and Agricultural Index*, August 1983-July 1984, p. 1 (main entry). (Copyright © 1984 by The H. W. Wilson Company. Material reproduced with permission of the publisher.)

Classified Indexes

Classified indexes have been popular as guides not only to specialized situations, such as taxonomic names, but also to general subjects. They are especially useful for generic searches when the retrieval is aiming for classes of documents. A classified index is arranged in a hierarchy of related topics, starting with generic topics and working down to the specific. Clearly, the scheme comes before the indexing, since every concept has a fixed place in the hierarchy.

Classified indexes have advantages and disadvantages. The most obvious advantage is that they are conceptually an aid to a search. The subject arrangement, which attempts to pull together related subjects, is based on the assumption that users are accustomed to a logical arrangement of knowledge and thus it is natural for them to search this way. Classified indexes make searching simple if the user wants to conduct generic searches, since the hierarchy is visually presented. When an entry is located, the user is immediately made aware of items closely related to that concept. It is similar to what happens when we browse a library stack — we become interested in books in the immediate area; this is the argument that has always been made for having open library stacks. Serendipity is a very legitimate way to search an information file.

The major disadvantage of the classified index is that a secondary file, an alphabetical list, is necessary, so that a search will generally require a two-step procedure of going to the alphabetical list to identify the right position in the classified list.

The literature is full of discussion about the superiority of either classified or alphabetical indexes (or combinations), but the fact remains that there are strong and weak points in each, and we come back to a point often made here: Who is the user?

The following are examples of classified indexes:

Engineering Index. New York: Engineering Information, Inc., 1884- . (See examples 21 and 22.)
This is an example of an arrangement by a primary heading based on a separately published authority file, *Subject Headings for Engineering.* The monthly publication is called *Engineering Index Monthly* and the annual publication is called *Engineering Index Annual.*

Index Medicus. Bethesda, Md.: National Library of Medicine, 1960- . (See example 23.)
This is a comprehensive index to the medical literature. It is a classified index that uses MeSH (Medical Subject Headings) as an authority list. This is an example of a highly specific list of subject headings.

Index to Theses Accepted for Higher Degrees in the Universities of Great Britain and Ireland. London: AsLib, 1953- .
This index has a classified arrangement. It is alphabetical by university within subject categories, and it has subject and author indexes.

(Text continues on page 60.)

A

ABLATION See ELECTRIC CIRCUIT BREAKERS—Materials; LASERS, EXCIMER—Applications; PLASMAS—Heating; MIXTURES—Ablation; ROCKETS AND MISSILES—Launching.

ABRASIVES See Also CERAMIC MATERIALS—Grinding; HONING; METAL FINISHING.

000001 ABRASIVE MINERALS: HARD WORK IN SOFT MARKETS. Traditional minerals used by the abrasives industry are facing strong competition from new, harder, but more costly materials. The article highlights developments among producers of natural and synthetic hard abrasives - emery, corundum, garnet, bauxite and fused alumina, silicon carbide, diamond, and cubic boron nitride. Market trends and future prospects for such materials are also examined. (Author abstract)

Toon, Steve. *Ind Miner (London)* n 231 Dec 1986 12p between p 53 and 73.

Applications See CUTTING TOOLS—Cubic Boron Nitride.

Bonding See Also GRINDING WHEELS—Cubic Boron Nitride.

000002 NOVEL TECHNIQUE FOR PRODUCING A GLASS-CERAMIC BOND IN ALUMINA ABRASIVES. Alumina abrasives bonded by a glass-ceramic were produced by the method of sintering a glass powder of fine particle size. A technique was found to overcome a long-standing problem in the use of devitrifying bonds, that being poor wetting and flow. The fracture strength of abrasives containing a glass-ceramic bond measured by the diametral compression test was equal to that of commercial vitreous bonded material, and the fracture toughness was 40% higher. (Edited author abstract) 16 refs.

Clark, Terence J. (Alfred Univ, Alfred, NY, USA); Reed, James S. *Am Ceram Soc Bull* v 65 n 11 Nov 1986 p 1506-1512.

000003 BONDED ABRASIVES - THE UNIVERSAL ANSWER. The bonded abrasives industry makes abrasive wheels, segments and blocks with vitrified, resinoid, rubber or shellac bonds: it has seen a severely declining market for its products over the past 10 years or so in all the major industrial countries. Capability and productivity of the grinding machine and abrasive wheel combination have remained relatively static until recently. Yet cutting tool technology has advanced considerably with new carbide grades and coatings, as well as ceramic tool materials, being applied in an increasing variety of insert-type tools. With the market for bonded abrasives now actually down to about a half its former volume, it is very interesting to observe how a major UK supplier, Universal Grinding Wheel Company, has met the situation.

Cookson, Jim (Metalworking Production, London, Engl). *Metalwork Prod* v 131 n 2 Feb 1987 p 69-70.

Coated Products See Also CAST IRON—Grinding. DIAMONDS—Lapping; GRINDING WHEELS—Diamond; METALS AND ALLOYS—Grinding.

of finishing to close tolerances with minimum part distortion and no temperature damage. The process is based on developments in metal grinding with coated-abrasive belts that have been under study at 3M since the mid-1960s. This includes the development of tough, new abrasive materials that stand up under the punishing impact of the grinding process. Developments in this area have been aided by close cooperation with machine builders who were willing to help pioneer the process. The high-pressure-grinding concept (at 3M it is called Rapid Grinding System or RGS) is based on the fact that long belt life and efficient metal removal depend on the belt contacting the workpiece at a proper rate of speed and under high pressure. The article discusses the techniques and case history applications.

Miller, D.E. (3M, St. Paul, MN, USA). *Mach Tool Blue Book* v 81 n 10 Oct 1986 p 56-59.

Efficiency See GRINDING—Mathematical Models.

Fatigue

000005 CYCLIC FATIGUE AND RELIABILITY OF RESINOID-BONDED ABRASIVE MATERIALS. The cyclic fatigue behavior of several types of resinoid-bonded abrasive material was determined in ambient air (22°C and 50% relative humidity) and in a standard coolant at 35°C. The fatigue behavior was not affected by the material hardness; however, the susceptibility to fatigue was significantly increased by the presence of a coolant. A power law relationship between the median number of cycles to failure and the maximum cyclic stress best described the effect of mean stress on the cyclic fatigue data. The use of cyclic fatigue data in determining the likelihood of fatigue failure is discussed and an overspeed proof test is suggested to assure the reliability of resinoid-bonded grinding wheels operating at high speeds and subject to a large number of stress cycles. (Author abstract) 9 refs.

Ritter, J.E. (Univ of Massachusetts, Amherst, MA, USA); Service, T.H. *Mater Sci Eng* v 82 Sep 1986 p 231-239.

Friction

000006 FRICTIONAL BEHAVIOR OF SUPERABRASIVES. Friction test results of diamond and CBN abrasive grains to various metallic and ceramic discs are shown, and also, recent studies on the friction of these superabrasives were reviewed. The present frictional test was conducted at sliding speeds of 5.0 to 15m/s under a load of 2.5 N or 4.5 N. The coefficients of friction under seady state were measured and discussed. The diamond grains indicate usually very low coefficients of friction of 0.06 to 0.15, whereas alumina and SiC grains show high coefficients of friction of 0.3 to 0.5 or higher. However, the coefficient of friction of diamond to cemented carbide was unexpectedly high. Also, CBN grains showed relatively high coefficient of friction. The values of the frictional coefficients of diamond grain generally agree well with various data obtained by other investigators. (Edited author abstract) 19 refs. In Japanese.

Matsuo, Tetsuo (Kumamoto Univ, Kumamoto, Jpn); Kawabata, Noriji. *J Jpn Soc Lubr Eng* v 31 n 10 1986 p 691-696.

Example 21. *Engineering Index* (main entry).

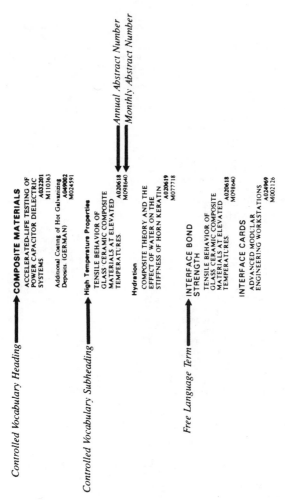

Example 22. *Engineering Index Annual* (subject index).

A-23187

PHARMACOLOGY

Enhanced generation of leukotriene B4 by neutrophils stimulated by unopsonized zymosan and by calcium ionophore after exercise-induced asthma. Arm JP, et al. **Am Rev Respir Dis** 1988 Jul;138(1):47-53

Eicosanoid production in isolated perfused lungs stimulated by calcium ionophore A23187. Westcott JY, et al. **Am Rev Respir Dis** 1988 Oct;138(4):895-900

The calcium ionophore A23187 is a potent stimulator of the vitamin D3-25 hydroxylase in hepatocytes isolated from normocalcaemic vitamin D-depleted rats. Benbrahim N, et al. **Biochem J** 1988 Oct 1;255(1):91-7

The biological dynamics of lipoxygenase in rabbit red cells in the course of an experimental bleeding anaemia. Unexpected effects of the calcium ionophore A 23187. Ludwig P, et al. **Biomed Biochim Acta** 1988;47(7):593-608

Effects of calcium ionophore and phorbol ester on class-II-restricted virus-specific human cytotoxic T cell clones. Richert JR, et al. **Int Arch Allergy Appl Immunol** 1988;87(2):178-83

Calcium ionophore A23187 induces differentiation of HL-60 cells into macrophage-like cells. Toyokawa Y, et al. **Nippon Ketsueki Gakkai Zasshi** 1988 Jul;51(4):746-51

A FIBERS see NERVE FIBERS, MYELINATED

ABATE see under INSECTICIDES, ORGANOTHIOPHOSPHATE

ABATTOIRS

Prevalence of disease conditions and pregnancy in sheep and goats seen over a three year period in Enugu abattoir, Nigeria. Wosu LO. **Arch Roum Pathol Exp Microbiol** 1988 Jan-Mar;47(1):57-64

ABBREVIATIONS

Proposed list of abbreviations [letter] Felson B. **Radiology** 1989 Jan;170(1 Pt 1):283

ABDOMEN

Periarteritis with intra-abdominal bleeding [letter] Sabo D, et al. **Ann Emerg Med** 1988 Dec;17(12):1368

Circadian rhythms in patients with abdominal pain syndromes. Roberts-Thomson IC, et al. **Aust N Z J Med** 1988 Jun;18(4):569-74

Diagnostic investigation and special treatment of chronic abdominal ischaemia. Petrovsky BV, et al. **Int Angiol** 1988 Jul-Sep;7(3):214-8

The impact of routine admission abdominal sonography on patient care. Verbanck JJ, et al. **JCU** 1988 Nov-Dec; 16(9):651-4

[The centenary of Obraztsov's method of deep palpation of the abdominal cavity] Gubergrits AIa. **Sov Med** 1988; (8):124-5 **(Rus)**

[Abdominal echography in recurrent abdominal pain: study in 100 cases] Rubio Quiñones F, et al. **An Esp Pediatr** 1988 Sep;29(3):217-9 (Eng. Abstr.) **(Spa)**

Example 23. *Index Medicus* (subject section). (Reprinted with permission of Executive Editor, *Index Medicus*.)

Coordinate Indexes

Coordinate indexes are created by combining two or more single index terms to create a new class. For example, if the individual index terms "Black," "Polecats," and "Texas" are combined, the result is a distinctive class: *Black Polecats of Texas*. Obviously, these types of indexes are basically Boolean models for searching, and the result is the logical product of the terms.

A classic example of a coordinate index is the marginal-hole punched card system. Index terms were represented by notching out holes in known positions around the card as shown in the following illustration.

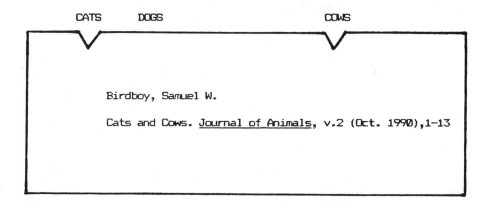

In the example, the article has been indexed by notching out the positions where the correct index terms are located. Notice that there is no notch for the term "Dogs," since it is not an index term for this particular document.

To search this type of coordinate index, a needle was inserted through a file of cards at the desired position (e.g., "Cats" and "Dogs") and the cards were shaken so that the notched cards would fall. In this case all cards with notches for cats and dogs would drop out, thus identifying the papers that were indexed under those two terms.

The natural evolution of these systems led to punch-cards computer systems and finally to modern, online databases, which are sophisticated descendants of the old postcoordinate indexes.

Coordinate indexing was the natural consequence of the application of punch-card techniques to information retrieval, since the presence or absence of a hole in a card can represent a binary indication of a specific bit of information. For example, the presence of a hole in a card position representing "Cats" would mean that the information unit "Cats" was indeed there.

In England in the 1940s, W. E. Batten, a chemist, indexed chemistry documents with this technique. He developed his system while he was head of the Patents and Intelligence Department of the Plastic Division of Imperial Chemical Industries in England. He made a card for each term in his vocabulary and designated fixed positions on the cards for particular documents. Then when a certain term was assigned to a document during the indexing process, the term card was pulled and a hole was punched in the position representing the document.

In 1947 Calvin Mooers, a pioneer in information retrieval, approached it the other way around by representing the *document* with a card. Terms used to index the documents were then notched-out on the edges of the cards in a randomly coded way, and at the searching stage rods that resembled knitting needles were threaded through a deck of cards. The cards with the desired Boolean combinations would drop out of the card deck because of the notched edges. A strong point with the Mooers system, which was called Zatocoding, was that it saved storage space by coding the hole combinations.

Another approach was tried by Mortimer Taube with his so-called uniterm system. He developed this system in 1951 for the Armed Services Technical Information Agency, and by 1956 the system had received wide attention in the information retrieval field. This technique was a variation on the Batten system except that the spaces on the cards were not specified for particular documents. Numbers representing documents were posted on the cards, and then the search visually matched the correct combinations. Taube sorted the document numbers in numerical order of the last digit (all numbers ending in zeros together, all ending in ones together, etc.) to facilitate searching. He took the uniterms directly from the text and advocated no vocabulary control mechanisms; however, it soon became clear that concept terms made up by combining two or more free-standing words introduced significant semantic difficulties into the retrieval process. Little by little, vocabulary control devices crept into Taube's system. As the size of the collection grows, multiword terms become necessary.

Taube's idea of indexing freely with the text words gives a fuller range of terms, but Mooers's technique asserts that not all text words are automatically useful as content descriptors. Words are at best imperfect communication devices, and Mooers felt that we should attempt to overcome the semantic difficulties with vocabulary control.

The three techniques above are called postcoordinate indexing methods, meaning that the coordination is done by the user at the searching stage, not by the indexer at the indexing stage. In other words, the user forms a searching strategy by combining the terms with Boolean operators to express the information need as closely as possible. Postcoordinate indexes are also called manipulative indexes.

Nonmanipulative indexes, where coordination is done at the indexing stage, are known as precoordinate indexes. This type of indexing is necessary in traditional printed indexes, since a printed page is final and allows no after-the-fact manipulation. For example, in searching a document on the teaching of indexing in an information science program, one might approach a precoordinated index with a generic heading "Information science." Under this term a subterm "Education" would be found, and a further modification would show "Indexing and abstracting." A postcoordinate index treats each term independently of every other term, and each term represents a unique entry point into the index. In actual practice, several of the terms are combined with Boolean operators to specifically identify a user's need. In the example above, an *and* Boolean combination of the three terms would filter out a set of all the documents that had been indexed with all three terms.

Indexes to books and indexes in book form are examples of precoordinate indexes. KWIC and KWOC indexes (to be discussed later) are precoordinate indexes that automatically rotate the terms so that each one will appear as a first term in an alphabetical list, but the terms are precoordinated when the index is created.

The greatest potential problem in using postcoordinate indexes concerns what is known as false coordinating or false drops. That is, we obtain the conceptual opposite of what was expected when the search request was formed. For example, a coordination of "Car polish" will also retrieve information about "Polish cars."

Some of the problems in postcoordinate searching can be minimized with a little forethought about the potential problems. A good general rule is to begin with a query stated as specifically as possible. The user should attempt to choose the correct terms and employ all of them, thus taking advantage of any generic searching capabilities the system may have built in. For example, most of the widely used online retrieval systems now have the ability to trace out species under generic terms on the command of the searcher.

Where do users get the search terms? They come from subject-author lists that go with the system, from printed indexes in the subject area, and from users' own knowledge, background, and experience. Before users begin, they should list all the possible terms and initially select the ones they consider most appropriate. They should not use terms they know are not related or terms with multiple meanings that users might not be aware of. Relating the terms in a precise way is essential for an adequate search of postcoordinated indexes. An imprecise and unclear formulation will quickly bring a truckload of irrelevant documents.

The user should keep in mind that the Boolean logical sum formulation will retrieve more documents; that is, it will broaden the search response. On the other hand, the logical product will narrow the search by requiring the presence of all the terms in the query to appear in the document under consideration. Logical difference is aimed at specifically excluding documents with certain subject terms, and the user must be cautious here, as difference may also indirectly throw out relevant information. For example, suppose a search request said "Cats *but not* Siamese." Any document with the term Siamese would be passed over, but it is possible that an excellent paper about cats in general (what the user wanted) had only a passing reference to Siamese cats, just enough to get the term assigned. The difference operator will reject this paper and a lot of good information. As this example illustrates, the difference formulation must be used with great care.

Postcoordinate indexes are popular and useful and are the basis of most online retrieval systems. However, there are some drawbacks. For one thing, there is the danger of losing relevant documents without ever knowing it (e.g., using negation as just mentioned). Also, a too narrow search can do this, so it might be safer to retrieve some limited amount of irrelevant material in order not to miss needed material. This, of course, is related to the personal preference of the user. Some people prefer to have a limited amount of highly relevant material, whereas other users do not want to miss anything. Irrelevant material, unless overwhelming, is not as major a tragedy to the average user as the information handlers sometimes believe. Generally, the user worries considerably more that something has been missed, that the "great document" that will totally solve the information need lies untouched in the black box.

Permuted Title Indexes

From the time that computing machines were first tried as information processing machines rather than merely scientific number-crunchers, information people have tried to use the words in the titles of documents as content indicators. The premise of a permuted title index is that titles effectively indicate the content of documents. Since it reflects the content of a document, a permuted title index helps users decide if that document would satisfy their information needs. Permuted title word indexes, created by systematically rotating information-conveying words in the title as subject entry points into the index, have had a long history. All along there have been strong advocates and equally strong critics of this technique. Clearly, the success of this kind of approach depends on how well the authors reflect the subject content in their writing of the title. The title is the only component of a document in which the author tries to indicate what the text is about. Generally speaking, the abstract is concerned with describing the way the subject is approached and what new information might be revealed, but its purpose is not as a pointer to a specific subject. One of the important recommendations of the famous Weinberg Report (U.S. President's Science Advisory Committee, 1963) was that the scientific community be urged to write specific titles that clearly convey the subject of papers. Information people have always felt that the title is an important subject indicator and could be the basis of a useful index. However, some of the early enthusiasm has been somewhat dulled, although there are numerous permuted title indexes in existence that serve useful purposes.

The best argument for creating permuted title indexes is simple: it can be done quickly, with a minimum of cost, and entirely by computer. There is little delay because of indexers, index editors, and production backlog. On the other hand, a permuted title index is not as useful as a subject index based on analysis of the major portions of a document. The main drawbacks of title indexing are: (1) the titles may not accurately reflect content, (2) the limited number of terms in the titles restrict complete subject indication, (3) most of the indexes are unappealing to the eye and are difficult to scan, and (4) the lack of vocabulary control can increase the retrieval of irrelevant documents. Since permuted title indexes are concordances, they suffer from the weaknesses of concordances, such as the scattering of synonyms and generic terms, causing user frustration and missed entries. There is little, if any, controlled consistency, since the indexes reflect content only as much as the title words represent conceptual subjects. To be fair, their effectiveness varies widely from subject field to subject field. In some areas title words are impracticable and virtually useless.

Over the years a number of variations have been tried to improve the effectiveness of permuted title indexes. For example, indexers have attempted to supplement the title with additional words, derived from the text itself or from a vocabulary list. A title is constrained by the number of words it can reasonably have, so indexers may add words, or give cross-references to related terms, particulary from synonyms. Indexers add words they consider to be related to the title words, but any such technique increases the cost and time necessary to prepare the index and works against the main argument for constructing permuted indexes.

The most popular permuted title indexes are the so-called KWIC and KWOC indexes. The former means key word in context and the latter, key word out of context. Both refer to the form of the index entry.

As an example of KWIC index, let's suppose we had the following titles:

Blue-eyed Cats in Texas
The Cat and the Fiddle
Dogs and Cats and Their Diseases
The Cat and the Economy

The KWIC index is an alphabetical list, ordered on each subject-conveying word in the title. Thus, taking the above titles, a KWIC index might contain the following entries:

In Texas,	*Blue-eyed* Cats	23
The	*Cat* and the Economy	12
The	*Cat* and the Fiddle	17
Dogs and	*Cats* and Their Diseases	3
Blue-eyed	*Cats* in Texas	23
and Their	*Diseases*, Dogs and Cats	3
Their Diseases,	*Dogs* and Cats and	3
and the	*Economy*, The Cat	12
and the	*Fiddle*, The Cat	17
in	*Texas*, Blue-eyed Cats	23

The number in the right-hand column will lead the user to the document entry in the index that gives the necessary bibliographic information to the document.

On the other hand, a KWOC index doesn't rotate the title, but lifts out the keyword of interest and lists it separately to the side. For example:

Blue-eyed	Blue-eyed Cats in Texas	23
Cat	The Cat and the Economy	12
Cat	The Cat and the Fiddle	17
Cats	Dogs and Cats and Their Diseases	3
Cats	Blue-eyed Cats in Texas	23
Diseases	Dogs and Cats and Their Diseases	3
Dogs	Dogs and Cats and Their Diseases	3
Economy	The Cat and the Economy	12
Fiddle	The Cat and the Fiddle	17
Texas	Blue-eyed Cats in Texas	23

Permuted title indexes, like other concordance indexes, often use stop-lists. These are words that are unsuitable as subject indicators. Clearly, such words as *the* and *an* belong on such a stop-list. However, in individual subject areas, words other than articles and prepositions may be included. For example, in a permuted title index in the field of chemistry the word *chemistry* may be eliminated because it bears no informational content in that environment.

Although there has been some disillusionment with permuted title indexes, they still serve a useful purpose.

Faceted Indexes

A faceted scheme is a type of synthetic classification and is often called an analytico-synthetic system. Facet analysis is a tightly controlled process by which simple concepts are organized into carefully defined categories by connecting class numbers of the basic concepts. This is in contrast to enumerative classification systems like Dewey, which are mostly prestructured before use.

Facet, by definition, means one side of something that has many sides. In other words, any subject is not a single unit but has many aspects; thus a facet index attempts to discover all the individual aspects of a subject and then synthesize them in a way that best describes the subject under discussion.

Enumerative systems are fixed and can accommodate new knowledge in limited ways, whereas faceted systems are much more flexible. For example, suppose the concept *air-to-ground missile* was a part of our knowledge scheme, but not *ground-to-air missile*. In an enumerated scheme, a category would exist:

AIR-TO-GROUND MISSILE

but not the other term. A book on ground-to-air missiles would have to be classified under a more general term, such as "Weapons."

In a facet scheme these terms would exist:

AIR
GROUND
MISSILE

and this would allow us to easily fit together each type of classification:

AIR-TO-GROUND MISSILE
GROUND-TO-AIR MISSILE

A faceted system is precoordinated at the time of indexing and is arranged in classification order, rather than in straight alphabetical order. It differs from enumerative classification systems in that its terms are not exhaustive, but are intended to be used as building blocks.

S. R. Ranganathan first used the term and introduced the idea of a faceted classification system. Ranganathan, a major pioneer of modern librarianship, began his work in classification research in 1925 and in the 1930s he published his basic works in facet classification. The principle of facet classification is similar to that used in zoology and other sciences that work heavily with classification problems. We start with a class and derive individual subclasses, or species, by determining the properties that *differ* between one group of elements and another. In other words, we start with a class and then, one by one, eliminate all elements except those that contain the properties that particularly interest us. The aim of this approach is to systematically identify the aspects or facets of a complex subject and then objectively synthesize those aspects so that we do not have an improper mixture of subjects, as we often have in other classification systems.

The philosophical basis is that a paper is a new creation in which an author looks at a subject in a different way, or brings out new ideas or a new discovery. Since each paper is in a sense a new way of exploring knowledge, it cannot truly fit into a preexisting category, as with the traditional classification schemes. The contents of the new document cannot be accurately revealed in a classification scheme built on previous knowledge; rather, a dynamic scheme is needed to reflect the dynamic nature of the knowledge itself. With a faceted system, we put together—on the spot, so to speak—the class most closely representing the informational concepts in the new paper.

The classes produced when a subject is divided by one, and only one, facet characteristic and then combined with other facets are represented by words; thus, a facet is a list of words with each term having an exact relation to the subject of which it is a part. A facet can be forms, or entities, operations, states of being, and so forth. Ranganathan proposed a set of basic notions, including time, space, energy, matter, and personality, which are the fundamental block terms that make up the faceted classification scheme. In some sense they are like individual terms in a coordinate index. The arrangement of the facets is based on assumed user needs and the way users will approach the system. A letter code is assigned to the facet terms to save space and aid in manipulation if the retrieval system is mechanical.

Let's look at a more detailed example of what a facet system is. Suppose we wish to construct a facet scheme for cats. First, we break our subject into the concepts that interest us most. For our purpose, we might assume that the facets are (a) type of cat, (b) color of cat, and (c) IQ of cat.

Next, we list the possibilities under the three facet headings:

Type	Color	IQ
Abyssinian	white	0-10
Burmese	black	11-20
Himalayan	blue	21-30
Manx	gray	31-40
Persian	brown	41-50
Siamese	green	above 50
Alley		

Once this is done, we need a code or notation. To keep things simple, we utilize a simple numeric code of 1,2,3, ...etc., and we have the following:

Type		Color		IQ	
1	Abyssinian	1	white	1	0-10
2	Burmese	2	black	2	11-20
3	Himalayan	3	blue	3	21-30
4	Manx	4	gray	4	31-40
5	Persian	5	brown	5	41-50
6	Siamese	6	green	6	above 50
7	Alley				

The next step is to build classes as we analyze our actual cats. The classes are synthesized at the time we pick up a real cat and turn it over in our hands. However, in order to do this, we must have decided on an order for the facets and also on an order for the resulting schedule of notations. Let's suppose, for both, we have:

$$Type \longrightarrow Color \longrightarrow IQ$$

Now we are ready to deal with our subject. We might pick up a blue Siamese cat with an IQ in the range of 11-12. Our class number then would be:

6 (Siamese) + 3 (blue) + 2 (11 -20 range) = 6 3 2

A black Alley cat with an IQ above 50 would be:

7 (Alley) + 2 (black) + 6 (above 50) = 7 2 6

Order in putting together the facets is not haphazard but critically important, and for that reason complex rules and procedures are necessary. This order will determine the physical arrangement of the collection, and, again, it should reflect user demands and needs. Clearly, the citation order will affect both the order of the individual terms in the index headings and the access points of the entry. The core facets are arranged with the most important one first, the second most important next, and so forth.

Finally, as was pointed out previously, any classified scheme needs an index to facilitate its use. When the document set is small and the concepts are simple, it probably is possible to scan the classification schedules, but as the system becomes more complex it will need an alphabetical index so that particular concepts can be quickly located in the schedule.

Chain Indexes

Index users run the risk of missing useful entries by failing to search the most specific subject of interest. Chain indexing is a method that attempts to minimize this by presenting the single entries in a classified index, one by one, in an alphabetical list. That is, chain indexes provide that every concept becomes linked, or chained, to its directly related concept in the hierarchy system. As it turns out, the terms form a citation pattern in the chain from general to specific, and all terms or subject names for which an item can be indexed are included.

Searchers who use index terms to find information, need to know the correct terms to use and the correct relationships that exist between the terms. Chain indexing was invented to make sure that the latter is given proper attention. A paper might be indexed with more conventional methods and be tagged:

Elephants
Man
Fat

Is the paper about elephants and a fat man? Or a fat elephant and a man? A chain index attempts to show relationships. Such an index might show:

Elephants
    Fat man

where the second unit indicates relational concepts. Fat man would appear elsewhere in the index with its relationship to elephants shown.

Thus, the argument for chain indexes is that the system uses both the classification terminology and its structure. It moves systematically through the hierarchy and reveals the weaknesses and strengths in the classification structure as one works with it. For example, a user can readily see subordinate classes that are not truly species of a genus. It draws together the many aspects of a subject that are otherwise dispersed in a classification scheme.

Chain indexing was one of the results of Ranganathan's theories of classification. In the beginning he proposed that every term in an indexing chain should be included as an entry term in the index, but he later changed his idea to eliminate unimportant terms.

Clearly, chain indexing helps overcome one of the problems of generic entry into a classified index by using all significant terms as entry points. Chain indexing is also highly mechanical, which relieves the indexer of a lot of decision making. On the other hand, it is still basically a classified system, and chain indexing reflects the faculties of classified systems, particularly in the way human choices are made: the compiler of the indexing system decides what the systematic order of human knowledge should be.

String Indexes

A string index is usually, but not necessarily, output by a computer. The idea is to display a series of rotating index entries from a basic list of index terms that make up the "string." The objective is to give the user an entry point for all index terms and to display them in context with each other.

Although *string indexing* is a modern term, its antecedent of trying to bring out the best in a classified scheme goes back many years. Historical links can be traced to the theoretical work of Farradane, Ranganathan, Cutter and others. Craven (1986) has defined string indexing as follows:

A string index is a form of indexing with two main characteristics: (1) each indexed item normally has a number of index entries containing at least some of the same terms and (2) computer software generates the description part of each index entry according to regular and explicit syntactical rules. The description part of a string index entry is called an *index string*; the computer software that produces it, an *index string generator.*

It should be made clear that the rotation of terms as entry points does not mean that the entries are all the same. In fact, if the system works as it should, each entry will be unique in the sense that the string itself modifies each lead term in proper sequence to preserve its contextual meaning. This, of course, is a major purpose of string indexing. In a standard uniterm alphabetical subject index the entries are generally semantically isolated, leading to retrieval problems.

By relating entry terms to other subject descriptors, users can avoid false starts right at the entry point. By observing the connected terms they can see where they stand. Let's suppose we have the topic *The use of computers in television animation in the United States*. Concept analysis gives a linear string of index terms; these terms are fed to the computer, which produces indicators of relationships. The computer rotates the terms, taking into account the relationships, and produces a series of entries. For example:

UNITED STATES
    Television industry. Computers. Animation.

TELEVISION INDUSTRY. United States.
    Computers. Animation.

COMPUTERS. Television industry. United States.
    Animation.

ANIMATION. Computers.
    Television industry. United States.

String indexing is a form of computer-aided indexing. Intellectual decisions are made by the indexer and the heavy manipulation work is done by the machine. Research and development is under way to see just how far the machine can be programmed to take over more and more of the manual part of the activity.

String indexing systems range from simple word rotations with few rules, to complex, highly structured systems. Some of the better-known, more complex examples of string indexing systems are POPSI, NEPHIS, CIFT, and PRECIS.

POPSI, Postulate-based Permuted Subject Indexing, was developed in India at the Documentation Research and Training Center. It follows the classification ideas of Ranganathan. Its coding rules are relatively simple and quite a bit like KWOC indexing with certain enhancements.

NEPHIS, Nested Phrase Indexing Systems, was developed by Timothy C. Craven. The input string is designed to be a phrase in ordinary language and "the emphasis in NEPHIS is on economy and on ease for the programmer, for the indexer, and for the searcher" (Craven 1986, 38).

CIFT, Contextual Indexing and Faceted Taxonomic Access System, is a special-purpose string indexing system developed for the Modern Language Association (MLA). Alphabetical subject entries are created from strings by indexers who assign facets derived from literature and linguistics. It is published to be used with the *MLA International Bibliography*.

PRECIS, Preserved Context Index System, is probably the best-known string indexing system. It is closely related to computer manipulation, and, in fact, evolved out of the British National Bibliography's interest in using MARC records and their involvement in chain indexing techniques. It was developed to provide subject index data for UK/MARC records and to produce an alphabetical subject index for the National Bibliography (See example 24).

4WORD. Lotus 123
5 Star *(Group)*. Pop music
   to 1987   784.5'0092'2
8-bit microprocessor systems   004.165
8mm films. United States
   8mm cinema films: Feature films — *Filmographies*
                      016.79143
16-bit microprocessor systems   004.16
16mm films
   — *Filmographies*   011'.37
   Editing — *Manuals*   778.5'35
16mm films. United States
   16mm cinema films: Feature films — *Filmographies*
                      016.79143
21-thiosteroids. Organisms   574.19'243
27 MHz waveband
   See also
      Citizens' band
35mm cameras
   See also
      Canon cameras
      Exakta cameras
      Leica cameras
      Minolta cameras
      Nikon cameras
35mm cameras
   — *Manuals*   770'.28'22
1900-1986 paintings
   1900-1986 portrait paintings. Special subjects: Nudes —
      Critical studies   757'.4'0904
1900 Club
   to 1985   324'.3
A-6 aeroplanes
   Grumman A-6 aeroplanes   623.74'63
A-7E aeroplane
   Chance Vought A-7E aeroplane. Markings   623.74'63
A-10 aeroplanes   623.74'64
À Becket, Thomas, *Saint See* **Becket, Thomas,** *Saint*
A-Ha *(Group)*. Pop music   784.5'0092'2
A la recherche du temps perdu. Proust, Marcel, *1871-1922.*
   Fiction in French
   Composition   843'.912
   Special subjects: Communication & interpersonal
    relationships   843'.912
A level *See* **G.C.E. (A level)**
AACR 2 *See* **Anglo-American cataloguing rules**
   2nd ed
Abbey of Farfa
   Architectural features   726'.771
Abbey of Saint Mary the Virgin *(Kenilworth, England) See*
   Kenilworth Abbey
Abbey Theatre
   to 1985 — Personal observations — Collections
                      792'.092'2
Abbeys. Barrow-in-Furness *(District)*. Cumbria
   Furness Abbey — *Visitors' guides*   914.27'81
Abbeys. Berwickshire *(District)*. Borders Region. Scotland
   Dryburgh Abbey — *Visitors' guides*   914.13'95
Abbeys. Cerne Abbas. Dorset
   Benedictine abbeys: Cerne Abbey. Ecclesiastical estates, *to*
    1625   333.3'22'0942331

Abbeys. Sibton. Suffolk
   Sibton Abbey. Ecclesiastical estates — *Cartularies*
                    333.3'22'0942646
Abbeys. Tewkesbury. Gloucestershire
   Tewkesbury Abbey — *Visitors' guides*   914.24'12
Abbeys. Titchfield. Hampshire
   Titchfield Abbey — *Visitors' guides*   914.22'775
Abbreviations. Education. Great Britain
   — *Lists*   370'.941
Abbreviations. Electrical engineering
   — *Lists*   621.3'0148
Abbreviations. Système International d'Unités.
    Measurement. Biology   574
Abbreviations. Système International d'Unités.
    Measurement. Medicine
   — *Dictionaries*   610
ABC Mile End
   to 1985   791.43'09421'5
'Abd Allah ibn al-Husayn, *King of Jordan See* **'Abdallāh,**
   King of Jordan, 1882-1951
'Abd Allāh ibn Husain, *King of Jordan See* **'Abdallāh,** *King*
   of Jordan, 1882-1951
'Abdallāh, *King of Jordan, 1882-1951*   956.95'04'0924
Abdomen. Man
   Acute abdomen. Diagnosis   617'.55075
   Acute abdomen. Surgery   617'.55
   Anatomy   611'.95
   Diagnosis. Radiography   617'.550757
   Diagnosis. Ultrasonography   617'.5507543
   Hernias. Surgery   617'.559
   Muscles. Exercises — *Manuals*   613.7'1
Abduction *See* **Kidnapping**
Abdullah, *King of Jordan See* **'Abdallāh,** *King of Jordan,*
   1882-1951
Abelian groups
   See also
      Modules. Algebra
      Rings. Algebra
Abercromby Square
   history   942.7'53
Aberdare. Mid Glamorgan
   history   942.9'73
Aberdare Hall
   to 1985   378'.19871'0942987
Aberdeen. Grampian Region. Scotland   941.2'350858
Aberdeen. Grampian Region. Scotland
   1700-1800   941.2'3507
   Cathedrals: St Andrew's Cathedral *(Aberdeen, Scotland)*
   — *Visitors' guides*   914.12'235
   Cinemas, *to 1987*   791.43'09412'35
   Economic conditions. Effects of exploitation of petroleum
   deposits in North Sea   330.9412'350858
   Electorate. Voting behaviour, *1979* 324.9412'350857
   Environment planning — *Proposals* 711'.4'0941235
   Geological features   554.12'35
   Granite products industries — *Biographies* 338.7'6912
   Intellectual life, *1714-1837*   941.2'3507
   Libraries: King's College, Aberdeen. *Library, to 1860*
                    027.7412'35
   Social life, *1915-1935*   941.2'35083
   Suburbs. Railway services, *to 1987* 385'.09412'35
Aberdeen Airways   387.7'065'41
Aberdeenshire. Grampian Region. Scotland
   Churchyards. Monumental inscriptions 929.5'09412'32
   Churchyards. Monumental inscriptions — *Collections*
                    929.5'09412'32
   Poll tax. Taxpayers, *1696*   336.2'5

Example 24. *British National Bibliography* (a PRECIS index). (Reprinted with permission of The British Library.)

In using PRECIS, the patron enters the alphabetically arranged index with a significant term and can see the use of the term by the author in its context. In other words, there is a précis or summary statement of the subject of concern under any term the indexer decided was important enough to be an entry term.

The rationale of PRECIS is that it is possible to go into an alphabetical index with any of the individual terms that are a part of a compound subject and see a full statement. PRECIS has a dynamic vocabulary that takes in new terms immediately after they occur in the literature being indexed. The primary objective of a PRECIS index is to allow users to enter the system with whatever term they have in mind and to immediately establish that term in context with the author's discussion. For example, a paper on the training of cowboys for Texas cattle ranching might be output as follows:

Entries

TEXAS
>Ranching. Cowboys. Training.

RANCHING. Texas.
>Cowboys. Training.

COWBOYS. Ranching. Texas.
>Training.

TRAINING. Cowboys. Ranching. Texas.

References

United States
>*See also*
>>Texas

Cattle Industry
>*See also*
>>Ranching

Ranching
>*See also*
>>Cattle Industry

Personnel
>*See* Cowboys

Employees
>*See* Cowboys

Cowhands
>*See* Cowboys

The above example shows the main idea of PRECIS. Notice that all the entries in the string contain all the terms used to index the document, and that each term in turn is made an entry point. The order of the modifying terms maintains the original meaning of the index string, and the entry usually occupies two or more lines to ensure readability. PRECIS is a popular indexing system and its computer programs are constantly being improved to deal with new situations.

The phenomenal growth of online database information systems and the accompanying development of computer-assisted indexing has fostered a continuing interest in string indexing. Ironically, the output of most string indexing is a printed index, and the online search services have not used string indexing extensively, although researchers are investigating how best to apply string indexes to online retrieval systems. Workers in string indexing are only slowly making progress toward setting standards for the procedure, agreeing on common terminology, and integrating the software. It appears unlikely that string indexing will be immediately introduced into commercial databases services.

However, a number of string indexing software programs are available, and others are appearing regularly. Much interest continues in string indexing, and its future seems to be secure.

Citation Indexes

A citation index consists of a list of articles, with a sublist under each article of subsequently published papers that *cite* the articles. It is not a new idea; over a century ago the legal profession developed such an index, *Shepard's Citations*, which gives accounts of decisions and later citations. Clearly, this is a fundamental searching tool for the law profession because of its reliance on precedent. However, citation indexing is relatively new as a general reference tool.

The premise of citation indexing is that citations reflect document content and that an author's citations can therefore be substituted for the judgment of indexers. Citations link together papers on a specific topic, and a citation index is built on the basis of this internal structure of subject literatures.

As we have seen, most indexes are prepared by the procedure of choosing index terms from documents or conceptual terms from a vocabulary list and arranging the terms to indicate the subject contents of the document. To improve on these indexes, syntactical and semantic devices are used to clarify the relationships in the way the terms are used. For example, such a device might be a parenthetical modifier:

Base (math)

Base (Ft. Bliss, Texas)

Base (Tiffany lamps)

Citation indexing is a different approach entirely. It does not depend upon index words at all, thus avoiding the intellectual problems of meaning and the interpretation of meaning by conventional indexing. The underlying assumption of a citation index is that we rely on the author of a document to tell us what the subject is, rather than on an indexer, who must decide without consulting the writer. With citation indexes we see that authors are the most qualified persons to define and delineate material most relevant to their subjects. Because the citation index is not based on index term assignment and needs no interpretation or any kind of terminology, it gives a clear channel between the author and the user, without the introduction of artificial language.

For example, suppose the following paper is published:

Scratch, B. W. "Cats and Their Idiosyncrasies." *Weirdo Animals*, vol. 100, no. 9 (January 1980), pp. 216-20.

Also, suppose the paper included the following references:

Abels, Cain. "Cats." *Cats and Dogs*, vol. 1, no. 1, (June 1880), pp. 1-16.

Adam, Eva. "Felines." *Animals and Kids*, vol. 10, no. 3 (February 1920), pp. 30-37.

The citation index would have the following entries:

Abels, Cain. "Cats." *Cats and Dogs*, vol. 1, no. 1 (June 1880), pp. 1-16.
    Scratch, B. W. "Cats and Their Idiosyncrasies." *Weirdo Animals*, vol. 100, no. 9 (January 1980), pp. 216-20.

And, later on:

Adam, Eva. "Felines." *Animals and Kids*, vol. 10, no. 3 (February 1920), pp. 30-37.
    Scratch, B. W. "Cats and Their Idiosyncrasies." *Weirdo Animals*, vol. 100, no. 9 (January 1980), pp. 216-20.

In other words, given a particular paper, a citation index shows who cited that paper at a later point in time. In addition to this basic index there may be supplementary indexes arranged by author or keyword subject term, but such approaches are not considered to be the primary approach to a citation index. Basically, this kind of index implies that a cited paper has an internal subject relationship with the papers that cite it, and we use this relationship to cluster related documents.

Examples 25 and 26 show the source index and the permuterm subject index from *Science Citation Index*. The source index contains bibliographic description of items in the *Science Citation Index*, and by looking up an author's name, the user can locate a full bibliographic description of the document. When the user finds a name, then the primary authorship items are first described and *see* references leads to other authors. Book reviews are found in the *Citation Index* portion of the *Science Citation Index* (not shown).

The *Permuterm Subject Index* comes from the title words of source items indexed in the *Science Citation Index* and is an example of a keyword index.

The primary advantage in using a citation index is that it leads the user to the latest articles; that is, unlike conventional indexes it goes forward in time rather than backwards. At a certain point, the user can discover how the ideas in a certain paper were received and what later developments were reported. Another advantage is that only the author's judgment of relevancy is involved, and therefore the production can be entirely mechanized.

The two obvious disadvantages of citation indexes are that (1) the production of such an index is expensive, and (2) the foundation of the index is based on the assumption that the authors of the papers are consistent and knowledgeable in their citations.

Citation indexing is more than an aid to users seeking information. It is also a research tool for studying the behavioral characteristics of the literature and, indeed, for studying the structure growth of science itself.

first source author ——— **CHAUDHARY BN** _____
  •UV SPECTRAL STUDIES OF A FEW NUCLEAR SUBSTITUTED ———————————— *article title*
  PHENOTHIAZINES   E3462
source journal ——— **ANN NUC SCI**   90(4):339-343   89   4R
  LOHIA COLL CHEM LABS, CHURU 331001, INDIA

CHEATHAM TJ _____
  •SMITH JR—REGULAR AND SEMISIMPLE MODULES —BIBLIOGRAPHY
                                                           F6479
  PAC J MATH   65(2):315-332   89   •R — *Indicates that references to this*
  SAMFORD UNIV, BIRMINGHAM, AL 35209, USA   *item were not processed.*
                                                       (Bibliographies which contain
                                                       only a listing on a given
coauthors ——————— **CHEDID A** _____   *subject).*
  •BUNDEALL.AE MENDENHA.CL—INHIBITION OF
  HEPATOCARCINOGENESIS BY ADRENOCORTICOTROPIN IN
  AFLATOXIN B1—TREATED RATS   A2694
  J NAT CANC   58(2):339-349   89 —— 49R
  UNIV CINCINNATI, COLL MED, DEPT PATHOL, CINCINNATI,   —— *source journal year*
  OH 45267, USA

language code ——————

  CHEKUNOV AV _____
  •KUCHMA VG—(RS) ABYSSAL ASYMMETRY OF GEOLOGICAL
  STRUCTURES   C6491— *ISI® Journal Accession Number.*
  DAN SSSR   233(1):211-213   89   8R
  ACAD SCI UKSSR, GEOPHYS INST, KIEV, USSR   *Indicates that copies of indi-*
                                                          vidual articles can be ordered
                                                          through ISI's The Genuine
cross referenced   *Article® service.*
secondary author _____ **CHENG LC** _____
  see ROGUS EM   BIOC BIOP A   484   347   89

  CHENG TC _____
  •SULLIVAN J—ALTERATIONS IN OSMOREGULATION OF PULMONATE
  GASTROPOD BIOMPHALARIA GLABRATA DUE TO COPPER ► NOTE —— *term indicating type of*
                                                           A4684   *source item*
volume (issue):page-span —— **J INVER PAT** |29(1):101-104| 89   5R
  LEHIGH UNIV,CTR HLTH SCI,INST PATHOBIOL,
  BETHLEHEM, PA 18015 USA

  CHRISTEN DK _____
  •KERCHNER HR SEKULA ST CHANG YK—
  OBSERVATION OF THE FLUX-LINE LATTICE IN SUPERCONDUCTING
  V3S1   A6981
  PHYSICA B + C   107(1-3):301-302   89   4R —— *number of references*
  OAK RIDGE NATL LAB, DIV SOLID STATE, OAK RIDGE, TN,
  37830, USA

  CHURCH DG _____
first source author ——— see WHOMON MM   NAUTILUS   3   20   89

  CIMPL A _____
  •KOSEK F HUSA V SVOBODA J—REFRACTIVE-INDEX OF ARSENIC
  TRISULFIDE ► LETTER   A4982
  CZEC J PHYS   31(10):1191-1194   89   3R
  UNIV CHEM TECHNOL PARDUBICE, DEPT PHYS, CS-53210, ——— *author's address*
  PARDUBICE, CZECHOSLOVAKIA

author of book review ———**COHEN IB** _____
(from The Scientist®*,*
Science *or* Nature)   •THE RISE OF MILLIKAN, ROBERT—PORTRAIT OF A LIFE IN
  AMERICAN SCIENCE — KARGON, RH► BOOK REVIEW   A2621
  NATURE   301(5897):270   89   1R
  HARVARD UNIV, BOSTON MA 02138 USA   *author of book being*
                                                      reviewed

Example 25. *Science Citation Index* (source index). (Reprinted with permission.)

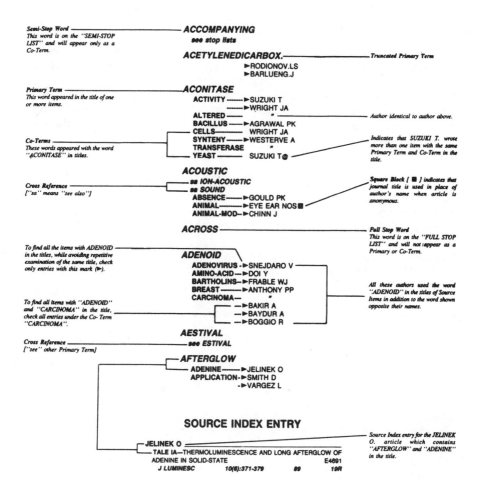

Example 26. *Science Citation Index* (permuterm subject index). (Reprinted with permission.)

Eugene Garfield (1979) has written, "Although it was developed primarily for bibliographic purposes, and in spite of its recognized utility as a search tool, the most important application of citation indexing may prove to be non-bibliographic. If the literature of science reflects the activities of science, a comprehensive, multi-disciplinary citation index can provide an interesting view of these activities. The view can shed some useful light on both the structure of science and process of scientific development" (p. 62). Garfield believes that this use of citation indexing may offer some "intriguing possibilities" for the study and management of science.

SUGGESTED READINGS

Bernier, Charles L. "Alphabetic Indexes." In *Encyclopedia of Library and Information Sciences*, vol. 1. New York: Marcel Dekker, 1968, 196-201.

Cleveland, Donald B. "An n-Dimensional Retrieval Model." *Journal of the American Society for Information Science* 27 (September-October 1976): 342-47.

Craven, Timothy C. *String Indexing*. Orlando, Fla.: Academic Press, 1986.

Cross, Ruth C. *Indexing Books*. Cambridge, Mass.: Word Guild, 1980.

Garfield, Eugene. *Citation Indexing*. Philadelphia: Institute for Scientific Information, 1979.

Hartley, James, Lindsey Davies, and Peter Burnhill. "Alphabetization in Indexes: Experimental Studies." *The Indexer* 12 (April 1981): 149-53.

Milstead, J. I. *Subject Access Systems: Alternatives in Design*. New York: Academic Press, 1984.

U.S. President's Science Advisory Committee. *Science, Government, and Information: The Responsibilities of the Technical Community and the Government in the Transfer of Information*. Washington, D.C.: The White House, 1963.

IV
Vocabulary Control

INTRODUCTION

When librarians became concerned with subject approaches to their stored knowledge records, they quickly came face-to-face with a stubborn fact of life: the complexity, variability, and richness of natural language, rather ironically, leads to ambiguity. An abundant vocabulary allows a depth of expression that gives humans the ability to communicate at a high level, but it also has a semantic complexity that opens the door to faulty understanding. Simply allowing any word in the language to represent content produces problems that were not immediately obvious. Using an unlimited, or an uncontrolled, set of words or phrases to index and to search a library leads to wasted effort and a certain degree of searching failure due to the enormous range of word choices. It is true, of course, that no two words in a language mean exactly the same thing. There are no true synonyms. But words are often very close in meaning, and more often, not clearly understood. The inconsistent use of words can lead to failure or partial failure in searching, for the simple reason that users are unlikely to choose all the terms that might be used by the indexer or the writers of the documents. And, in many cases, the user would choose the terms used by the indexer but with a different understanding of their meaning.

As a result, many forms of controlled vocabularies have been developed over the years, such as classification schedules and subject authority files. A controlled vocabulary is a consistent list of words to be followed when indexing. A search request is then stated using the same consistent word list.

The goal of a controlled vocabulary is to enhance conceptual accord between the indexer and the index user. The indexer examines a document, mentally filters through the author's intent, and then chooses terms from the thesaurus that represent the appropriate concepts and relationships as the indexer interprets them. The user approaches the index with personal concepts and terms. The function of the thesaurus mechanisms is to eventually lead both the indexer and the user to the same point. Vocabulary control is a complex activity and one of the fundamental issues in indexing. This chapter will discuss this activity in detail.

GENERAL NATURE OF
INDEXING LANGUAGES

An indexing language is much more than a list of index terms that are acceptable to users. An indexing language also contains mechanisms for structuring and using those terms. The purpose of the structuring mechanisms is to minimize the ambiguity of isolated vocabulary terms that may be totally out of context. In the ideal situation, the mechanisms reduce the obscurity and redundancy of a general vocabulary but, at the same time, do not reduce the effectiveness of the user's personal vocabulary.

The phrase *indexing language* is generally defined as all the words permitted either to describe a specific document or to construct a query to search a document file, along with the rules describing how the terms are to be used and in what relation to each other. In other words, the vocabulary of an indexing language is the list of words allowable in that indexing language. It is the complete set of terms in the natural language that are employed in the collection of documents, and therefore are necessary as keys for entry into files of knowledge records. The list includes all required synonyms that are used in the process of indexing a set of documents.

This does not mean that all the terms in the list can be used to actually index the documents. Some words serve to lead the user to the controlled terms that could be used by the indexer. These "pointer" terms, along with the allowable index terms, make up what is called the *entry vocabulary*. The total entry vocabulary tries to predict as accurately as possible all the ways that a patron may approach the knowledge base. The importance of a full and varied entry vocabulary cannot be overemphasized, because an inadequate one will limit users' ability to connect their own words with the controlled list and this will ultimately restrict their access to the document file.

Indexing languages can be categorized into a number of fundamental types. An initial breakdown would include assigned-term and derived-term systems. In the former, an indexer must assign terms or descriptors on the basis of subjective interpretation of the concepts implied in the document, and in so doing will have to use some intellectual effort. Indexers determine the subject matter of the document and then decide what terms in their own filtered vocabulary are appropriate. In derived-term systems, all descriptors are taken from the item itself. Thus, author indexes, title indexes, citation indexes, and natural-language indexes are derived-term systems, whereas all indexing languages with vocabulary control devices such as subject heading lists, thesauri, and classification schemes are assigned-term systems. Since there is more intellectual effort involved with assigned-term systems, they will normally involve greater time and effort and therefore will cost more at the indexing stage of the operation. Derived-term systems are generally thought of in terms of mechanical devices, such as the computerized title KWIC indexes, which allow the whole process to be reduced to a clerical task.

According to the advocates of assigned-term indexing languages, vocabulary-controlled systems are more consistent and therefore more efficient, but the many tests that have been run on indexing languages and systems over the years fail to be convincing. As a matter of fact, there is strong reason to believe, from those tests, that natural-language systems may have considerably more to offer than we have believed up to this point. The following sections will go into more detail about these approaches to indexing.

NATURAL-LANGUAGE INDEXING

Derived-term systems are sometimes called natural-language or free-text indexing, because the system allows the indexer to select the terms to be used directly from the text being indexed, or, in automatic systems, the terms are selected by the computer. Since the terms are picked out of the text itself, this approach may also be called indexing by extraction. The uniterm systems developed in the early days of information retrieval are examples of natural-language indexing. The rationale for this approach is based on the idea that the authors are using words that conform to the subject field under discussion. They are communicating directly to the reader in a commonly understood language. Such a language is dynamic and constantly in vogue, and anything else is a contrived, artificial language that may constitute an unnecessary communication barrier between author and reader.

However, such languages have inherent weaknesses. The primary use of free-word vocabularies occurs in coordinate indexes and their derivatives. Such vocabularies begin from scratch, so to speak, and are accumulated. Words are optionally selected by indexers, and when they are indexing the first document, they can freely choose all of the words they believe are necessary to convey the intended meaning and subject content of the document. Naturally, indexers must rely upon their own backgrounds and knowledge of the meanings of the words in the text, or they might use standard dictionaries and general thesauri for definitions. Eventually, this means that the vocabulary tends to grow of its own accord as new documents are added to the system.

As more and more documents are indexed, the indexer's definitions begin to broaden or become more specific so that the selection and use of words are controlled only by a sense of discipline. This discipline is a function of the indexer's point of view. For example, a general in the army will use the word *base* in an entirely different way than a baseball player uses it.

As the free word vocabulary grows, the relationship between its expansion and the growth of the collection is clear. When a collection of documents is interpreted in various ways and there is no attempt at vocabulary control, complete chaos can eventually develop, rendering the index basically useless. The conclusion, then, is drawn by some that even free word vocabularies must be controlled in some way. For example, natural-language indexing may be related indirectly to a thesaurus. Indexers may index with words directly from the text without strictly following the controlled vocabulary in a subject thesaurus, but users, when they are searching, may use an accepted subject thesaurus to find the terms needed to identify relevant information.

On the other hand, work continues steadily on improving natural-language approaches. More and more machine-readable databases, which are increasing in popularity and success, are being designed to utilize natural-language form. The reason for this is that such systems simplify the user's searching task and put the burden on the machine. As online terminals to these databases become increasingly popular and eventually move out from the immediate control of librarians, they will be designed to accommodate natural language. Operational online systems utilizing natural-language indexing appear to be working quite well in a variety of fields, and parallel to this is a rapidly growing technology that will make the storing and searching of full text more feasible. The ultimate goal is the development of computer programs that are capable of effectively processing natural language and hardware that can input and manipulate full text efficiently.

THE NEED FOR VOCABULARY CONTROL

A natural-language system may take index terms directly from titles, abstracts, or full text. The words of the author are used directly, with no distortion or indexer interpretation. There is little room for indexing error and new terms can be immediately incorporated into the vocabulary.

However, the trade-off is that the burden of accurate retrieval comes at the searching stage because of the problems of synonyms and generic relationships, which a controlled vocabulary attempts to overcome. A controlled vocabulary brings together like concepts into the same index term so that these concepts will not be scattered throughout the index under many synonymous or equivalent terms.

We seem to be facing an intellectual dilemma here. On the one hand, if we are going to bring the files in direct contact with users through computers, then we need to develop ways of letting the user resort to unrestricted natural language as closely as possible. On the other hand, the problems of such systems are real. Searching a natural-language system generally requires more time and effort and necessitates a great deal more pondering in order to retrieve all relevant documents simply because the searcher must try all possible terms a writer may have used. Semantic imprecision, a constantly changing vocabulary, and the variety of language underlie the need for a controlled vocabulary.

Related to controlled vocabularies are two concepts that have been around for a good while and are important to the discussion of the usefulness of a controlled vocabulary, because they concern the appropriateness of terms selected for an indexing vocabulary. These are the concepts of *literary warrant* and *user warrant*. An index term in a book or in a vocabulary control list has literary warrant if there is sufficient literature on the topic represented by that word. If a substantial literature does exist and the word is not included in the index or vocabulary control list, this particular subject is submerged in a broader literature under a more generic term. User warrant is a similar concept. We say a term is warranted if it is a term that will be used somewhat regularly by the users of the index in their search for information. Clearly, user warrant is a key to designing a vocabulary control device and requires that the designer know who the users are.

A controlled vocabulary is characterized in the following way:

1. It represents the general conceptual structure of a subject area and presents a guide to the user of the index.

2. The terms are derived as nearly as possible from the vocabulary of use; that is, they closely reflect the literature vocabulary and the user's own technical usage. Although the terms cannot, by definition, be as specific as natural-language indexing, they should allow as much precision as is necessary for adequate retrieval.

3. It employs a considerable number of precoordinated phrases to reduce false drops to a minimum. For example, by precoordinating "Venetian blinds" there will not be a false drop of "Blind Venetians" papers from the document file.

4. It supplies a standard vocabulary by controlling synonyms and near synonyms in order to increase consistency. This, of course, is a primary function. This provides a mechanism that will ensure that only one term from a list of similar terms will be used in indexing a given concept.

5. Where necessary it defines ambiguous terms and distinguishes homographs.

6. Through cross-references it shows horizontal and vertical relationships among terms.

A controlled vocabulary is needed to represent the user's request with the same terms that represent the document contents, to bring together semantically related terms, and to make a search more efficient and effective. By controlling synonyms it systematically manages the semantic erratic behavior of natural language. An uncontrolled vocabulary has the obvious advantage of being totally specific, and often substitutes one term to represent many of the author's terms.

A controlled vocabulary of some kind is also desirable in a computer-based system. But the important point is that the confining aspect of a controlled vocabulary is removed from the vision of the user, and the machine now converts and probes for the user.

From the discussion thus far, it should be clear that problems of language are the focal point of the indexing activity. These language problems may vary widely, encompassing a native language such as English, the special jargon of an academic area such as psychology, or the selected words used exclusively in the system of concern. One of the exciting and primary contributions from other disciplines to library and information science comes from linguistics, and perhaps the approaches used in this field are a key area for research efforts in information science.

The major requisite for vocabulary control is the construction and maintenance of a thesaurus, term list, or word association list that makes the elements or words acceptable and instantly accessible to both the indexer and the user. It is not unusual to see dictionaries of terms alphabetically arranged and complete with definitions used by technical information systems. This dictionary type of term list often is an adaption of existing or published technical dictionaries. On the other extreme, there are highly structured word association matrices that describe frequency of use or other criteria and are essentially thesauri even more technically arranged than *Roget's*.

As with natural-language indexing language, there are some problems associated with controlled vocabularies. For example, human beings find it difficult to confine themselves to constrained definitions in their native tongue or technical jargon. That is to say, habits of language persist, and arbitrarily imposed limitations are resented. Quite often, issue is taken with the way an authority list collapses several words into one; it is argued that each word is distinct and that the generic word is inappropriate. When constraints are applied to a vocabulary, human beings become uncomfortable, since deductive reasoning and creativity are directly related to the flexibility and extent of human vocabularies. Also, relationships between an index vocabulary and the complete vocabulary of the collection are not easy to determine, and the retrieval power of certain words with respect to a group of users is difficult to ascertain and keep current.

In the absolutely ideal situation, a terminal would interface with a completely natural-language system. A patron could present a query in the form of a conversational sentence, and the computer would search the texts, reduce the problem of synonymity to an acceptable minimum, and provide a sufficient group of documents. This undoubtedly will come, and much progress is pointing to it, but at the present we must work with less than the ideal and must address the problems that are to be solved. Therefore, at the present stage we have to consider the choice of requiring the user to be bound by a controlled vocabulary or to use a limited natural-language system. A controlled vocabulary handles synonyms and brings semantically related terms together, thus requiring less word guessing on the part of the searcher. This, in turn, minimizes false drops. On the other hand, a controlled vocabulary can never be as specific as a natural language. A user asking for specific information on sparrows does not want to "*see* Birds." In this case, an indexer's attempt to index concepts rather than words has done the user a disservice.

A controlled vocabulary is an artificial language that puts an information specialist between the text and the user. Users must then conform to this new language rather than to their day-by-day practitioner's language. Often they believe that the rules and word choices in the controlled list are, at best, a nuisance, and at worst, stupid. Controlled vocabularies, then, are best utilized when an information professional is involved with the system, while natural language is best employed when the system is used directly by subject practitioners.

Dictionary Requirements

The purpose of an indexing language is to help users discriminate between terms and to reduce ambiguity in the language. The index language designer, then, cannot simply report on usage, but must guide or dictate usage. We are concerned that the role of a dictionary in an information retrieval system, should be to assist both indexers and searchers in using and manipulating the system's index language. In particular, information retrieval systems have the following requirements for a dictionary-like tool, which explains or defines word usage.

1. *Association.* One of the principal problems of using language is that of discriminating between words that are similar or between similar ideas. We need to resolve the problem of synonyms and near-synonyms. Confusion over word meanings can be resolved by going to an authority, provided all language users agree on the same authority list. What words are associated with each other and in what relationship?

2. *Use of appropriate words.* Even if there were no synonyms and near-synonyms in a language, users would often find themselves in a situation where they would be unsure of the exact words to select to convey some concept. In this case, they would need the same device that the indexer used in order to resolve the problem, that is, a list of the vocabulary of the language and some definition of each word so they could choose among them. Even if two words do not have exactly the same definition, as long as there is any possible likeness of meaning, there needs to be an

explanation of the difference, hence an opportunity for the users to decide for themselves which forms are appropriate.

3. *Decision record.* There should be a history of word use decisions. This requirement refers to the need for, or utility of, a single, final authority, accessible to all system users and containing all vocabulary usage rules and decisions. Since the index language is not normally the same as the natural language spoken by the system users, users may have some difficulty when first learning the language until they fully understand that the retrieval system has its own language and its designers have the right to make their own rulings on word usage. Problems may arise when novice patrons persist in using words in the way they usually employ them without understanding that the information retrieval system works within a different framework. For example, the system may have a highly structured vocabulary and will work only if the prescribed entry terms are selected by the user. The user must adapt to this vocabulary. Either an indexer or a patron may request that a change be made in the vocabulary of the dictionary, but before a change is made they must understand what rulings are currently in force and why those rulings were made.

Again, we emphasize the fact that an indexing language is more than a list of words. It is a list of terms along with the rules for building expressions that shows the relationships among compound constructions and the final arrangement of the expressions.

Types of Index Terms

A distinction should be made between types of index terms:

- *Keywords* are the raw words that come from the literature.

- *Descriptors* are terms that have been defined for use by the thesaurus.

- *Identifiers* are proper nouns, for example:
    Names of people
    Names of organizations
    Project names
    Nomenclatures
    Identification numbers
    Place names
    Trademarks
    Abbreviations and acronyms
  Identifiers are unique entities, not general concepts, and when they appear in documents, they must be used in the index as they are.

- *Entry terms* are words that allow the user to enter the vocabulary structure. If the entry term is not an allowable descriptor, it will refer the user to a term that is acceptable.

Synonyms

In general language there are few true synonyms, but in the indexing world synonyms and near-synonyms are a basic concern. For example, from *Roget's International Thesaurus*:

Dullness
   apathy
   bluntness
   grayness
   lackluster
   stupidity
   unimaginativeness

A check of a current dictionary finds that all the listed synonyms seem appropriate to the basic word, yet each concept has its own world of meaning. The point is that synonymous terms are defined in accordance with current language usage.

As was noted before, a controlled vocabulary means that equivalent terms are gathered together under one term and there is a consensus that that term represents all the other terms. When the thesaurus designer is deciding upon the representative terms, precedence should be given to current usage and the terms that are best understood by users of the system. Of course, cross-references should be given from the other equivalent terms.

Homographs

Homographs, words spelled alike but having different meanings, can be handled in one simple manner — by using a broader term. Another method is to combine the words into phrases that immediately reveal the intended meaning of the homograph. For example:

Polish (car)   Polish (nationality)

Base (math)   Base (military)

Pot (cooking)   Pot (smoking)

Generic Vocabularies

Generic vocabularies show vertical arrangements of words within classes. Words may appear in several classes. Generic vocabularies also indicate synonymous relationships, near-synonymous relationships, and related word groups. "Cat equals Feline" would be considered synonymous in some systems, but in others "Feline" is broader than "Cat." For example, in a general index "Feline" and "Cat" mean approximately the same, but in a book on biology, especially taxonomical zoology, there would be a clear understanding of the different meaning of the terms.

Relationships of words do not necessarily have to follow conventional generic forms but may be constructs, combinations, or syndromes common to a particular area or discipline.

Generic vocabularies allow terms that *should* be seen together to actually *be* seen together, whereas in an alphabetical index, they might very well be scattered.

Generic vocabularies allow terms to be seen immediately in their context. In fact, the user can see either a specific context or a very broad context by simply scanning up or down in the display.

For example, suppose a user is interested in weapons. In an alphabetical index he or she must search on individual terms, relying on memory and cross-references, but a generic vocabulary might offer the following display:

Weapons
    Nonconventional
        Blowpipes
        Boomerangs
        Spears
        Big rocks

    Guns
        Rifles
        Pistols
        Shotguns

    Bowie knives

Classification Vocabularies

Classification vocabularies are ordinarily used in conventional library systems. Examples of these are the Universal Decimal Classification and the Library of Congress Classification System. The use of these classification systems is limited because they are too broad and cover too wide a territory for the specific areas required in indexing languages, they lack precise definitions, and they lack flexibility.

At one time indexers believed that there was a clear distinction between a thesaurus and a traditional classification. As a matter of fact, the term *thesaurus* was adopted by indexers to deliberately make the distinction. The early thesauri were usually relatively simple alphabetical lists of terms showing exact relationships with straightforward codes. These thesauri were to be used in postcoordinate systems, while classification systems were to be used with precoordinate systems. However, over the years thesauri have evolved into much more complex tools, showing hierarchical relationships and/or fully faceted classification characteristics. Now, thesauri are used in precoordinated systems, and classification schemes are playing a role in postcoordinate systems.

AUTHORITY LISTS

Librarians created authority lists many years before information scientists invented thesauri for indexing. When hierarchical classification schemes were created, it was recognized immediately that such schemes would need some sort of supporting tool, so subject heading lists were built for this purpose. Without such lists cataloging would have to be done solely with the classification scheme, which would make the cataloging task somewhat more difficult than it needs to be. Of course, authority files and thesauri have the same objective of vocabulary control. Subject cataloging conceptually groups concepts, assigns identifying terms to these classes, and arranges those terms in an alphabetical sequence. These lists are the approved operating terms, or authority list. When the terms are brought together into a hierarchical structure with classes and subclasses evolving in a related manner, we have a second example of an authority list — the classification schedule. A third example of an authority list is the thesaurus, which is discussed in a later section.

An authority list is a formal list of the words in the controlled vocabulary, showing the formal relationships between words and spelling out how they are to be used. Ambiguity is solved by referring to the authority list as the final arbitrator in vocabulary control. If indexers or searchers are unsure of what terms are to be used, they consult this authority list for direction. This is a record of usage and formal decisions concerning usage.

VOCABULARY GENERATION

Where do authority lists come from? How are they generated? There are two ways to form and build vocabularies. Both are carefully planned and follow logical lines of development. First is the *evolutionary vocabulary*, which is edited or planned after the fact. This is the result of stopping the free vocabulary evolution at some point and trying to make some order out of the chaos. In the second case, the vocabulary is generated as the result of a special study or inquiry and a consensus of experts who predetermine what the vocabulary should be for an area of knowledge. This is called an *enumerated vocabulary*. Thus, the exact methods of vocabulary development depend on which type of vocabulary generation is used.

The evolutionary vocabulary consists of raw material supplied by indexers. After sufficient documents are indexed, alphabetic listings of words selected by indexers are surveyed in preparation for editing and acceptance procedures. Each term in the vocabulary, whether it be a single descriptor, a combination of terms, or a broad classification, becomes a candidate for inclusion in the list. The candidate word must be accepted on the basis of one or several criteria.

A new word common to the language or area of study may be a candidate if it can be defined well enough from any one of a number of points of view. Suppose the word *base*, defined from a military point of view, is added to a system. The specific definition of base is: "the locality or the installation on which a military force relies for supplies or from which it initiates operations." But this word can have other meanings, depending on the viewpoint. In math, base is "the number with reference to which a number system or a mathematical table is constructed," and in chemistry it is defined as "any of various typically water-soluble and acrid or brackish tasting compounds capable of reacting with an acid to form a salt," etc.

The word *model* may enter the system as a synonym for pattern, form, idea, measure, image, reproduction, mannequin, or paragon. It is necessary to decide whether there is a single dominant and most often used word, such as *paragon*, that may contain all document references.

The word chosen from the dictionary to represent a class of synonymous words is often called the "preferred" term. By definition, hierarchical languages do not have synonyms and they are not in subject heading or fixed keyword languages. Of course, in any of these word lists, near-synonyms are possible, since it is a subjective opinion as to whether or not two terms are synonyms. Control over the synonyms in these languages is accomplished by use of the dictionary, with careful definition of terms. Clearly, a free keyword language makes control of synonyms very difficult.

Entry Vocabulary

The words and groups of words that allow the user access to the indexing list are called the entry terms. The entry terms may or may not be the allowable terms for indicating content, but if not, they lead the user by relationship pointers to the terms actually used. The permissible index terms may also be entry terms; therefore, the list of entry terms will include both index terms and pointer terms.

One thing that all indexers and designers of indexing systems should not forget, but they often do, is that there is a wide range of needs of different users of the same index. A user who may want to find quickly one or two items has no need for an exhaustive, prolonged search. Almost any document with the query index term attached to it is relevant to the information need. On the other hand, a user may, indeed, need an exhaustive, highly specific search. An ideal indexing system will serve the needs of both these users and all users in the range between these two extremes.

The usefulness of an index is highly dependent on the entry vocabulary. A scant, obscure entry vocabulary will short-circuit the user in the preliminary check into the list, leading away from the path needed. A strong, full entry vocabulary will enhance the user's chances for finding the right words in the search.

It should also be pointed out that the stronger the entry vocabulary, the easier the indexing is to use by lower-level indexing personnel and the more effective the use of mechanized devices for searching. The searching can be a more routine, nonintellectual, clerical-type task.

Frequently, a user will find during a search that the word in mind is not a document descriptor; the same situation occurs with indexers when they are describing the document. Without an entry vocabulary, both the user and the indexer must select exactly the right term, while an entry vocabulary reduces the intellectual decision making.

Expressiveness

Hierarchical languages generally try to cover all aspects of a subject, even if it means liberally sprinkling "etc." and "other" throughout the hierarchy. Keyword languages usually do not claim full coverage, but instead are concentrated on those aspects that documents are expected to be about. Omissions can be easily corrected, which is not true of hierarchical systems.

Unfortunately, no language is capable of giving the level of broadness or exactness that may be wanted at a particular point. The subject coverage is stipulated and the resulting vocabularies are defined for these languages, and if the extent of coverage needs to be enlarged or its differentive power increased, it is done through the combinations of descriptors by the user. Thus, we have the ability, through the use of Boolean combinations, to increase the expressiveness of an indexing language. We utilize the synthetic qualities of the indexing language by postcoordination with Boolean operators. The danger, of course, is the likelihood of false drops since coordination permits errors or poor results by improper associations of terms, as discussed earlier.

Vocabulary Growth

By now it should be clear that an index vocabulary, free or controlled, is never static but is always a rapidly changing, dynamic entity. Knowledge itself is dynamic, changing moment by moment. It follows then that a subject literature, which reflects the subject, is also changing, and thus the indexing language that represents the contents of that subject literature is equally dynamic. If not, it soon becomes dated and inadequate.

Not only do terms change, but collections of documents grow, and the size of the index vocabulary must grow to accommodate the collection growth. For the most part, the indexing of a totally new subject presents no serious problem, as this process involves simply adding entirely new terms. The trouble is that in most collections the addition of wholly new subjects is not as frequent as is the situation where old subjects split or vary or cross over into another discipline; for example, biology and chemistry became biochemistry. Old terms are no longer sufficient, but at the same time they are still necessary for the old lines of thinking. Changes will have to be made in the indexing language to reflect these variations and subtle modifications in meaning and relationships. Indexing languages seldom, if ever, shrink; they inevitably grow larger, with more and more structural complexities.

THE THESAURUS

One of the results of active attempts to overcome the problems involved in using uncontrolled vocabularies in indexing was the evolution and subsequent development of the thesaurus. Thesauri are not an entirely new, radical approach to bibliographic control, but grew out of librarians' continued attempts at vocabulary control.

Too often librarians are overly conservative and they modify systems only when they receive jolts from users. The development of the modern thesaurus is a case in point. As users became computer-oriented they wanted ready access to highly specific subjects, and traditional library classification methods simply could not provide this service. Many of the concepts for thesaurus design have come from the feedback of users of retrieval systems, and this is the way it should be.

Taube's uniterm system, which indexed with unit words from the document texts and allowed the searcher to postcoordinate, was an extreme switch from traditional methods. This method used only single words, pulled from the document, and involved no control. The idea was alluring mainly because it promised a relatively inexpensive way to use clerical people as indexers. However, before long it became clear that this was not a fail-safe system. In fact, as collections grew, there was an insufferable increase in false drops. Also, as the vocabulary grew, the physical manipulation of the uniterm file became more and more unwieldy. The first remedy was to use a limited amount of precoordination for the most obvious word problems, e.g., putting together *Venetian* and *blinds* as "Venetian blinds" to avoid the obvious false drop from those two uniterms. This, of course, was a first step in vocabulary control. This evolution generally continued until finally, in the late 1950s, the entire vocabulary was regulated, at which time the indexing list became known as a thesaurus.

Classification schemes, subject headings, and thesauri are all authority control devices, but there are some differing characteristics. For example, classification schemes are generally hierarchical with secondary alphabetical indexes, while thesauri are generally alphabetical with hierarchical structure built in by the use of cross-references. The relationships between terms in the thesaurus are more specific. However, in thesauri, descriptors are often dependent on other terms and are intended to be combined with other terms, whereas in a classification scheme or a subject heading list the terms can stand alone. Also, most subject heading terms are independent of other terms, that is, the terms can conceptually stand on their own, whereas the terms in a thesaurus may be dependent on other terms. They are meant to be combined with other terms to express more specific concepts. In other words, we have on one hand precoordinated systems (e.g., classification and subject headings) and on the other hand, postcoordinated languages (e.g., descriptors and natural languages).

In addition, in some thesauri, descriptors can be manipulated. For example, they may allow for permutation of the individual words in a concept phrase. The thesaurus is a tool that is used to control alphabetical indexing languages. Originally, it was a control device for postcoordinate indexing systems, while the subject headings list controlled the more precoordinate alphabetical systems, but the degree or shade of difference between these two is now very slight.

The thesaurus controls the vocabulary in a variety of ways. In the first place, it determines the specificity of the language by giving the terms that can and cannot be used, thus restricting vocabulary size. The more specific the language, the higher the precision will be in the documents selected.

Construction

As with any controlled list, the construction of a thesaurus follows a basic approach. It begins with a free list of natural-language words from which groups of synonyms are gradually formed, representing as nearly as possible single concepts. This may be done in one of two fundamental ways, either by building top-down with a theoretical, enumerative approach the same way traditional classification schemes are created or by building bottom-up with an empirical approach. The latter begins with the literature and the users of the literature and often includes such quantitative methods as a count of the frequency of word use in the subject area.

Actually, the construction of a thesaurus is often somewhere in between the theoretical approach and the empirical one, with a committee working on the thesaurus with both approaches.

In the first approach, the committee is usually made up of subject specialists who provide words they think are appropriate, drawing the terms from their own expertise, from previously constructed indexing languages, from dictionaries, and other such basic reference tools in the field. The alternative method is to go directly to the current literature, the subject literature itself, accumulate representative samples of the kinds of items that are likely to be indexed, and compile a list of words to work with. This is an empirical approach and has the advantage of identifying the actual terms now being used by the writers themselves. As with any empirical approach, it has the disadvantage of being limited to a particular point in time, and we can say nothing about the relative permanence of its representation. The jargon of a particular subject area can be ephemeral and trendy, and thus serve little useful purpose in an authority list.

If the first approach is adopted, a number of tools may be used. For example:

1. *Classification schemes and subject headings*. These schemes and lists, especially those designed for special collections in the fields to be covered by the thesaurus, are very valuable sources. A good classification scheme is particularly useful, for the obvious reason that it shows hierarchical relationships. But it must be remembered that obsolescence is a weakness in classification, and care must be taken not to bring this into the thesaurus.

2. *Review articles*. Review articles are generally definitive works covering a broad field or a specific subfield. The advantage of review articles is that they provide current terminology and are relatively exhaustive.

3. *Monographs*. Monographs, particularly in science and technology, serve as periodical synthesizers of the primary literature. These publications, especially textbooks, introduce and define basic terminology in a field.

4. *Basic reference tools*. Handbooks, dictionaries, encyclopedias, and other such reference tools deal with terminology in a subject field. Again, one must be cautioned against obsolescence when using these tools. It is assumed that thesaurus builders will become familiar with the quality and coverage of any such tools they may consult.

Whichever approach is used, it must be remembered that a thesaurus is neither a dictionary nor a classification scheme. Dictionaries serve as a record to standard usage of words and terms, but this is not the primary purpose of a thesaurus. A thesaurus is the *result* of the understanding of proper usage.

Steps in Thesaurus Construction

The following general steps are suggested for constructing a thesaurus:

1. Identify the subject field. The boundaries of the subject field should be clearly defined and the parameters set to indicate which areas will be emphasized and which will be given only cursory treatment.

2. Identify the nature of the literature to be indexed. Is it primarily journal literature? Or does it consist of books, reports, conference papers, etc.? Is it retrospective or current? If it is retrospective, then it will be more complex to make changes in the thesaurus.

3. Identify the users. What are their information needs? Will they be doing their own searching or will someone do it for them? Will their questions be broad or specific?

4. Identify the file structure. Will this be a precoordinated or postcoordinated system?

5. Consult published indexes, glossaries, dictionaries, and other tools in the subject areas for the raw vocabulary. This should not be done necessarily with the idea of copying terms, but such perusal can increase the thesaurus designer's understanding of the terminology and semantic relationships in the field.

6. Cluster the terms.

7. Establish term relationships.

Term Relationships

One of the key points of a thesaurus is that it indicates the relationships among terms. This is achieved by showing under each term the broader, narrower, and related terms, indicated by BT, NT, and RT, placed alongside the words being considered. For example:

INTELLIGENCE
- BT: Ability
- NT: Comprehension
- RT: Talent
- RT: Aptitude

The *broader term* reference shows hierarchical relationship upward in the classification tree. It differs from the *use for* reference in that both the basic term and its broader term are descriptor terms and both can be used.

The *narrower term* reference is similar to the broader term reference, except it goes down in the classification tree.

The *related term* reference refers to a descriptor that can be used in addition to the basic term but is not in a hierarchical relationship. By having the related terms displayed, both the indexers and the searchers are in a better position to cover the full range of options that may be possible in either indexing or searching.

Another important guide in a thesaurus is the *use* concept. The *use* reference refers to a preferred descriptor from a nonusable term. In a sense it is reciprocal of a *use for* (UF) term, which is discussed below. For example:

Persian cats
    USE CATS

Siamese cats
    USE CATS

The *use for* reference deals primarily with synonyms or variant forms of the preferred descriptor. It is also used to lead the indexer to more general terms. For example:

CATS
    UF   Persian cats
            Siamese cats

Another example:

PROMOTION POLICIES
    UF   Automatic promotion

            and

Automatic promotion
    USE: PROMOTION POLICIES

In the last example, the preferred term is "Promotion policies," and the UF points this out. The UF instruction will enable the thesaurus to control vocabulary size by posting specific terms on the more general term. In some cases, UF references are also used to deal with synonyms and near-synonyms.

Another useful cross-reference in the thesaurus is the *scope note* (SN). A scope note is used to restrict the usage of a descriptor or to clarify one that is ambiguous. For example, it may be used with homographs to declare which word is intended, or it may support the use of narrower terms.

As a rule, scope notes are given in a thesaurus to avoid ambiguities. They serve to explain the scope of a term as well as to delimit it. These indicators are not necessarily straight dictionary definitions, but more like brief descriptions of the sense or framework in which the terms should be used. For example:

CULTURAL BACKGROUND
> SN: The total social heritage and experience of an individual or group, including institutions, folkways, literature, mores, and communal experiences.

Thus, a thesaurus provides the control of terminology by showing a structural display of concepts, supplying for each concept all terms that might express that concept, and presenting the associate and hierarchical relationships of the vocabulary. Generally, the result is an alphabetical list of all the words and phrases making up the controlled vocabulary.

Term Forms

There are a few general rules for deciding on the form of terms used in the thesaurus. There may, of course, be exceptions to the rules, but in most cases:

1. Descriptors should be nouns, either single nouns, noun phrases, or nouns with qualifiers indicated in parentheses.

2. Multiword terms may be either precoordinated or formed by postcoordination of existing terms.

3. Generally, the singular form of the words is used for processes and properties and the plural is used for *classes* of people who do the actions involved. For example:

    Processes
    > Liquidation
    > Indexing

    Classes
    > Teachers
    > Preachers
    > Candlestick makers

4. Multiword terms should be entered in their natural word order with cross-references to the inverted forms.

5. Abbreviations should be used if their meanings are known to the users.

At this point in the thesaurus construction, consideration should be given to combining terms into multiword forms as necessary. The important issue here is to draw a fine line between how much precoordination will be done and how much will be left to the thesaurus user, who may be either the indexer or the searcher. Although the objective of the thesaurus is vocabulary control, too much control will make the device nonmanipulative and thus defeat its purpose, if the purpose of the thesaurus is to have a manipulative system. Careful rules must be laid down as to how terms are to be combined and defined. Criteria must be established for handling synonyms and related terms, both vertical and horizontal. The handling of cross-references must be described. And, finally, the list must be alphabetized with a consistent alphabetizing procedure.

Updating

A thesaurus is not a one-shot effort but a continuing enterprise. If the thesaurus is not maintained, updated, and carefully monitored, its usefulness quickly deteriorates and its advantages over an uncontrolled indexing language are soon lost. The vocabulary of the literature and of the subject specialist is constantly changing, and the thesaurus must reflect these changes.

With a controlled vocabulary, indexers cannot use any word in the language. They must follow the thesaurus. On the other hand, a thesaurus cannot be a static tool with a permanent vocabulary; therefore, there should be procedures for changing the terms. At some point the indexers will sense the need to add a new term, because they see it reappearing in the subject area literature as the subject evolves. Usually the indexers will recommend the addition of the term and will describe the purpose and scope of the new term. The biggest question is, of course, whether or not the term is necessary. Could the same indexing results be obtained by coordinating existing terms? Also, the indexer will need to suggest cross-references and recommend where in the hierarchy the term belongs. Generally, the term will be reviewed by senior editors or by a committee before it is added to the thesaurus.

Updating is more than just adding new terms; it involves replacement and changes in the structural relationships of the old terms as well. The approaches and considerations that went into creating the list in the first place must be used in the same way to update. Time and again thesauri that were originally excellent tools have been allowed to become useless, suffering strong criticism in their declining days. Over time, a thesaurus that is not kept current has very little chance of surviving.

Display

A display is the final, usable form of the thesaurus or index. The thesaurus may be in a number of physical formats, such as printed (e.g., on cards), in microform, or in a machine-readable medium. It is generally an alphabetical list, but often will have some kind of secondary arrangement such as classified or hierarchical by descriptor sets, or, occasionally, with permuted displays. Some typical thesaurus displays are:

Alphabetical with cross-references

Alphabetical with general subject categories

Alphabetical with hierarchical displays

Alphabetical with faceted classification

Classified with index

The advantage of the dual display, first alphabetical, then hierarchical, is that when the entry term is selected, the thesaurus will immediately show the broader and narrower terms, along with whatever semantical relationships are present. This type of display is not universal. Sometimes a thesaurus will be divided into two distinct parts, with the first being a classification layout, showing detailed hierarchical forms, and the second being a necessary alphabetical entry tool. A good example of this type of thesaurus is the thesaurofacet.

THESAUROFACET

The thesaurofacet is a combination of a conventional faceted classification scheme and an alphabetical thesaurus, with each term in the thesaurus also appearing in the faceted classification schedule and tied together with a code, which is usually a classification number. The information provided for each term is not the same in both lists, but complementary. The two parts of a thesaurofacet are designed to be used in conjunction with each other, not separately. The alphabetical thesaurus is used when searchers have a specific term. When they enter with that term, the display will provide a hierarchical order showing the term's primary position. On the other hand, the classification display is used when a searcher has a broad subject in mind. The alphabetical thesaurus serves as an index to the faceted schedule, taking care of synonyms and alternative word forms. A thesaurofacet is an excellent means of combining the advantages of a detailed faceted classification with the language-control potentials of a thesaurus.

THESAURUS EVALUATION

On the surface, the evaluation of a thesaurus is rather straightforward. How well does it help indexers and users select the exact terms they need and how well does it show structural relationships between vocabulary terms? Unfortunately, like other aspects of information retrieval, the final judgments are usually subjective, despite the quasi-quantitative methods of recall and precision.

A thesaurus can be used at the indexing stage or the searching stage, or both. Generally, indexers use the thesaurus to select approved terms to represent the document concepts, and the user of the index uses the thesaurus to find the correct term that will give entry to the index. In the ideal situation the terms will be broad enough to pull together relevant related information, but specific enough not to produce nonrelevant information. Seldom is this situation totally realized because of the many variables involved in the indexing and retrieval process.

Although user satisfaction (or the lack of it) may be helpful in determining the quality of a thesaurus, it is essential that certain criteria be established beforehand. When deciding what criteria are to be used, it is important to remember exactly what it is that the tool is designed to do. A thesaurus is a device to control vocabulary, based on the premise that such control is a fundamental problem in indexing. We attempt to establish a link between concepts and terms by grouping natural-language words into sets of similar words and picking a "preferred" term to stand for the meaning of the entire group. Because of the ambiguity of language and its use, this can never be absolutely accomplished, but the degree of correspondence is an indicator of the quality of a thesaurus. Some questions that might be asked are:

1. How good is the subject coverage of the concepts displayed? Is it adequate to allow proper indexing and searching?

2. How well does the thesaurus handle broader terms, narrower terms, and related terms? In other words, are all the structural relationships between terms treated adequately?

3. How adequate is the display of the thesaurus? Is it easy to see, understand, and follow through on? Does it lead to efficient and effective indexing and searching?

Most of the failures of a thesaurus can be linked to these three basic areas. However, another pragmatic factor to be considered in evaluating a thesaurus is its cost. Creating and maintaining a thesaurus is costly, and the question is whether or not its benefits equal or exceed that cost. In maintaining a thesaurus, a key point to keep in mind is that as more specificity is allowed the word list grows in size, which in turn complicates the structure and thus costs more to maintain. Exactly how specific the thesaurus will be is a basic construction decision, and cost cannot be ignored while making this decision.

Constructing a thesaurus is a complex, labor-intensive job, and the work on a particular thesaurus is never finished. We have learned a lot about these valuable tools in the past few decades, but we have a great deal more to learn. It is one of the truly interesting and challenging areas of our profession.

EXAMPLES

It might be useful for the reader to examine some classification schemes, subject heading lists, and thesauri. The following is a short list of some of these items that will most likely be available for examination. Illustrations of selected thesauri are given in chapter XII where online systems are discussed.

Aitchison, J., comp. *UNESCO Thesaurus*. Paris: UNESCO, 1977. (See examples 57 and 58, chapter XII.)

This is a structured list of descriptors for indexing in education, science, social science, culture, and communication. It has four primary displays: a classified thesaurus, a permuted index, a hierarchical display, and an alphabetical thesaurus.

Merwe Van de, with others. *Thesaurus of Sociological Research Terminology*. Rotterdam: University Press, 1974.

This tool is an example of a classified vocabulary displayed in columns. The columns include category descriptors, unauthorized terms, and related terms.

Thesaurus of Agricultural Terms. National Agricultural Library. Scottsdale, Ariz.: Oryx Press, 1976.

This thesaurus is the basis for the subject index of the *Bibliography of Agriculture*. In the list, word variants are grouped together in parentheses following the key term.

National Computing Centre. *Thesaurus of Computing Terms.* 8th ed. Manchester, U.K.: The Centre, 1977.

This is an example of a thesaurus compiled from other thesauri and subject glossaries. It contains an alphabetical list, a hierarchical list, and an index to the hierarchy.

Organization for Economic Cooperation and Development. *Macrothesaurus for Information Processing in the Field of Economic and Social Development.* Paris: OECD, 1986.

The purpose of this tool is to provide detailed terminology for indexing, processing and retrieving documents issued by the United Nations. Its primary arrangement is alphabetical with each descriptor accompanied by the foreign-language equivalent. Secondary indexes include a hierarchical list and a KWOC index.

The UNESCO: IBE Education Thesaurus, 4th ed. Paris: UNESCO, 1986.

This is an example of a faceted index. It is a list of terms for indexing and retrieving documents in education and has four primary divisions: a classified thesaurus, a permuted index, a hierarchical display, and an alphabetic thesaurus.

Beck, C., and others, comp. *Political Science Thesaurus.* Washington, D.C.: American Political Science Association, 1975.

This is an example of a standard type thesaurus, with a main section of terms, each of which is followed by broader, narrower, or related terms.

American Psychological Association. *Thesaurus of Psychological Index Terms.* 5th ed. Edited by R. G. Kinkade. Washington, D.C.: American Psychological Association, 1988. (See example 59, chapter XII.)

This is an example of a thesaurus where subject experts reviewed the list of terms before they were included. There is a section where preferred thesaurus terms are rotated in alphabetical order by each word in the term string.

Engineers Joint Council. *Thesaurus of Engineering and Scientific Terms.* New York: Engineers Joint Council, 1969.

This has four divisions, the most important being a main heading listing and a permuted index. The main heading descriptors include hierarchical structuring, cross-references, and scope notes. The permuted index presents each significant thesaurus term in alphabetical order.

Educational Resources Information Center. *Thesaurus of ERIC Descriptors.* 11th ed. Phoenix: Oryx Press, 1987. (See example 51, chapter XII.)

This tool has three main sections including the alphabetical descriptors in the thesaurus file, a rotated descriptor display (which is an alphabetical index to all significant words that form descriptors), and a two-way hierarchical term display, which shows the broader-narrower relationships of all main terms.

Medical Subject Headings (MeSH). Bethesda, Md.: National Library of Medicine, 1963- . (See examples 48 and 49, chapter XII.)

This tool has three primary uses. It is the subject heading authority file for indexing the biomedical literature in *Index Medicus*, the authority list for cataloging at the National Library of Medicine, and the searching thesaurus for *Index Medicus* and for the online system.

Schultz, C. K., ed. *Thesaurus of Information Science Terminology*, 3rd ed. Metuchen, N.J.: Scarecrow Press, 1978.

This thesaurus is based on an extensive examination of the literature. It is notable, also, because of the seven chapters on thesaurus construction and use.

Sears, Minnie Earle. *List of Subject Headings*. 10th ed. Edited by Barbara M. Westby. New York: Wilson, 1972.

U.S. Library of Congress, Subject Cataloging Division. *Subject Headings Used in the Dictionary Catalogs of the Library of Congress from 1898 through December, 1984*. 10th ed. Washington, D.C.: Library of Congress, 1986.

Dewey, Melvil. *Dewey Decimal Classification and Relative Index*. 20th ed. 4 vols. Edited by John P. Comaromi. Albany, N.Y.: Forest Press, 1989.

U.S. Library of Congress, Subject Cataloging Division. *Classification Classes A-Z*. Washington, D.C.: Library of Congress, 1986- .

Ranganathan, Shiyali R. *Colon Classification: Basic Classification*. New York: Asia Publishing House, 1963.

Roget's Thesaurus of English Words and Phrases. London: Longman, 1982.

It would be sacrilegious to have a list of thesauri and not include Roget. Although this is not an indexing thesaurus, it certainly is a useful tool to anyone who is trying to cope with the variegation of natural language.

Thesaurus of Scientific, Technical and Engineering Terms. New York: Hemisphere Publishing, 1988.

Thesaurus of Sociological Indexing Terms. San Diego: Sociological Abstracts, Inc., 1986. (See example 56, chapter XII.)

SUGGESTED READINGS

Aitchison, Jean, and Alan Gilchrist. *Thesaurus Construction: A Practical Manual*. 2nd ed. London: AsLib, 1987.

American National Standards Institute, *American National Standard Guidelines for Thesaurus Structure, Construction, and Use*. New York: ANSI, 1980.

Austin, Derek. "Vocabulary Control and Information Technology." *AsLib Proceedings* 38 (January 1986): 1-15.

Calkins, Mary L. "Free Text or Controlled Vocabulary? A Case History Step-by-Step Analysis ... Plus Other Aspects of Search Strategy." *Database* 3 (June 1980): 53-67.

Kaula, P. "Chain Indexing." *Herald of Library Science* 9 (1970): 318-25.

Kazlauskas, E. J., and T. D. Holt. "The Application of a Minicomputer to Thesaurus Construction." *Journal of the American Society for Information Science* 31 (September 1980): 363-68.

Markey, Karen, Pauline Atherton, and Claudia Newton. "An Analysis of Controlled Vocabulary and Free Text Search Statements in Online Searches." *Online Review* 4 (September 1980): 225-36.

Perez, Ernest. "Text Enhancement: Controlled Vocabulary vs. Free Text." *Special Libraries* 73 (July 1982): 183-92.

Richmond, Phyllis A. *Introduction to PRECIS for North American Usage.* Littleton, Colo.: Libraries Unlimited, 1981.

Svenonius, Elaine F. "Unanswered Questions in the Design of Controlled Vocabularies." *Journal of the American Society for Information Science* 37 (September 1986): 331-40.

Townley, Helen M. *Thesaurus-making: Grow Your Own Word-Stock.* London: Andre Deutsch, 1980.

V

Indexing Methods and Procedures

INTRODUCTION

How is an index made? How does one learn to index a book or a document? A good starting point is to study existing indexes and to use them at length, because indexing is as much an art as a formal procedure, and thus it is a strong function of experience. A person who examines and uses indexes will gradually learn what an ideal index should be like, although indexes vary widely in their characteristics and quality. The different types of printing and displays are immediately apparent. Outlay of main headings and subheadings will differ. Location indicators and bibliographical information will vary. Sometimes instructions for using the index are poor or nonexistent, so that the user must discover how to use it by trial and error. Each index and its arrangement must be studied individually if full utilization is to be realized.

Good indexing is not a casual clerical job. It is the result of a professional activity carried out by people with proper training and experience. There are procedures and techniques, worked out over the years, that can be learned and followed. This chapter will explore some of those methods.

INDEXING RULES

Simply stated, indexing is the procedure that produces entries in an index. That procedure includes a number of basic activities: analyzing content, assigning content indicators, adding location indicators, assembling the resulting entries, and choosing the physical form in which the final index will be displayed.

Closely associated with this procedure are rules designed to guide the indexer's work. Although rules are necessary for quality control, two fundamental facts of life concerning indexing rules should be mentioned. First, rigid obedience to rules will not always ensure total consistency. We cannot control the language of a subject area, and indexers will tend to adjust to the language changes of a user group. The important thing is the control of the changing word usage by these indexers (consistency of indexer usage), which may be more desirable than strictly following the letter of the law in the rule book. Second, it is impossible to spell out a list of indexing rules that will completely cover every possible situation. If this were possible, indexing would have been totally automated long ago. Indexing cannot be reduced to a few simple rules because of the numerous variables involved. For example, do scientists require a different approach than the social scientist or the artist? Should encyclopedias be indexed differently from journal articles or films? Subject literatures have different structures, formats, and users, making it extremely difficult to compose any universal rules for indexing.

However, experience and reflective study have given us some guidelines and some approaches that seem to work. Actual rules are written for specific indexing operations, but the following, *not be taken literally*, are some examples of what general rules might look like.

1. Refer singular to plural terms:

    Cat, *see* Cats

2. Include prepositions and conjunctions at the beginning or at the end of headings, but include them only when they are required for ease of understanding. For example:

    Cats   Cats

    Types   *not*   Types of

3. Use modifying phrases of subheading to differentiate blocks of reference numbers:

    This: Cats
               Diseases, 7, 42, 87, 109
               Domesticated, 19, 29, 36, 87
               Types, 1, 19, 62, 93, 120, 210

    Not this: Cats, 1, 7, 19, 29, 36, 42, 62, 87, 93, 109, 120, 210

4. To avoid the ambiguity of homographs, use scope notes in parentheses:

    Bases (military), 23, 17, 19
    Bases (baseball), 97, 108

5. When writing modifications of terms, introduce the phrase with a word that stands out and catches the attention of the user:

    Sex, the use of TV in the teaching of

6. For multiple authorship, list only the first three authors:

    Jones, A., Jones, B., Jones, C., and others

7. Use initials of authors:

    This: Jones, A. F.

    Not this: Jones, Albert Fitzgerald

8. Alphabetize word by word:

    This: New York
               Newark
               Newton

    Not this: Newark
               Newton
               New York

9. Choose terms consistently.

10. Use location indicators that are as precise as practical.

11. Index to the maximum specificity signified by the author. (Don't post up to a more generic term if the author's specific word has an acceptable term at that level.) For example, if the author is talking about B-52 bombers and that is an acceptable term, don't substitute "Airplanes."

12. Do not scatter similar entries. (The user wants to find related entries in one place, as much as possible, not strung out from *A* to *Z* in the index.)
    For example, if we have the terms

    City government
    County government
    State government

    then it might be better if a single entry is given with subheadings:

    Government
        City
        County
        State

Of course, cross-references should be given from important entry terms.

These are merely examples of what rules may look like. There are generally many such guides, and in practice the rules may be the opposite to the examples given here. Rules are not universal laws, but reflect the local policy—the goal is always intelligent consistency.

One type of rule that is generally inflexible is that of format. Format rules usually are prescribed by editors, and an indexer must be concerned at all times about what is expected. Users, especially of periodical indexes, come to expect a particular form and style, and they hope to use the index without having to read new and complicated instructions. Ideally, rules are designed to facilitate understanding and use, not merely to cut production costs.

A number of manuals are available that give rules for indexing. The following are some examples:

Aitchison, J., and A. Gilchrist. *Thesaurus Construction: A Practical Manual.* 2nd ed. London: AsLib, 1987.

This is a revised edition of a useful, step-by-step guide for creating a thesaurus. Although it is *not* directly a guide to indexing, a reader can learn a great deal about the indexing process and rationale by moving through the steps in the manual.

American National Standards Institute. *American National Standard Guidelines for Thesaurus Structure, Construction, and Use.* New York: ANSI, 1980.

Again, this is directed at thesaurus building, but the rationale given in the preceding entry is true here also.

American National Standards Institute. *American National Standard for Library and Information Sciences and Related Publishing Practices—Basic Criteria for Indexes.* New York: ANSI, 1984.

Borko, Harold, and Charles L. Bernier. *Indexing Concepts and Methods.* New York: Academic Press, 1978.

As discussed in chapter I, Borko's book is a straightforward presentation of the indexing process.

British Standards Institution. *British Standard on Indexing: Preparation of Indexes of Books, Periodicals and Other Publications.* London: BSI, 1976; BS3700, 1976.

Both this British Standard and the American Standard (see above entry) are useful learning tools. Obviously, a standard is a brief statement and not a detailed discussion, but a great deal can be learned by carefully reading these two publications.

Speight, F. Y. *Guide for Source Indexing and Abstracting of the Engineering Literature.* New York: Engineers Joint Council, 1961.

Although somewhat dated, this brief guide is clearly presented, is highly readable, and logically lays some guidelines for indexing.

United Nations Educational, Scientific, and Cultural Organization. *UNISIST Indexing Principles.* Paris: UNESCO, 1975.

Some more popular guides to indexing include:

Harris, E. T. *A Guide for the Preparation of Indexes.* Santa Monica, Calif.: Rand Corp., 1965.

Bakewell, K. G. B. "How to Let Your Fingers Do the Walking and Not Lose the Way (Index Compilation)." *Times Higher Education Supplement* 412 (September 26, 1980): 12.

Bingham, W. V. "How to Make a Useful Index." *American Psychologist* 6 (1951): 31-34.

STEPS IN INDEXING

The task of an indexer is to provide guides to the subject content of knowledge records, the result of which is a subject index. Probably only an indexer can really understand the total process, which is a combination of formal rules, common sense, and an elusive thing called talent. Like people in other creative fields, indexers, even those with years of experience, often have a difficult time describing what they do. Subjective judgments play a major role.

The first step in the indexing process is deciding whether or not the document is worth indexing. The item is scanned quickly, probably superficially, to see if it meets the criteria for being indexed. These criteria are not necessarily a universal judgment of merit but a value judgment based on the objectives and policies of the indexing agency. The policies and purposes of a large general indexing service will be geared to a large user group with a broad subject interest, while in a special library or a narrowly defined information center the users will have a distinct, more specific type of information need. In other words, the decision to index or not to index is based on the information needs of the clientele. Incidentally, the needs of the clientele will also affect the indexing process proper as regards depth and specificity of indexing, and the number of terms allowed per document.

The next decision is what parts of the document will be indexed and what parts will be passed over. Then the decision must be made about how exhaustively the material will be indexed. That is, will every minute aspect of the indexable material be reflected or only applicable facets? Related to this is how specifically the material will be indexed. Once these decisions are made, the actual indexing begins and the following steps are suggested.

Recording of Bibliographic Data

Good bibliographic form can be summed up simply—it includes all useful data, leaves out useless data, and is consistent in format. For example, if using only the initials of an author's given name fulfills the needs of the users and causes no ambiguity, it would be foolish to waste space or time verifying the full name. Generally, bibliographic form will be specified by rules of format, and these rules should be followed closely. Care must be taken to see that the data is recorded accurately, for the obvious reason that incorrect entries cause the document to become inaccessible. Even if an error is not critical, it can be irritating to the user.

Content Analysis

Once the recording of the essential bibliographic data is completed, it is time to examine the paper more closely. Not every document has to be read completely; spot reading may be sufficient for the indexer to understand what concepts are dealt with. On the other hand, some documents may have to be read completely, maybe more than once, before the indexer feels confident in identifying the subject content.

Clearly, the content analysis stage can be affected by the environmental situation. The process may be hurried if there is a labor shortage or other critical time factors. Also, the amount of time involved in content analysis will depend on the nature of the document and the experience of the indexer.

But the major factor will be policy decisions. Indexers generally work under guidelines imposed by the agency they work for, or under self-imposed guidelines if they work alone. Often these guidelines are concerned with the selection of certain content indicators and the rejection of others. For example, indexers of scientific literature may be told to concentrate on methodology, measurement, equipment used, and new results and to ignore historical material. Indexers attempt to represent every possible concept only in very general information systems. Clearly, the more familiar the indexer is with the field in general, the easier content analysis is.

Following the familiarization phase, indexers must decide which aspects of subjects will be emphasized and which aspects will be deemphasized. Some of the facets will be basic to the needs of the index users, some will be of marginal interest, and some will be of no importance. These decisions are made at the analysis stage. As these decisions are being made, indexers jot down the concepts, either using words directly out of the text or drawing on their own vocabulary or a combination of both.

Where do the concepts come from? Formal papers can be broken down into basic units, each of which is examined below.

The title. The use of permuted titles as indexes was discussed earlier. Surely titles (and subtitles) give important clues to subject content, but they do have certain drawbacks. In order to be concise, titles often generalize. The purpose of a title is to convey to the potential reader an understanding of the paper's major topic. Specific aspects of that topic may or may not be conveyed.

We are assuming in the foregoing that titles are indicative of document content. Unfortunately, good title writing is not always a strong point in science papers and even less so in scholarly writings. Titles may be vague, either because they are too generalized or because the author is aiming for a "catchy" title or is trying to be cute. In too many cases, the titles, unfortunately, are simply not related at all to the subject dealt with. Despite these drawbacks, titles are a basic indexing unit and they are the first stop in determining subject content.

The abstract. The second important unit to be considered is the abstract. Whereas index terms simply indicate subject content, abstracts are actual surrogates of documents, and good abstracts can be fundamental indicators of subject content. Abstracts should strip away ephemeral material and deal with the key subjects in the paper. Most of the words in the abstract should heavily convey subject content.

Extracted abstracts, that is, abstracts that simply string together sentences lifted from the text, are less useful than original abstracts. In the latter case, the abstract writer expresses concepts using words not directly used by the author. Really good abstracts of this kind come close to being all that is necessary for adequate indexing, but a wealth of studies over the years tends to show that abstracts alone are not consistently as good for indexing as using *all* the indexable units in a document. Unfortunately, abstracts, like titles, can be badly written and misleading.

The text itself. By convention, most technical and scholarly papers follow a certain pattern that gives the indexer an important short-cut to understanding subject content. First, the introduction, the summary, and the conclusion should be read. As the old saying goes, the introduction explains what is *going* to be said, and the summary and conclusion explain what *has* been said. At least the overall intent of the paper can be ascertained from these units.

Section headings should also be observed, since these are, in a sense, minia-ture titles to the major parts of the paper. As content indicators, they have the same strengths and weaknesses as titles.

In addition, first and last sentences of paragraphs should receive primary attention since, by convention, these sentences carry the message of the paragraphs. Numerous indexing studies have empirically demonstrated that the first sentences, especially, carry the message of the paragraph.

A number of other things in the text should be considered. The historical and theoretical background of the paper's topic should be studied, if present. The methodology and sources, if described, can be important. Charts, diagrams, graphs, photographs, and other such illustrative materials may be a key factor for understanding content. Knowing what to read and what to skim comes from expe-rience, but these items should be helpful in examining the text of the document.

The reference section. Most technical and scholarly papers are accompanied by a list of references. In the past decade or so there has been a growing interest in the contribution of these references to content analysis. A great deal of study has been done on references and their importance for indexing. Citation indexing and bibliographic coupling techniques are two results of this study that come to mind. It is generally conceded that writers take referencing seriously and that these lists reflect the subject content of the papers. Authors cite other writers who have written on the same topic, both to support themselves and to give the reader an opportunity to go to other works that are closely related. Of course, the subject indicator in the reference list is again the title, although the names of the authors may also be keys to subject content, especially if they are recognized as experts in particular subject areas. Although the weaknesses and strengths in title indexing are still present, the range and variety of titles in the reference list can add substantially to an understanding of subject content.

Subject Determination

After examining and analyzing the document, the indexer must determine the subject(s) covered — simply put, what the document is about. Concepts in the document must be identified and expressed in words and a list of possible descriptors for the index prepared.

So the indexer scans a document, looking at sentences, phrases and words that reveal what the document is about. Then a subjective decision is made concerning the meaning of the document and what is relevant to the users of the index. How does an indexer make these decisions? We have little understanding of indexers' mental processes, but there appears to be two general types of indexers. One type reads a paper and understands what the paper is about. The other type may not totally understand the paper but has the talent for selecting appropriate keywords from the text.

The objective now is to form a mental picture of what the author is saying. The author is not present, and all the indexer has to go on are those black, printed symbols on the paper. Language is ambiguous and metaphorical, and the indexer must now make the best possible subjective decisions. For example, "The mosquitos attacked with the ferocity of a tiger" is about mosquitos, not tigers, and tigers would be an incorrect term (with the possible exception that there might be a language professor who is studying metaphor in scientific writings).

The indexer is now making intellectual decisions—decisions that will make or break the indexing of that document. The fundamental problem here is that the concept of a subject is an elusive one. All writers in an area have a unique understanding of what that subject is and also a unique way of expressing themselves and choosing words when they write. And the situation is the same when it comes to the indexer, and eventually to the reader. If we were all robots, programmed to write the same way, there would be no indexing problems.

So indexers must form a mental image of what the author is saying and then state in their own words, or in words borrowed from the writer, what that subject is. This word list, which we might call a *concept list*, should be as complete as possible, but concise. Final document descriptors will be filtered from this list.

A naive indexing rule at this point might be "index all important subjects." But what is important? For one thing, how often an idea is repeated may be an indication of its importance. Most of the automatic indexing techniques, using a computer, are based in one way or another on the frequency of occurrence of words in a text, and this comes from the intuitive feeling that major ideas are repeated and minor ideas are only mentioned.

Another clue is style and grammatical structure. For example, in the sentence "The mosquito attacked with ferocity," the word *mosquito* is an important word, but in the sentence "The queen looked at me with her mosquito eyes," *mosquito* is probably not important. Also, the author will often tell us, either implicitly or explicitly, that a topic is an important point in the paper, and generally we can believe it.

The selection of subjects is closely related to the policies of the indexing agency. For example, the rules of a particular indexing operation may flatly state that historical background is not to be indexed since it offers nothing new to the discussion in the paper. Underlying this process is a very important premise: the subject matter of each and every document is assessed in terms of the information requirements of the users. The user is the ultimate judge of what subjects are important. If indexers keep this premise in mind, it will make their task easier by providing an intellectual framework within which they can work.

Conversion to the Indexing Language

The next step involves converting the concept list into a list of acceptable index terms. If a controlled vocabulary is being used, this implies using an authority list to do the conversion. The indexer translates, so to speak, the concepts into standard index terminology so that the correct terms will be found and used, even when the user looks in the wrong place in the index. The terms in the concept list are matched against the thesaurus or other authority lists with the goal of choosing final descriptors within the accepted framework of the prescribed indexing language.

Each concept word from the list is checked in the thesaurus or other authority lists for several possibilities:

(a)   Is there an exact equivalent available?

Concept list	Thesaurus
Cats	Cats

Thus, "Cats" becomes the index term.

(b)   If not, is there a synonym or near-synonym?

Concept list	Thesaurus
Student grouping	USE: Grouping (instructional purposes)

"Grouping (instructional purposes)" becomes the index term.

(c)   Is there a narrower term that might be used?

Concept list   **Thesaurus**

Inspection

Inspection
    USE: Supervision

Supervision
    UF: Inspection
    NT: School supervision

Thus, either "Supervision" or "School supervision," or both, might be used, depending on policy and on exactly what the original concept *inspection* conveyed.

(d)   Should a broader term be used?

Concept list   **Thesaurus**

Labor organizations

Labor organizations
    USE: Trade unions

Trade unions
    UF: Labor organizations
    BT: National organizations

(e)   Should a related term be used?

Concept list   **Thesaurus**

Information science

Information science
    RT: Library science

Thus, both terms might be used, again according to the content of the paper and its use of the term "Information science."

(f) Should two or more terms in the thesaurus be coordinated?

Concept list	**Thesaurus**
Polish car	Car
	Polish

A good thesaurus will have careful rules for how and when to combine terms.

(g) Place names can cause problems. For example, the names may be different in different languages. The names sometimes change. In the first case, the general rule is to spell it one way and have cross-references from variant spellings. In the second case, the general rule is to use the latest form and have cross-references from earlier spellings.

(h) Since no word in the thesaurus will convey the meaning, should a new term be added to the thesaurus?

Reexamination

The final step in indexing a document is to examine what has been done. Do the final descriptors assigned cover all the important concepts derived from the document? Do the descriptors accurately reflect the subjects? Could the terms be used to recreate the meaning and intent of the document? That is, could the indexer or an outsider use the words to write a synopsis of the document?

CHOOSING DESCRIPTORS

In the preceding section we discussed some of the mechanics of indexing a document, although indexing a document is clearly not a mechanical activity. A number of factors are related to the decisions an indexer makes in carrying out the basic steps described.

Selection

A quality index is the result of a series of good indexing decisions. Indexers must be certain that all the right terms have been selected, but also that no needed terms have been excluded. Including the wrong terms will lead the user to information not wanted or needed, and leaving out the right terms will keep needed information from being discovered. In many ways, indexers are trying to second-guess what the users need and how they will react to the index entries. If users have a particular information need, what term will they use to identify the document the indexers have in their hands? And closely related to this, if the users decide to use that term, will they be satisfied?

The ideal index term clearly reflects what the document is about. It is precise enough to locate specific information, yet it is broad enough to identify related material. It is at this point that a good thesaurus will tie terms to related terms by showing semantic and hierarchical interrelationships through cross-references, term qualifiers, and scope notes.

The point has been made that selectivity is partly based on the policies of the indexing agencies, which often describe the kinds of subjects to be selected for indexing. Clearly, indexing is not based solely on the words that appear in the text of the document. For example, if the index is aimed at mathematicians, the indexing rule will probably instruct the indexers to emphasize mathematical subjects and viewpoints and to ignore concepts unrelated or ephemeral to mathematics.

Selection policies will vary, depending on the audience to which the index is directed. Obviously, an index aimed at a homogeneous group of specialists will serve a different purpose than an index aimed at a general audience with a wide range of information needs. Other factors in selectivity include the nature of the material itself (is it technical or nontechnical?) and the type of index. A back-of-the-book index presumably has all the information available immediately, whereas a periodical index may index material remote and possibly unavailable to the user. This can affect choices of selection.

Entry Points

Entry terms are terms that give users an access to the database. The term may be a proper term, that is, a term that was used to index, or the term may direct the user to a proper term. The relationship established by entry terms with allowed index terms is important to successful indexing and searching. The user who thinks of a possible subject term and then cannot find that term as an entry term either thinks of another term or gives up.

Entry terms are often near-synonyms of an acceptable term. They may also be permutations or pluralization. Often entry terms are colloquial and the cross-reference leads to the more formal term.

From the viewpoint of the users, entry points into the index are extremely critical, perhaps the most important aspect of an index. An ideal index would be responsive to any word users might select when they begin the information search. Such an index would probably be impractical because of construction costs and the physical size of the tool. At the same time, an index with skimpy entry points is less effective, and the burden, both in cost and time, then shifts to the user.

Suppose, for example, that a document under analysis is about three-legged, near-sighted, black cats in Denton County, Texas. Possible words that a user interested in this topic might use are:

Cats

Black cats

Animals

Handicapped cats

Handicapped animals

Vision problems in cats

Denton County cats

Texas cats

There are six terms in the original indexing string and if we permuted all six terms there could be more than 100 entry points. If every possible concept were used as an entry point, the index would grow rather rapidly. There is always a trade-off in how far we can go.

Depth of Indexing

Descriptor choice is always influenced by depth of indexing or exhaustivity. This simply means the number of topics that will be covered in the indexing of a document or the amount of detail covered for a particular topic. It is the degree to which all the separate subjects touched on in a given document are acknowledged in the indexing activity and converted into the indexing language of the system. Suppose we have a document that covers five topics (X_1, X_2, X_3, X_4, X_5) and no others. If we acknowledge all five topics during the analysis stage and assign descriptors to represent these five topics, we can say our indexing of this particular document is complete and that we have indexed in depth. The more indexing depth, the more index terms will be employed. Of course some documents simply do not contain many different ideas, and deep indexing will not produce many terms, no matter how exhaustive.

For some twenty or so years a great deal has been written on the effects of exhaustivity on indexing performance, and a considerable amount of unsettled debate goes on. We seem to agree that there might be an optimal level of exhaustivity for a particular situation, but, unfortunately, no one is quite sure how to determine that optimal point.

Depth of indexing is related to how well a retrieval system pulls out all documents that are possibly related to a subject. Extremely deep indexing will retrieve a high proportion of the relevant documents in a collection, but as more and more documents are retrieved, the risk of getting extraneous material rises. Therefore, when indexers are aiming for exhaustiveness they must keep in mind that at some point they may be negatively affecting the efficiency of the system.

Then why even bother with trying to achieve exhaustivity? Simply because we run the risk of not uncovering information for a user. Generally, users are more worried about missing something than being inconvenienced by having to examine irrelevant material. Up to a point.

The ideal system will give users all documents useful to them and no more. Since this ideal balance is seldom, if ever, realized in practice, the goal is to balance the two; adding more and more terms, trying to cover every facet and nuance of those facets, can throw the balance off.

Precision of Indexing

The preciseness with which we describe a document (often called specificity of indexing) is another dimension in choosing descriptors. This refers to the generic relationship between index terms. The more specific the term, the more precise the results, i.e., more of the retrieved items will be precisely related to the searcher's inquiry. On the other hand, more generic terms will retrieve a greater number of items that are generally related to the searcher's inquiry. If the descriptors used are parallel to the subject concepts in the documents and reflect these concepts precisely, then we say the indexing is specific. As the indexing becomes less precise and less parallel to the exact concepts, the descriptors will apply to a broader range of documents that are farther apart in informational overlap. For example, "Cats" is a more specific term than "Animals," and if searchers use the term "Animals" they will receive a wide range of information on all kinds of animals, hopefully including their desired information about cats. "Cats" is a more precise term. Clearly, a very specific indexing language will have a large vocabulary with more potential descriptors.

The use of a specific term will enable the searchers to zero in on the exact topic they want, but once again they risk the possibility of missing information. Suppose, for example, they are interested in diseases in cats and they use the search term "Cats," which is a reasonable term to them. There is a possibility that a document not described by this term deals with diseases in animals in general, giving important information that certainly applies to cats but is indexed with the term "Animals." The searchers will miss this document. Specific indexing and searching will retrieve a small set of documents, concentrating on exact ideas. Broader, more general documents are excluded. So once again we are faced with the problem of balance, since a less specific search leads to the possibility of giving the users material they consider unrelated to their need.

The problem of specificity begins at the point where the indexing language is designed and must be considered in selecting the vocabulary and designing the thesaurus. Once the thesaurus is constructed, the only way to change its specificity is to make major changes in the vocabulary. It is difficult for an indexer to be nonspecific if the language is designed for specificity.

It should be pointed out that exhaustiveness is a decision made at the indexing stage and can be controlled by limiting the number of terms allowed for an individual document and by the indexer's decision to ignore certain facets, based on the understanding of what the user's information needs are.

Weighting

Indexers are keenly aware that descriptors assigned to a document are not equally important in reflecting content. Some descriptors are absolutely necessary and describe the main thrust of the document, but indexers hesitate to assign descriptors to what may be of minimum importance. Yet a searcher does not know the importance of many descriptors until the paper is examined. To help overcome this problem, the concept of weighting was proposed, whereby a term is given a value, on some kind of scale, to identify its relative importance.

The device of weighting index terms developed in the early days of information retrieval. The technique is usually based on the frequency of occurrence of words and can range all the way from simple word counts to some rather complex statistical models. For example, several techniques attempt to relate the frequency of occurrence of words in a particular document to the frequency of occurrence of these words in the collection as a whole or to natural language. The idea is that the words in the document will be weighted according to how they vary from the normal frequency of occurrence. If there is a significant increase in the frequency then that concept must be a meaningful term.

Making the Choice

A popular approach to the problem of specificity is simply to index to the specificity of the author. If the writer talks about cats, then the indexer has no right to post up to "Animals" as an index term, since this moves content analysis away from what the document is really about, thereby reducing the relevance of the documents.

Choices should be made on the basis of the clientele. As a general rule, an indexing agency aimed at a general user will go with the broader term approach and with more exhaustivity, whereas a specialized indexing service will use narrower terms and will decide what facets are important and what facets can be ignored.

INDEXING SYNTAX

General Problem

A thesaurus is a vocabulary control device basically aimed at overcoming the semantical problems in language. And it has proven to be successful at this. However, indexing also has syntactical language problems that go beyond semantic control.

Simply stated, syntactical ambiguity occurs when term combinations create counterfeit concepts for a document. For example, a document might be indexed with the terms "Dogs," "Cats," and "Diseases," and it might be about dogs and about cat diseases but say nothing about diseases in dogs. However, if the users request information using the terms "Dogs" and "Diseases" they will be lead to irrelevant material. As depth of indexing increases, more terms are available, with more possible combinations, increasing the possibilities for syntactical error.

When uniterm coordinate indexing was first proposed, the idea was to index with single terms from the documents and allow users to form term combinations to fit individual needs, thereby avoiding elaborate cross-references and complex authority lists. Neither the indexer nor the user would have to take the time to consult any such lists. This indexing method was basically a revolt against the cumbersome procedures involved in traditional library approaches and sounded like a neat system. But its simplicity failed to take into account the vagaries of natural language, and the "pure" uniterm system never worked and probably never actually existed in a real-world system of any size. Very early, Taube was using multiword or "bound terms." This was the first step toward syntactical control, and from it evolved the idea of links and roles.

Links and Roles

Uniterms and postcoordination introduced the problem of false coordination and spurious relationships into indexes. In order to bring back some of the vocabulary control lost by replacing precoordination with postcoordination, links and roles were introduced. The idea was that the devices would specify the specific function, or role, of a term for the particular document being described.

Linking is a technique that reduces the comprehensiveness of a term, restricting its coverage for the document under consideration. Often several concepts will appear in papers that have certain, fixed relationships to each other and the relationships cannot be inverted. Let's use as an example "The use of mountain equipment for camping in the desert." Uniterms for this document are "Camping," "Equipment," "Desert," and "Mountain." Someone interested in using desert equipment for mountain camping would retrieve this document, which would be irrelevant to the query. The problem is that the correct relationship is not evident because at least two counterfeit combinations can be formed:

Desert equipment   Mountain camping

The first link (called *A*) would be between "Camping" and "Desert," and the second link (called *B*) would be indexed by "Equipment" and "Mountain." If the document being considered is numbered 29, then we have:

Doc. Number	Term	Links
29	CAMPING	A
29	DESERT	A
29	EQUIPMENT	B
29	MOUNTAIN	B

Generally, links are found in uniterm type systems because precoordination tends to ease the problem of false coordination.

The negative trade-offs in using links include the difficulty of making the right connection between pairs of terms and the redundancy caused by this technique, which increases the size of the index and rapidly runs up the indexing costs. Also, links merely show that certain terms have a relationship, but they do not clearly indicate what that relationship is. A better device for easing the problem is the use of roles.

Roles are used to minimize syntactical ambiguity by modifying terms to indicate their usage in a particular context — that is, they indicate the "role" of the terms. For example, suppose a document about school accounting was indexed with the terms "School" and "Accounting." Using links alone would not prevent "Accounting school" (where accounting is taught) from being retrieved. Links, in this case, would not remedy a false drop, but a role indicator for accounting, such as "types of," would modify the term properly.

The negative points of this technique are that role indication can be difficult to develop, and extensive use of the technique increases indexing costs rather dramatically. Roles are hard to apply consistently, and they have the effect of making searching more complicated as well.

Also, there are doubts that the added cost of indexing that results in using links and roles is worth the slight increase in retrieval effectiveness. Studies indicate that the devices increase precision somewhat but decrease the recall effectiveness of the indexing. At the same time, there is an expense increase in the indexing, storage, and retrieval operation.

INDEX PRODUCTION

The Mechanics

The physical mechanics of indexing can vary considerably according to the size and policies of the indexing agency. Some agencies use preprinted forms, and the indexing procedure culminates in the completion of the form. The following is an example of what such a form might look like.

SPEEDY INDEXING SERVICE

Indexer _____ Indexing Date _____ Publication Date _____

Type of Document _____ Publication Source _____

Author 1 _____ Author 2 _____ Author 3 _____

Title _____

Descriptor 1 _____ Descriptor 2 _____

Descriptor 3 _____ Descriptor 4 _____

It should be noted that such forms are often filled in on a computer screen now that computer-aided indexing is becoming a preferred method of operation.

Cards are also popular, especially in book indexing. Generally, one subject index entry is allowed per card. After the initial indexing is completed, the cards are alphabetized for modification, adding of cross-referencing, and general editing.

Editing is necessary to bring together scattered similar entries and to remove errors. A number of check points should be considered during this process:

- Check *see* type references. It is necessary to be sure that cross-references actually appear in the index and that page numbers are correct.

- Check spelling.

- Check punctuation.

- Check headings and subheadings for correctness and form.

- Check typography (e.g., caps).

- Check alphabetical order.

- Check for excessively long blocks of undifferentiated references.

- Check for missing entries.

- Check for unnecessary entries.

Arrangement

An index must be arranged in some acceptable way if a search is going to be possible. An alphabetical index may be arranged letter by letter or word by word. For example:

Word-by-Word	Letter-by-Letter
Air bag	Air bag
Air base	Air base
Air brake	Airboat
Air chamber	Airborne
Air command	Air brake
Air door	Airbrush
Airboat	Airburst
Airborne	Air chamber
Airbrush	Air command
Airburst	Aircushion
Aircushion	Air door
Airdry	Airdry

Numbers and punctuation may be handled in different ways. For example, punctuation may be ignored or it may be treated as a space. It is unwise to treat punctuation as a separate character. The following examples illustrate the two different approaches.

Letter-by-Letter	Word-by-Word
(Hyphen ignored)	(Hyphen as space)
MAR-ARR-776	MAR-ARR-776
MARHQ-64-861	MAR-SM-812
MAR-SM-812	MARHQ-64-861

As far as numbers are concerned, numbers are usually before letters. For example:

11
114
212
a
b
c
m
n

There are also some special cases where the index covers numerical data or historical periods. In these cases the arrangement may be numerical or chronological.

Classified indexes are arranged in a logical order based on content, rather than on an arbitrary alphabetical order. To be properly used, classified indexes require auxiliary devices. Often these devices include a separate alphabetical index. Other devices include codes, either alphabetic or numeric, and typographical devices, such as varying typefaces and spacing between terms. For example:

Using codes

500	Science
510.1	Mathematics
510.2	Geometry
510.2	Algebra
510.21	Abstract algebra
510.212	Number theory
510.212	Prime numbers

Using indention

Science

    Mathematics

        Geometry

        Algebra

            Abstract algebra

            Number theory

            Prime numbers

    Biology

    Chemistry

Many indexes do not have secondary entries under terms. However, if such subarrangements are present, then the arrangement of these secondary entries must be decided on. Typically these entries are titles, subject subheadings, modifiers, abstract numbers, order numbers, or location indicators. If the second level entries slow down the searching, then careful reconsideration is in order.

The manner in which an index is displayed—on a printed page, in a card drawer, or on a computer terminal—is an important factor. Regardless of the form, the term order must be immediately discernible. The terms, along with subheadings, must be legible and recognizable. Indentation or various typefaces can be used to discriminate main headings from subheadings. In printed indexes, continuation headings make life easier on the user, while in a card index, guide cards must be used often. The general rule is that discrete units should be quickly recognizable and the whole display easy to browse quickly.

INDEXING SPECIFIC FORMATS
AND SUBJECTS

Indexes deal with many forms of documents and with many specific subject areas. Recorded information can be represented by marks on stone, ink swirls on papyrus, blocked letters on a printed page, magnetic charges of electricity on a computer disk, or depth-dependent light images on a compact laser disk. The media may be the message to some people, but not to the indexer. The bottom line to the indexer is that units of information exist on whatever the media is, and if the information is not carefully identified and indexed, it cannot be retrieved.

Do specific subjects and specific formats have anything to do with the indexing process? Or is indexing just indexing and all the rules and procedures are the same? This is an area where much more research is needed. Professional indexers, relying on their knowledge and experience, have differing opinions on this point, but there is a lesson to be learned from catalogers who give a lot of attention to the differences in cataloging when it comes to specific subjects and to particular forms of materials.

Bibliometric studies have taught us, among other things, that subject literatures have different structures, and user studies have taught us that subject specialists have different needs. Given these conditions, it is unlikely that all indexing rules and procedures are universal.

The general assumption is that specific subjects and various physical forms need individual consideration when being indexed.

Rationale

Is the indexing of special formats or specific subject areas different from indexing in general? The answer is both yes and no.

First, the field of indexing has derived some general principles, based on experience and basic research. Although it is true that we do not yet have any general "theories," we have a substantial amount of empirical data and shared common sense. It is not true that some subject areas or unique formats are exempt from our general notions of indexing. At the same time, indexing must be adjusted to fit the needs of users and to best cover the subject.

Adequate indexing begins with an understanding of both the user and the peculiar aspects of the literature being indexed. Special subject knowledge, or knowledge and experience about the physical form of the document, may be needed to index the material adequately. Each subject literature has its own nomenclature, traditions, and internal structure, and a good indexer respects and reflects these peculiarities. Appropriate aids, such as thesauri, may be needed for the indexing task.

Each information retrieval system for individual subject areas has unique aspects. For example, (1) a defined set of people are interested in that subject and have information needs related to that subject, (2) each subject area has its own vocabulary, and (3) each subject area has a variety of subspecialties, each of which has its own peculiar aspects. Therefore, the indexing process and the subsequent successful retrieval of information in that subject area depend on the attention given to the particularities of the individual subject areas and the users interested in that subject.

Indexing, in the global sense, has common problems, regardless of the format of the materials or the type of information conveyed by the documents. At the same time, for each format and type of material there are specific indexing concerns. A good index is tailored to fit the situation.

Fundamentally, all indexing *is* the same, in the sense that content is analyzed and represented as clearly as possible to the users. And it should be emphasized that indexing is concerned with the content of the information record, and the form is a secondary concern. However, form is often related to ease of storage and ease of use, and there can be a relationship between form and the index that is created. For example, users frequently express a desire to have a separate index to "what's in microform." Librarians often dismiss this as being an illogical way to approach a search, but it is not illogical to the user. The user may want to work in the microforms room with an index to the information *in that room*, then move from bound periodicals to unbound issues. If an index on the basis of form expedites the search, then it is not "illogical" to create indexes based on the form and location of the material.

Specific Subject Areas

Science

When a subject field has a well-defined and unambiguous vocabulary, the indexer has a strong foundation for constructing an indexing language. On occasion, the science literature meets this criteria, but not always, because scientific information has vocabulary problems like any other literature. For example, the pharmacological literature contains elements of mathematics, physics, chemistry, and other basic sciences. The nomenclature is a complex combination from these areas. Acronyms, generic names, popular names, trade names, and molecular and structural formulas present problems in selecting entry terms and in constructing adequate cross-references.

Medicine

A good example of indexing science is the medical literature. The problem in indexing the medical literature is the complexities of the vocabulary of the subject. Not only does the terminology have intrinsic subcategories, but it is not static. Furthermore, medical terminology also includes terms from the supporting basic sciences, engineering, and a number of the social sciences.

In medicine the journal literature and books are both important. The books include encyclopedias, handbooks, textbooks, and other such fundamental tools that medical personnel turn to every day. On the other hand, the journals contain current reports of continuing developments in the field. Unfortunately, not all the journal literature is adequately indexed. Many times the "index" is a list of contents or a keyword title index.

Like other scientific literature, the biomedical literature has a large number of different concepts. Thus, complex thesauri are required in order to have a controlled vocabulary. The generic relationships involve many classes of concepts, many of which are rigid nomenclature.

Law

Lawyers are often well versed in using indexes, for the simple reason that a great deal of what the lawyer does is what a reference librarian does: looks for information in the literature. Fortunately, most of the publishers of law materials understand the critical necessity of an index in retrieving law information and, as a result, there are many good indexes to the law literature.

A large portion of the law literature is a group of reference tools, such as dictionaries, encyclopedias, treatises, regulations, legal journals, loose-leaf services, and, of course, statutes, digests of cases, and judicial decisions. The main concern of an indexer in this field is that word-by-word specificity is necessary because the literature is extant and the lawyer usually is searching for a very particular case or legal precedent.

Indexes to the law literature often are a combination of types of indexes. The index has subject descriptors, which may come from a controlled vocabulary, but at the same time those descriptors may be concordance-type words or phrases. Many times the index is an annotated index, because a full citation and description will save a lawyer time.

In law indexing there are often some strict practices that are followed because of the inherent importance of the language itself to the practice of law. For example, phrases cannot usually be broken down into single words as they are in other indexing systems, because legal phrases will lose their meaning. Dorothy Thomas (in Feinberg 1983, 153-79) gives an example of using the phrase *burden of proof*, which is a legal expression that is familiar to all of us. The total concept must be brought out, and it should be in the index as a phrase if it appears anywhere in the text.

Definitions in law are extremely important, and a law index should lead to all words in the text that are defined or described or have to do with "meaning."

Synonym and homonym control is very critical in law because legal decisions are often made on the precise definition of the meaning of words. This can be a very tricky situation for the nonlegal information professional, and the indexer must proceed with caution. Related to this, a good law index has an elaborate cross-referring structure.

All subject areas have distinct vocabulary. But in law, the language itself is a vital part of the professional activity in ways unlike other areas. The very words chosen decide the destiny of people and nations. The indexer must be keenly aware of this.

History

Another good example of indexing concern in specific subject areas is history. Without indexes, the searching of historical material reduces itself to a rummage hunt where serendipity and random luck play a major role.

Before the turn of this century, archival material was simply stored away, often in a careless way, and subject retrieval devices, if they existed, were mostly primitive. After the turn of the century, more serious attention was given to this type of material, both in how to preserve it and in how to retrieve it on demand through adequate indexing devices. However, good retrieval devices were slow to evolve, and often they were partially complete and rather makeshift. Many good indexes now exist, both general and local, but there is still a long way to go.

Historical material exists in many different forms: records, manuscripts, documents, books, photographs, photocopies, newspapers, microforms, artifacts, etc. It is often useful before indexing such materials to divide the different types into subtypes based on form. For example, manuscripts could be grouped into originals and transcriptions. Records and documents might be divided into bound and unbound. The idea here is to make separate indexes to the material on the basis of accessibility. This will make it much easier for the user to physically locate the material once the index has identified the information desired.

Music

A final example of specific subject area indexing is music. There are several categories of music indexing: musical scores, various forms of recordings, subject areas, and historical information about music and musicians. Each of these areas, in turn, has its own peculiarities. Because of the highly specialized nature of the field, a music indexer must know something about music. For example, a large part of a music score is visual, and the indexer must be able to understand the visual notations. Also, when musical instruments are involved, the indexer must have considerable technical knowledge about the instruments and their relationships.

Another example is musical recordings. The first impulse when indexing records is to index every possible heading, but subsequent thought will make it clear that an unwieldy and generally unusable index will result. For example, a country/western record could be entered under the writer of the lyrics, the composer of the music, the band, the soloist, the title, and the date of composition. If it is a mixed album, then it becomes even more complicated. If the record is jazz, the complication increases, because jazz enthusiasts want to know everything about it, including who played the high note in a particular passage.

Again the problem of exhaustivity and specificity arises when indexing musical recordings. For example, if the work is an opera, are all the soloists indexed? With jazz, as mentioned above, how far does the indexing go in making entries for the performers or the various instruments?

Another important question concerning recordings is arrangement of the entries. In the case of classical music, a likely choice is by the name of the composer, although it could be by the name of the orchestra or soloist. Another approach is to construct a classified arrangement with appropriate subdivisions. The major classes, for example, could be orchestral works, vocal works, or instrumental works. Second-level divisions might include type of opera, song, sacred work, etc.

Specific Formats

As discussed earlier, the format of the material should be given consideration when constructing an index. Below are several examples of specific formats of material and some comments about special problems they present.

Encyclopedias

Indexing an encyclopedia presents a number of special problems. The first one, of course, is size. The completed work has thousands of pages and hundreds of thousands of references. The resulting index may be one or more large volumes. Another problem is the diversity of the subject matter to be indexed, which may run literally from *A* to *Z*. Also, the ages of the users may extend from cradle to grave and the educational level from semiliterate to *cum laude*.

Indexes to encyclopedias are very seldom created by single individuals, but are constructed by a staff of indexers made up of specialists and nonspecialists. The editorial complexities are formidable.

The first question that should be asked is whether or not an encyclopedia needs an index. Size may be the determining factor. A small encyclopedia of a few volumes can usually rely on cross-references to provide adequate subject entry points. But as size increases, details increase, and an index becomes inevitable.

Obviously, all aspects must receive attention. A vast range of subjects, topics, persons, places, and things must be addressed. A clear decision must be made concerning the scope of the index. For example, will all entries be included, no matter how small? Will all people mentioned in the encyclopedia be entered? Will this include people referred to in charts, pictures, and other graphics?

Many complex decisions have to be made when constructing an index to an encyclopedia.

Newspapers

Newspapers existed many years before they were indexed. Slowly, the media began to realize that newspapers needed retrospective access, although many editors still need to be convinced. The newspapers believed in the "morgue" (the collection of past issues), but, with some notable exceptions, such as the *New York Times Index*, the average newspaper editor did not view indexing systems as important.

There are now four general categories of retrospective searching systems: (1) the morgue, which is usually a clipping service of articles from the newspaper being served, although sometimes it will include articles from other newspapers or serial publications; (2) local indexes, which are mostly prepared by the local public library, but sometimes are maintained by the newspapers; (3) published indexes, which are professionally prepared and published, such as the *New York Times*, the *London Times* and the *Washington Post*; and (4) online indexes to newspapers, such as *Newspaper Abstracts* from University Microfilms International.

Vocabulary control is a continuing problem with newspaper indexing. A story may contain names, places, and perhaps subjects that may not occur again in a hundred years or ever. This is most obvious for personal names.

Conceivably, name, place, and event can occur once and never occur again. On a day-by-day basis a newspaper can cover the entire universe, which means that the possible indexing vocabulary is most of the words in the language. Since newspapers carry stories about everything in this life and the next, the possible vocabulary has no limits. Clearly, there is a major conflict here because on the one hand there is a need for universal vocabulary, and on the other hand the nature of the material demands a high degree of specificity. If an index is both highly specific and highly exhaustive, then the only possible solution may be to use a computer to search it.

Another problem that the indexer has is with the multiple editions that newspapers tend to have. Major newspapers may come out with several editions each day. This means that stories get added, dropped, or shifted to different pages. Generally, the solution is to select which edition will be indexed and stick to it, although this is not always the most satisfactory way to handle the problem.

Finally, it should be pointed out that computers are being used very successfully for indexing newspapers. In chapter XI a number of computer-aided indexing systems will be discussed.

Trade Literature

A major problem with trade literature, particular product data, is a lack of standardization among the publishers of the literature. This type of information comes in a variety of forms: catalogs, brochures, exhibitions, direct mail, and journals.

The common way to handle this material is to file it alphabetically by manufacturer and then turn to buyers' guides as a subject approach. As every special librarian knows, this is not a very satisfactory way to handle this important information. At the same time, the indexing of this material can be tedious, time-consuming and costly.

In conclusion, although formats and specific subject areas warrant special consideration, the basic principles of indexing remain the same.

SUGGESTED READINGS

Bakewell, K. G. B. "How to Let Your Fingers Do the Walking and Not Lose the Way (Index Compilation)." *Times Higher Education Supplement* 412 September 26, 1980: 12.

Barber, John, Sheena Moffat, and Frances Wood. "Case Studies of the Indexing and Retrieval of Pharmacology Papers." *Information Processing and Management* 24 (1988): 141-50.

Brenner, Everett H., and Tefko Saracevic. *Indexing and Searching in Perspective.* 2nd ed. Philadelphia: National Federation of Abstracting and Information Services, 1985.

Coates, E. J. "Scientific and Technical Indexing." *The Indexer* 5 (1966): 27-34.

Collison, Robert L. *Indexes and Indexing.* 4th rev. ed. London: Ernest Benn; New York: J. De Graff, 1972.

Feinberg, Hilda, ed. *Indexing Specialized Formats and Subjects*. Metuchen, N.J.: Scarecrow Press, 1983.

Grodsky, Susan J. "Indexing Technical Communications: What, When, and How." *Technical Communication* (Second Quarter 1985): 26, 28-30.

Jillson, Willard Rouse. "The Indexing of Historical Materials." *The American Archivist* 16 (1953): 251-57.

Langridge, D. W. *Classification and Indexing in the Humanities*. London: Butterworths, 1976.

Rada, Roy, Hafedh Mili, Gary Letourneu, and Doug Johnston. "Creating and Evaluating Entry Terms." *Journal of Documentation* 44, no. 1 (March 1988): 19-41.

Simpkins, Jean. "Indexing Loose-leaf Publications." *The Indexer* 14 (October 1985): 259-60.

Svenonius, Elaine F. "The Effect of Indexing Specificity on Retrieval Performance." Ph.D. dissertation, University of Chicago, 1971. (ED 051 863)

Van Rijsbergen, C. J., D. J. Harper, and M. F. Porter. "Selection of Good Search Terms." *Information Processing and Management* 17 (1981): 77-91.

VI
Book Indexes

INTRODUCTION

A good book index sorts and classifies the contents of the book into a form that allows immediate access to specific items a user needs.

In 1969 Robert L. Collison wrote, "The only way of discovering whether one is an indexer or not is to index a book," (Knight 1969, 29). There is a great deal of truth in that statement. Almost all the problems and associated decisions in indexing can be illustrated with book indexes.

When the general public thinks of an index they usually think of a book index. Modern indexing began with book indexes, and they still constitute a major portion of indexing output. A separate chapter on book indexes should not imply that these indexes are dissimilar to other indexes, because all indexing has the same fundamental principles, and the concepts and procedures developed thus far apply to book indexes. However, book indexing is a special genre, and this chapter will highlight certain fundamentals and point out some important differences.

THE NATURE OF BOOK INDEXES

An index to a book is a self-contained information retrieval system. The information database is between the covers of the book, and the purpose of the index is to recall the information with an acceptable level of precision.

The dictionary defines an index as a list arranged on the basis of some specified datum. Examples are proper names, dates, and subject terms. These headings give the index both order and purpose. Also, all but the simplest book index will have subheadings. The extent and complexity of the headings and subheadings structure will depend on the length of the book, the length of the index, the subject matter, and the personal style of the indexer.

A book index rearranges the information in the text, most often into an alphabetical order. Its objective is to serve as a pointer to specific details discussed in the book, in the same way that a periodical index leads to specific details in the journal literature. A book index is not a contents list, in the sense of a table of contents, although its purpose is to denote content. When authors write books, they follow a certain order, arranging their material in some sort of logical sequence, and the table of contents follows that order exactly, outlining chapters, sections, and appendix materials. The index does not follow the author's word order, but arranges it in a way that allows a reader to go directly to specific details.

The facetious example used earlier of an index saving users the task of having to read a million documents to find what they want applies to a book index—users can locate details in a book without having to read or reread the entire book. One of the characteristics of a poor book index is that it is more a contents list then a true index.

One of the differences between a book index and other types of indexes is that each book index is as unique as the book itself. It is a single work serving only the book in hand and generally is changed only if the book changes with a new edition. In a sense it is a more personal piece of work than other types of indexes. In most cases it is done by a single individual, whereas other indexes (e.g., periodical indexes) are created by many workers over a relatively long period of time. This means that book indexers are solely responsible for the total task, including forming their own rules and planning their own procedures. And most good indexers feel a great deal of personal responsibility for the results.

Unfortunately, book indexes are too often created with less than ample commitment from the book's publisher. In a periodical indexing service the index is the product of concern, and the full operation is aimed at creating that index. But in the book publishing world the index is often one of those nuisances that holds up publication. As a result, the indexer works under unreasonable time and space requirements with little appreciation for the product. In many cases the indexing is given to an editor or an office clerk to be done over the weekend. Worse still, the book may be put on the market without an index.

In some cases the author of the book prepares the index. Over the years there has been much controversy about the wisdom of an author-created index. On the one hand, it is pointed out that nobody knows more about the book's content than the author; therefore, correct index entries can be expected. On the other hand, it is pointed out that an author sometimes cannot see the forest for the trees. That is, the author may not understand a reader's perspective. Also, simply knowing what the book is about does not guarantee that an author knows how to create an index.

Indexing a book is not a job for an amateur. It is a demanding task requiring a knowledge of the book's content, its subject, the terms and synonyms of the subject, and the basic procedures and methods of indexing.

As mentioned earlier, most books need an index, but not all, unless we take the position that all books are potential reference tools. It is not clear that Dr. Seuss' *Cat in the Hat* would need an index, although many children's books do need one. We cannot categorically rule out any book. James Michener writes lengthy, historical novels that are full of facts and indexes to his fiction might be useful. But the converse is also true. We all read popular works and very seldom do we find an index necessary. The immediate access to specific information in these books is not a consideration. We sit down with the book, read it, and absorb the ideas as they are presented. Great numbers of people who read books don't care if the books have an index or not.

However, having made this point, there is another facet. When we read a worthy book, that book becomes in our minds a personal reference tool, and we want it to have a good index. We want to be able to retrieve specific information without having to read the entire book. That's the purpose of an index.

PROCEDURES

The first practical step in indexing a book is to go to the closet and find a sturdy shoebox, since the work is done easily using the old-fashioned card method. Of course, we are talking about thousands of such cards.

Although cards and slips, of various sizes, continue to be a first choice for many indexers, there are alternative devices. For example, some indexers prefer loose-leaf notebooks. Notebooks can be bought with built-in marginal letter tabs, or the tabs can be added. Although notebooks are compact and easy to use, they lack the flexibility of cards.

These traditional manual methods have served indexers well and will continue to be a way to do it. For some, the card method will always be totally adequate. However, times are changing and more and more computer-aided tools are being developed, including some good ones for book indexing. These computer-aided indexing tools will be discussed in chapter XI.

Besides a stack of cards and a shoebox (or a microcomputer), the book indexer needs some basic reference tools. A standard, up-to-date dictionary and a general thesaurus are basic. In addition, dictionaries, handbooks, and a thesaurus in the subject area are recommended. For some books, a good place-name gazetteer and a dictionary of proper names are essential.

Also, just as reference tools are vital in indexing the book, so are good models. If possible, the indexer should have on hand one or more indexes from books on the same subject.

Step One

The first formal step is to open a clear communication line with the editor of the book, who will probably have space limitations and occasionally a rigid format to be followed. If the book is one of a series, the editor may want to keep a uniform format among all the volumes, including the index. The size of the index is a more critical issue, and it is usually a trade-off between the publisher's economic constraints and what the indexer considers optimal. Professional indexers often advocate that a book index should have five pages for every 100 pages of text, but this is not always possible. Of course, if indexers feel they don't have enough space or freedom to do a proper job, they can reject the assignment. This is not an infrequent occurrence.

Also, an editor, for various reasons, may not send along the accessory material to a book—the table of contents, preface, illustrations, appendices, and the like. Quite often these items are being prepared parallel to the indexing process, but the indexer should ask the editor for these items, at least in crude form, because they often hold important indexable information.

In addition, the author may be working on proofs while the indexing is going on, and changes, especially drastic ones, can lead to indexing errors. The editor should communicate these changes as soon as possible. For example, the addition of several lines to the text can throw off the index pagination, perhaps for dozens of pages.

Although indexers are not assistant editors, they have responsibility to alert the editor to errors they have discovered, such as inconsistency in spelling that stands out when the index pulls together scattered information in the book.

Step one, then, is to establish and maintain a communication line between editor and indexer so that neither will experience any surprises when the index is turned in.

Step Two

The second step is to read through the book quickly. A fast scan of the book, without any attempt to actually index at this point, will give the indexer an overall feeling for the text. Obviously, the indexer should be thinking of the indexing that will be done, but no attempt should be made to record concepts. A few general notes might be useful, but the note taking should not detract from the basic purpose of getting a broad understanding of what the book is about. The indexer who fails to do this basic preliminary step may begin with a sense of uncertainty about the content of the text, and the development of the index may be conceptually wrong.

Some note taking and underlining may be done concerning such matters as the relative amount of space devoted to various topics or what minor points may be omitted. But the primary objective is to obtain an understanding of the nature of the book and to develop a feeling for who the readers of the book will be and what they will need from the index. A second, more careful reading is suggested, with extensive note taking on the kinds of headings a reader might look for. For example, if the work is a biography or travel book, indexers will realize that proper names and geographical references will constitute a major part of the index. Also, they can get a feeling of whether the index will lean toward general entries or will need to be high in specificity. What we learned earlier about exhaustivity and specificity will now be useful, since these concepts apply to book indexes as well as to periodical indexes. In this reading the indexer will want to note information that is fresh and unique so that it will receive proper attention in the index. This second reading will put the indexer in the position to plan the index.

The indexer's basic objective in reading the book is to get a grasp on the subject matter, but there are other important objectives. First, the indexer must try to mentally sort out the significant concepts, the minor concepts, and the insignificant points. It is helpful to understand what the author's objectives were in writing the book, what kind of information is being presented, who the reading audience will be, and how readers will use the information. Often some of this information can be obtained from the introduction or preface, but the indexer must be on guard, because sometimes authors claim that they are doing a certain thing when in reality they are not.

The actual indexing should not begin until a clear plan is developed. The exhaustivity and specificity of the index must be determined in terms of the subject content, the potential reader, and the length of the index. It should be remembered that high exhaustivity and high specificity will increase the number of entries substantially, and this will increase the length of the index proportionally. The plan should include decisions about the structure and appearance of the index, since entry selection and form will be closely related to these factors. An index is a permanent tool, forever a part of the book, and if extensive use is anticipated, its structure and appearance are of considerable consequence.

Reading the book through several times is critical because later on, when going page by page, the indexer may be unable to see the forest for the trees.

A good devise is to write a 500-word abstract of the book. The indexer who cannot write such a summary may have problems indexing the book.

Step Three

Now the indexer is ready to go page by page, sentence by sentence, and actually do the indexing. The majority of book indexing is done from proofs. If the book is in this stage, the editor will be able to tell the indexer how much space will be allocated for the index. We emphasize this point because nothing is more exasperating than trying to slice an index in half.

The indexer will occasionally be expected to work from a manuscript, and while this is not the most desirable of circumstances, it can be done. If the editor has not numbered the paragraphs in the manuscript, the indexer can do so and create the index by referring to paragraph numbers. Just before the book goes to press, the paragraph numbers can be translated to page numbers. However, this is a tedious task and introduces another possibility for error.

It should be mentioned that in some types of indexes references are made to paragraphs. For example, a number of large encyclopedic works often have pages crowded with complex information and the index will refer to specific areas or paragraphs on the page. Some specialized books, such as poetry, may need references to individual lines. This kind of indexing can be done from the manuscript.

Now comes the task of choosing the entries that will guide the reader to what is needed. There may be dozens of ways to work, but the time-tested card method allows the indexer to keep the entries in alphabetical order right from the start. This is important, because it is foolish to keep hunting back through earlier entries, especially when the pile of cards has grown to many hundreds. And, of course, a computer can keep things sorted and readily available on demand.

Also, this is the time to start keeping track of synonymous terms and the inclusion of *see* references, so that the indexer can go to entries he or she has decided to use.

As the indexing progresses, the indexer will make many decisions concerning form of entry, needed cross-references, generic/species relationships, and so forth. These decisions should be recorded, either on slips at the beginning of the indexing stage, or separately in a notepad. This device will help to ensure consistency in the indexing.

It should be emphasized that correlation and consolidation of terms may be temporary decisions, because as the index grows the wisdom of earlier decisions may be questioned.

In the beginning, it is probably best to simply list terms on cards with little regard to the problem of synonymous terms. Decisions about which synonyms will be cross-references and which will be actual terms should not come too early in the process, because all the evidence is not in about which is the preferred term.

However, at some point, say after a few cards, these structural decisions will start to be made. At this point the indexer will need to sort through the cards, pulling ideas together, copying page references onto the preferred term, and making cross-references out of the others. Every few hundred cards or so, this process should be repeated. As more and more terms are collected, it may be desirable to reverse earlier decisions and make changes.

Indexers should not fool themselves into believing that they can remember these decisions, especially after forty or fifty pages of text, or after they have been absent from the task for a while. Consolidation of terms will make the final revision and editing task much more tolerable. The important thing is to keep track of what is going on and to be consistent. For example, don't have one entry "French Foreign Legion," another "Foreign Legion, French," and a third "Military units, France."

An extended period of time is usually required to construct a book index, and it can rarely be done in a single sitting. Because of this, continuity in thinking is lost when the indexer leaves the project. Therefore, it is a good practice to spend a little time when returning to the project to flip through the cards to remember the direction the index is taking. This is where the general note taking will prove very useful.

In book indexing, how closely should the indexer stay to the vocabulary of the user? Most book indexes, especially of single-author, single-volume books, reflect rather closely the words used by the author. If the book is of a highly technical nature, readers will probably expect the terminology to be technical. The problem comes when a book is of a scholarly or scientific nature but is written for a wide range of readers. To meet the reasonable expectations of all readers the index may have to include not only exact author terms, but also concept terms not used by the author.

Also, authors often tend to be inconsistent in their choice of words; but the index must be consistent. In this case, numbers and carefully chosen cross-references are absolutely necessary.

As a general rule, every meaningful word in the text should be included in the index. Synonyms are then cross-referenced to the keyword. However, on occasion the indexer will determine that the actual text word would not be an appropriate one for the user of the index. In this case the actual text word becomes a cross-reference to a synonymous term.

The following sections will discuss the selection of both name and subject entries, but some general remarks might be in order at this point. Every book index is unique and will have individual construction problems requiring good judgment on the part of the indexer. Indexers must have the wisdom, experience, and imagination to visualize the whole book, with all its ramifications, and to relate this understanding to the information problems of all who read the book.

The obvious indexable items in a book should be covered carefully. Chapter titles of the book and section headings are a good place to begin, but these may not always be useful. Care must be taken when indexing from chapter titles and section headings to index the subject and not just the words. For example, a title such as "Where I Spent My Summer Vacation," which might be a description of a world cruise, could lead to such inane entries as:

Where I Spent My Summer

or

Spent, Where I, My Summer

or

Summer, Where I Spent My

Books need to have tables, graphs, diagrams, and other such material indexed in most cases, because these complementary additions may very well contain information that may not be discussed directly in the text. Also, such things as the preface, footnotes, and appendices should be examined carefully for possible indexable information. Many times this information is redundant, especially in the preface and the introduction, but often it is not.

The indexer will likely have to do investigation beyond the text of the book to resolve inconsistencies and to fill out incomplete information. For example, the author may use more than one form of a name or may use only a last name, assuming that everyone is familiar with the full name. The indexer cannot make such assumptions. "Disraeli" in the text becomes "Disraeli, Benjamin, 1st Earl of Beaconsfield" in the index. It is the indexer's duty to fill out the name so that the index user will know the entry is not about Disraeli, Homer, who runs the local delicatessen. Book indexes are heavily used by people who never read the book, at least not completely. This type of user browses a library stack, pulling book after book, searching for entries on a certain topic. The index must convey complete information, regardless of the whimsy or writing style of the author.

The indexer must also look to reference tools for vocabulary clarification and for words that are unfamiliar. A subject thesaurus can be used to suggest terms readers might recognize first, but that were not used by this particular writer.

The indexer must avoid negative entries. For example, a book may contain a sentence such as the following: "This account will not discuss Abraham Lincoln." Obviously, in such a case "Abraham Lincoln" would not be an entry. Imagine the reaction of a reader doing research on Lincoln finding a Lincoln entry, only to be told the book will not discuss the topic.

At the same time, indexers must be careful in their judgment of what is minor information to be left unindexed. It may be possible that the preface holds some key point, or the reader may remember some detail that actually appeared on a map; that is why the accessories to the main text must be included in the indexing. At the same time, some information is useless and will never be sought, and the indexer has to find the right balance for what to include and what to exclude. Probably a good practice is to lean toward including too much rather than too little.

Step Four

Once the indexer has made entries for the entire text, it is time to begin the exacting task of reviewing the work. The objective is to check consistency of entries, duplicate subject cards, proper cross-referencing, spelling, and blatant omissions. The revision should be done with the text in hand, with special attention given to correct page references. Ideally, a second person should do the mechanical checking, since by this time the indexer is bleary-eyed and undiscerning. Final alphabetizing is then done, following some standard procedure such as the ALA filing rules.

Step Five

The last step is the typing of the information from cards to paper for submission to the editor. This step should be taken *only* after the indexer feels certain nothing more can be done to improve the index. Changes at the typing stage can become self-defeating and confusing. The acceptable format is a single column, double- or triple-spaced, on good quality paper. It should be unnecessary to mention that the typing should be done with a new ribbon, with clean keys, and not on colored or onionskin paper. And the retention of a second copy is an unbreakable law. Imagine the chagrin if your mailed index ends up in the dead letter box in Peoria.

Once the typing is done, the pages must be checked for omissions and typing errors. The importance of checking and rechecking at every stage cannot be over-emphasized if a quality index is to result. It goes with the territory.

All of this makes indexing sound like an exacting task. It is.

NAME ENTRIES

Inexperienced indexers might believe that name indexing is the easiest part of indexing. If so, they are in for a surprise, because name entries are troublesome, and the seemingly endless variations thwart even experienced indexers. Certain conventions have developed over the years, influenced partly by cataloging rules and partly by the practices of book indexers and publishers. The examples given below are by no means exhaustive but will cover some of the major patterns of usage.

The trouble starts with the practices of the book's author. He or she may begin by mentioning "Lincoln," then later "A. Lincoln," then "Albert Lincoln," and end up talking about Abraham Lincoln. The only sensible approach for the indexer is to identify *which* Lincoln is being referred to at every point and spell out the name in full in the index.

People with "normal" names are indexed by surname, with titles and first name following, separated by commas. For example:

> Disraeli, Homer
> Disraeli, Homer, Jr.
> Eisenhower, Gen. Dwight David
> Schweitzer, Dr. Albert

Famous people who are recognized by forenames are indexed by these fore-names, and cross-references are made if there is a possibility that they may be looked up by either. For example:

> Edward V., King of England
> John XXIII, Pope
> Patrick, St.

If surnames have a prefix and the name is anglicized, they are indexed under the prefix. For example:

De Mille, Cecil Blount
La Follette, Robert Marion
St. Laurent, Louis Stephen

Initials may be used for middle names, if desired, but full first name is recommended if it is known. However, if the person is known by a middle name, it should be spelled out. For example:

Use: Fitzgerald, F. Scott
Not: Fitzgerald, Francis S.

Compound surnames are not broken up, even if they are not hyphenated. For example:

Ben-Gurion, David
Dervish Pasha, Gen. Ibrahim

Noblemen, such as dukes, earls, counts, and so forth, are generally indexed under titles, with a cross-reference made from the family name, although sometimes common sense dictates the opposite.

Kelvin, 1st Baron, Thomson, William
Thomson, William. *See* Kelvin, 1st Baron

Foreign names that keep their original form and are not generally anglicized are indexed that way. Otherwise, they are entered under the anglicized form. For example:

Juan Carlos
   but
Joan of Arc
Jeanne d'Arc. *See* Joan of Arc

Pseudonyms are usually referred to the real name if it is known. For example:

Geisel, Theodor Seuss
Seuss. *See* Geisel, Theodor Seuss

If more than one person is involved in an endeavor, such as joint authorship, entry should be under both, but *both* are in each entry. For example:

Smith, Homer, and John Williams
and
Williams, John, and Homer Smith

Corporate bodies should be the entry for publications they create, with cross-references to anyone who had a major responsibility in creating the document. For example:

> Ghost Valley Parapsychology Association, Report of the
>   Social Director

and

> Disraeli, Homer, Report of the Social Director. *See* Ghost
>   Valley Parapsychology Association

Branches of government are indexed under the name of the country, government, or place. For example:

> Texas, State Legislature of
> United States, President of

Modification of this usage occurs when the index starts growing with numerous entries under one of these headings. The heading is then broken down into specific offices.

Famous historical events are indexed by the names by which they are generally known. For example:

> Missouri Compromise
> Pearl Harbor

Natural places and landmarks are indexed under explicit name and not the prefix, unless the inversion is an equal part of the name. For example:

> Griffin, Ft.
> Rushmore, Mt.

but *not*:

> York, New

Again, if these entries are extensive, it pays to set up categories. For example:

> FORTS
>   Davis
>   Dodge
>   Griffin
>   Sumter National Monument

When business firms have the name of more than one individual, the firm is indexed under the first surname in the title, with cross-references from the names of the other persons. For example:

Disraeli, Homer and Company
Green, Williams. *See* Williams and Green
Williams and Green

Newspapers, local institutions, and so forth should be entered under place name unless they are widely known. For example:

Denton County, Texas, Fine Arts Council
but:
Musée du Louvre

National institutions, political parties, universities, and so forth are entered under the official name. For example:

American Society for Information Science
Harvard University

Finally, very common names should be differentiated by description notes or dates. For example:

Doe, John (1790-1843)
Doe, John (Baker)
Doe, John (Tailor)
Doe, John (Thief)
Doe, John (Tinker)

SUBJECT ENTRIES

Of course, the problem of selecting subjects is more formidable than the problem of proper names. Proper name selection can be controlled reasonably well by establishing rules and developing a list of models to follow. The problem of subject headings is less susceptible to fixed rules and canned examples because of the elusiveness of what "aboutness" means in subject analysis. However, form of entry and internal structure can be codified well enough to be useful to an indexer.

Most book indexes do not extensively index ideas, but stick mostly to the words used by the author, trying to create vocabulary control close to the natural language of the text. As a result, a majority of the indexes are stronger in place-name entries and personal names than in subject interpretation. The most obvious explanation is that the indexer seldom has enough time to do a proper job with subject analysis, which is unfortunate because the objective of the index is to make the information in the book completely available. This includes careful content analysis and subject description.

Analyzing Content

As with any subject indexing, the indexer begins with the words of the text, scanning each sentence and underlining the key subject words used by the author. The indexer then evaluates these words within the framework of the total paragraph to determine the subject being discussed. Clearly, not every underlined word in a paragraph is a major subject and indispensable. Many words are minor and would be useless in the index. What important topic or topics are discussed in this paragraph? What words are simply modifiers and not actually subject indicators? For example, in "The mosquitos attacked with the ferocity of a tiger" only "mosquitos" is a subject indicator.

Choosing Entries

How many terms should the index have? Often a length will be imposed by the editor, but there is also a common sense limit. That is, the index covers what would be expected by the scholarly needs and common sense of the index users. Every word in the text should not be arranged alphabetically as an index. In fact, an index entry that leads to little or no information does a disservice to the user. Related to this, an index may be burdened with excessive cross-references. It is possible for an index to be overdone.

So, how many headings should a subject be given? A general rule is to use as many entries as needed to completely cover the subject and any major approaches a reader might use. For example, if the topic is "The use of computers for the indexing of books and periodicals," it will probably require entries under "Computers," "Books," "Periodicals," and "Indexing." Immediately, the question arises concerning ideas *implied* but not actually stated; in this example, "Automatic indexing" comes to mind. Already the indexer faces the problem of synonyms and "preferred" terms. Those decisions are made on the basis of subject knowledge and the usage of the language in that subject. Generally, the subject is indexed with the same specificity of the text, with perhaps a cross-reference from the class name.

The caution against "posting up" to a more generic term holds, but it certainly is not a rigid rule. For example, if "The mosquitos attacked with the ferocity of a tiger" is in a paragraph that discusses only mosquitos and nowhere else in the book are there any other topics on insects, it would be unwise for the indexer to have an entry under "Insects." However, if the book also discusses ants, bees, beetles, wasps, grasshoppers, and cockroaches, then the index will have an entry under "Insects" with subheadings under the individual types, although the term *insect* is never used by the author.

In some cases, a generic term may be used with cross-references from the components if the larger term would likely be a preferred term by the reader. For example: "The Presidential campaign debate between Kennedy and Nixon" might have these entries:

Presidential Campaign Debate, 97-120, 305
Kennedy, John F. *See* Presidential campaign debate
Nixon, Richard M. *See* Presidential campaign debate

Often the complexity of a subject will lead to many entries, and a good practice is to include in each entry only the facet of concern at that point. For example, the index entries for "The use of computers in business, government, and education" would be:

Business, use of computers in
Government, use of computers in
Education, use of computers in

and *not*:

Business, government, and education, use of computers in
Education, business, and government, use of computers in
Government, business, and education, use of computers in

Synonymous or near-synonymous terms are cross-referenced to the selected terms. For example:

Telephone operator, 19, 47-49, 106
Phone girl. *See* Telephone operator
Telephone girl. *See* Telephone operator

Often there are pairs of synonyms and antonyms that conceptually go together, and the reader will search for their combinations. Such terms should be combined as entries. It still may be advisable, however, to have cross-references from the individual components. For example:

Sickness and health
Love and hate
Plague and pestilence

Sickness. *See* Sickness and health
Health. *See* Sickness and health

The indexer should be alert for combinations that can be made that are not combined by convention of usage. This is suggested when a minor amount of space is devoted to certain subjects. If the discussions are extensive, then separate entries are called for. For example, if there are a few references to "Libraries" and some other references to "Librarians" then:

Libraries, 107, 110
Librarians, 87, 110

becomes:

Libraries and librarians, 87, 107, 110

However, judgment has to be used in combining topics, since if the practice is carried too far, the indexer does the reader a disservice. For instance, in the above example, if both topics are discussed somewhat extensively and a reader is looking for information on libraries and couldn't care less about the people who operate them, then separate entries are preferred.

Homographs require separate entries with interpretative notes, usually in parentheses. For example:

Bases (military), 93, 97-120
Bases (mathematics), 190-96, 201
Bases (lamps), 309-12, 315

The indexing of subject content is a difficult part of the job, requiring skill, experience, and subject knowledge, and when the right terms are selected, a major step is taken toward creating a quality index.

FORM AND INTERNAL GUIDANCE

The first concern of the indexer is to select the right name and subject entries so that readers will find all the details they need. The exhaustivity and specificity of this selection will affect both the use and the length of the index. However, there are other factors involved: the practice of using *see* references and the general form of the index. For example, scattering is a perpetual curse on indexing. Basically, scattering of terms means that closely related ideas are not connected in the structure of the index and the user must constantly play a second-guessing game in order to find the relevant terms. Scattering can take several forms. The most obvious and probably the most prevalent type of scattering occurs with synonyms, but scattering can also be related to generic/specific entries. In the latter case, users might be forced to search for more generic or more specific terms to avoid missing relevant entries.

Saving Space

There are many ways that space can be saved in an index, but a basic one is in the arrangement of the entries. The danger of too much space saving in entry arrangement is that readability may be sacrificed, thereby making the index difficult to use. Arrangement can vary all the way from one entry per page, surrounded by a great expanse of whiteness, to entries and references jammed together to resemble a page of text out of a ponderous encyclopedia. The happy medium is elusive, but it can be approximated. Consider the following example:

Computers, 71-72, 279
Computers, development of, 79-80
Computers, educational uses of, 69, 201-5
Computers, library use of, 309-15
Computers, programming of, 320-31

Several possibilities are available. One way is to optimize space and block subheadings under the generic term:

> Computers, 71-72, 279; development of, 79-80; educational uses of, 69, 201-5; library use of, 309-15; programming of, 320-31

This arrangement may be appropriate when the list of subheadings is short and there are few references.

Here is another approach:

> Computers, 71-72, 279
>   Development of, 79-80
>   Educational uses of, 69, 201-5
>   Library use of, 309-15
>   Programming of, 320-31

A third alternative is to list the indented subheadings and block the page numbers with dots to lead the reader's eye to the reference. For example:

> Computers.....................................71-72, 279
>   Development of................................79-80
>   Educational uses of.........................69, 201-5
>   Library use of....................................309-15
>   Programming of.................................320-31

There is a tendency in our society to use acronyms and abbreviations, and these can save some space. The key is to use these short forms only if they will be understood by the reader, and, in any case, they should be used sparingly. Otherwise the index will soon resemble a medieval Chinese manuscript.

In addition, the collapsing of terms and the proper use of *see* references can save space here and there. Beyond this, the saving of space is in the hands of the publisher and printer, and they make decisions concerning the number of spaces in an indention, the number of columns on a page, the size of type, and so forth. Indexers' opinions are not usually considered in such matters, but it is important for them to know before the index is typed what these decisions are, since they can influence the formatting.

References

Cross-reference is a primary function of entry selection, of course, but there are a few niceties that can make the difference between clear, direct internal guidance and a mesh of circumlocution and dead ends. There are no absolute rules for entry assignment, and therefore none for the use of cross-references. There are, however, some situations where the use of cross-references is almost certain. For example:

Differences in spelling
Labour. *See* Labor

Foreign words/names
Bretagne. *See* Brittany

Archaic words
Cordwainer. *See* Shoemaker

Colloquial words
Doc. *See* Physician

Synonyms and antonyms
Doctor. *See* Physician
Unemployment. *See* Employment

From genus to subclass
Insects. *See also* types of insects by name

From subclass to genus
Battle of Gettysburg. *See* Civil War

Name Variations
Becket, Thomas. *See* Thomas à Becket, Saint

Abbreviations and acronyms (if there is any chance they might be accessed either way)
UNESCO. *See* United Nations Educational, Scientific, and Cultural Organization

Finally, all *see* references should be checked to be sure that no circumlocution ("Cats." *See* "Felines"; "Felines." *See* "Cats") or dead ends (*see* page 500 of a 400-page book) exist.

OTHER POINTS

1) In technical books symbols will often be used as preferred terms. The best way to handle this situation is to spell out the words (when they exist) and put the symbols in parentheses. For example:

Pi (π), 107, 109

2) When bibliographic information becomes an index entry, care should be taken to clearly differentiate between elements, such as series volume numbers and pages, so that they cannot be confused with the page references of the indexed book.

3) Headings should be distinguishable from subunits, preferably by being in capital letters.

4) If a main heading stands alone, it has no punctuation. Neither do subheadings.

5) References to pages are separated by commas, but have no end punctuation.

6) Parenthetical notes are followed by a comma, but no punctuation is used before.

7) Use of singular or plural forms in entries should be decided on at the planning stage and should be consistent throughout. For example:

> Dog
> Cat

but *not*:

> Dog
> Cats

Much ado has been made about the use of singular versus plural headings. Generally, indexers prefer to use one form or the other and they argue that by choosing one form it at least gives a sense of consistency. However, it turns out that sometimes it is preferable to actually use both forms in the same index. Clarity and purpose should be the guiding principle rather than absolute consistency.

8) Often a geographical name has a different form in other countries. This may make it necessary to enter the name in several ways, although this is not automatically true. Some alternate forms are so universal that multiple entry is not necessary.

9) A word of caution when indexing biographies: Indexers often make the mistake of trying to compile every facet of the biographee's life under the name heading of the main character. Since the entire book is about this person, the aspects should be separate headings and not pages and pages under the name entry.

10) Often a compound heading must be inverted to be useful:

> Dogs, wild
> Professors, eccentric
> Disraeli, Homer
> Cartoons, animated

The reasons for inverting the first three examples are obvious. However, there might be some question about the last example. If the user is an animator, then "Animated cartoons" might be a better choice, but the more general user thinks of "Cartoon" in a more generic way. In general, natural language order is preferred when possible and when the natural order begins with content-bearing words.

Probably in no other area of indexing can quality vary as much as in book indexing, from 0 percent to 100 percent. At the top of the scale is a scholarly, almost faultless piece of work, and at the zero end is a confused, misleading list of words. Notice that the absence of an index is not zero on the scale, since *no* index can be better for the reader than a poor one. However, a book without an index is incomplete. Several years ago a British politician introduced a bill that would have denied copyright and imposed a fine on a publisher who issued a book without an index, but the bill failed. Perhaps that was unfortunate.

SUGGESTED READINGS

Anderson, James D., and Gary Radford. "Back-of-the-Book Indexing with the Nested Phrase Indexing System." *The Indexer* 16 (October 1988): 79-84.

Bakewell, K. G. B. "How to Let Your Fingers Do the Walking and Not Lose the Way (Index Compilation)." *Times Higher Education Supplement* 412:12, September 26, 1980.

_____. "Why Are There So Many Bad Indexes?" *Library Association Record* 81 (1979): 330-31.

Bell, H. K. "Publishers and Indexers: A Colloquy." *The Indexer* 12 (April 1981): 141.

Collison, Robert L. "The Elements of Book Indexing, Part II." In: Knight, G. Norman. *Training in Indexing*. Cambridge, Mass.: M.I.T. Press, 1969, 28-39.

_____. *Indexing Books: A Manual of Basic Principles*. London: Ernest Benn; New York: J. DeGraff, 1962.

Cross, Ruth C. *Indexing Books*. Cambridge, Mass.: Word Guild, 1980.

Diadato, Virgil P. "Table of Contents and Book Indexes." *Library Resources and Technical Services* 30 (1986): 402-12.

Gibson, John. "The Indexing of Medical Books and Journals." *The Indexer* 13 (April 1983): 173-75.

VII
Index Evaluation

INTRODUCTION

Anyone who can read, knows the alphabet, and has a modicum of horse sense can make an index. However, there are good indexes and there are bad indexes, and making a *good* index requires more than common sense. It requires an understanding of the empirical knowledge base that has developed over the centuries and an appreciation of the methods that have worked. The definition of a good index is simple: It is an index that leads a user to the exact information that is needed, with no hurdles and no irrelevant material.

The purpose of evaluation is to determine the effectiveness, efficiency, and value of what we have done by careful study and appraisal. We evaluate indexes to determine how good they are, and our work is not complete until such evaluations are made. And this must be a continuing activity.

An examination of the literature makes it clear that the evaluation of indexing and indexes always has been of major importance. However, no totally acceptable methods of evaluation have been agreed upon. Indexing is more of an art than a science, and, as such, it depends heavily on experienced judgment. Until such time that indexing can be based on an established theoretical body of knowledge, it is not likely that the procedures and results can be quantitatively assessed. At the same time, it is essential that we have some method, quantitative or not, that will help us evaluate what we are doing.

The entire information retrieval process is a series of interrelated steps, each of which is critical to the success of the total system. The indexing step itself can be broken down into a series of substeps that are similarly critical. Thus, when we attempt to evaluate indexing, we are dealing with many variables. One of the shortcomings of our methods of evaluation has been the lack of control of the many variables involved when we look at the entire process. Often, in past situations, only one, or sometimes two, variables were controlled in the so-called experiment, and the many related or intervening variables were politely ignored.

A good or bad index is not the result of a single component but of many factors, ranging from human judgment to economic constraints. The evaluation methods that have been developed are not quantitatively precise but are fraught with subjective factors. However, a great deal of thought has gone into the problem and some workable methods exist.

THE GENERAL PROBLEM

What is an indexer supposed to achieve? The final product is an index that works, resulting from the assignment of descriptors to identify the subject content of a knowledge record. How well the indexer does this determines the quality of the index as a retrieval tool.

It would be desirable, then, to have an objective, quantifiable way to ascertain quality. We generally judge quality by simply saying that the "indexing is good" or "the indexing is bad," but it is difficult to define what we mean by *good* and *bad*. Attempts are then made to define good in terms of objectives, e.g., the *purpose* of the index. Does it fulfill its stated purposes? Are its scope and coverage adequate? However, once again we are not quite sure how to make those judgments. Generally, when we say purpose, for example, we are talking about how sufficient the descriptors are in meeting the information requirements of the user.

So we begin with user needs and then examine the index for accuracy, consistency, form, and internal structure. Generally, an index can be evaluated either as an individual unit or in comparison with similar indexes. The objective of the first approach is to rate the index in terms of the needs of the clientele, the subject areas covered, its stated purpose, and its cost. When the latter approach is used, we stand it up in like company and compare its relative quality and cost. To do this, we must have made a previous judgment about the other indexes.

USE OF INFORMATION

Although much has been said about how indexing must be aimed at the user, little is understood about the needs of the users in terms of the information conveyed by the documents and the effects of that information on the user once the document is read. Throughout the history of bibliographic control, librarians have focused on the object itself, developing content indicators according to what they conceived the document to be about. The situation did not change significantly with the advent of information retrieval.

How do users approach an information file? How do their perceptions or their problems color the interpretation of the index they use? Almost nothing is known about how users react or use the information provided. How does this use influence or change their future needs? If these questions could be answered, indexing quality would improve rather dramatically.

There is a cynical view that users approach our libraries and information retrieval systems only as a last resort when there is absolutely nowhere else to turn. When they do come in, they have low expectations, silently demanding very little more than they usually find. Therefore, we continue to operate in the same old way, never fully understanding what is meant by the term "use of information."

CATEGORIES OF USE

Use of *materials* is a different thing. It is an objective concept that can be observed and quantified, and this kind of use is what is meant, generally, when talking about the needs of users. What we must understand is that when a user opens an index, there is no assurance that he or she will find the material useful.

People have many objectives in mind when they approach a library. One user wants a grand sweep of a topic that pulls together every tidbit of information written about it, a second person wants only a general survey of a topic, and a third one wants to verify a single fact.

To take care of all three, an index must be complete. That is, it must alert the user to everything on the topic. The index must have enough specificity for the third user to get a fact quickly, and in all cases the index must retrieve only relevant materials. Clearly, users will differ in their demands for completeness and specificity, but all of them want to avoid having to examine irrelevant materials.

It should be clear, then, that before evaluation can be carried out, some criteria of users' needs and demands concerning an index must be established. The goal of a good index is to aid the user in finding information in documents within a reasonable boundary of time and personal effort. And, above all, the retrieved information must be relevant. This is where evaluation begins.

RELEVANCE

Over the years almost every possible indexing comparison has been made. Human indexing has been intercompared for consistency. Human indexing has been compared with machine indexing. Numerous tests have been conducted to compare the relative utility of using different parts of a document for indexing, for example, indexing only with titles, or titles and abstracts or using the full text of the document. Statistical methods and quasi-mathematical models have been proposed to ascertain the quality of indexes.

The problem has not been a lack of testing models. The problem has been the subjective nature of what a "good" index is and this problem begins with the concept of what relevance is.

Those who have dedicated time and deliberation to the topic seem to agree that indexing evaluation will never be totally effective until there is an understanding of the precept of relevance. It is the fundamental notion in evaluation, not only of indexing, but of all bibliothecal enterprises.

The notion of relevance comes about in a logical way. When users make a search of the information store, they have in their own minds an image of what information they need. Given that image, the total information file is dichotomized, with one part having the documents that they need and the other group having documents that don't concern them. The validity of this dichotomization depends solely on how the content of the documents matches the image of the user. In other words, relevance is in the eye of the beholder. It follows, then, that relevance is the crux to evaluating an index on its performance, even though relevance is clearly a relative notion. As the index points and guides the searcher to information and presents directions about what should be retrieved and what is not to be retrieved, it works under the user's mandate of relevance.

Relevance, as a notion, was not original with indexers and information retrieval practitioners but has been of concern to philosophers and logicians since antiquity, and over the years extensive theories have been developed and discussed. When a logician makes an inference from A to B, it is maintained that for this to be valid, A must be *relevant* to B. In fact, the basic relationships in logic, including deduction, implication, entailment, and logical consequence, are all closely constructed around the notion of relevance. Thus, it is not surprising that relevance is a theoretical problem of interest to information retrieval in general and to indexing in particular.

Problem Relevance

People use information sources because they face a problem. An information problem can range from the trivial to the profound, can be simple or complex, but to the user it is always important. Unfortunately for the indexer these problems are seldom completely or even partly defined. Every information professional knows that the hardest part of the job is finding out exactly what the information seeker is asking. People often are not sure what they are asking for, and they approach the information professional in all stages of both problem understanding and question formulation.

So, one begins the task by asking the question, How do you design an index that can effectively react to any stage of the searcher's problem, varying from simply a dim, obscure fancy all the way up to the scholar's well-defined fact? An index that is based on the assumption that all problems are well defined and that queries are straightforward is doomed for extinction.

Relevance Assessments

The classical way to formally appraise the relevance of documents retrieved using a particular indexing system is to form a panel of experts in the subject areas indexed and gather a bank of relevant responses to a number of fixed questions. Nothing could seem more reasonable, and indexing system after indexing system has been evaluated this way. However, the simplicity of this method began to worry some of the more astute professionals in the field during the 1960s.

A serious look at relevance began with the 1958 International Conference for Scientific Information, where it was suggested that (1) the idea of relevance should be considered independently and prior to any particular method of representation or information retrieval system; (2) relevance is multivalent, a matter of degree and not a simple yes/no decision; and (3) the relevance of given documents may change as a result of other documents, as stock of knowledge at hand changes. However, it was some time before these ideas became widely considered. Early on, Cleverdon (1967) noted that these panels of experts were not homogeneous but formed different groups, each with its distinct judgment bias. In the first place, a panel expresses relevance judgment on a set of contrived questions and tends to be less critical than users with their own distinct problems. Panelists are likely to accept documents that relate in only a general way to the question, but real users have particular notions of what constitutes acceptable answers.

One approach has been to take large numbers of panel relevance judgments and average them, but differences between panel judgments and real user judgments are so great (up to 50 percent in some cases) that error cannot be averaged out with any true validity.

A little later on, it was realized that even real users can vary in their relevance judgments. Two people, approximately equal in background, could approach a system with exactly the same question, get the same answers, and be poles apart in relevance judgments. Even the same user may vary his or her judgment on different days. Clearly, relevance is not an absolute concept, and not surprisingly it has been the object of considerable contention.

In the early days of information retrieval, it was acknowledged that not every document retrieved for a given query would be relevant to that query. However, the workers always considered the problem to be the result of system malfunction. We have come a long way in realizing that evaluation is a tricky business and that the whole concept of relevance is a fundamental problem.

Does this leave us with no leg to stand on? Not quite, if we consider briefly the nature of quantification and measurement. Relevance evaluations probably will never be as exact as measurement in the physical sciences, but physical measurement can never be as perfect as mathematical proof, and this has not prevented the physical sciences from devoting enormous energies to quantification. In fact, the maturity of a science is usually judged on its measurement techniques. When physical scientists detect inconsistencies, they resort to statistical techniques while trying to improve their measurement tools. We must learn this lesson and move ahead, because relevance judgments are all we have to work with at this time when theoretical constructs are almost totally lacking in the field.

Pertinence

Evaluation terminology has been somewhat fuzzy over the years. Lancaster (1977) has written an excellent article that attempts to clarify the terminology.

There is a notion, which seems rational, that relevance exists on at least two levels. The first level is relevance, *per se*, and the second level is sometimes called *pertinence*. This is based on the idea that there are two aspects to the evaluation of a subject index: (1) The relevance of the retrieved information as expressed by the index terms used, and (2) the usefulness of the information to the user who made the request. The first aspect deals with the degree to which the retrieved information reflects the index terms used. Does the index term reflect what the retrieved document is "about"? If users search under a particular term, will the information be about the topic suggested by the index term? In the second case, will users actually find the retrieved information pertinent to their information needs?

Users base their judgment of the relevance of a document on much more than the accuracy of how the index term used pulled a particular document. The document that was retrieved might be exactly what the index term described, but the user does not find the document useful. For example, the document may not be timely, it may not be in a language the user understands, it may be written on a level of comprehensibility that is beyond the user, or it may be information the user already has. All these factors will adversely affect the user's judgment.

So, relevance is most closely associated with the relationship between the document and the index, and pertinence is most closely associated with the relationship between the document and the user.

The first aspect of relevance can be quantified by letting a subject expert evaluate the results. But, the second aspect, pertinence, is the reflection of a single user and is highly personal. The only way to measure pertinence is to survey users and ask them how useful they found the information. This is usually done with a scaled, rather than a yes/no, questionnaire, since most users will find a degree of pertinence in the retrieved documents.

In trying to evaluate how well an index is working, we could let three types of people make a judgment: an information intermediary, a subject specialist, and the requester of the information. The information intermediary is the one who forms the searching strategy and can judge the results within the framework of how the question was asked. The subject specialist has a more global response in that he or she is concerned with whether or not the information in the document is sufficiently close to the subject matter of the request. These first two judges are evaluating how well the index matches the document, but information need colors the user's judgment.

On the surface it would appear that the only thing we can expect of an index is that it retrieves documents relevant to the information requested and expressed with an index term; we have no way to control the pertinence variable. But this stance fails to recognize that, in the end, it is the pertinence of the information to the user that counts. If the index never retrieves pertinent information, the entire information system has failed, including the index. Thus, it is essential that we evaluate indexes on all levels, no matter how difficult the methodology.

RECALL AND PRECISION

The people who developed information retrieval were quantitatively inclined because they were primarily scientists and engineers; as a result, they wanted to test their systems with quantitative measures. What they proposed is known as *recall* and *precision*.

When users approach the library to solve an information problem they may find that a single document is all they need. Or they may be satisfied with several core items. At other times they want a full literature search, both current and retrospective, and they will be satisfied with nothing short of total retrieval of everything related to their query. When users take the last option, the capability of the indexing system to identify relevant documents is known as its *recall* power. As far as these users are concerned, recall is their primary requirement of the system, since their stated goal is to find everything that the system has to offer related to the questions asked. How well did the system do? Of course, the extent to which individuals worry more about recall or precision will depend a lot upon their particular information needs.

The recall measure is a simple quantitative ratio of the relevant documents retrieved to the total number of relevant documents potentially available. If there are 100 documents in the library, for example, relevant to the user's needs and the indexing system leads to 75, then the recall ration is 75 out of 100 (75/100). Recall for this search was 75 percent effective.

However, recall is not the only thing users may be concerned with, although users tend to worry about it more. If they want to be absolutely sure of total recall, they can always ignore the index and go directly to the material (read all one million documents in the library). They can examine the documents one by one until they have filtered out what they want. But this is the whole point of bibliographic control in general and indexing in particular—the filtering has already been done for the user. The index decreases the number of items users must examine, but since it is an artificial device, thrown between them and the material, there is the risk of not getting total recall. Therefore, the recall measure is a test of the index's ability to let relevant documents through the filter.

What we're leading up to is that there is another side to the coin: the index must not allow nonrelevant documents through the filter. The capability of the indexing system to hold back documents not relevant to the user is known as its *precision* power.

The precision measure is a ratio of the relevant documents retrieved to the total number of documents retrieved. For example, if 100 documents are retrieved and 50 of those items are relevant to the request, the precision ratio is 50 to 100 (50/100). Precision for this search was 50 percent effective. For a given system, all possibilities can be represented with the following matrix:

Query

System Response	Relevant	Nonrelevant	Total
Retrieved	a	b	a + b
Not retrieved	c	d	c + d
Total	a + c	b + d	a + b + c + d = N

where a, b, c, and d are the number of documents in each class. Thus we have:

$$\text{RECALL} = \frac{a}{a+c}$$

and

$$\text{PRECISION} = \frac{a}{a+b}$$

Referring to the earlier example:

$$
\text{Query I:} \quad
\begin{aligned}
a &= 75 \\
c &= 25 \\
a+c &= 100
\end{aligned}
$$

and

Query II: a   = 50
              b   = 50
            a + b   = 100

Then:

Query I: RECALL = $\dfrac{a}{a+c}$ = $\dfrac{75}{100}$ = 75%

Query II: PRECISION = $\dfrac{a}{a+b}$ = $\dfrac{50}{100}$ = 50%

When successive recall and precision calculations are plotted on a two-dimensional graph, it will generally follow this pattern:

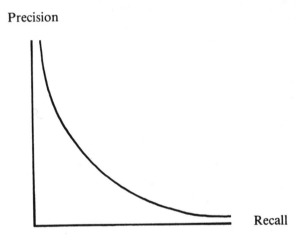

As recall increases, precision goes down.

The Effects of Exhaustivity and Specificity

In a previous chapter the concepts of exhaustivity and specificity were discussed. What effects, if any, do these two concepts have on the recall and precision ratios? Exhaustivity and specificity are recognized as being two factors affecting the response of an index language, the first defined as the number of separate subjects indexed, and the second as the power of the index to precisely define the topic. Generally, extensive exhaustivity gives high recall and low precision. Conversely, restricted exhaustivity gives low recall and high precision. On the other hand, deep specificity gives low recall and high precision, and scant specificity results in high recall and low precision. This is why it is believed that there is an optimum level of exhaustivity and specificity, some mystical point where recall and precision are in the best balance possible.

Ascertaining the Recall Quantity

One of the problems in using recall and precision ratios is determining the value of the recall measure. Users can respond to retrieval results and indicate which documents they feel are relevant, but the problem is in ascertaining what unidentified relevant documents are still left in the file. The precision measure is not handicapped this way, because the user has in hand all that is necessary for the precision calculation.

Since the recall measure is a ratio of relevant documents retrieved to the total number of relevant documents in the system, it is implied that the total number of relevant documents in the file must be known for each query tested. In operational systems, which may have many thousands, perhaps millions, of documents, this ideal situation is simply not possible. The only solution is to establish some sort of proximity of the ideal, since we cannot hope to examine the full collection of documents to calculate recall for each query.

Sampling would appear to be the logical solution. A proper sampling method allows us to statistically establish a representation of relevant documents in the total file by examining a relatively small number of actual documents. The procedure involves submitting a question to the system and obtaining retrieval results, then pulling a controlled sample from the collection to ascertain the proportion of the sample that is relevant to the query. The results of the sample are extrapolated to the total collection to statistically suggest the total number of probable relevant documents in the file. The user's query results are then examined against the sample results and the recall value is calculated.

For example, suppose a user approaches the system wanting information on cats, and the search turns up 80 documents, 60 of which are relevant to the topic. Precision is quickly calculated as $60/80 = 75$ percent. Now, a sample is taken of the total document file (including, of course, the 80 documents just identified). Suppose the sampling pulls 10,000 documents (say 5 percent of 200,000) and it is discovered that 10 documents are about cats. Since the sample is 5 percent of the file, we multiply 10 (the number of relevant documents in the sample) by 20 (to get 100 percent) and we assume that our total file has 200 documents about cats. Now we are ready to calculate the recall for the query: Recall $= 60/200 = 30$ percent. Our user will probably be a little unhappy with our index.

A second approach is to "plant" source documents in the file. That is, mark documents as being relevant to certain topics and then search the file and calculate a value on the basis of the proportion of these marked documents that get pulled by the index. This is an easier approach, but is somewhat artificial.

The Use of Recall and Precision

Recall and precision must be used together to obtain a true picture of how the index is performing. And to be meaningful, a significant number of searches must be run to get an accurate measure of recall and precision. Ideally, many results, representing all levels of users over a span of time, will go into the evaluation. The astute reader has realized that in the foregoing discussion we have alluded to evaluation of both indexes and total retrieval systems. This was intentional, since recall and precision can be used for either. One word of caution is in order if only the index is to be evaluated: the results cannot be modified by any intermediary, such as the librarian who might eliminate any obvious junk. This is perfectly all right, of course, in evaluating a total system, since the human filtering is a part of the retrieval system and should be a part of the evaluation process. But when evaluating the index only, it is necessary to work with exactly the results the index produces.

In a sense, the precision measure is an evaluation of the penalty we pay to get an acceptable level of recall. If we insist on 100 percent recall, the precision ratio will likely drop to a troublesome level, because of the inverse relationship between recall and precision.

In using these measures to evaluate an index, we must remember that users are affected in their attitudes and relevance judgments by many factors. For example, relevance can begin at the stage of document acquisition. If a subject is inadequately covered, the finest index in the world will not satisfy users. They will question the system's recall power, not realizing that no system can recall what isn't there. Such subjective factors as the amount of effort that is required of them and the general procedures they must go through color users' opinions.

Retrieval ability is only one aspect of index evaluation. Some other factors are discussed in the next section.

INDEX QUALITY

Certain aspects of indexes that need to be evaluated, such as errors, omissions, general carelessness in construction, and poor display, do not directly require the opinions of the users, although these factors are of concern to them.

There are many good indexes and their quality continues to grow, but basic problems remain in the construction and production of indexes. No one in the field will concede that there are enough good indexes to cover adequately the vast information store potentially available to the world. Partly responsible for this, of course, are the limited resources available for indexing activities. Despite dramatic changes in attitude in some quarters, the research and development enterprises in business, government, and academia still fail to accept the fact that information is a major link in their activities, and the money for personnel, facilities, and research in the information endeavor is seriously lacking. It has been observed that the lack of resources to produce an outstanding network of indexing services is analogous to the financial plight science itself suffered until the middle of this century.

Perhaps a reason for the lack of interest in quality indexes is that it has been difficult to define quality, and users have no benchmark to compare against, no sense of standards for accuracy. Consequently, users tend to believe that all is being done for them that can be done. Quite frankly, too many people are poor users of indexes and do not understand how to fully benefit from their potential. If the makers of indexes and librarians were to educate users, increase their awareness of indexing power, perhaps this would lead to adequate support for the activity.

Subject Error

Inadequate resources are not alone responsible for poor indexes. Errors are not uncommon, beginning with errors in choosing subject descriptors. A careless indexer may choose words that change meaning. In the science field, for example, it is not unusual for an editor to change up to a fourth of the indexer's entries. Many of these are serious errors, such as totally wrong entries and/or the omission of major ones. The purpose of the index editing process is to minimize these kinds of errors.

Choosing the right index terms to represent information is difficult, in both manual and machine indexing. Human indexers try to circumvent the subtle pitfalls of natural language in order to represent true meaning, and machines must rely on semantic and syntactical algorithms in an attempt to do the same. Neither approach is error free.

Omission errors are troublesome in that they are time-consuming and difficult to detect. To catch these errors, editors have to practically re-index the document. Although editors can immediately detect blatant omissions, they must rely on intuition and their own subject experience to catch most omission errors. One technique they can use is to set up a routine procedure of randomly selecting certain documents to be automatically re-indexed by a senior, experienced indexer. This, of course, can be a way to check the incidence of all kinds of errors, and it is certainly a helpful way to see how extensive omission errors are among the indexing crew.

Incorrect descriptors are somewhat easier to catch, since editors can see the relationships involved. For example, they may see the concept *muffler* indexed under the descriptor "Winter clothing," when they know the paper is about automobile equipment. Wrong descriptors are not as subtle as omission errors. Policy, rather than indexer error, may also lead to the omission of needed descriptors. For example, the rules may say to omit historical background, but complaints may start coming in because users want to study the historical framework of a particular subject. The solution here is to reexamine the policy on historical content.

Another descriptor error that is difficult to catch is the use of a too broad or too narrow term. We have already discussed the effect this has on recall and precision, but in the absence of a user's relevance assessment, indexers and editors have to second-guess each other about the choices made. Feedback from users will help give both indexers and editors experience in making these decisions.

Unfortunately, once subject descriptor errors slip by the indexer and the editor, they may go unrecognized for years by users who simply plod along with what they have before them.

Generic Searching

Alphabetical indexes have always presented difficulties in promoting generic searching. The basic problem is that when maximum specificity is allowed, the user must look up a long string of entries to run out the generic tree. Preparing a full list of these entries is also burdensome to the indexer. While it may be a little unfair, alphabetical indexes should be evaluated as to how well generic searching can be done.

Terminology

Terminology evaluation is primary in the domain of thesaurus construction, but since the end point of bad nomenclature is the index, evaluating terminology is one method of evaluating an index. What must be understood is that thesaurus construction and indexing activities are interdependent—or at least they should be. Certainly, if writers and users reject the terminology of the thesaurus, it will make life difficult for the indexer, who will be hard pressed to find words in the controlled list; and users will find the index unsatisfactory from their frame of reference. In a quality index, users will locate the terms they expect to find.

Internal Guidance

The purpose of notes and cross-references in an index is to guide a user who has looked in the wrong place to look in the right place, or to check out an alternate possibility. One quick and dirty technique for evaluating an index is to scan its pages for *see* type references. The absence of such references immediately makes the index suspect.

Another type of internal guidance is the printed instructions on how to use the index. A quality index will have concise, clearly written instructions with examples covering the major points. Although it is probably true that users generally ignore instructions totally, or only flip to them when they become frustrated, instructions should always be provided.

Accuracy in Referring

Index users depend on cross-references to effectively find the information they need; thus, the nature, number, and accuracy of cross-references will reflect the quality of an index. Nothing will irritate a user faster than finding mechanical inaccuracies, such as a wrong year or volume number in a citation or a wrong page number in a book. Mechanical errors often appear in indexes, because of the many opportunities for errors to slip by.

Errors lose the audience immediately. Probably nothing is more irritating than to find an index entry that tells us to "*see also* Dogs," and upon scanning the *D*'s we find that there is no such descriptor. Or to have an entry say "*see* page 502" when the book has only 205 pages. Circular references are also frequent. For example, the "Dogs" entry says to "*see* Animals," and the "Animals" entry says to see "Dogs." Confidence in that index quickly slides in the popularity poll. Such errors make the entry useless and increase users' time and effort because they must start their search all over again. These are careless errors that can be minimized by thorough checking by both indexers and editors.

Of course, the burden should be on the indexer. Editors reasonably anticipate some of these inadvertent errors, but they can't be expected to redo the entire job. The simplest way to test accuracy in referral is to look up a number of entries and see where they lead. When the indexers review their work, they should check out every branch that they have proposed for the user. Poetic justice should require indexers to use their own indexes.

Entry Scattering

One of the problems of an alphabetical index is scattering, that is, having similar entries spread out from *A* to *Z*. For example, suppose we had these entries: "National planning," "Regional planning," "State planning," "County planning," and "City planning." An alphabetical index would scatter the entries into five places in the index. A simple remedy in this case is the inversion of terms:

Planning, city		Planning
Planning, county		City
Planning, national	or	County
Planning, regional		National
Planning, state		Regional
		State

What about people who want to look under the noninverted terms? Cross-references should guide them.

Scattering can generally be minimized by having clear rules and by good indexer training. And a first-class thesaurus can be a major positive influence.

Entry Differentiation

It is frustrating for users to turn to an entry and find five or six lines of undifferentiated references. They are then faced with the task of examining the references one by one to find the subset needed. If an entry has more than five or six entries, it should be broken down. For example, this is very disconcerting to a user:

PLANNING, 1-2, 5, 23, 25, 28-31, 42, 53-60, 73, 82, 109-11, 119, 120, 131-32, 143, 152, 160-68, 170, 190, 199, 303-4, 316

This is better:

PLANNING, 28-31, 73, 152, 190, 199
    City, 5, 119, 131-32
    County, 1-2, 120, 170, 316
    National, 23, 25, 303-4
    Regional, 53-60, 82, 143
    State, 42, 109-11, 160-68

Spelling and Punctuation

Incorrect spelling quickly puts a cloud over the quality of an index, not because it is actually all that critical, but because it suggests carelessness to users and reduces their confidence. Indexers and editors of quality indexes make strong efforts to avoid spelling errors.

Incorrect punctuation is a similar type of error. The goal here is consistency. Again, errors in punctuation (or inconsistency) may not be tragic, but they can affect the image of the index and can also be misleading. For example, if a dash delineates one thing and a comma another, then these uses should not be interchanged throughout the index. Certain conventions of use have been accepted, such as using parentheses to show synonyms and sometimes to set off *see* type references, and commas to show inverted entries. The secret here is to have punctuation rules spelled out for the indexer.

Punctuation is a major problem in alphabetizing. The letters of the alphabet all have a known position in a defined sequence and as long as we are dealing only with letters, a few simple rules will suffice. But when numbers, symbols, and punctuation are introduced, more complex rules must be established. For example, punctuation marks do not have an inherent sequence. It might be suggested that indexes be made without punctuation, but for most indexes this is impractical because punctuation plays an important role in clarifying meaning and in making indexes readable.

Filing

There has been no shortage of filing rules in the library profession, but for many years most of the rules have followed the same general pattern. Cutter's *Rules for a Dictionary Catalog* (4th edition) has a long list of filing rules. Cutter set the standard for a hundred years, and only since the advent of computers have we made any drastic changes in his precepts. For example, Cutter gave us the rule that when the list to be alphabetized contains words that are exactly alike (London, Jack, and London, and London Bridge) we should put person, place, and thing in that order. He also gave us a rigid order for filing forenames of titled persons such as noblemen, popes, kings, and so forth.

The good news is that there is now a trend to simplify rules. For example, the ALA rules have now relaxed a number of the more rigid rules and there is no evidence that effectiveness of retrieval has suffered.

If anyone believed that filing is a trivial problem, a surprise was in store when computers were brought into the picture. Trying to program a computer to follow the ALA filing rules (or any filing rules) proved to be formidable. Filing rules are necessary, but a good thing can be carried too far. With computers, as the rules and exceptions increase, there comes a point where ambiguity is no longer reduced, but increases. For example, if the rule states that *Mc* is to be filed like *Mac*, then the computer, the ever-obedient servant, will put "Machine" in an awkward place.

Layout

A quality layout depends heavily on typographic conventions. For example, punctuation, type size, and font can quickly differentiate between units. Main entries are generally in heavy print, often in capital letters, and subheadings are in lighter print and smaller letters. *See* references are often italicized and perhaps set off with parentheses to make their appearance unique. It is also standard practice to use indentation to set off subheadings from main headings, since a straight column of words is confusing and difficult to read.

Layout is concerned with how space is used on the page, and a balance must be found between wasting space and providing easy-to-read entries. It is possible to have too much space. For example, if lines are too short, the reader has to read long columns; on the other hand, long, unbroken lines slow down scanning.

The printing itself can vary in quality, ranging from a beautiful work of art down to a slipshod product that convinces the user that the entire index is slovenly constructed. Quality layout is the result of indexers, editors, and printers taking pride in what they are doing.

Cost

Economics is an unavoidable factor in producing quality indexes. Stringent cost constraints may result in a poor index, or at least cause it to fall short of what it might have been.

Cost can have two meanings. In addition to the cost of creating an index at the production end, there is a "cost-effectiveness" at the user's end. In the first case, the major cost will be the indexing itself, including the salaries of professional indexers. Although indexers are probably paid less than they are worth, they should be paid salaries worthy of their training, experience, and subject expertise. In addition, clerical people are needed, as are materials, equipment, space, and so forth. One of the major costs for an indexing operation is the authority list. Constructing a thesaurus is a costly project, and maintaining it is a continuing expense. The maintenance cost of an authority list is why some are allowed to become obsolete, but upkeep is absolutely imperative if quality indexing is to be maintained.

It is often said that there is a functional relationship between the cost to the index producer and the cost to the user. This relationship has two aspects: if the index production cost is exorbitant, so is the selling price; and if corners are cut in creating an index, the buyer "pays" for it in the additional time and effort it takes to retrieve information when using the index.

The finest, highest-quality index in the world is merely an oddity if nobody can afford to buy it. Naturally, index producers are keenly aware of this, and they generally try to know what users needs are and what they are willing to pay to have those needs met. Inflation has hit the indexing enterprises, like everywhere else, and this, along with library budget cuts and the availability of online databases, is causing concern among indexing services about the future of printed indexes. Occasionally, index producers have cut back on the frills in their services, focusing on fundamentals, and have still been able to continue producing reputable indexes that are acceptable to their clientele. What is the worth of an index to the public? Maybe a better question to ask is — What will it cost the public not to have this information?

Standards

Indexing and abstracting standards are essential. Standards promote consistency and uniformity and they attempt to codify experience and successful tradition. If we do not consider experience and successful past effort, we reinvent the wheel with the same bumpy lumps. It is likely that our descendants are going to write a highly unflattering account of how we repeatedly recycled old ideas under new terms, for example, *subject authority control* versus *thesaurus*. We indexers know the difference, but most librarians are skeptical.

Standards are the result of our collective history of experience. They represent the criteria by which we measure and assess our indexes and our indexing activity. And yet, they are not absolute laws. Indexers are a very independent-minded group of professionals with very definite ideas of what is right and wrong in indexing. They promote standards, but they reserve the right to break the law if it means that a better index will be created.

Modern society is structured around standards. Without standards, film wouldn't fit our cameras, wheels would fall off automobiles, buildings would collapse, and so forth. So it appears reasonable to have standards for indexing — some guidelines for quality. Standards are important to indexing activities for the same reason they are important to any area of endeavor: they provide consistency and guidelines.

Indexing standards have been developed both here and abroad. The U.S. publication is called *Basic Criteria for Indexes*. The last edition was published in 1984 by the American National Standards Institute and the following purpose of the publication was stated:

> This standard provides guidelines and a uniform vocabulary for use in the preparation of indexes.... The standard is not designed to teach basic indexing practices. It presents guidelines for the results to be achieved, not how to go about achieving them.

The standard defines what an index is, describes the nature of indexes and the various types of indexes, and then makes recommendations concerning the presentation and style of indexes; it does not attempt to regulate procedure. Clearly, procedure is the prerogative of the indexer.

The American National Standards on Library and Information Science and Related Publishing Practices has published more than three dozen standards, some of which are directly useful to indexers and abstractors. For example:

- Basic Criteria for Indexes

- Writing Abstracts

- Guidelines for Thesaurus Structure, Construction, and Use

- Proof Corrections

- Bibliographic References

- Development of Identification Codes for Use by the Bibliographic Community

The issuing of standards by these bodies does not ensure uniformity or even suggest compliance, since there is no force of law. But it is certainly a step in the right direction, and a great deal of indexing operations follow these standards to a large extent, either deliberately or by convention.

Reputation

The traditional method reference librarians use to evaluate indexes is still very useful. This method asks a series of questions:

- Who is the publisher? (The quality publisher who consistently produces good indexes will soon have a good reputation in the profession.)

- What is the scope of the index? Does the index cover what it should cover and what it claims to cover?

- Does it duplicate other indexes that might already be available?

- Does it cover gaps in other indexes?

- Does it have gaps in the subject it is supposed to cover?

- Is the depth and exhaustivity of indexing adequate for the user of the index?

- Is the index timely and current?

- Is it worth its cost?

We must accept the fact that there will never be a perfect index. Too many variables are involved, the most important one being the idiosyncrasies of human beings. Besides, even if a "perfect" index is proclaimed to the world, surely a number of indexers will step forward and point out enough faults to discredit its perfection.

An index is a quality one if it allows users to quickly and easily find all information pertinent to their information needs and if it rejects nonrelevant and nonpertinent information. This is the bottom line.

SUGGESTED READINGS

Ajiferuke, Isola, and Clara M. Chu. "Quality Indexing in Online Databases: An Alternative Measure for a Term Discriminating Index." *Information Processing and Management* 24 (1988): 599-601.

American National Standards Institute. *Basic Criteria for Indexes*. New York: ANSI, 1984.

Bernier, Charles L. "The End Users." In *Proceedings of the 25th Annual Conference of the National Federation of Abstracting and Information Services.* Arlington, Virginia, 1983. Philadelphia: NFAIS, 1984, 48-51.

Cleverdon, C. W. "The Cranfield Tests on Index Language." *AsLib Proceedings* 19 (1967): 173-94.

Lancaster, F. W. "Pertinence and Relevance." In *Encyclopedia of Library and Information Science*, vol. 22. New York: Marcel Dekker, 1977, 70-86.

Line, M. B. "Secondary Services in the Social Sciences: The Need for Improvement and the Role of Librarians." *Behavioral and Social Science Librarian* 1 (Summer 1980): 263-73.

Svenonius, Elaine F. "Directions for Research in Indexing, Classification, and Cataloging." *Library Resources and Technical Services* 25 (1981): 88-103.

VIII
The Nature and Types of Abstracts

INTRODUCTION

Abstracting, like classification and indexing, is a procedure for representing the content of knowledge records so that users can find the information they need. Abstracts can be written for books, journal articles, computer software, art, or any other information-bearing media.

Abstracting differs from classification and indexing by providing some of the actual information contained in the information record. An abstract summarizes the essential contents of a particular knowledge record and is a true surrogate of the document. Classification systems and indexing systems point to where likely information is located, but, except for the limited information conveyed by titles, indexes and classification schemes require the user to examine the material. Abstracts reduce considerably the amount of legwork required to locate information.

The underlying fundamentals of abstracting are closely related to indexing. Abstracting involves content analysis and the representation of that content, but this time with natural-language prose rather than index terms. However, abstract writers are also concerned with selecting the right concept words and then expressing them effectively in writing. They often must choose synonyms and more generic or more specific words to convey meaning and intent to the abstract user. In addition, abstracting journals will generally have indexes, so indexing is a direct part of the abstracting process.

THE ABSTRACT AND ITS USE

Modern abstracting can be traced at least as far back as the beginning of printing, and with a liberal definition of the term, much farther than that. In 1665 the first abstracting journal, *Le Journal des Scavans*, was published in Paris, with Denis de Sallo as its editor. The publication was not totally an abstracting journal since it served as a chronicle of events of concern to the scholarly academies, but it carried critical abstracts of books and other communications. It was a successful enterprise, surviving over the centuries and evolving into a publication for primary literature.

After a relatively slow start, the publication of journals grew exponentially, and the growth of abstracting journals followed the same type of incremental curve. Today there are thousands of abstracting and indexing services, producing millions of abstracts annually at a total cost that runs into millions of dollars.

Use and Users

Scholars have many avenues for finding information, in addition to the literature. They attend professional conferences, visit other research centers, talk on the telephone, write letters, and use electronic mail. Numerous studies over the years have tried to describe the communication patterns of scholars, especially scientists. One of the interesting observations made repeatedly is that availability and ease of use are primary factors in communication. It may be easier for a scholar to twist his chair around and ask a colleague than to put on an overcoat and gloves and slosh through the snow to the library.

Most scientific communication depends on the published primary literature, and this system was a key to the development of science over the last 300 years. Likewise, the development of abstracting devices played a vital role, because without such devices access to the primary literature would be a formidable task, given the size of the scientific literature and its fragmentary and derivative nature. Individual papers in science are seldom of monumental consequence; but taken together, these small tidbits, some more important than others, create a scientific knowledge base. Abstracts are devices that guide us through the maze and help us find what is important and relevant to our information needs.

Studies over the years have shown that scientists *do* use abstracts, although how often has been difficult to ascertain. D. J. Urquhart (1948) did a use study that showed that scientists used abstracts and digests for 33 percent of their references, but other studies have shown variations from 8 percent to 60 percent. So, it is clear that abstracts are important, but the actual extent of their use may vary from discipline to discipline.

Abstracts are written to decrease the time and effort it takes to search the overwhelming output from research and scholarship around the world. An inestimable number of new papers are published each year, with the number increasing annually. It is unlikely that practitioners in any field come even close to reading this outpouring in their own field of interest, no matter how specialized. But that is exactly the point in using an abstract. It is quite likely that the users neither need nor want to read everything. They are concerned with finding that minute portion of the bulk that relates to their current activity or individual interest at a given point. Their specialty may be turtles, but of the hundreds of turtle articles published they want only a few dozen, perhaps, and the rest do not fill any information need. An abstract helps them to decide. Instead of obtaining and examining a 3,000-word paper, they can read a 150-word abstract and then either request the paper or forget about it. Occasionally the abstract will carry all the information a user needs, and thus it serves an additional function.

Clearly, abstracts satisfy users' needs for both current and extensive retrospective information. Users simply scan abstracts as they are published to see what new papers have been written and then turn to older abstracts when they want to go back through the literature.

Abstracts are also used to overcome the language barrier, since many foreign language abstracts are published in English. Knowing an additional language enhances a user's situation, since other abstracts may be translated into or originally written in that other language. These translated abstracts will convey needed information, or they can help the user decide whether to obtain a translation of the paper.

Although we often think of the audience for abstracts as consisting solely of scientists, this is far from true. Doctors and other medical professionals use abstracts to filter through the extensive and complex health sciences literature. Teachers and students use abstracts in their daily activities. Patent lawyers would be hard pressed if they had to operate without abstracts to the millions upon millions of patents issued for centuries all around the world. And what an unpleasant task it would be if we had to read the full papers delivered at a professional conference rather than the abstracts we pick up at the registration desk.

Abstracts also play an important role in the structure of computer-based systems. In a natural-language system it is usually impractical to have the full text of the documents in the computer, so title and abstracts are often stored and the natural-language search is made on the title and abstract.

Finally, abstracts are used by indexers. As we learned in a previous chapter, a well-written abstract is loaded with content-bearing words and is a valuable resource for the indexer.

Types of Materials Abstracted

Ideally, any information record, regardless of its source, form, or purpose, could be served by an abstract if the record is worth preserving. There are a number of general categories of materials that should be abstracted.

Journals. The majority of abstracting is done on journals, since this is the source of publication for most of the primary literature. Abstracts are made to all the papers in the journal, including theoretical papers, research papers, technique papers, speculative essays, and tutorials. Also, discussions, review articles, letters to the editor, communications, and editorials should be included if these items contain significant material.

Technical Reports. During and after the Second World War, the growth of the research and development enterprise, supported by an unprecedented influx of government money, created a "Third World" of information records in the form of technical reports. For a while, traditional librarians were either unprepared or unwilling to handle this type of material. Their almost complete lack of bibliographic control of such material made them uneasy. Citations could not be looked up in "standard" bibliographical tools, and no one was sure if this material, often in flimsy form, should be cataloged or stored in the basement in the hope that nobody would ever request it. As far back as the mid-1940s, scientists, some of national stature, became seriously concerned. This situation was one of the factors that led to the rise of information retrieval, since the early workers in this field were scientists and engineers who naturally turned to mechanical devices as possible solutions.

Happily, the situation has improved. While it is true that every year thousands of technical reports are buried, some devices have been developed for bibliographic control of these rich sources of original research. For example, the National Technical Information Service is a government operation that identifies and makes available many thousands of technical reports every year. These are primarily reports required by the recipients of federal grants, but many reports are received from other sources, such as foreign researchers. Major indexing and abstracting services are also including increasing numbers of these reports in their output.

Dissertations. Despite the cynical opinion of the general public, important original research can originate from Ph.D. candidates at universities. While it is true that many of these efforts are motivated only by a desire to obtain a degree and are sometimes of no great consequence, serious, dedicated effort is often expended and meaningful results are obtained. *Dissertations Abstracts International* is the primary tool for identifying these items, but dissertations are also indexed and abstracted by many other services. For example, *Chemical Abstracts* makes an effort to cover dissertations of interest in the field of chemistry.

Monographs and Books. Generally, if a book is about a single topic, a single abstract is written, but if the volume is a collection of individual papers or each chapter covers a different topic, several abstracts are written to cover the separate units.

Patent Specifications. As mentioned earlier, abstracts are essential to workers who are concerned with patents. In addition to patent lawyers, business executives, industrial research and development personnel, and, of course, inventors all need abstracts.

Conference and Symposium Proceedings. Often the abstracts to conference and symposium proceedings are the only records that are available, which makes the abstracts especially valuable.

Reviews. Reviews usually do not lend themselves to extensive abstracts, but such an abstract should briefly discuss coverage and the number of entries in the review. An exception may be made for definitive and highly significant works.

TYPES OF ABSTRACTS

Abstracts can be classified in several different ways—by the way they are written, by their use, and by who writes them.

By Internal Purpose

One way to classify abstracts is to divide them into three types: indicative (or descriptive), informative, and critical.

Indicative or descriptive abstracts disclose that significant information and specific data can be found in the document. For example, an indicative abstract might state that "the number of onions grown in California was determined and reported in this article."

On the other hand, an *informative* abstract actually presents the specific data. In this case, the abstract would read: "According to this article, a billion seventy-five onions were grown in California."

A *critical* abstract makes a value judgment or editorial comment on the paper. In our example, the abstract would now state: "This article reports on the number of onions grown in California, but since it doesn't indicate which years, the information is not of much value." A good example to look at is *Anbar Management Services Abstracts*. These abstracts are indicative abstracts with critical comments italicized in the abstracts.

An indicative abstract simply describes what type of record is being abstracted and what it is about. This kind of abstract is generally used on general papers with broad overviews, on reviews, and on monographs, but is also used for single papers. In most cases, the indicative abstract is somewhat shorter, is written in general terms, and does not give the user a progressive account of the paper's development. It has often been described as an alerting device and is never expected to replace the paper itself. It guides users to the paper by telling them what can be found there. However, to do this, the abstract cannot be too general. It must give essential information, such as the purpose of the paper and the results.

An *informative* abstract tries to present as much quantitative and qualitative data as it can. This type is the most useful for documents reporting on experimental investigations. It abridges the principal ideas and facts and contains actual data. Informative abstracts have been compared to a skeleton with all the flesh missing—the viewer is given enough detail to accurately reconstruct what the departed soul must have looked like. The user should not have to retrieve the paper for further information, since such things as formulas, statistical results, and parts of tables are often included in the abstract.

The *critical* abstract is generally recognized as a third type of abstract, although it is questionable if it is indeed a third category. If it is heavily editorial, it cannot convey much basic information and is really a review of the document rather than a true indicator of document content. Some abstractors feel strongly that a good abstract avoids the bias and personal viewpoint of critical comment, and that the abstractor, whose job is solely to reveal content, should be remote and invisible in the final product. It is difficult enough to keep bias out—why deliberately introduce it?

On the other hand, information professionals sense a growing need for new techniques that will allow more complex and in-depth analysis and synthesis of information. Information funding agencies, such as the National Library of Medicine, are calling for research in this direction. Such techniques will include more and more qualitative evaluation at the indexing and abstracting stages of bibliographic control. So, the future for critical abstract writing appears to be very strong. There is a need for sophisticated methods. The traditional, bland (just state the facts) type of abstracting will become unacceptable.

Not all people agree with the idea that an abstract can properly take the place of reading the paper. Many feel that it is presumptuous to think that a 150- to 250-word abstract can carry enough information from a well-written 3,000-word paper to be of much use except as a guide. The inclusion of data merely serves to let the user have a better indication of what will be found in the paper. It alerts users to the existence of new data and gives them an indication of what that data is like, but it is not to be used as an original source.

An informative abstract should cover four essential points: (1) objective and scope of the work, (2) methods used, (3) results, and (4) conclusions. Item (1) is important because it may allow users to determine, without reading any more of the abstract, that they have no use for the paper. Item (2) must cover equipment used and all the methodological details so that the user will gain a good understanding of the investigation.

Although many abstracts are clearly either indicative or informative, in actual practice they are often combined and perform both an indicative and an informative function. Indexing and abstracting services often indicate that the abstracting will be indicative, informative, or a combination of both, according to the nature of the material being abstracted.

Actually, all three types of abstracts serve useful purposes, although the most popular one, and probably the most important one, is the informative type. A vast majority of abstracting results in informative abstracts, since a majority of abstractable materials lend themselves to this form. On the other hand, reviews, books, essays, and the like lend themselves to indicative abstracts and occasionally to critical ones. Once again, the type of material and the eventual users are the basis for a decision on which type of abstract should be used.

At this point it might be well to enlarge on the example given at the beginning of this section. The following are fictitious abstracts, illustrating the various types.

Indicative

"Onion Raising in California." Homer Disraeli. *Agriculture Happenings*, v. 201, no. 2 (April 1989), pages 7-19.

Deals with all aspects of the onion crop in California and touches onion production in other states, mainly for comparative purposes. All types of onions are discussed, with figures given for each category and for the total production. There are breakdowns for how much of the product is consumed in the state and how much is exported. There is also a detailed discussion of (1) farming techniques, (2) wholesale practices, (3) transportation, and (4) general economics of the onion business. A large portion of the paper is devoted to the social and medicinal implications of eating onions.

Informative

"Onion Raising in California." Homer Disraeli. *Agriculture Happenings*, v. 201, no. 2 (April 1989), pages 7-19.

According to this article, California raised 170,000,019 onions, while its closest competitors, Oregon and Texas, combined could manage only 70,000,017 onions. Rhode Island was almost out of contention with a little over 2 million. Big, white, sweet onions are the best sellers, with yellow onions second, and small green onions close behind. Some 120 million white onions, 30 million yellow onions, and 20 million little green onions were put on the market. Californians consumed 70,000,035 of these onions, with the rest being placed on the out-of-state market. Most onion farming is highly mechanical and is done by large-scale farming enterprises. The main mode of transportation is by truck, although some is by rail and a minute part by Ford station wagon. The onion business is economically stable and is generally a money-maker. According to the article, persons who eat onions with every meal have a life expectancy of some 1% above the national average, but they are invited to only 20% as many parties, and their divorce expectancy is 200% above the national average.

Critical

"Onion Raising in California." Homer Disraeli. *Agriculture Happenings*, v. 201, no. 2 (April 1989), pages 7-19.

Deals with all aspects of the onion crop in California and discusses various aspects of the crop, from farming to consumption. Although many figures and "facts" are given, important details are missing. For example, the author never says *what year* he is talking about, thus making the figures meaningless. A check of *Statistical Abstracts* showed no figures comparable to those of the author. The paper discusses the farming techniques, transportation, and economics of the onion industry. A large part of the paper deals with the social consequences of heavy onion eating and with the medicinal benefits, but it does not support the claims with any reliable data.

Although it is useful to describe these different types of abstracts, in actual practice any particular abstract often does not fall neatly into any one of the categories. The nature and amount of information will vary according to the length of the document, the importance of its information, and the abstracting policies being followed.

By External Purpose

Another way to classify abstracts is by external purpose: discipline-oriented, mission-oriented, or slanted. Any one of these may be indicative, informative, or critical in their internal construction.

When an abstract is written for a specific area of knowledge (e.g., mathematics), it is said to be *discipline-oriented*. When it is written to support application activities that may or may not be interdisciplinary in nature, it is a *mission-oriented* abstract. A mission-oriented group is defined in terms of an assignment rather than a subject area. The *slanted* abstract is often a form of the mission-oriented abstract and is one that highlights or concentrates on a selected portion of a document's subject content. For example, a paper that discusses diseases in dogs, cats, and chickens might have only the part about dogs abstracted if the user group is doing research on diseases in dogs.

By Author

Abstracts may be written by three fundamental groups: authors of the papers, subject area experts, or professional abstractors. The ideal abstractor would probably be the author of the paper who is a recognized expert in the subject and has training and years of experience in writing abstracts. Obviously, relatively few abstracts are written by such rare individuals.

On first thought, it might appear that an author would be the best person, since presumably the author knows more about the paper than anybody else. However, authors do not necessarily make good abstractors. It is somewhat analogous to a playwright who takes the lead part in the play, although someone else might be a much better interpreter of the writer's work. On the positive side, author-prepared abstracts are on time, since they generally accompany the manuscript, and they are cheaper, since no additional expense is necessary if the author's abstract is used. A number of indexing and abstracting services give their abstractors the option of using author indexes published with the papers if they judge them to be satisfactory. On the negative side, authors generally are not versed in the procedures and methods for writing good abstracts and do not have the experience required to do a good job. Equally serious, authors often are too close to the paper to give it an objective treatment. Authors can fail to see that what they think is important may not necessarily be the most important information for the user. Authors as abstractors have been known to use their abstracts to promote the paper; this can create a misleading abstract and is unfair to the user. The upshot has been that author-prepared abstracts vary considerably in quality.

Many abstracting journals rely on subject specialists, who are not professional abstractors but are professionals in their subject, to write abstracts. If these experts are trained and experienced in the procedures and methods of abstracting, they generally produce excellent, high-quality abstracts. An outstanding example is *Excerpta Medica*, which relies extensively on experts in the health sciences field. A few cautions are in order, however, in using subject experts. In the first place, the expert may not be absolutely expert in all the ramifications of an area, especially if he or she is assigned topics across a wide range of the subject. For example, there are specialized areas of mathematics that other highly competent mathematicians know absolutely nothing about, and they would be unable to follow even a proof in that area. Also, it must be remembered that since experts represent the establishment in a subject area, they may be intellectually reluctant to accept an offbeat new idea from an upstart young author. It is also possible that the paper was written by a professional opponent whose views are diametrically opposite to those of the abstractor. Obviously, such factors can affect the results.

The third group consists of full-time professional abstractors. Generally speaking, it is easier for a subject expert to be trained in abstracting than to make a professional abstractor competent in a subject field, but professional abstractors, as a group, produce high-quality abstracts, especially if they are assigned to areas with which they have become familiar. Although professional abstractors demand higher wages, they do the work on time, often have foreign language expertise, and can cover areas in which subject experts cannot be found.

In chapter III a list of representative indexes was given, which the reader was encouraged to examine to become familiar with the different types. Following is a list of representative abstracting tools, and once again the reader is urged to examine these examples and others.

Biological Abstracts. Philadelphia: BIOSIS, 1926- . (See examples 27-30.)

This service monitors approximately 9000 serials from over 100 countries. References are arranged into broad subject categories. Four indexes allow access to citations using author name, biosystematic grouping, genus name, and subject terms.

(Text continues on page 172.)

ABSTRACTS

AEROSPACE AND UNDERWATER BIOLOGICAL EFFECTS

ECOLOGY AND PSYCHOLOGY

12324. LEIMANN PATT, HUGO O. (Prevent. Med. Branch, Natl. Inst. Aviataion and Space Med., Belisario Roldan 4651, Buenos Aires, Argent.) AVIAT SPACE ENVIRON MED 59(10): 955–959. 1988. **The right and wrong stuff in civil aviation.**— Aircrewmembers (ACMs) enter a mortally hostile environment when they take off from Earth in their flying machines. Their physiological adaptation has been augmented and supported through ergonomics, avionics, and engineering, but no such technological aid helps them adopt their minds to that atypical condition. They must rely upon their own psychic resources, i.e. "aeronautical motivation" in the three levels of consciousness, and defense mechanisms to counteract their "aeronautica: anxiety. \ arious relatio ıships oi motivation and defense give rise either to the flying adaptation syndrome or the various forms of the secondary flying disadaptation syndrome when ACMs must face the dangers of flight. These alterations of the ACMs' psychic balance may cause temporary or permanent medical disqualification due to the impairment of safety which they provoke. This paper proposes an analysis of the interplay between motivation, psychic defenses, and aviation stress to explain the manifestations of flight adaptation and disadaptation seen in some aircrewmembers.

PHYSIOLOGY AND MEDICINE

12325. OKUDA, SHINYA*, SHIGEAKI MATSUOKA and MOTOHIKO MOHRI. (Dep. Neurosurg., Sch. Med., Univ. Occupational and Environmental Health, Japan, Kitakyushu, 807 Japan.) J UOEH 10(3): 247–262. 1988. [In Engl. with Engl. and Jpn. summ.] **Topographic electroencephalographic studies in a hyperbaric environment: Specific reference to high pressure nervous syndrome.**—Hyperbaric chamber dives at various equivalent depths below sea level, i.e. 7, 14, 19 and 31 atmosphere absolute (ATA) with helium–oxygen or helium–nitrogen–oxygen have been performed at the Japan Marine Science and Technology Center. A two–dimensional (topographic) disply of the scalp EEG was used during simulated underwater experiments to determine; (1) Whether there are any characteristic EEG patterns in high pressure nervous syndrome (HPNS), (2) the relationship between the EEG changes and the compression rate, and (3) the relationship between the EEG changes and the characteristic signs and symptoms of HPNS. A two–way analysis of variance and a distribution analysis technique revealed that the topographic brain patterns depended on the diving depth and indicated the most affected brain areas during compression and decompression. Significant correlations between the diving depth and the EEG potentials were observed at different brain locations. Alpha waves showed a diffuse cortical distribution. Theta wave activity was more localized in the frontal midline region. These waves developed paroxysmally in relatively brief bursts supplanting or intermixing with normal background EEG rhythms. In our subjects, frontal midline theta activity was associated mostly with some of the characteristic features of HPNS, such as a transient episode of laughter or euphoria at depths greater than 21 ATA. An intimate correlation between frontal midline theta wave and laughter was observed. Frontal midline theta waves may be related to emotional activities induced by helium under high pressure. There were significant individual variations in susceptibility and subjective signs and symptoms. The EEG is of great value in studying man's physiological reactions in an undersea environment and also very important in selecting divers who are relatively more tolerant of a severe hyperbaric environment.

Example 27. *Biological Abstracts* (main entry). (Copyright Biological Abstracts, Inc. [BIOSIS®]. Reproduced with permission.)

Biol Abstr 88(12):GI-1

A

Genus-species	Major Concept	Ref. No.
ABEDUS-INDENTATUS	BEHAV ANIMAL	126848
ABELIA	ECOL ANIMAL	128845
	FLOWER HORT	130619
ABIES-ALBA	PL DIS OTHER	134856
	PL DIS OTHER	134857
ABIES-CONCOLOR	ECOL PLANT	128988
	PALYNOLOGY	133670
ABIES-FIRMA	FORESTRY	129859
ABIES-GRANDIS	PL NUTRITION	135132
ABIES-MAGNIFICA	ECOL PLANT	128988
ABIES-PINDROW	FORESTRY	129880
ABUTILON-THEOPHRASTI	ECOL PLANT	126584
ACACIA-CAVEN	ECOL PLANT	129045
	ECOL PLANT	129046
ACACIA-MYRTIFOLIA	BEHAV ANIMAL	126851
ACACIA-PULCHELLA	ECOL PLANT	129052
ACACIA-VERTICILLATA	ECOL PLANT	129050
ACANTHASPIS-PEDESTRIS	INSECT MORPH	131266
ACANTHEPHYRA-PURPUREA	CRUSTAC SYST	131435
ACANTHOCYCLOPS-ROBUSTUS	CRUSTAC SYST	131440
ACANTHODIAPTOMUS-DENTICORNIS	CRUSTAC SYST	131440
ACANTHOGOBIUS-FLAVIMANUS	ASCHEL SYST	131562
ACANTHOPANAX	DICOT SYST	127457
	PHARM CV	133883
ACANTHOPANAX-GRACIUSTYLUS	INSECT SYST	133883
ACANTHOPHILA-LATIPENELLA	ECOL ANIMAL	131495*R
ACANTHOPLEURA-JAPONICA	ECOL ANIMAL	128881
ACANTHURUS-NIGRICANS	ECOL ANIMAL	128854
ACANTHURUS-XANTHOPTERUS	CRUSTAC EXPT	128854
ACARTIA-TONSA	PL DIS OTHER	131248
ACER-OPALUS	TOXIC GEN	134851
ACER-PSEUDOPLATANUS	LIMNOLOGY	136889
ACER-SACCHARUM	BAC PHAGE	128964
ACETOBACTER-METHANOLICUS	FD MICR FOOD	137215
ACETOBACTER-XYLINUM	BAC PHYSL	129656
ACETOBACTERIUM-WOODII	INSECT PHYSL	134654
ACHAEA-JANATA	MOLLUSC EXPT	131302
ACHATINA	MOLLUSC EXPT	131356
ACHATINA-FULICA	PHARM NEURO	131359
	PHARMAC BOT	134450
ACHILLEA-MILLEFOLIUM	PL CHEM CNST	133790
	PL GROWTH	134933
ACHLYA-BISEXUALIS	FD MICR DET	135046
ACHROMOBACTER	GENET BAC VI	129591
ACIDIPHILIUM-FACILIS	CHEMO BAC	130052
ACINETOBACTER-ANITRATUM	GENET BAC VI	128097
	GENET BAC VI	129994
ACINETOBACTER-CALCOACETICUS	PH VECT ANIM	130025
ACINETOBACTER-CALCOACETICUS-		135560

Genus-species	Major Concept	Ref. No.
AGROBACTERIUM-RHIZOGENES	FLOWER HORT	130610
	PL DIS MISC	134818
	PL METB	135086
AGROBACTERIUM-TUMEFACIENS	CROPS GRAIN	126537
	GENET BAC VI	130015
	GENET BAC VI	130019
	GENET BAC VI	130024
	GENET PLANT	130081
	GENET PLANT	130522
	PL DIS MISC	134817
	PL DIS MISC	134818
	PL DIS RESIS	135086
AGROPYRON-CRISTATUM	CROPS FORAGE	126439
AGROPYRON-RIPARIUM	SOIL PHY CHM	136542
AGROSTIS	SOIL MICRO	136621
AGROSTIS-VINEALIS	ECOL PLANT	129084
AGROTIS-SEGETUM	ENT FLD CROP	129192
AGYNETA-RAMOSA	ARACHN SYST	131409*R
AHAETULLA-NASUTA	REPT SYST	128272
AJUGA-DECUMBENS	ENT BIO CONT	129151
AKATOPORA-CIRCUMSAEPTA	ECTOP SYST	131574
ALBIZIA-FALCATARIA	FORESTRY	129878
ALBIZIA-LEBBEK	CROPS FORAGE	126448
ALCALIGENES	BAC PHYSL	134648
	FD MICR DET	129591
ALCES-ALCES	ECOL ANIMAL	129597
ALCHEMILLA	FLOR DISTRIB	128891
ALCHEMILLA-BABIOGORENSIS	FLOR DISTRIB	127511
ALCHEMILLA-DE'LII	FLOR DISTRIB	127511*R
ALCHEMILLA-FIRMA	FLOR DISTRIB	127511
ALCHEMILLA-FISSA	FLOR DISTRIB	127511
ALCHEMILLA-GORCENSIS	FLOR DISTRIB	127511*R
ALCHEMILLA-INCISA	FLOR DISTRIB	127511
ALCHEMILLA-ZAPALOWICZII	FLOR DISTRIB	127511
ALDROVANDA	DICOT SYST	127509
ALECTORIS-GRAECA	IMMUN BAC VI	130799
ALEURITES-FORDII	PHARMAC BOT	133780
ALLACOPHORA-FOVEICOLLIS	PL CHEM CNST	134954
ALLIUM	PL CHEM CNST	134927
ALLIUM-CEPA	PL CHEM CNST	128372
	PL CHEM CNST	134934
	PL CHEM CNST	134869
	VEGETAB HORT	130703
ALLIUM-SATIVUM	PL DIS CONT	134711
ALLOCHERNES-LWA	ARACHN SYST	131410*S
ALLOTEUTHIS	MOLLUSC SYST	131596
ALNUS	FD SUGAR	129849
ALNUS-GLUTINOSA	ENT TREE WD	129238
	PL CHEM CNST	129238
	FORESTRY	129873
ALNUS-INCANA		

ABEDUS- to ARISTOLOCHIA-

Genus-species	Major Concept	Ref. No.
ANASTREPHA-FRATERCULUS	ENT FRUITS	129195
ANAULUS-AUSTRALIS	ECOL PLANT	129055
ANAULUS-BIROSTRATUS	ECOL PLANT	129055
ANCYLOSTOMA-CANINUM	CHEMO PARAST	128131
ANCYLOSTOMA-DUODENALE	ASCHEL EXPT	131333
ANEMONE-CORONARIA	FLOWER HORT	130609
ANEMONE-RADDEANA	PHARMAC BOT	133814
ANGELICA-DAHURICA	DICOT SYST	127456
ANGUILLA-ANGUILLA	NERV ANAT	133028
	PISCES SYST	128259
ANNAMANUM	COLEOP SYST	131470
ANODONTA-CYGNEA	MOLLUSC EXPT	131380
ANOLIS-CAROLINENSIS	ENDOCR PINL	129386
ANOMALA-CUPREA	ENT BIO CONT	129149
ANONYX-NUGAX	ECOL ANIMAL	128852
ANOPHELES-ALBIMANUS	INSECT PHYSL	131290
ANOPHELES-DARLINGI	ENT AN PESTS	129128
ANOPHELES-QUADRIMACULATUS	PH DISINFECT	135570
ANOPHELES-SPP	DIPTERA SYST	131489
ANOPLOCEPHALA-PERFOLIATA	ENT AN PESTS	129127
ANOPLOPHORA	PARAST VET	133724
ANOPLOPHORA-CHINENSIS	COLEOP SYST	131470
ANOPLOPHORA-DAVIDIS	COLEOP SYST	131470
ANOPLOPHORA-GLABRIPENNIS	COLEOP SYST	131470
ANOPLOPHORA-HORSFIELDI	COLEOP SYST	131470
ANOPLOPHORA-IMITATRIX	COLEOP SYST	131470
ANOPLOPHORA-LEECHI	COLEOP SYST	131470
ANOPLOPHORA-MACULARIA	COLEOP SYST	131470
ANOPLOPHORA-NOBILIS	COLEOP SYST	131470
ANOPLOPHORA-VERSTEEGI	COLEOP SYST	131470
ANOUS-MINUTUS	AVES SYST	128224*R
	ECOL ANIMAL	128863
ANTEON-EPHIPPIGER	HYMENOP SYST	131504
ANTHERAEA-PERNYI	INSECT PHYSL	131292
ANTHERAEA-POLYPHEMUS	INSECT PHYSL	131308
ANTHERAEA-PROYLEI	INSECT PHYSL	131304
ANTHERAEA-YAMAMAI	ENT SERICLT	129220
ANTHRONIA-ANOMBROPHILA	LICHEN SYST	127573*S
ANTHROPOIDES-VIRGO	VIRUS AN	137191
ANTIRRHINUM-MAJUS	GENET PLANT	130550
	GENET PLANT	130588
ANTRICOLA	ACARINA SYST	130419
AOTUS-TRIVIRGATUS	GENET HUMAN	130410
APANTELES	HYMENOP SYST	131506
APANTELES-ASAVARI	HYMENOP SYST	131506*S
APANTELES-SP	LEPIDOP SYST	131526
APHELENCHOIDES-COMPOSTICOLA	PL DIS CONT	134732
APHIS-GOSSYPII	ENT TREE WD	129239
APHODIUS	COLEOP SYST	131462
APHODIUS-ANTHONYI	COLEOP SYST	131462*S
APHODIUS-INCOMMODUS	COLEOP SYST	131462*S

Example 28. *Biological Abstracts* (genus name index). (Copyright Biological Abstracts, Inc. [BIOSIS®]. Reproduced with permission.)

ORGANISMS
Ecology, General
46319
Pharmacological Metabolism
51911

MICROORGANISMS
Animal Production, Feeds, Feeding
44140
Animal Production, General
44155 44160 44161 44162
Anthropology, Physical; Ethnobiology
52344
Bacteriology, Medical and Veterinary
49336 49369
Blood Cell Studies
44472
Blood Vessel Pathology
45054
Blood, Hematopoietic Agents, Pharmacology
51686
Blood, Lymphatic, Reticuloendothial Pathologies
44539
Cancer Therapy
50704
Carcinogens, Carcinogenesis
49874
Chemotherapy, General
45604 45606 45610 45611 45612
45613 45614 45615
Digestive Pathology
46016 46101
Ecology, Animal
46211 46241
Environmental and Industrial Toxicology
54156 54194
Epidemiology, Communicable Diseases
53344
Food Spoilage and Contamination
47107 47111
Forestry, Forest Products
47224 47247 47253 47260
Immunopathology
48480 48496 48558 48603 48679
Industrial Microbiology, Biodegradation, Deterioration
47060
Insecta, Physiology
48904
Integumentary Pharmacology
52078

● **Pedoviridae**
Genetics, Bacteria, Viruses
47519
● **Styloviridae**
Bacteriophage Studies
54576 54578
Genetics, Bacteria, Viruses
47392 47432 47454 47467 47476
Nucleic Acids, Purines, Pyrimidines, Biochemical Methods
44273
Virology, Animal Host
54561

Animal Viruses
● **Animal Viruses—Unspecified**
Blood, Hematopoietic Agents, Pharmacology
Blood, Lymphatic, Reticuloendothial Pathologies
54542
Cancer Pathology, Clinical Aspects, Systemic Effects
50494
Cancer Therapy
50637
Digestive Pathology
46048
Digestive Pharmacology
51870
Economic Entomology, Biological Control
46648
Epidemiology, Communicable Diseases
53349 53358 53372
Epidemiology, Organic Disease, Neoplasms
53436
Food Technology, Meat, Meat By-products
Genetics, Bacteria, Viruses
47394 47463
Genetics, Cytogenetics, Animal
47819
Immunology, Bacterial, Viral, Fungal
48321 48365
Immunopathology
48490 48565
Pharmacology, General
52029
Virology, Animal Host
54565 54567
Virology, Medical and Veterinary
49435 49437 49451 49465 49466
49484

Immunology, Allergy, Pharmacology
52072 52073
Immunology, Bacterial, Viral, Fungal
48320 48337 48338 48342 48344
48354 48372 48386
Immunology, General
48436 48458
Immunopathology
48510 48534 48566 48654
Lymphatic Tissue, Reticuloendothelial System
44607
Radiation Health
53281
Sense Organ Pharmacology
52326
Serodiagnosis, Medical and Veterinary Microbiology
49410
Virology, Animal Host
54555 54559 54572
Virology, Medical and Veterinary
49415 49418 49422 49427 49434
49439 49440 49443 49448 49449
49452 49457 49458 49478 49480
49482 49497

● **Orthomyxoviridae**
Epidemiology, Communicable Diseases
53355
Genetics, Bacteria, Viruses
47456 47501
Immunology, Bacterial, Viral, Fungal
48325 48339 48341 48343 48382
Microbiology, Medical and Veterinary, General
49387
Serodiagnosis, Medical and Veterinary Microbiology
49411
Virology, Animal Host
54563
Virology, Medical and Veterinary
49420 49477

● **Papovaviridae**
Cancer Immunology
50394
Carcinogens, Carcinogenesis
49775 49787 49799 49800 49869
49980 50002 50061 50063 50065
50066 50072 50080 50176 50177
50220 50233 50243 50245 50246
50247 50249 50254

Example 29. *Biological Abstracts* (biosystematic index). (Copyright Biological Abstracts, Inc. [BIOSIS®]. Reproduced with permission.)

MEETING

103061. SWANN, JOHN W. and ANNE MESSER (Ed.). (Birth Defects Inst., Wadsworth Cent. Lab. Res., New York State Dep. Health, Albany, N.Y.) Alan R. Liss, Inc.: New York, New York, USA. Illus. ISBN 0–8451–4265–8. xiii + 277p. 1988. Albany Birth Defects Symposium, 18. Disorders of the developing nervous system: Changing views of their origins, diagnoses, and treatments; Albany, New York, USA, September 28–29, 1987./BOOK

PAPERS

103062. NELSON, KARIN B. (Neuroepidemiol. Branch, Natl. Inst. Neurol. Communicative Disorders Stroke, Bethesda, Md.) 1–18. **Antecedents of cerebral palsy and childhood seizure disorders.**/HUMAN, CONGENITAL MALFORMATION, PRENATAL INJURY

103063. SWANN, JOHN W., ROBERT J. BRADY, KAREN L. SMITH and MARTHA G. PIERSON. (Wadsworth Cent. Lab. Res., N.Y. State Dep. Health, Empire State Plaza, P.O. Box 509, Albany, N.Y. 12201–0509.) 19–50. **Synaptic mechanisms of focal epileptogenesis in the immature nervous system.**/RAT, GAMMA–AMINOBUTYRIC ACID

103064. CHUGANI, HARRY T.*, MICHAEL E. PHELPS and DION BARNES*. (Dep. Neurol., UCLA Sch. Med., Los Angeles, Calif.) 51–68. **PET in normal and abnormal brain development.**/CHILDREN, POSITRON EMISSION TOMOGRAPHY, LENNOX–GASTAUT SYNDROME, REFRACTORY PARTIAL EPILEPSY, CEREBRAL PALSY

103065. JOHNSTON, MICHAEL V.*, JOHN W. MCDONALD and FAYE SILVERSTEIN*. (Dep. Pediatr., Univ. Mich. Med. Sch., Neurosci. Lab. Build., 1103 E. Huron, Ann Arbor, Mich.) 69–92. **Role of synaptic mechanisms in hypoxic–ischemic brain injury and birth defects.**/RAT, HUMAN, ENCEPHALOPATHY, NEUROTRANSMITTERS

103066. COURCHESNE, ERIC. (Neuropsychol. Res. Lab., Child. Hosp. Res. Cent., 8001 Frost St., San Diego, Calif. 92123.) 93–110. **Cerebellar changes in autism.**/HUMAN, PURKINJE CELL

103067. MESSER, ANNE*, BONNIE EISENBERG and DAVID L. MARTIN*. (Sch. Public Health Sci., State Univ. N.Y., Albany, N.Y. 12201.) 111–124. **The role of timing and cell interactions in cerebellar development.**/MOUSE, PURKINJE CELL, MUTATION

103068. KEMPER, THOMAS L. (Dep. Neurol., Med. 9, Boston City Hosp., 818 Harrison Ave., Boston, Mass. 02118.) 125–154. **Neuroanatomic studies of dyslexia and autism.**/HUMAN

Example 30. *Biological Abstracts* RRM (Reports, Reviews, Meetings). (Copyright Biological Abstracts, Inc. [BIOSIS®]. Reproduced with permission.)

Chemical Abstracts. Columbus, Ohio: American Chemical Society, 1907- . (See examples 31 and 32.)

This very comprehensive abstracting tool publishes over 500,000 abstracts per year. It has an author index, a numerical patents index, and a keyword index in the weekly issues. The semiannual volumes have a chemical substance index, a general subject index, a formula index, an index of ring systems, an author index, and a patent index. This is an example of a comprehensive indexing and abstracting service.

Dissertation Abstracts International. Ann Arbor, Mich.: University Microfilms International, 1938- . (See examples 33 and 34.)

The abstracts are of doctoral dissertations submitted for microfilming to University Microfilms. The basic list is arranged alphabetically by subject field and then by university. There is also an author index and a subject index. These are good examples of author-prepared abstracts.

Excerpta Medica. Amsterdam: Excerpta Medica, 1947- . (See example 35.)

This is a major abstracting service for the medical literature. The primary coverage is human medicine and the supporting basic sciences, although there is some coverage of related medical subjects, such as nursing. It is published in sections, covering particular specialties, and some abstracts will appear in more than one section when it is appropriate. There are author and subject indexes, which cumulate annually.

Fertilizer Abstracts. Muscle Shoals, Ala.: Tennessee Valley Authority, National Fertilizer Development Center, Technical Library, 1968- .

This is an example of an abstracting journal in a specialized field and published primarily for a mission-oriented research group. The abstracts appear in three basic parts: technology, marketing, and use.

Historical Abstracts. Santa Barbara, Calif.: Clio Press, 1955- . (See example 36.)

These abstracts are written by scholars in the field and are signed. The publication has a classified arrangement with annual author, biographical, geographical, and subject indexes.

Mathematical Reviews. Providence, R.I.: American Mathematical Society, 1940- . (See examples 37-39.)

This is a good example of critical abstracts that are signed by the reviewer. The critical comments in the illustrations are typical of this journal. Coverage includes both pure and applied mathematics. It is arranged by subject with a detailed table of contents showing the subjects. Author and key indexes are included.

Physics Abstracts. London: Institution of Electrical Engineers, 1898- . (See examples 40 and 41.)

This heavily used abstracting tool is an example of broad coverage, e.g., bibliographies, books patents, reports, conference proceedings, reports, periodicals, and dissertations. The basic arrangement is by subject classification, with author and subject indexes and indexes to the types of materials covered.

(Text continues on page 184.)

1—PHARMACOLOGY

C. PAUL BIANCHI

This section includes the biochemical, physiological, and toxic effects of drugs or potential drugs, their metabolism. analysis in biological systems, and structure-activity relations. Drug formulations are included in Section 63; analysis of drug formulations appears in Section 64; the pharmacology of hormones and agents affecting reproduction, e.g., contraceptives, in Section 2; radiopharmaceuticals, in Section 8; effects of antibiotics, bactericides, etc., on microorganisms in vitro are placed in Section 10; studies emphasizing the synthesis of drugs are included in the appropriate synthetic organic or inorganic section; drugs used only as investigative or diagnostic tools appear in the section appropriate to the organism or process under investigation.

110: 204859m **Correlations between phencyclidine-like activity and N-methyl-D-aspartate antagonism: behavioral evidence.** Koek, W.; Woods, J. H. (Dep. Pharmacol., Univ. Michigan, Ann Arbor, MI 48109 USA). *Sigma Phencyclidine-like Compd. Mol. Probes Biol.,* [*Proc. U.S.–Fr. Sponsored Int. Semin.], 2nd* 1987 (Pub. 1988), 357–72 (Eng). Edited by Domino, Edward F.; Kamenka, Jean-Marc. NPP Books: Ann Arbor, Mich. A review with 54 refs.

110: 204860e **Biochemical mechanisms of the biological activity of alkylxanthines.** Kulinskii, V. I. (Krasnoyarsk. Gos. Med. Inst., Krasnoyarsk, USSR). *Usp. Sourem. Biol.* 1988, 106(3), 347–62 (Russ). A review with 139 refs., discussing the inhibition of cAMP phosphodiesterase, adenosine receptor blockade, and other possible mechanisms involved in the action of alkylxanthines (esp. Me analogs).

110: 204861f **Kidney disease, proteinase, and proteinase inhibitors.** Nakayama, Shuei; Koide, Hikaru (Med. Sch., Juntendo Univ., Japan). *Chiryogaku* 1988, 21(5), 625–30 (Japan). A review with 21 refs., on rules of proteinases and proteinase inhibitors, esp. chymopapain, subtilisin, gabexate mesilate, and camostat mesilate, in pathogenesis and therapy of kidney diseases, esp. glomerulonephritis.

110: 204869q **Lovastatin: An HMG–CoA reductase inhibitor for lowering cholesterol.** Frishman, William H.; Rapier, Roderick C. (Albert Einstein Coll. Med., Hosp. Albert Einstein Coll. Med., Bronx, NY USA). *Med. Clin. North Am.* 1989, 73(2), 437–48 (Eng). A review with 46 refs. examg. the assocn. between total cholesterol, low-d. cholesterol, and very-low-d. cholesterol and heart disease and the pharmacol. of lovastatin, which lowers serum cholesterol levels.

110: 204870h **Cocaine-induced coronary artery disease: Rec= ognition and treatment.** Frishman, William H.; Karpenos, Alexander; Molloy, Thomas J. (Albert Einstein Coll. Med., Hosp. Albert Einstein Coll. Med., Bronx, NY USA). *Med. Clin. North Am.* 1989, 73(2), 475–86 (Eng). A review with 62 refs. examg. the pharmacol, effects on the sympathetic nervous system, cardiovascular effects, and cardiovascular complications of cocaine use.

110: 204871j **Computer modeling of anthracycline– and anthr= aquinone–DNA interactions.** Brown, Jeffrey R.; Neidle, Stephen (Fac. Pharm. Sci., Sunderland Polytech., Sunderland, UK SR1 35D). *Bioact. Mol.* 1988, 6(Anthracycline Anthracenedione–Based Anticancer Agents), 335–69 (Eng). A review with 79 refs.

Example 31. *Chemical Abstracts* (main entry). (Reprinted with permission of Chemical Abstracts Service.)

A
  23187 heart electrophysiol calcium
    205370g
  23187 lung bronchi constriction 205403v
Ab
  initio cyclopropane fluoro 211763d
  initio dimethylbenzamide ortholithiation
    211737y
  initio ion mol reaction 211830y
  initio mol electrostatic potential
    211750x
  initio MP2 hydride transfer 211753a
ABA
  biosynthesis corn embryo xanthophyll
    209411u
Abnormal
  Hb human structure detn 208769e
  Hb phenotype review 210069v
Abortifacient
  RU 486 aromatase inhibitor 205971d
Abortion
  epostane 205972a
  gonadienone deriv P 213172j
  RU 486 review 205766r
Abs
  configuration aurovertin B 213210v
  configuration CD acyclic triol 211792n
  configuration isoquinuclidine carbometh=

Acanthopanax
  biocem constituent seasonal variation
    209362d
Acaracide
  milbemycin prepn P 212499j
Acaricide
  benzoylthienylurea prepn P 212601m
  benzyl propyl ether P 212342c
  detn honey gas chromatog 211108u
  household cyhexatin carboeulfan bromo=
    propylate P 207848t
  methylaminophenylpyrazole prepn
    P 212815j
  nicotinaldehyde aryldithiohydrazone
    prepn P 212616v
  Rhipicephalus 207779w
  sulfonamide deriv P 207856u
  triazinylthiophosphorylurea 212931u
Acceptor
  donor electron transfer review 211690c
Accessory
  cell T lymphocyte antigen 210739p
  dendritic cell interleukin 1 210605a
  gland male Drosophila protein sequence
    206856a
  gland proctolinergic innervation cricket
    209638y
Accident

Acetanilide
  atrazine resin secretion stimulant
    P 207829n
  bromination P 212389y
Acetate
  aminomethylenecyano intermediate
    prepn P 212152r
  bridged palladium complex 213030m
  catalyst oxidn acetaldehyde P 212136p
  glycerin bacon curing P 211290x
  magnesium tilapia feeding expt 211362x
  nitrile deoxyhexosulose 211133y
  olfaction age Pseudaletia 209595g
  tetradecanoyl phorbol inducible gene
    mouse 206975v
Acetatobistrimethylsilylmethyltungsten
  complex 212993r
Acetatocyclohexylstannane
  solvolysis kinetics trifluoroethanol
    212967k
Acetazolamide
  anticonvulsant tolerance brain carbonic
    anhydrase 205501a
Acetic
  acid 212086x
  acid additive acyloxyalkylarene oxidn
    P 213374q
  acid bacteria vinegar manuf P 211297e

Acetonylpyran
  tolylthiopropanal aldol stereochem
    212438p
Acetophenone
  condensation azafluorenone phenacylide=
    neazafluorene 212585j
  hydroxynaphthylimino 212310r
  semicarbazone IR 211960r
Acetorphan
  analgesia brain electrostimulation
    205560u
Acetoxyacetylaminofluorene
  lymphoblast cell cycle death 205572y
Acetoxyalkanoic
  acid enantioselective hydrolysis catalyst
    212096a
Acetoxybenzoic
  acid P 213374q
Acetoxybutenyl
  allylamine intramol cyclization palladium
    212533t
Acetoxydienyl
  amine intramol cyclization palladium
    212533t
Acetoxyhydroxyethylazetidinone
  prepn antibiotic intermediate
    P 212454a
Acetoxylation ˙

Example 32. *Chemical Abstracts* (keyword index). (Reprinted with permission of Chemical Abstracts Service.)

COMMUNICATIONS AND THE ARTS

ARCHITECTURE

High rise office buildings in the Transvaal, 1950–1976: A study of their form-giving factors. Brittan, Philip, D.Arch. *University of Pretoria (South Africa),* 1988. Promoter: D. Holm

Although Broadbent's four form-giving factors—pragmatic, iconic, analogic and canonic—were found to be interrelated, it was established that the icon dominated as a form-giving factor in high-rise office building design of this period.

Initially the Chicago School skyscraper was the model, followed by the commercial stepped New York model. These were replaced by Mies van der Rohe's Alexanderplatz icon as built in the much publicized American glass curtain-wall Lever House and Seagram's Building. Alternatively Le Corbusier's Barcelona project icon, as built in the Brazilian Ministry of Education and Health Building, was followed. All these icons were built and published prior to the Transvaal high-rise period.

Pragmatic form-giving factors like safety, comfort, established practice, building technology, energy and cost were overruled by the iconic symbols of progress, power and prestige. Surprisingly even townplanning regulations were redrawn to accommodate building icons.

Canonic form-giving factors appeared in the form of standard, repetitive modules, not as differentiated proportional designs. These repetitive grid modules were both part of the high-rise icon and pragmatically convenient.

Analogic form-giving factors, normally associated with creative design, were practically absent in the work of the architectural firms responsible for high-rise buildings.

When the energy crisis and recession halted the high-rise fashion overseas, the Transvaal again followed suit, being also influenced by political problems and an anti-high-rise sentiment.

Procurement of rural primary schools in Southern Africa: An approach to resource optimization. [Afrikaans text]. de Villiers, Adriaan Jacobus, Ph.D. *University of Pretoria (South Africa),* 1988. Promoter: D. Holm

This approach to resource optimization is directed towards the particular needs and resources of rural communities. It is a procedure for optimizing both the provision of facilities and the use of resources to meet the requirement for acceptable and appropriate primary schools within budget and time constraints.

Example 33. *Dissertation Abstracts International* (main entry). (Published with permission of University Microfilms International, publishers of *Dissertation Abstracts International*, copyright © 1989 by University Microfilms International.)

AAA SCHOOL DISTRICTS
ADMINISTRATIVE PRACTICES CONCERNING SINGLE-
PARENT FAMILIES: A STUDY OF MISSOURI AAA
SCHOOL DISTRICTS (EDUCATION, ADMINISTRATION)
TORGERSON, JOY L., p.3233–A

ABC
THE RELATIONSHIP OF THE K-ABC'S SIMULTANEOUS
AND SEQUENTIAL PROCESSING SCORES TO READING
COMPREHENSION IN FOURTH, FIFTH, AND SIXTH
GRADE CHILDREN (EDUCATION, PSYCHOLOGY) LEWIS,
BARRY GORDON, p.3309–A

ABILITY
A STUDY OF THE RELATIONSHIPS AMONG FOURTH
GRADE STUDENTS' PERCEPTIONS OF WRITING,
LANGUAGE SKILLS ACHIEVEMENT, AND THE ABILITY
TO PRODUCE A WRITTEN TEXT (EDUCATION,
CURRICULUM AND INSTRUCTION) BROWN, VICKI
RENEE, p.3244–A
AN EVALUATION OF THE ABILITY OF MANDATORY WORK
PROGRAMS TO REDUCE WELFARE CASELOADS
(POLITICAL SCIENCE, GENERAL) BRASHER, CHARLES
NIELSEN, p.3487–A
AN EXPLORATION OF THE RELATIONSHIPS BETWEEN
DIAGNOSTIC REASONING ABILITY AND LEARNING
STYLE IN UNDERGRADUATE NURSING STUDENTS
(EDUCATION, TESTS AND MEASUREMENTS) OLIVIERI,
RITA J., p.3342–A
COGNITIVE STYLES: THEIR CONSOLIDATION AND
RELATIONSHIP, BEYOND COGNITIVE DEVELOPMENTAL
LEVEL AND CRITICAL THINKING ABILITY, TO
UNDERSTANDING SCIENCE (EDUCATION, SCIENCES)
BOSTIC, JEFF QUINN, p.3320–A
LEARNING THE ECONOMIC CONCEPTS OF DEMAND,
SUPPLY AND PRICE: A STUDY OF THE COGNITIVE
LEARNING ABILITY OF THIRD AND SIXTH GRADE
CHILDREN (EDUCATION, ELEMENTARY) HAIL, JOHN
MARTIN, III, p.3264–A
THE EFFECT OF SEMANTIC MAPPING STRATEGY ON
PROSE LEARNING ACROSS TIME AND ABILITY
(EDUCATION, PSYCHOLOGY) AL-BAILI, MOHAMED
ABDULLAH, p.3304–A

ABSTRACTION
LEVELS OF ABSTRACTION IN EXTENDED DISCOURSE
AND RECALL-RECOGNITION TASKS (EDUCATION,
READING) TILLMAN, MONTAGUE KAY, p.3318–A
ON ABSTRACTION: A SOCIOLOGICAL ANALYSIS
(SOCIOLOGY, SOCIAL STRUCTURE AND
DEVELOPMENT) LEE, JASON SANDFORD, p.3523–A

ACADEMIA
COMPETENCIES FOR DIRECTORS OF ALLIED HEALTH
PROGRAMS IN ACADEMIA (EDUCATION, HIGHER)
RINES, JOAN T., p.3282–A

ACADEMIC
AN INVESTIGATION OF THE EFFECT OF MUSIC UPON
THE ACADEMIC, AFFECTIVE, AND ATTENDANCE
PROFILES OF SELECTED FOURTH GRADE STUDENTS
(EDUCATION, ELEMENTARY) KOOYMAN, REBECCA JOY
KING, p.3265–A
AN INVESTIGATION OF THE IMPACT OF BUDGET
REDUCTION ON ACADEMIC SUBUNITS OF
INSTITUTIONS OF HIGHER EDUCATION (EDUCATION,
HIGHER) ROSE, LINWOOD HOWARD, p.3282–A
THE RELATIONSHIP BETWEEN TYPE/DEGREE OF
ACCULTURATION, ACADEMIC ACHIEVEMENT, AND
ACCULTURATIVE STRESS AMONG VIETNAMESE
COLLEGE STUDENTS (EDUCATION, GUIDANCE AND
COUNSELING) LOPEZ, NATHANIEL JOSEPH, p.3271–A

ACADEMIC ACHIEVEMENT
ACADEMIC ACHIEVEMENT AND OTHER SELECTED
VARIABLES OF LATCHKEY CHILDREN WITH AND
WITHOUT MAJOR AFTERSCHOOL FAMILY
RESPONSIBILITIES (EDUCATION, ADMINISTRATION)
CARPENTER, STEPHANIE WALLS, p.3214–A
ACADEMIC ACHIEVEMENT OF HAITIAN LIMITED ENGLISH
PROFICIENT STUDENTS IN NEW JERSEY PUBLIC HIGH
SCHOOLS (EDUCATION, LANGUAGE AND LITERATURE)
RORRO, GILDA BATTAGLIA, p.3292–A
MOTIVATIONAL INFLUENCE OF CAREER INFORMATION,
EMPHASIZING RELATIONSHIPS BETWEEN
SCHOLASTIC AND CAREER SKILLS, ON THE ACADEMIC

Example 34. *Dissertation Abstracts International* (keyword title index). (Published with permission of University Microfilms International, publishers of *Dissertation Abstracts International*, copyright © 1989 by University Microfilms International.)

FORMAT OF ABSTRACT SECTION

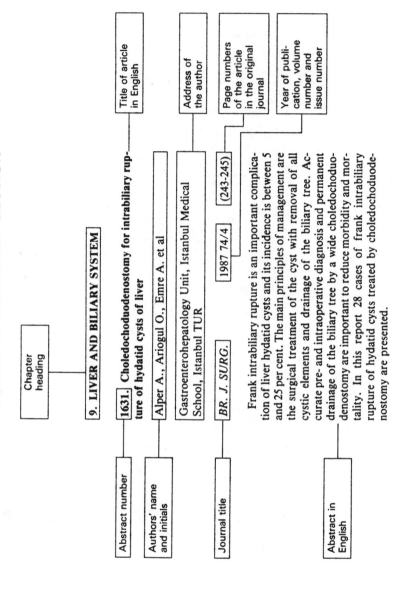

Example 35. *Excerpta Medica* (abstract format). (Excerpta Medica/Embase Publishing Group, Amsterdam.)

A

Abakanowicz, Magdalena. Poland. Sculpture.
1954-87. *11102*

Abbey Theatre. Deevy, Teresa. Dramatists.
Ireland. 1930's. *6564*

Abdallahi ibn Muhammad. Sudan. 1885-1986. *8686*

Abdication. Edward VIII. Great Britain. Political
Crisis. 1930's. *2508*

Abdullah ibn-Hussein. Foreign Relations. Great
Britain. Invasion. Jordan. Palestine. 1943-48.
3912

Abelshauser, Werner. Economic Development.
Germany, West. 1945-48. *10715*

Abgarovicz, Kaetan. Antoniewicz, Jan Bołoz.
Armenians. Authors. Literary Criticism.
Poland. 1856-1922. *11041*

Aboriginal Education Unit. Australia
(Wollongong). Teacher Training. Wollongong,
University of. 1982-85. *5772*

Aborigines. Assimilation. Australia. Geographic
Mobility. 1920's-70's. *5765*

—. Australia. Canada. Indians. Suffrage. Voting
and Voting Behavior. 1970's-85. *9455*

—. Australia. Central Australian Aboriginal Media
Association. Glynn, Freda (interview). Women.
1946-86. *9469*

—. Australia. Demography. Public Opinion.
Research. 1971-81. *1768*

—. Australia. Land. Legislation. Political Protest.
1950's-86. *1774*

Abortion. China. Population policy. 1970-82. *9224*

—. Human rights. Policymaking. Western Nations.
1973-85. *4384*

Abragam, Anatole. France. Personal Narratives.
Physics. 1960-84. *8548*

Abraham (biblical character). Bible. Genocide.
Jews. Literature. Revisionism. World War II.
1942-70. *8173*

Abraham, David. Germany. Political instability
(review article). Sociology. 1920's-33. *6912*

Abraham, Edward. Medical research. Penicillin.
Personal narratives. 1929-86. *849*

Abraham Lincoln Brigade. Americans. Civil War.
Gordon, Joe. Gordon, Leo. Letters. Spain. ca
1930-42. *2727*

—. Americans. Civil war. Personal narratives.
Spain. Veterans. 1936-39. *6685*

—. Civil War. France. Prisoners of War. Spain.
USA. 1936-39. *6694*

—. Civil War. Spain. USA. 1930's-85. *2738*

Example 36. *Historical Abstracts* (subject index). (Reprinted with permission from *Historical Abstracts*, Part B, Vol. 39, 1988, p. 863. ABC-Clio, Inc.)

89f:00037 00A25
Parkinson, Claire L. (1-NASA4)
Paradigm transitions in mathematics.
Philos. Math. (2) **2** (1987), *no.* 2, 127–150.

An interesting attempt is made to apply the concept of "paradigm" and "paradigm-shift" from T. S. Kuhn [*The structure of scientific revolutions*, Univ. Chicago Press, Chicago, Ill., 1970] to the history of mathematics. The broad range of historical topics considered is indicated by the following sub-headings: 2. Euclidian geometry and the concept of proof; 3. Non-Euclidean geometries; 4. Algebra; 5. Noncommutative algebras; 6. Solution by radicals; straight edge and compass constructions; 7. Probability theory; analytic geometry; calculus; 8. Foundations.

A further weakness is the lack of any awareness of the work of I. Lakatos [e.g., *Proofs and refutations*, Cambridge Univ. Press, Cambridge, 1976; MR **58** #122]—the key figure in contemporary philosophy of mathematics—who explicitly builds his system on a detailed exegesis of historical cases. Lakatos, unlike this paper which merely applies labels, illuminates the mechanisms underlying the developing of mathematics. It should be added that the reviewer enjoyed reading the paper and enjoyed being provoked by it.   *Paul Ernest* (Exeter)

89f:00038 00A25 00A69
Tseytin, G. S. [Tseĭtin, G. S.]
The relationship between mathematical and ordinary thought.
Soviet J. Comput. Systems Sci. **26** (1988), *no.* 1, 163–166;
translated from Izv. Akad. Nauk SSSR Tekhn. Kibernet. **1987,**
no. 2, 193–196, 224 (*Russian*).

Mathematical thought, in the sense of mathematical reasoning, is contrasted with ordinary thought. The author suggests that neither is derived from, nor attempts to model, the other. He sees mathematical thought not as completely objective, but as depending on reproducibility. He claims that ordinary thought is richer in its diversity of subtle distinctions which mathematics treats as equivalent, but that the application of mathematical methods to other sciences serves as an index for a certain level of maturity of that science, though without the presence of a suitable base in the science, introduction of mathematical apparatus reduces to science-like but useless exercises.

It seems that the author is attacking some unspecified and (to the reviewer) unknown philosophical position or trend in nonmathematical disciplines. A good deal may be lost in the translation of what is a very succinct article.   *John H. Mason* (4-OPEN)

Example 37. *Mathematical Reviews*, June 1989 issue 89f (main entry). (Reprinted with permission of the American Mathematical Society.)

Example 38. *Mathematical Reviews*, May 1989 89e (key index). (Reprinted with permission of American Mathematical Society.)

00	General
01	History and biography

03	Mathematical logic and foundations
04	Set theory
05	Combinatorics
06	Order, lattices, ordered algebraic structures
08	General mathematical systems

11	Number theory
12	Field theory and polynomials
13	Commutative rings and algebras
14	Algebraic geometry
15	Linear and multilinear algebra; matrix theory
16	Associative rings and algebras
17	Nonassociative rings and algebras
18	Category theory, homological algebra
19	K-theory

20	Group theory and generalizations
22	Topological groups, Lie groups

26	Real functions
28	Measure and integration
30	Functions of a complex variable
31	Potential theory
32	Several complex variables and analytic spaces
33	Special functions
34	Ordinary differential equations
35	Partial differential equations
39	Finite differences and functional equations
40	Sequences, series, summability

41	Approximations and expansions
42	Fourier analysis
43	Abstract harmonic analysis
44	Integral transforms, operational calculus

Example 39. *Mathematical Reviews*, June 1989 issue 89f (major classes). (Reprinted with permission of American Mathematical Society.)

FORM OF ENTRY

All entries in *Physics Abstracts* follow the same basic pattern. The following example identifies the individual parts of a typical entry for an article from a journal.

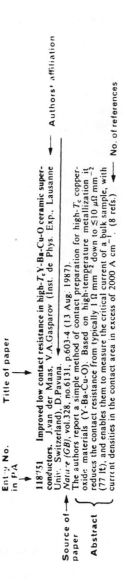

Example 40. *Physics Abstracts* (entry format). (Reproduced with permission from INSPEC, Institution of Electrical Engineers, London, England.)

CLASSIFICATION AND CONTENTS

The abstracts are arranged by subject in accordance with the following scheme. The page number for each section is given. The CLASSIFICATION AND CONTENTS is followed by an alphabetical guide to the scheme, the SUBJECT GUIDE.

The classification scheme is the result of cooperation between INSPEC, the American Institute of Physics, the European Physical Society and the Physics Working Group of the ICSU-AB.

Example 41. *Physics Abstracts* (classification outline). (Reproduced with permission from INSPEC, Institution of Electrical Engineers, London, England.)

Psychological Abstracts. Washington, D.C.: American Psychological Association, 1927- .

Coverage includes journal articles, books, and technical reports, with a signed abstract for each item included. The arrangement is classified, with major areas of psychology then broken down into narrower topics. Each issue has an author index and short subject index.

LIMITATIONS

Abstracts, like all devices for bibliographic control, are imperfect. Productive scientists and other scholars have come to recognize the value of information in their work, and they consider the publication, storage, and retrieval of this information an integral part of their activities, not as something incidental. As a result, they have learned to depend upon bibliographic control to speed their work.

Two points should be kept in mind. First, the abstracts themselves can vary in quality from worthless to superb. They can be affected by errors, policy, omissions, and abstractor bias — or be so poorly written that they are difficult to use. Second, not all users are equally proficient in using abstracts and other bibliographic tools, and thus the user imposes a self-limitation on the tools.

And it must be remembered that users do not depend solely on libraries for information. Scientists turn first to colleagues, then to their own journals, books, and reports and to conference information and the "invisible college" (personal network of unprinted information that flows back and forth). The abstractor must keep this in mind and strive for a product that will be a priority choice of information seekers, which at present it is not.

SUGGESTED READINGS

Ashworth, Wilfred. "Producing and Using Abstracts." In *Handbook of Special Librarianship and Information Work*." 4th ed. Edited by W. E. Batten. London: AsLib, 1975, 124-52.

Bakewell, K. G. B., and G. Rowland. "Indexing and Abstracting." In *British Librarianship and Information Work, 1981-1985, vol. 2*. London: Library Association, 1988.

Bates, Marcia J. "Locating Elusive Science Information." *Special Libraries* 75 (April 1984): 114-20.

Borko, Harold, and Charles L. Bernier. *Abstracting Concepts and Methods.* New York: Academic Press, 1975.

Neufeld, M. Lynne, Martha Cornog, and Inez L. Sperr, eds. *Abstracting and Indexing Services in Perspective: Miles Conrad Memorial Lectures, 1969-1983*. Arlington, Va.: Information Resources Press, 1983.

Urquhart, D. J. "The Distribution and Use of Scientific and Technical Information." *The Royal Society Information Conference* (1948): 408-19.

IX
Abstracting Methods and Procedures

INTRODUCTION

The primary use of an abstract is to give scholars access to the literature in their disciplines, and it does this in several ways. First, it is a current awareness device that allows users to scan quickly the literature in their field. Abstracts also give the user a retrospective search tool so that noncurrent literature can be examined for pertinent information. Often abstracts allow users to identify information that exists in another language because there are English language versions of the abstracts.

Abstracting and its cousin summarizing are as old as story telling. The ancient peoples attached content abstracts to papyrus rolls. Runners returned from battle with summaries of the events. When we tell our friends about our vacation we select and condense what we think might be of interest. The ability to summarize and abstract is important in nearly all aspects of our lives, including the bibliographic control of our literature.

STEPS IN ABSTRACTING

It makes some sense to say that the process of abstracting begins with deciding if the material is worthy of an abstract. Many things are published that simply are not worth the effort and expense, and often the abstractor is put into a position of having to make that decision. This does not imply that the abstractor becomes a publication referee, trying to second-guess decisions already made by editors and their supporting referees, but abstractors may very well be working under established policies that exclude certain items. Pressures of time and money, and specific objectives of the abstracting agencies, determine these policies. Suppose, for example, that an abstractor has a guideline that says not to abstract "notes and short communications" from journals unless the material is *significant* to the subject area of the journal. When indexers come across such items they must make a decision.

Some people believe that an indexer and/or abstractor cannot know everything a user might need, and therefore everything should be indexed and abstracted. The premise of this stance is false, since all bibliographic control implies that information professionals will make decisions about what users need. This concept permeates all bibliothecal activities from start to finish, especially indexing and abstracting. Granted, the systems are far from perfect, but the professional selection responsibility, at any point, is clearly there.

In an abstracting agency articles are screened before they go to an abstractor, and the abstractor will probably have guidelines for subject coverage in the abstract. The guidelines will list areas to be covered and areas to be excluded, but the abstractor will be the one making judgments during the abstracting process; the quality of those judgments will depend largely on the abstractor's experience.

Papers in refereed journals are probably of better quality than conference reports. However, a large number of conference reports are published and are an important part of the literature. Special care must be taken in abstracting this type of document. In many cases the abstract will be longer than usual and will convey more details, since long after the conference is over, the abstract may be the only information available on the document.

Also, reprints and abridgments of previously published articles are generally not abstracted, and the abstractor must be on the lookout for these items.

What are some of the factors involved in deciding which materials should have abstracts?

Economic constraints. On a priority list of items to be abstracted, the cost, in terms of time and production, may cause low-priority items to be left out.

Significant material. Notes, communications, and letters to the editor may have minimal significance. For example, a letter to the editor complaining that the journal's format is bad is probably not critical to the concerns of the investigators who read the journal.

Publication source. Items from disreputable publishers may be ignored, whereas items from respected publishers would always be abstracted. Although it is perhaps a little unfair, items from new and unknown sources may be temporarily ignored, since no one knows if they are worthy publications. This is why indexing and abstracting services do not immediately add such publications to their bank. As a matter of fact, information professionals are taught that one way to judge the quality of a journal is to see if it is covered by a reputable indexing and abstracting service. Of course, this could develop into a vicious circle with everybody waiting for everybody else to judge the hapless journal.

Subject interests of the users. Some things will clearly be of interest, others clearly not, and some items will be of marginal interest. The problem arises when the abstractor does not have a clear image of the user. Again, policy guidelines are helpful. It should be emphasized that the item itself may be of value, possibly earning the author a Nobel Prize, but it may be of no interest to the users of this abstracting service.

Now comes the actual abstracting.

Step One

The first step is to accurately and fully record the reference. Incorrect reference entry is an unpardonable sin, since the purpose of the entry is to give exact steerage to the original paper from the abstract. Completeness and accuracy are essential. If the reference is wrong, readers will either give up and turn elsewhere or be burdened with additional work.

The type of abstract — indicative, informative, or critical — does not affect the need for full bibliographic entry, since no type of abstract can always replace the original document. Indicative abstracts can seldom replace the original because they are summary in nature and only alert readers to the type of information contained in the paper. Informative abstracts cannot carry all the data presented in the paper. Therefore, each and every abstract must be complete and accurate, with no exceptions.

The elements to be included are fairly well standardized, but the order of presentation can run the gamut and is usually an individual choice of the abstracting agency. There is a general consensus that the reference section goes at the head of the abstract, before the body, so that users can decide if they want to read further. In other words, they choose on the basis of the title, much the same way they decide when using an index.

In writing the reference entry, it is not unusual to abbreviate to save space, but abbreviations should be consistent and follow established rules. A list of the abbreviations should be available to the user.

Careful attention should be given to the following elements in the entry:

Title. A good title can be a key device in identifying information for retrieval, and users have learned this. Good titles are heavily loaded with strong content-bearing words, and users will often depend on the titles to help them decide if they need the paper.

There is more to handling the title than simply copying it correctly from the paper to the worksheet. First, if the title is vague or misleading, the abstractor should take corrective action by adding modifying words in brackets. For example, the author's title might be "Controlling eating," but the abstractor's title reads, "[The use of hypnosis in the] controlling [of compulsive] eating." Occasionally, the title carries no indication of content. For example, the author's title might be "Eureka!" whereas the abstractor's title is "Eureka! [The discovery of a calorieless beer]."

However, too much of a title change can mislead users when they begin to look for the document itself. As a general rule, titles should be retained as they are published, with the exception of augmented titles as just described. A good title is descriptive, clear, and brief, stating exactly what the topic of the paper is, and such a title requires no augmentation by the abstractor.

In the case of a foreign language paper, many abstracting agencies will translate it. Most agencies simply use the translated English version alone, but some run both the English and foreign titles.

Author. Some abstractors believe that the author should be the first element in the bibliographical reference, their reasons being that (a) the author's name is usually placed first and its placement anywhere else would look strange, (b) users often base their searches on authors who are leaders in the field, and (c) if the user enters the file of abstracts with a citation in hand, the citation is easier to locate by author. The last two arguments are valid, except that indexing and abstracting tools are generally subject-identifying devices and if the title is given prominence, it will serve that subject need best. Most readers will be looking for subject guidance, and the title is what they are interested in first.

The form of entering the author's name varies, but a standard way is to invert the first name and add additional authors in the normal order. The use of initials for given names cuts down on space but can lead to ambiguity of authorship. As we know, a number of J. Smiths write and publish. Generally, it is best not to use initials.

Author affiliation. An author's organization is often of interest to a user because it helps in judging the author and makes communication easier if the reader wants to contact the author for reprints or for any other reason. Affiliation is usually located after the author's name, sometimes with an address attached. For example: Disraeli, Homer (Disraeli Delicatessen), or Disraeli, Homer (Disraeli Delicatessen, Muleshoe, TX).

Funding agency. If the document is a technical report or a paper based on the results of funded research, the agency giving the money should be noted in the reference section. In the journal literature it is customary for the paper to carry an acknowledgment of funding support. The information should include the name of the agency and the grant or contract number.

Publication source. This, of course, is the key unit in the reference because it provides the location of the paper. It is important that it be accurate and consistent and that it follow some standard conventions for citing. For journals, the following is suggested:

Journal titles (abbreviated titles may be used if they are standard abbreviations and can be understood)
Volume number
Issue number
Inclusive pagination
Year

For example:

J Amer Soc Inf Science 30(5)
290-95 (1979)

Monographs and books should include:

Title
Author
Publisher and place of publication
Date
Pages
Price

For example:

Think Green. Thumb, Tom, Jr. and Homer Disraeli (ABCD Press, Muleshoe, TX) 1989. 250pp. $30.50.

Although these two forms will cover most material indexed, a third form, patents, should be mentioned. A patent reference might follow this order:

Title
Inventor
Organization
Issuing country
Patent number
Issue date

For example:

> "A sausage-stuffing computer." Disraeli, Homer (Disraeli Delicatessen), U.S. 0000000000, 1 April 1988.

Foreign languages. Following the source, information should be given about foreign language documents. The original language should be indicated, and if it has been translated the translation source information should be supplied. Obviously, if the paper is not available in translation, the user must be aware of this. Otherwise, if users cannot read the foreign language and the paper cannot be translated easily, their time is saved by consulting the abstract.

Other. Some additional information that might serve a user is descriptive notes (e.g., available only in microfiche), sources for obtaining the document, and price.

Step Two

When the reference section is complete, it is time for the content analysis of the document. The content analysis of a document for abstracting purposes is similar to the analysis done for indexing, but since the final purpose is different, there are some differences in the analysis procedure. When indexing, the objective is to identify key concepts with the goal of creating a word list, a column of controlled descriptors that will point to a document's content. On the other hand, the objective of the abstractor is to create a narrative of that document's content. The abstractor wants to construct a miniature surrogate of the document, which will be a skeletal representation of the document.

Abstracting is the process of expressing the ideas of other people in one's own words. It also involves reviewing all the points in a document and deciding which ones are important, keeping in mind who the readers of the abstract will be and what they will be seeking. For example, suppose we had the following simple account:

> Smith carried out the experiment on Tuesday because Monday was a holiday and on Wednesday he had a dentist appointment. Right after lunch he mixed four grams of the Red Stuff with eight grams of the Purple Stuff, put it to boil, and set the timer for exactly four minutes. While the mixture was cooking, he called the dentist's office to confirm the time of his appointment. At exactly the time that the timer rang, the mixture exploded and destroyed the lab. Smith concluded that four minutes is too long to cook the mixture.

The important points to be worked into the abstract are:

- Used four grams of the Red Stuff

- Used eight grams of the Purple Stuff

- Cooked the mixture exactly four minutes

- Mixture explosion resulted

- Conclusion: Don't cook the mixture for four minutes.

The nonrelevant points to be ignored are:

- The day he did the experiment

- The time of day he did the experiment

- The dental appointment

- The time of the dental appointment

The trick, of course, is to know enough about the subject and to understand the paper well enough to be able to know what is important and what is not.

There are five overall indicators that the abstractor looks for first in preparing the content analysis:

1. *Objectives and scope.* Why was this document written? What purpose did the author have in mind? In most scholarly and scientific papers, the objectives and scope are discussed in the beginning of the paper.

2. *Methodology.* For papers reporting experimental work, some of the techniques and methods used should be described, but not all. Enough should be given to allow the reader to understand how the work was carried out. In analyzing documents, the abstractor should note carefully any new methods the authors have developed or used in their work. For documents that are not reporting experimental work, the abstractor should note data sources and how these data were handled. For example, attention should be given to any statistical techniques that were employed.

3. *Results.* What were the outcomes? What relationships and correlations were observed? Were the data raw, collected data only? Were the results obtained from a single measurement or were they obtained from replication? Does the abstractor see any factors that might affect the validity, reliability, or accuracy of the results? All these things should be noted for inclusion in the abstract.

4. *Conclusions.* What hypotheses were accepted or rejected? What evaluations? What applications or suggestions? How are the implications related to the objectives of the paper?

5. *Other information.* Supportive information should be noted, such as results that are not directly related to the main topic but that might be important in other areas. For example, if the paper is historical, the scholar may have discovered a new source of data useful to other areas. This type of information belongs in the abstract but should not dominate it.

These are the things abstractors will surely include in the abstract and the things they concentrate on when analyzing the document. But what does the abstractor leave out? If the purpose of an abstract is clear, it becomes obvious that a number of elements in a paper can be safely ignored. The inclusion of these elements would make the abstract complete, but they would have low informational value. For example, the abstractor can usually overlook the general introduction (except if it presents objectives and scope) and historical background. Historical summary is not new to the field and is not a unique contribution of the paper being abstracted. Redundancy, old information, and a complete discussion of the methodology can also be passed over.

In the process of analysis, the abstractor should omit information a potential reader of the paper is expected to know. For example, a paper in psychology may take a paragraph to explain who Freud was, but the abstractor can safely assume that the readers of a scholarly journal in psychology do not need this information. Another example would be discussions of the author's promises of the wonderful research he or she is going to do in the future. This, perhaps, is acceptable in the original paper, but it has no place in the abstract.

As a rule, graphical material, such as drawings and tables, should not be worked directly into the abstracts, but the abstractor certainly should use the information in the graphics to write the abstract. If the drawings and tables are of special significance to the paper, the abstractor should note this.

Step Three

The third step is to write the annotation. At this point the abstractor has notes on the highlights of the paper and has a mental picture of the contents and concepts of the paper. Now those concepts must be constructed into a short narrative. The results of the analysis must be expressed in natural language.

For most people an outline is a useful device when writing anything, no matter what the length. Other people cannot be convinced that an explicit outline is necessary, although we would suspect that an outline exists in their head as they construct the abstract. Dennis and Sharp (1966) suggest an outline that lists main points with subsidiary points underneath, as follows:

I.   Main point
   a. Secondary point
   b. Secondary point

II. Main point
   a. Secondary point
   b. Secondary point
   c. Secondary point

III. Main point

Clearly, this will not be a perfectly balanced outline, since some main points may not have secondary points or a main point may have many secondary points.

A good working premise is that the abstract will be seen and read by someone who knows nothing about the existence of the original document or what it contains. Everything is in the hands of the abstract writer.

How long should an abstract be? Just exactly long enough to do a proper job and not one word more. This is not a facetious statement because length of the abstract is determined by the length of the document, the nature of the topic, the facts discussed, the technical details, and many other factors. A key element is the quantity of information and its complexity and originality. The abstract should be a model of brevity, yet it should not read like a night letter that is costing the abstractor $500 a word. Generally, it will run less than 250 words, and less than 100 for such things as communication notes and editorials. Beyond 500 words, the abstract has possibly become a review. However, there is no law about length.

The first sentence of the abstract is critical. It should be a topic sentence that tells what the paper is all about. It is a concise, informative thesis statement and resembles the lead sentence in a news story. It should convey the type of information that allows readers to decide if they want to continue reading the abstract or not. The first sentence should not repeat words that the user has just read in the title. It is not only an insult to the reader's intelligence but wastes critical space. For example, if the title of the paper is "The History of Cats in Denton County, Texas," the abstract should not begin, "This paper is about the history of cats in Denton County, Texas." The title need not be repeated, and "This paper is about" is an unnecessary space waster.

The abstract should be complete, and it should reflect the full meaning and purpose of the paper, rather than just focusing on an isolated concept. For example, an abstract of a paper that summarizes the American Civil War should cover more than the Battle of Gettysburg. This does not imply exhaustivity. The complete basic informational content of the original document is to be presented but not every detail or topic discussed. The goal is to make the abstract self-contained and understandable to readers in a way that makes it unnecessary for them to consult the original document. Readers should *know* what the document is about solely from reading the abstract.

Abstract writers, especially authors who abstract their own papers, constantly worry about what is being left out, but it must be remembered that an abstract, by definition, will not be as complete as the original paper. It is not supposed to be, since it serves a different purpose.

The structure of the abstract should be unified and logically developed. In other words, there should be a beginning, a middle, and an end, with the final sentences leaving the reader with the feeling that nothing more needs to be said.

Logical development is not ensured by simply following the order of the paper, because not all published papers are straightforward. This does not necessarily mean that the paper is poorly written; it may simply be a reflection of the author's writing style. The author may be the type that launches a paper at the heart of the matter, and then fills in background, jumping to the next key issue, filling in background, and so forth. In the full paper this can be an acceptable presentation and is certainly "logically" written within its own framework. However, if the abstract is presented this way, it will be extremely difficult to follow.

Is the actual writing done with a pen in one hand and a finger of the other hand moving along the original text? It is recommended that the abstract not be written while reading for content. This will almost always guarantee a bad abstract. Definitive notes should be taken in the analysis stage and the first draft of the abstract written from the notes, thus reducing the temptation to "extract," that is, to lift sentences and phrases straight out of the text. An abstract is a carefully constructed, condensed representation and interpretation of the paper, written with selected, high-content-bearing words and phrases, not simply a string of sentences taken directly from the text. If extracts were as useful as abstracts, we would simply retire all abstractors and turn the business over to a computer.

Abstractor writers should try to avoid vague expressions and long, rambling sentences. In fact, complete sentences are not always necessary, because phrases can often convey the message. But a steady diet of rapid-fire phrases will soon sound like a cryptogram and will be irksome to read. A phrase must convey a complete thought.

The abstract should be one paragraph only, except in the case of extraordinarily long documents. Brevity is aided by a little consideration for common sense style. For example, redundant phrases should be minimized.

Don't say:	"The results of the study lead one to the conclusion that..."
Instead:	"The conclusion is..."
Don't say:	"After the experiment was completed the following data were compiled..."
Instead:	"Resulting data were..."

The abstract writer should avoid using words that can have different meanings depending on the context in which they are used. Abbreviations can be used for brevity, but care must be taken to use standard ones so there will be no chance for misunderstanding.

Finally, critical abstracts should not take sides on controversial questions or preach sermons. A critical abstract is still an abstract, and it should be an objective piece of work. At the same time, bias and an author's strong opinions may be noted, but abstractors should take care that their biases do not distort what the author is *really* saying. Certainly, such items as accuracy, validity, and relationship to other works with different viewpoints should be brought out in a critical abstract.

Step Four

The last item of the abstract, the abstractor's name, gives credit (and responsibility) for the abstract. Often only initials are given, with the full name appearing elsewhere in the abstract publication, but full names are also used frequently.

Step Five

The last step is the arrangement of the abstracts. A common form is alphabetical by title, but some alternatives are alphabetical by author; alphabetical by subject descriptors; classified; and dictionary. In nearly all cases the abstracts will require indexes to support the basic file, and this is especially true of classified abstracts.

INDEXES TO ABSTRACTS

When a collection of abstracts is compiled into a bibliographic unit, there is immediately an access problem. In all bibliothecal activity the first move is to collect and arrange, and suddenly access is dependent on that particular arrangement. If we arrange our personal library on the basis of authors, then we are in trouble if we need to know who is buried in Grant's tomb and can't remember who wrote about Grant and his final disposal. Our only option would be to read through the collection until we find a discussion of Grant. The point is that a collection of abstracts is a hopeless collection of human endeavor unless there are indexes to get the user on the right track.

If abstracts are to be utilized to their maximum extent, they need high-quality indexes to back them. There should be indexes to authors and all personal and proper names, as well as to editors, translators, illustrators, and the like.

More important is the need for a detailed and accurate subject index. The fundamental issue is subject approach, and the success or failure of an abstracting service may depend on this entity. This is the most critical point of any abstracting endeavor. The aim of the index should be to include every aspect that a user might need. Often abstractors are responsible for recommending possible indexing entries, and thus they must be proficient in indexing as well as in abstracting. Abstractors may not be expected to be indexers, but they can be instructed to look for identifiers such as proper names, catch-titles, and key terms that will be fundamental to an index.

Any classification approach will require indexes for proper use. In the case of abstracts, there may be indexes to:

Subjects
Names
Titles of periodicals
Book reviews
Classification formats
Abbreviations

Name indexing will include personal and corporate names mentioned in the titles, in bibliographic references, and in the body of the abstract.

In summary, indexes to abstracts follow all the fundamental principles of indexing discussed earlier. The important thing to remember is that a poorly indexed abstracting endeavor will minimize the usefulness of the abstracts.

EDITING

The editing of abstracts is absolutely essential. Since abstracts are short literary pieces, they must be edited carefully, the same way any prose is edited before it is published. Abstracts have omissions, deviations from policy, errors in references, meaningless abbreviations, poor diction and grammar, punctuation absurdities, and endless other editorial nightmares. Generally, in an abstracting operation, the editor's task goes beyond "careless" errors. The editor serves, in a sense, as a master abstractor, concerned with content analysis and quality of the abstract. Ideally, the editor assumes the position by promotion from the ranks and knows a good abstract from a bad one.

The first editing task is to check the reference section against the original paper. Author names, titles, journal names, sources, and volume and issue numbers are often incorrect.

Numerical data in the abstract should be scrupulously compared with the document text because the accuracy of such data is essential and because transcribing numerical data is easily susceptible to error.

In the text itself, the editor sees to it that standardized terminology and nomenclature conform to the rules given to the abstractor. Grammar is corrected, redundancies are slashed, words are abbreviated, ambiguous abbreviations are spelled out, ephemeral subjects are eliminated, and clumsy diction is improved.

The editor is not obligated to redo the abstract, and if such is required, the professional competence of the abstractor must be questioned. Of course, it is imperative that the editor work directly with the original document to determine the quality of the abstract.

The abstract editor's primary worry, like the editor of an index, is the error of omission. This is the invisible error that is difficult to detect. Most editors develop a second sense for this—they can sense that something is missing.

The novice abstractor should understand that editors are not ghouls who must have raw meat thrown to them before they issue a check. They are colleagues who are as concerned as the abstractor about creating a quality product.

Editors are a bridge between the abstract writer and the printer. On the one hand, they fuss with the content and intellectual quality of the abstract; on the other hand, they prepare copy that conforms to the constraints of the publishing world. They must not sacrifice informational integrity or author creativity to mechanical or economical expediency, yet they know that publication practices require certain uniformities of presentation. For example, each title, cross-reference, entry, and subentry must follow a consistent pattern and appear in the same position and typeface; no exceptions can be allowed, regardless of an abstractor's creative urge.

The editor is responsible for separating the various units for publication, such as main files, various indexes, lists of abstractors, an outline of any classification scheme pertinent to the abstract, and instructions on how to use the abstracting publication. Guides to the use of the abstract are critical and are a major area of responsibility for the editor.

The editing process is a specialized, professional activity, involving an undefinable affinity between the abstractor and the ghoul behind the desk.

MANAGING ABSTRACTING OPERATIONS

Producing abstracts is much more than just having a group of well-trained abstractors producing copy and having editors correcting their work. Abstracting is usually done within the framework of an organization. This organization may be a one-person operation in a special library or a large, internationally known indexing and abstracting agency. What are some of the elements common to any abstracting activity?

First, there must be some policies concerning acquisition and procedures, even if the operation is a one-person endeavor. Abstracting policies are closely related to acquisition policies. Decisions about what to acquire and what not to acquire for an organization are based on the objectives of the organization. The same criteria carry over into the decision concerning the bibliographic access of these materials. Clearly, every item that an organization acquires cannot receive equal treatment. Some items require exhaustive analysis, and some need only passing identification. This concept is fundamental at any level, from the one-person library up to the large indexing and abstracting organization. The point is that policies regarding acquisition and importance need to be established, regardless of the level of the operation. Many factors are involved in establishing policy for what to abstract and what not to abstract. What areas are important for the objectives of the organization? Does coverage mean all languages and countries or only English and the United States? What about including abstracts in English of foreign language publications? Should popular papers be abstracted or only scholarly works? If Linus Pauling writes an article for *Playboy*, should it be abstracted? What about patent literature and conference proceedings? Textbooks? Letters to the editors and editorials? The management of an abstracting operation, large or small, begins with a written, specific policy statement of the operation's range of inclusions and exclusions.

Guidelines are important to an abstracting operation, even if it consists of a single librarian in a small special library. Guidelines help to maintain consistency and give directions when decisions must be made. They also are valuable training tools for new abstractors.

Guidelines can range from a few general comments to long and detailed explanations. The guidelines should cover such points as (1) what subjects are to be emphasized or omitted, (2) how to handle special materials, e.g., patents, (3) how to handle symbols and abbreviations, and (4) writing style.

The assignment of papers to individual abstractors is not a random process that is based solely on the workload. The primary concern is to see that assignments cover overlaps and gaps and are directed toward individual competencies. One way is to assign on the basis of document types, such as technical papers, reports, or philosophical essays. The key to good assignment is to match the paper to the technical background and experience of the abstractor. Foreign language papers, obviously, are assigned to people who can handle the language.

Assignment by journal is a common practice, and this makes sense if the journal covers specialized topics that are familiar to the abstractor. Experience with a number of journals can be developed by abstractors so that they can handle the areas and idiosyncrasies peculiar to those journals.

Another approach is assignment by category. An abstractor who works for years on papers about dogs develops some affinity toward the literature. Types of documents, such as patents, or reviews, can be assigned to people with experience in these areas.

The operation may not be so extensive that each abstractor can work in a narrow niche. In smaller operations, it may be considered the abstractor's professional obligation to accept any assignment within the realm of reasonability. But when possible, abstractors should be assigned to what they do best.

Abstractors learn by doing. They read, absorb, and take interest in the subject matter they deal with. Good abstractors are intellectually curious, want to know about the areas they deal with, and are concerned with performing a service to the workers in that area. An organization has a responsibility for training abstractors, overseeing their work, explaining editorial corrections, and discussing candidly the abstractors' mistakes. A good editorial practice is to return an edited abstract to the abstractor explaining why changes were made. The purpose is not to chastise, but to improve abstracting skills.

EVALUATION

What is a good abstract, or a good abstracting operation? In the field of library and information science, evaluation has been an elusive entity. Our primary measure has been a subjective pronouncement of "good" or "bad." We use a number of error-detection devices, such as correct citations, factual description, and omission of critical points. We also criticize poor diction and grammar, redundant phrases, and obscure writing.

Some additional evaluation measures are conformity to abstracting policy and rules, promptness in the publication or availability of the abstracts, the cost, the quality of supportive indexes, the authoritativeness of the abstracts, and brevity.

The cost of an abstracting operation is a quality factor in the sense that if no one can afford it, it is useless. Use is affected by its economic inaccessibility. Much grumbling is currently heard among librarians about how they simply can no longer afford such and such indexing and abstracting services because the price is astronomical.

Authoritativeness is closely related to the prestige of the abstracting services, and this prestige comes by performance over a period of time. It is related to the manner in which abstracts are written, edited, and published. Also correlated to this is the reputation of the people who write the abstracts. Abstractors do not win Nobel Prizes, but they do build reputations. Quality abstracting services take pride in their corps of abstractors.

More important than editorial, mechanical evaluation is how users judge the abstracts. The ultimate test is how well the abstracts do their job in satisfying users' information needs.

SUGGESTED READINGS

American National Standards Institute. *American National Standard for Writing Abstracts*. New York: ANSI, 1987.

Ashworth, Wilfred. "Abstracting." In *Handbook of Special Librarianship and Information Work*. 4th ed. Edited by W. E. Batten. London: AsLib, 1975, 124-52.

_____. "Abstracting as a Fine Art." *The Information Scientist* 7 (June 1973): 43-53.

Borko, Harold, and Charles L. Bernier. *Abstracting Concepts and Methods*. New York: Academic Press, 1975.

Collison, Robert L. *Abstracts and Abstracting Services*. Santa Barbara, Calif.: Clio Press, 1971.

Defense Documentation Center. *Abstracting Scientific and Technical Reports of Defense-Sponsored RDT/E*. AD 667000. Alexandria, Va.: Defense Documentation Center, March 1968.

Dennis, G. W., and D. W. H. Sharp. *The Art of Summary*. London: Longmans, 1966.

Doyle, Lauren B. "Indexing and Abstracting by Association." *American Documentation* 13 (October 1962): 378-90.

Dronberger, G. B., and G. T. Kowitz. "Abstracting Readability as a Factor in Information Systems." *Journal of the American Society for Information Science* 26 (March 1975): 108-11.

Hall, Deanna Morrow. "Writing Abstracts: The American National Standard." *Bulletin of the American Society for Information Science* 13 (October-November 1986): 35.

Line, M. B. "Secondary Services in the Social Sciences: The Need for Improvement and the Role of Librarians." *Behavioral and Social Science Librarian* 1 (Summer 1980): 263-73.

Maizell, Robert E., and Julian F. Smith. *Abstracting Scientific and Technical Literature*. New York: Wiley-Interscience, 1971.

Mohlman, J. W. "Costs of an Abstracting Program." *Journal of Chemical Documentation* 1 (1961): 64-67.

Polisskaya, O. B. "Improving the Content Structure of Abstracts on the Basis of Queries from Workers in New Technology." *Scientific and Technical Information Processing* 12 (1985): 16-27.

Ratteray, O. M. T. "Expanding Roles for Summarized Information." *Written Communication* 2 (1985): 457-72.

Weil, B. A., I. Zarember, and H. Owen. "Technical Abstracting Fundamentals." *Journal of Chemical Documentation* 3 (1963): 86-89, 125-36.

Wood, N. W. "Abstracts and Their Indexes—Style, Presentation, and Uses." *AsLib Proceedings* 18 (1966): 160-66.

X

Indexing and Abstracting a Document

Indexes and abstracts serve as systematic guides to recorded information. The point has been made in the previous chapters that the indexing and abstracting processes are based partly on some empirical guidelines that have evolved over the centuries, but the quality of an index or an abstract is determined in large part by the talent and skills of the professional. Many decisions are made by the indexers and abstractors as they move through the process of appraising the document in hand and in trying to match it to the needs of a potential user.

The purpose of this chapter is to give a practical example of how to index and abstract a technical paper. No two people would handle this paper in exactly the same way, but, this example shows at least one logical and procedural way to do it.

First comes the text of a technical paper, followed by a description of the train of thought that went into the abstracting and indexing endeavor.

EXAMPLE OF A TECHNICAL PAPER

AN n-DIMENSIONAL RETRIEVAL MODEL*
Donald B. Cleveland

Introduction

Search strategies for automatic document retrieval systems are usually based on Boolean functions, although it has been shown that such functions are inadequate (1, 2, 3). In these models the assumption is made that a relation between each document and the query is a sufficient condition for optimal retrieval results. It is also assumed that each document in a file is independent of other documents.

Goffman (4) has shown clearly that documents are *not* independent of each other. In fact, a search strategy which takes account of document relatedness and mutual dependency results in a retrieval model that is superior to traditional models.

*Reprinted from *The Journal of the American Society for Information Science*, edited by Arthur W. Elias, v. 27, no. 5 (September-October 1976), by permission of John Wiley & Sons, Inc.

The experiment reported in this paper presents a technique of combining Goffman's search strategy with means other than index terms for reflecting document content. The results suggest that such a combination may be used to construct effective retrieval systems.

Document Relatedness

The concept of the inter-relatedness of documents in a file has been discussed for a number of years. One example is *probabilistic indexing* which associates a probability of relevance with index terms. Maron and Kuhns (5) proposed this technique, which essentially works as follows: A request for information is given to a computer which makes a statistical inference and derives a number called the relevance number for each document. This relevance number is a measure of the probability that the document will satisfy the request. The result of the search is an ordered list of those documents that satisfy the request, ranked according to their probable relevance.

Also, given a request consisting of one or more index terms, the computer can elaborate on the request to increase the probability of selecting relevant documents that would not have been selected otherwise. An *a priori* statistical distribution connects related documents in a file.

Another idea was suggested by Doyle (6). Concerned with the idea of interdependence of documents in a file, Doyle proposed that the documents in a file be displayed in an *association map* which would express the relationship of the subject matter in the documents. The user is presented first with a map of concepts which are expressed in the file. He then chooses specific direction according to interest and need. The available documents are then displayed so that he can decide which to investigate.

One of the classical proposals for structuring retrieval files independently of index terms is *bibliographic coupling* attributed to M. M. Kessler (7) who worked with citations in the early 1960s at M.I.T. Documents are linked together by the references the authors include in the paper to form networks of papers on a subject.

Another idea, called "context clues" was proposed by a group of researchers at the Institute of Library Research, under M. E. Maron (8). Context clues are those items of information that describe various objective properties and relationships which hold for individual documents, e.g., authors, reviewers, professional societies and the like.

Likewise, there is a "context" that surrounds each library user who comes in for service. Indeed, there seems to be a total, complex environment in which librarian, documents, and users interact and this environment can give "clues" to documents that are relevant.

These ideas, and others like them, are attempts to break out of the constraints imposed by classical indexing approaches.

Goffman's Method

Basically, the Goffman *Indirect Method* model reflects the concept that the exposure of a user to any given document modifies for him the relevance of succeeding documents. Thus, a file of documents can be classed (or ordered) on the basis of conditional probabilities between each pair in the file in terms of one being relevant to a stated query, given that its *predecessor* is relevant to that query. Content relatedness between each pair is the basis of the file structure.

For a given query this search strategy selects answer sets, chained together on the basis of a quasi-distance between each pair of documents. The chain represents the logical reading order of the documents.

The file is structured independent of any query. Obviously, a major key to the success of this model lies in determining, or measuring, the relatedness property between pairs of documents. Goffman used the co-occurrence of index terms as the measure. The present experiment extended the *Indirect Method* by representing documents in an n-dimensional Euclidean space with n measures of relatedness.

The Notion of Document Distances

In the literature dealing with statistical indexing approaches, especially the associative retrieval methods, there are many references to index spaces, vectors and distances. Such discussions are usually launched without any clearly defined spaces or any indication that the conditions for a distance exist. The space is not defined and an essential ingredient is usually missing — an axiomatic definition of distance based on the properties of the objects involved. A distance function is often implied without a properly defined unit or any valid assignment rule.

In the experiment reported here, a distance function between documents is defined based on the properties of the documents. It is then shown that these documents can be thought of as existing in n-dimensional Euclidean space, with n representing n measures of the content relatedness between pairs of documents. The proximity between pairs of documents is then determined by calculating the Euclidean distance.

The Mathematical Model

The Mathematical Model is the simple, ancient one of a distance in Euclidean space. The use of index terms as a measure of document-relatedness might be represented as a directed line segment between document X_i and document X_j. Suppose a second measure is added so that two measures are used to determine the relatedness of each pair of documents in the file. Now there is a relatedness measure between document X_i and document X_j expressed in two dimensions. Using the formula for distance, we can express the distance between X_i and X_j as

$$D(X_i,X_j) = \sqrt{(X_j-X_i)^2 + (Y_j-Y_i)^2}$$

where (X_j-X_i) is the first measure and (Y_j-Y_i) is the second measure. In general, the measures could be N and the distance would be expressed as

$$D(X_i,X_j) = \sqrt{(X_j-X_i)^2 + (Y_j-Y_i)^2 + ... + (N_j-N_i)^2}$$

It is assumed that the measures are linearly independent and mutually orthogonal, creating an orthonormal reference system in n-dimensional Euclidean space.

This is a true distance function between documents based on the *properties* of the documents. The proximity between pairs of documents is determined by calculating the Euclidean distance.

The Experimental Model

The objective of the experiment was to test relative retrieval effectiveness using different measures of document relatedness. In order to carry out such a test, certain ingredients are needed. These are:

1. One or more queries.

2. A document file which contains answers to the queries.

3. Some way of measuring the content-relatedness between the documents.

4. A means of determining relevance.

Two randomly selected scientific papers were taken to be queries for the system. That is, the topics in those papers were considered as areas about which information was to be sought.

Usually, scientific papers have a set of references which the author dealt with when he was writing the paper. These were the items he felt were relevant to his topic. They include the authorities and the previous works he used to write the paper, and those out of a probably much larger set he chose as being the most important or relevant. We can consider these references as being answer sets to the query, which is the paper itself.

Thus, we have queries, files of documents, various means of measuring relatedness (to be tested) and authoritative judgments of relevance. Taken together, these elements may be considered as a simulated information retrieval system for testing a search strategy and its relatedness measures.

Measures

The measures of document proximity used to structure the file in order to carry out the *Indirect Method* search strategy can be expressed in terms of Cartesian coordinates as follows:

1) *X-axis*—Keyword co-occurrence between the documents in the file. This is the measure used in the original *Indirect Method* experiment and is, of course, the most obvious measure. Documents with similar index terms probably have similar information content.

2) *Y-axis*—The relatedness between the journals in which individual documents appear. If the articles in journal i cite articles in journal j more than any other, then it is reasonable to assume that the subject matter of j is more like the subject matter of i than is the subject matter of any other journal *in the sample*. This is an indication of the relatedness of the articles in the two journals.

3) *Z-axis*—The relatedness between the authors of the documents. The relatedness among the authors in the data set was established by determining the extent of common authorship on various topics. If the author of document X_i usually writes about the same topics as the author of document X_j, there is a high probability that documents X_i and X_j are related in information content.

4) *W-axis*—The commonality of citations between the documents. It is assumed that closely related documents will have closely related citations.

An automatic word frequency technique was used to get the index terms measure. This technique has been used successfully in documentation studies at Case Western Reserve University for several years. Its basic form is described by Goffman (4).

The resulting lists of index terms were used to construct a matrix of relatedness between each pair of documents in the file. The numerical value was calculated as follows:

$$P_{ij} = \frac{m\,(X_i \wedge X_j)}{m(X_i)}$$

where $m(X_i \wedge X_j)$ is the number of index terms common to document X_i and document X_j. $m(X_i)$ is the total number of index terms for document X_i.

The second measure was based on the journals in which the documents appeared. There were 16 different journals in the data set. Approximately 30,000 citations, all the citations for a one year period, were examined. The result was a frequency list of citations for each of the 16 journals, giving the total citations to other journals in the data set.

For the purpose of constructing the measure, the top 3.5 percent of each distribution was arbitrarily chosen as representative of the most cited journals for each particular journal. Thus, connected with each journal was its journal citation profile. The measure between journal J_i and journal J_j was defined to be

$$Q_{ij} = \frac{n(J_i \wedge J_j)}{n(J_i)}$$

where $n(J_i \wedge J_j)$ is the number of cited journals common to the profile of journal J_i and journal J_j and $n(J_i)$ is the number of journals representing the journal citation profile of J_i.

Authors were the next concern. From SCIENCE CITATION INDEX® a list consisting of other authors who cited each author in the data set was compiled. The number of authors commonly citing authors A_i and A_j for a given topic suggested a profile of relatedness between A_i and A_j. The measure between each pair of authors in the data set was then determined as follows:

$$R_{ij} = \frac{\phi(A_i \wedge A_j)}{\phi(A_i)}$$

where $\phi(A_i \wedge A_j)$ is the number of citing writers common to the profiles of author A_i and author A_j and $\phi(A_i)$ is the number of writers representing the author profile of author A_i.

Finally, the measure of citations was calculated as follows:

$$S_{ij} = \frac{\theta(C_i \wedge C_j)}{\theta(C_i)}$$

where $\theta(C_i \wedge C_j)$ is the number of citations common to document C_i and C_j, and $\theta(C_i)$ is the number of citations representing document C_i.

Data Sources

The articles for the experiment were picked in the following way: A "random" walk was made through the open periodicals stacks of the Health Sciences Library at Case Western Reserve University and ended when a pleasing color of binding was detected. The nearest volume was pulled down and flipped open twice. This selection yielded Volume 123 of *The Journal of Infectious Diseases* and the two articles, "Precipitin Responses to Rubella Vaccine RA 26/3" by George L. Bouvier and Stanley A. Plotkin, and "In-vitro and In-vivo Studies of Resistance to Rifampin in Meningococci" by Theodore C. Eickhoff.

All the references in the two articles were used as the experimental data file, except one which was a monograph not readily available.

There were 26 articles, 13 from each of the two query articles. The 26 articles, plus the two query articles, represented 16 different journals and included 69 different authors.

The other data sources included a one year's run of each of the 16 different journals, and for the 69 authors, one year of the SCIENCE CITATION INDEX®.

Using the measures, four basic matrices resulted, showing the relatedness between the 26 documents in the file in terms of:

1. Closeness of index terms between the documents;

2. Closeness of the journals in which the documents appeared;

3. Closeness of the authors of the documents; and

4. Closeness of citations.

Vectors were also calculated showing the direct, or Boolean, relatedness between the two query articles and each document in the file. This was done for each of the four basic matrices.

Distance Matrices

At this point, the four matrices showed the relatedness between each pair of documents in terms of the four basic measures with values between 0 and 1.

It was now necessary to convert these matrices into distance matrices and combine them, using the Euclidean distance formula. If the measure value between document X_i and X_j was greater than some chosen threshold, then the distance between the pair was defined as being unit distance one. The following tactic was employed to convert each of the four basic matrices into distance matrices:

Step one: Arbitrary thresholds were picked for each matrix in terms of the calculated numerical values. In actual practice the thresholds would depend on whether a fine or a broad scope of retrieval is desired. For purposes of experimentation, it is only necessary that the thresholds be held constant throughout the experiment. The thresholds picked were .14 for the index terms, .50 for the journals, .08 for the authors and .01 for the citations. Any relatedness values that fell below these thresholds were considered zero.

Step two: Go along the row of document X_i and assign a unit distance of one to each document X_j which is above the threshold.

Step three: For each document X_j that is a distance of one from document X_i, go along the row of X_j and assign a distance of two to each document that is above the threshold, provided it is not already of distance one from document X_i.

Step four: Continue this procedure until all documents have a distance from document X_i. Those documents with zero relatedness values are considered to be of infinite distance.

Step five: Repeat the procedure for all i.

Step six: Repeat the total procedure for all n basic matrices.

The results are links of documents for each n basic matrix. These sequences reflect the smallest communication chain between elements, hence a quasi-distance. Graphically, it looks like this:

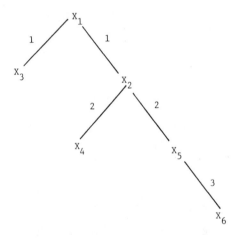

Thus, four basic distance measures were created, representing the four basic measures under consideration. Since a quasi-metric space existed, the objective now was to combine these orthogonal measures into various one, two, three and four-dimensional measures, using the Euclidean distance formula to determine the shortest chain between neighborhoods of documents in each dimension. Eleven matrices resulted.

Terms and Journals	Terms, Journals and Authors
Terms and Authors	Terms, Journals and Citations
Terms and Citations	Terms, Authors and Citations
Journals and Authors	Journals, Authors and Citations
Journals and Citations	Terms, Journals, Authors and
Authors and Citations	Citations

The rationale behind the testing was this: The document file consists of 26 documents. Thirteen documents form an exhaustive answer set for one test query and the other 13 documents form an exhaustive answer set for the other query, provided, of course, that none of the references in set *a* are relevant to query *b* and vice versa for set *b* and query *a*.

Therefore, a test consists of presenting queries to the system, using a particular relatedness measure or a particular combination of measures and observing how close the retrieval results approach the ideal.

Two points were important: (1) Exhaustiveness of retrieval, and (2) Exclusion of non-relevant documents.

The distinction between a "Boolean" search and an "*Indirect Method*" search should be made clear. Some form of Boolean operation is the most basic of techniques. (In the experiment reported here the index terms used to represent the "query" article made up the search vectors.) For a Boolean search, a query is compared with *each document* in the file, using any Boolean operation desired. The relevance of one document is entirely independent of the relevance of all other documents.

With the "Indirect Method," the query simply serves as an entry point to the file. Once a relevant document is found, the remaining retrieved documents are determined by internal file structure, *independently* of the query. Relevance is not a zero or one comparison between the query and each document, but is based on a conditional probability of relevance between the documents in the file.*

---

*For a full description of this technique, the reader is referred to Goffman's paper.

Measure	Relevant Retrieved	Relevant, Not Retrieved	Non-relevant, Retrieved
Authors	26	0	0
Authors-Journals	26	1	0
Authors-Terms	25	1	0
Authors-Terms-Journals	25	1	0
Citations	22	4	0
Journals-Citations	22	4	0
Authors-Citations	22	4	0
Journals-Authors-Citations	22	4	0
Terms-Journals-Authors-Citations	22	5	0
Terms-Citations	21	5	0
Terms-Journals-Citations	21	5	0
Terms-Authors-Citations	21	5	0
Terms (Boolean)	13	13	0
Terms-Journals	25	1	12
Journals	26	0	26

Fig. 1. Tabulation of results — both queries combined

Observations

1. The *Indirect Method* gave better results than a straight Boolean search. This was true both in the repetition of the original *Indirect Method* (using chains) and with the distance technique.

2. The *Indirect Method* distance technique gave better results than the chaining method with certain combined measures. This was not true of index terms alone.

3. The best retrieval results came from:
    a. Authors alone,
    b. Authors and journals in combination.

4. The next best retrieval results were:
    a. Authors and Terms,
    b. Authors, Terms and Journals.

Conclusions

Based on the results of this experiment:

1. Authors or authors with journals are the best measure of document relatedness. Measures other than index terms can be used for retrieval.

2. The *Indirect Method* is still best, no matter which form it takes (chains or distances).

3. The distance technique actually worked better than the chaining method, and it is simpler to use.

Implications

The importance of authors and the combination of authors and journals was the most interesting result of this experiment. It is an area that should be explored further.

For example, it is possible to visualize a library catalog based on author networks. Knowing an author on a subject of interest, a patron might enter the catalog with that author and find other authors who write on the subject. This is not a subjective subject heading cross-reference, but is based on a quantitatively determined author network. Such networks could be machine-constructed from existing data bases.

Another implication lies in the use of computers in information retrieval systems. Automatic indexing has never been completely successful. One reason is the input and processing problem involved with total text manipulation. Why not forget this full text approach and establish retrieval systems based on authors and the journals in which they publish? If desired, another dimension, based on abstracts or manually assigned index terms, might be used, but the index terms would play a secondary role.

Obviously, the experiment reported here is only a pilot project, based on a small set of documents. However, the positive results are encouraging enough to warrant a larger investigation, pointing toward possible operational systems.

References

1. Goffman, W. 1964. "A Searching Procedure for Information Retrieval." *Information Storage and Retrieval.* 1964; 2: 73-78.

2. Verhoeff, J.; Goffman, W.; Belzer, J. 1961. "Inefficiency of the Use of Boolean Functions for Information Retrieval Systems." *Communications of the Association for Computing Machinery.* 1961; 4: 557-59.

3. Goffman, W. 1964. "On Relevance as a Measure." *Information Storage and Retrieval.* 1964; 2: 201.

4. Goffman, W. 1968. "An Indirect Method of Information Retrieval." *Information Storage and Retrieval.* 1968; iv; (4): 361-73.

5. Maron, M. E.; Kuhns, J. L. 1960. "On Relevance, Probabilistic Indexing and Information Retrieval." *Journal of the Association for Computing Machinery.* 1960; vii: 3.

6. Doyle, L. B. 1961. "Semantic Road Maps for Literature Searches." *Journal of the Association for Computing Machinery.* 1961; viii.

7. Kessler, M. M. 1963. "Bibliographic Coupling between Scientific Papers." *American Documentation.* 1963 January; xiv.

8. Maron, M. E.; Shoffner, R. M. 1969. *The Study of Context: An Overview.* Berkeley, CA: The University of California. 1969.

* * * * *

THE ABSTRACT

The originally published version of this paper has with it an author-prepared abstract, but for the moment it has been left off. Let's see how we might go about writing an abstract for this paper.

The first order of business is to go over the paper and decide what it is about. Ideally, the abstractor will read the paper through several times.

Having read the paper, can we state, in one sentence, what this paper is about? It has to do with information retrieval, of course, but that is a very broad term. What specific aspect of information retrieval is dealt with here? It has to do with searching strategies, and, in particular, it seems to be carrying forward work done by a man named Goffman. At this point, it would be useful for the abstractor to scan the references to Goffman's work; an abstractor knowledgeable in the field would probably be somewhat familiar with Goffman's ideas. This is the kind of knowledge that supports the contention that indexers and abstractors should have subject background.

At any rate, we might now notice that in the last paragraph of the introduction the author has stated what the paper is about. However, we must maintain a degree of cynicism, since it's not unheard of for an author to say that a paper is about topic *A* when in reality it is about topic *B*. However, in this case it appears that the paper is about what the author says it is, so our first sentence might read:

> This paper reports a technique that expands W. Goffman's Indirect Method search strategy.

Having gotten this sentence on paper, we now have a launching pad.

In the chapters on abstracting it was stated that an abstract should point out what new ideas or techniques are presented in the paper. So we might look at the sentence and ask *what* and *how*? What "technique" was used and how does it "expand" on Goffman's method? It seems that Goffman's technique is based on the redundancy of content between each pair of documents in a file, and he uses the co-occurrence of index terms to establish the level of this redundancy. The author of the present paper is proposing some new measures. So now we can go back and expand on the basic sentence so that it now reads:

> This paper reports a technique that expands W. Goffman's Indirect Method search strategy by using means other than index terms to reflect document content.

At this point the abstractor again takes stock and tries to conceive what next piece of information would help readers decide if they want to read the paper or not. When we read our sentence again, the most obvious is: What "other" means? Again, the answer is supplied in the section on measures. So now we add a second sentence:

> The four basic measures of document relatedness were (1) index terms, (2) journals in which the documents appeared, (3) closeness of the authors of the documents, and (4) closeness of citations.

A decision has to be made at this point: Should the abstract elaborate here and go into detail about each of these measures? It is not clear from this sentence just how these measures were constructed.

The decision is made *not* to elaborate, for the following reasons. First, most people reading this abstract will recognize what is meant by each of these four terms and will know that it is of secondary importance to know exactly how the measures were constructed. This is not the major point of the paper. If readers choose to read the paper, there is a high probability they will learn the details. And, second, abstracts have space constraints, and to elaborate at this point would make the abstract long and give inordinate space to a secondary element.

But, what next? Is this paper a philosophical essay? A survey? Experimental research? Clearly, it is an experiment, and a good part of the paper discusses the experiment.

Now comes another decision. How much of the experimental model should be discussed in the abstract? It seems that the experimental model is *not* new but a replication of Goffman's model; therefore, its exact procedure should not be elaborated on in the abstract. If a new, unknown, innovative experiment had been used, then it should be noted with some detail.

However, there are some differences in the objectives of Goffman's experiment and in the new work. The new paper defines a distance function within Goffman's model and calculates relatedness of documents by using the Euclidean distance mathematical model. Consequently, we can add two more sentences to the abstract:

> In the experiment a distance function between documents is defined, based on the properties of the documents themselves. The proximity between pairs of documents is then determined by calculating the Euclidean distance.

The abstractor has told us what the document is about, what new idea is to be considered, and what new objective is built into Goffman's experimental model. All that remains is to state the major results:

> Based on the results of this experiment, authors or authors with journals are the best measures of document relatedness.

If we read over these sentences, we get a vague feeling that the narrative is left up in the air. We need some concluding remark, to leave the reader with a feeling of completeness. Suppose we add a short critical comment: "This aspect should be explored further."

Also, in the first sentence, "This paper" is unnecessary and so it is deleted, along with a few other superfluous words. Now our complete abstract reads as follows:

> Reports a technique that expands Goffman's Indirect Method search strategy by using means other than index terms to reflect document content. Four basic measures of document relatedness were (1) index terms, (2) journals in which the documents appeared, (3) closeness of the authors, and (4) closeness of citations. Distance functions between documents are defined, based on the properties of the documents.

The proximity between pairs of documents is then determined by calculating the Euclidean distance. Authors or authors with journals seem to be the best measures of document relatedness. This aspect should be explored further.

This is an abstract of ninety-one words, a rather standard length for the journal in which it was published.

INDEXING THE DOCUMENT

Proper indexing begins with a proper bibliographic entry for the paper. Following the selected model for entries the indexer must carefully and accurately include all necessary information and in the proper form.

Now the indexer is ready to read the document. With a pen or pencil or colored marker in hand, or better still, a computer-aided indexing program, the indexing begins. The indexer selects the significant concepts in the paper without being overly concerned with what the final indexing terms may be.

Where in the paper can the indexer find significant concepts? First, the title itself provides *n-dimensional* and *retrieval model*. Both of these concepts are very general and do not carry much specific information, but that is not the indexer's concern at this point.

Next comes the author-prepared abstract, from which emerges the following list of concepts:

Technique—in itself a vague word, but which later on could present an important concept if used in conjunction with one or more other terms

Indirect Method—a specific, unique concept in the field of information retrieval

Search strategy—one of the fundamental processes in an information retrieval system

Index terms—obviously a significant concept in a paper about information retrieval, and one that the indexer with subject background will know is used as a document relatedness indicator in Goffman's method

Citations—a significant concept both in information retrieval and in the present paper

Distance function—a popular concept in information retrieval for a number of years and central to the paper being indexed

Euclidean distance—the mathematical model used in the technique tested in the experiment reported by the paper

Document relatedness—again a popular information retrieval concept and also a key one in the paper

The next step is to scan the section headings, which provides the following terms for our concept list:

Goffman's method—term in which the man becomes the indicator

Document distances—a primary concept in most mathematical models of information retrieval systems

Mathematical model—which might become a subject entry term; "Mathematical models," a popular topic in information retrieval

Experimental model—also a recurring topic in information retrieval

Distance matrices—the technique that creates distances between documents in an Euclidean space, displayed in the paper in matrix form

After finishing the section headings, the indexer turns to the text proper and scans it for additional concepts. The following words are added to the list:

Automatic document retrieval
Retrieval systems
Probabilistic indexing
Bibliographic coupling
Measures of relatedness
Properties of documents
Simulated information retrieval system
Keyword co-occurrence
Journal relatedness
Author relatedness
Commonality of citations
Word frequency techniques

Only one part of the text remains to be scanned: the references. The indexer now examines the titles in the references for significant words. The premise here is that the references will reflect what the paper is about. The following words now complete the concept list:

Searching procedures
Literature searches

Our full list looks like this:

Technique	*Retrieval systems*
Indirect method	*Probabilistic indexing*
Search strategy	*Bibliographic coupling*
Index terms	*Measures of relatedness*
Citations	*Properties of documents*
Distance function	*Simulated information retrieval system*
Euclidean distance	*Keyword co-occurrence*
Document relatedness	*Journal relatedness*
Document distances	*Author relatedness*
Mathematical model	*Commonality of citations*
Goffman's method	*Word frequency techniques*
Experimental model	*Searching procedures*
Measures	*Literature searches*
Distance matrices	*N-dimensional*
Automatic document retrieval	*Retrieval model*

At this point the indexer may choose to add terms subjectively arrived at from personal knowledge of the subject and understanding of who the index users will be. Meaning cannot be totally conveyed from a list of words lifted from the text, since language is much more than a list of words. The arrangement of words, their proximity to each other, and the order of sentences and paragraphs are the proper context for words. When words are stripped away from these structures they lose much of their communication power. For this reason the exact words of the text are rarely sufficient, as naked symbols, to convey the full meaning of natural language. The indexer should understand this and try to add appropriate terms to bridge the gap as far as possible between the natural language intent and the bare list of "key" words. By adding a word here and there the indexer can restore, to a certain extent, the meaning lost when the text was dismembered.

The next step is to translate the concept list into the controlled vocabulary. The thesaurus we will use to index our example is *Thesaurus of Information Science Terminology*, compiled by Claire K. Schultz. In the entry examples from the thesaurus on the following pages, an allowed index term or phrase is indicated in capital letters and cross-referenced terms are indicated in lower case letters.

The first word on the concept list is *technique*. Intuitively we feel that this is a very broad term and probably will be a modifier to another term. Nevertheless, we should check the thesaurus to see if it is an indexable term. Page 197 of the thesaurus proves our intuition was wrong, because we find "Techniques" listed as an entry term. We write the term on our list of index terms. Now we ask the question, Does this term have a broader term? It does—the word *input*, but this term is clearly inappropriate to the paper we are indexing, so we pass it by. Does the term have a narrower term? It has six listed:

Communication techniques
Data processing techniques
Evaluation techniques
Manual techniques
Photograph
Printing

The only possibility here is "Evaluation techniques," but if we think back to the paper, the techniques talked about were those for structuring information retrieval files, *not* evaluation techniques. So we pass by this narrower term.

Next we observe that our entry term "Technique" has a list of related terms:

Applications	Modeling
Delivery of services	Publishing
Input-output equipment	Research
Instructing	Statistics
Measures (measuring techniques)	

Two possible candidates occur:

Measures (measuring techniques)
Modeling

The paper deals with a model of an aspect of information retrieval and also, most certainly, with measures. So we add these terms to the list. Now we should check the added terms to see if they have broader, narrower, or related terms. A check on pages 140 and 137 turns up no new terms that are related to the paper, so we are ready for our next term on the concept list.

The next term on the concept list is *Indirect Method*. It is not listed at all in the thesaurus. The term is not an identifier (place or proper name), so we ask if the concept of the phrase can be denoted by combining two or more descriptors from the thesaurus. After a pause we cannot think of any such combination, so we ask the next question: Is there a synonym we might use to enter the thesaurus again? We cannot think of one, so we will have to be content that perhaps the entry term "Technique" will be selected by a user wanting information on the Indirect Method. We realize that *Indirect Method* is not widely known in the field, and if we were to have any input on future revision of the thesaurus we might note it for possible inclusion in a revised edition.

Our next term is *search strategy*. On page 182 of the thesaurus we find:

Search Strategy
    Use   SEARCHING
             INTERRELATIONS
             TECHNIQUES

The paper is fundamentally concerned with searching techniques, so we add "Searching" to our list. Lower down on the same page we find the term with the following:

SEARCHING
    BT   Storage and Retrieval Processes
    RT   Comparing
             Selection
             Storage and Retrieval Systems

Two possible candidates here are:

Storage and Retrieval Processes
Storage and Retrieval Systems

The paper deals with both concepts, but to use either would be to "post up" on the term with which we are dealing. Later down on our concept list we see *retrieval systems*, but if we realize that the paper is dealing with processes and not specifically with systems we will reject "Storage and Retrieval Systems." Now, do we post up to "Storage and Retrieval Processes"? Yes, because it is a generic term that clearly defines the whole intent of the paper, and it is a term likely to be used by the reader. It is added to the list, and we turn to page 190 and find the following:

STORAGE AND RETRIEVAL PROCESSES
    BT   Data Processing
    NT   Inquiry Negotiation
            Searching
    RT   Evaluation
            Information
            Selection
            Techniques

No new usable terms are found, so we are ready for the text term on our concept list, which is *index terms*. On page 97 of the thesaurus we find:

INDEX TERMS (DOCUMENT SURROGATES)
    BT   Indicators
    RT   Concepts

    and

INDEX TERMS (FORMAT AND INTERRELATIONS)
    BT   Structure
    RT   Interrelations

The paper discusses a technique based on the structure and interrelationship of index terms. Given the meaning and intent of the paper, "Index Terms (format and interrelations)" will be a key descriptor. Should we also add "Structure" and "Interrelations"? "Structure" does not strike us as being a term a user interested in the information in the paper might select, so we reject it. However, "Interrelations" is, so we add it to the list and then turn to page 115 and find:

INTERRELATIONS
  BT   Administration
  NT   Associating
        Bias
        Collating
        Comparing
        Composing
        Consistency
        Constructing
        Extracting
        File Organization
        Meeting Organization
        Merging
        Opportunity
        Permutation
        Ranking
        Readiness
        Sequencing
        Sorting
        Structure
  RT   Change
        Coding Systems
        Data Analysis
        Electromechanical Data Processing Equipment
        Index Terms (Format and Interrelations)
        Interaction
        Randomness
        Relations

Out of this long list, "File Organization" is selected, since we remember from the paper that the Indirect Method and the new idea tested are both concerned with the organization of files for information retrieval. "File organization" is added to our descriptor list, and we now look up this new term in the thesaurus. On page 83 we have:

FILE ORGANIZATION
  BT   Interrelations

Nothing is to be added here, so we move on to the next term on the concept list — *distance function*. We find no listing for it, and since it is not an identifier, we try to think of two terms that might be combined to express the concept. Failing in this we try to think of synonyms, coming up with *vector space*, but there is no such listing. So we try *space* and find, on page 188:

Space (Allocated for Storage)
  Use   STORAGE SPACE

     and

Space (Outer Space)
   Use   AEROSPACE SCIENCES

and

SPACE (RESOURCE)
   BT   Resources
   NT   Storage Space
          Measures (Measuring Techniques)
          Priorities

and

Space (Topologic)
   Use   TOPOLOGY

The closest one of concern to us is "Space (Topologic)," but the paper deals with a metric space, not topological space, so this term is rejected.

Can we think of a broader term for *distance measures*? *Mathematical measures* comes to mind, so we search the thesaurus and find on page 133:

MATHEMATICS
   BT   Knowledge Areas
   NT   Algebra
          Geometry
          Logic
          Statistics
   RT   Coding Systems
          Cybernetics
          Evaluation Techniques
          Modeling
          Numeric Processing
          Symbolic Logic

The only possibility here is "Modeling," and since it is already on our descriptor list, we will settle for it. Ideally, a user wanting information on the use of distance functions will use "Modeling" as an entry term.

The next term on the concept list is *Euclidian distance*, which leads us along the same path as the last term.

Next on the list is *document relatedness*, which we cannot locate in the thesaurus. However, we do find two separate entry terms, "Documents" and "Relations," so we add these, presuming a postcoordinate search by the user.

Since we can find no useful broader, narrower, or related terms under either of these, we go to our next term on the concept list, which is *mathematical model*. On pages 132-33 we find

Mathematical Models
   Use   MODELING
            MATHEMATICS

Since "Modeling" is already on the descriptor list, we add "Mathematics" and turn to "Mathematics" on the same page. We have been over this ground before, so we move on to the next term on the concept list.

The term *Goffman's method* is not in the thesaurus, but it is clearly an indicator term, so we add it to the list and move to the next term, which is *experimental model*. On page 79 we find "Experimental research." Now the paper is not a discussion *about* experimental research in information science, but *is* experimental research, and its techniques and general approach would probably be of interest to a person concerned with experimental research in the field, so we add it.

The next term is *measures*, which is already on the descriptor list. The next is *distance matrices*. We realize that this concept leads us down the same path as an earlier concept, *distance function*.

The next term is *automatic document retrieval*. The closest we can come is:

Automated Retrieval
    Use   STORAGE AND RETRIEVAL PROCESSES
            COMPUTER APPLICATIONS

"Computer Applications" is inappropriate, and we already have "Storage and Retrieval Processes."

The foregoing procedure is repeated, in turn, for the remaining words on the concept list, resulting in the following terms being added to our list of descriptors:

Indexing	Citations
Indexes	Citation indexing
Performance	Authors

The complete final descriptor list, now alphabetized, looks like this:

Authors
Citation indexing
Citations
Documents
Experimental research
File organization
Goffman's method
Index terms (format and interrelations)
Indexes
Indexing
Interrelations
Mathematics
Measures (measuring techniques)
Modeling
Performance
Relations
Searching
Storage and retrieval processes
Techniques

In closing, four things should be noted about this descriptor list creation:

1. The indexing was exhaustive.

2. The indexing was specific.

3. The influence (good and bad) of an author-prepared index is evident.

4. The use of this particular thesaurus had good and bad moments. Some of the time the precise term could be found, or built, but at other times it was difficult to find the proper words. This is a good example of how a thesaurus can never be perfect, how it can never have terms that completely fulfill both literary and user warrant.

XI
Automatic Methods

INTRODUCTION

Society recognizes the need for information in the decision-making process. Information, accurately processed and delivered on time, is not a luxury but a necessity. We realized long ago that the solution to the information explosion was not simply to add more people, more filing cabinets, another wing to the library, or whatever. Centuries ago humans learned to build and use machines to augment physical abilities. Later came machines to augment mental abilities as well. Just as an ax makes it easier to chop down a tree, a computer makes it easier to handle data processing chores.

For a good number of years people have been asking if computers can do indexing and abstracting. If the text of the documents can be converted into machine-readable form, and if the correct rules can be programmed into the computer, then, clearly, the answer is yes. The first condition is rapidly becoming less and less of a problem, but the second condition remains a difficult one.

The purpose of this chapter is to give an overview of how computing machines may be useful in the chore of indexing and abstracting.

INFORMATION PROCESSING WITH COMPUTERS

It does not take very long to enumerate what makes a computer important, because it is a very specific entity, with a relatively simple mode of operation. It can find solutions only to problems that have been completely analyzed, described, and prepared in proper form by human minds. If the world is taken over by a computer in the foreseeable future, you can be sure that behind it is a diabolical human mind.

Why are computers useful?

Computers are fast. Everyone knows that computers are extremely fast, but the general public probably has no real concept of just how fast they are. It is common to talk about operations being done in nanoseconds (billionths of a second). How fast is a billionth of a second? Can the human mind conceive how fast that is? Speed allows computers to handle tasks that could never be done manually because it would take too long or would require an infeasible number of people. For the first time, problems can be solved that were too much to handle with pencils and paper or even with the aid of adding machines. The computer's speed makes these tasks ordinary. For example, let's say it takes you fifteen seconds to add up four three-digit numbers:

149
206
123
319

In that same fifteen seconds, a computer could have added several million such numbers. Or to put it another way, in fifteen seconds the computer could do what it would take you four or five months to do with pencil and paper if you worked day and night without sleeping, eating, or sharpening your pencil.

Computers follow instructions automatically. Programming a computer means preparing a detailed list of instructions (a program) that tells the machine what to do in a logical progression. The program tells the computer to test certain conditions throughout the program and then take alternative routes through the program according to those conditions. After the program has been prepared, it is stored in the machine, and the computer takes over. It faithfully carries out those instructions, one after the other. The only human action is a possible input of data at various points, but the machine no longer needs any outside intervention; thus it does its duties automatically.

Computers are accurate. They very seldom make mistakes. When the computer adds up the millions of numbers in fifteen seconds, it is unlikely that it will make an error in the calculation. This dependability makes the computer extremely useful in all segments of its application.

Programmers, however, do make mistakes. If they give the computer wrong instructions and the machine faithfully does what it is told, the error is not the fault of the computer. When we read in the paper about the little old lady on welfare who received a tax bill for $17 million, it is usually safe to assume that it was a human error and not the fault of the computer.

Computers promote meticulous problem analysis. A computer can work only a problem that has been meticulously analyzed and mapped out. A constant factor in computer system malfunction is the failure of its programmers to fully understand the problem. If the problem or the system being automated is not understood in the first place, then bringing in a computer is a mistake. This has happened over and over again in library automation. Librarians often realized that their computer was simply allowing them to make the same old mistakes — at an incredible speed.

Understanding a problem is one thing, but understanding it to the depth of detail and insight necessary to program a computer may be another matter. For example, if you are asked to get up and go open the door, very little instruction is needed. You may never have seen a door before, but if we speak the same language, I will say, "See that little round thing near the middle? That's a knob. Turn the knob and push on the door." I do not have to analyze the problem any further or give any more instruction.

But suppose I want to program a computer-controlled robot to do the same thing. Then the *major* steps (but not all the detailed steps) would be:

1. Raise your arm.

2. Move your arm until the hand is directly over the round ball sticking out of the door a little over halfway down.

3. Lower your arm until your hand touches the ball.

4. Close your fist and secure it around the ball.

5. Turn your wrist clockwise until the latch is extracted into the door.

6. Gently push the door, etc.

Can a computer be given these kinds of instructions to index and abstract a knowledge record? Computers have the ability to make simple decisions in the areas of number comparison, character comparison, and machine system testing. Their most fundamental ability is to make a decision on the basis of the relative magnitude of two numbers. Essentially, this is the limit of the machine's intellectual ability. The question that immediately arises is, How can computers accomplish such marvelous things if these are the only decision-making capabilities they possess? The secret lies in the skillful way a human programmer uses this simple, logical ability of the machine.

For example, suppose a company has a file of personnel information, including the number of children each employee has. If the manager needs a list of all those people who have seven or more children, the programmer can write a program that will tell the computer to start at the front of the file and pull down the first employee's record and go to the specified block of data that has the number of children. The computer then compares that number with seven and if it equals seven or is larger, the computer is told to print out that particular personnel record and then move to the next one. When the number in the block is less than seven, the computer is told *not* to print out that record but to move directly to the next.

We may look at the completed list and marvel at how smart the computer is — it knows all the families in the company and how many children each has. The truth is, the computer knows no such thing. It simply compared two numbers.

But upon this elementary principle, complex systems are built. The computer revolution has impacted every field of human activity and will probably go down in history as the most significant technological development since the invention of printing.

AUTOMATIC INDEXING

Human indexing is costly and can range in quality from excellent to appalling. With the rapid growth of information, the time lag between publication of a paper and the availability of indexes and abstracts to that paper has grown frightfully. Adding new people to the staff is not always a solution; it may be economically infeasible, and professionally qualified people may not be available. This is one of the practical reasons that interest turned to the possibility of automatic methods. Of course, there has been intellectual interest in such automatic means since the early days of information retrieval.

Unfortunately, we have not been able to write programs that will allow a computer to understand natural language as well as man does. A computing machine is an incredible device, but it is a poor substitute for the human brain.

The computer's power lies in processing mundane trivialities (man solves a complex problem by dividing it up into a long series of mundane steps, and *then* the computer takes over). There is no record of any computing machine that has made a valid value judgment without human direction, and such value judgments play a major role in the creation of quality indexes and abstracts.

However, a computer can be useful and is becoming increasingly important in indexing and abstracting. Promises and schemes have come and gone over the past few decades, but slowly we are obtaining an understanding of how to use these fantastic gadgets in indexing and abstracting. In the last two decades, considerable time and money have been spent on research in computer indexing of documents. In addition to the impetus the information explosion provided, computer technology rapidly advanced with a shift in emphasis from strictly scientific number-crunching to information processing. Computers became available that were compatible with the needs of information professionals. Also, for a number of years considerable funds were available, principally from the federal government, for research in this area. Most of this money was aimed at information storage and retrieval systems in general, not specifically at indexing and abstracting, but it soon became clear that indexing and abstracting are at the heart of the matter, involving considerable human endeavor, both mental and physical.

It was pointed out in an earlier chapter that there are basically two kinds of indexing: *assigned indexing* and *derived indexing*. Assigned indexing means that the indexer chooses descriptors to represent concepts in the document, whereas derived indexing involves use of the author's actual words as descriptors, without modification. Automatic indexing is based on the assumption that the words in the text and their relationships to each other are sufficient to represent content concepts. This is derived indexing.

Word Frequencies

The most extensive, if not the most successful, automatic indexing techniques are based one way or another on word frequencies – the number of times words occur in the text, the number of times they occur in conjunction with each other, the number of words that occur *between* two words, and so on.

In 1949 George Zipf published a book called *Human Behavior and the Principle of Least Effort*, subtitled "An Introduction to Human Ecology," which first drew attention to a behavioral factor related to frequencies of word occurrence in English language texts. Basically, Zipf believed that we can get a deeper understanding of human behavior if we look at it as a natural phenomenon, the same way we study biology or anything else in the universe. His purpose in writing the book was to support what he called "The Principle of Least Effort," which, he claimed, controls our individual and societal behavior, including language. We tend to take the path that entails the least effort.

Zipf supported this theory with data he collected for twenty-five years. For example, he believed that tools were created because of the principle of least effort. The caveman found out it required less effort to hit a saber-toothed tiger over the head with a club than to strangle him barehanded. It was Zipf's belief that society developed because it requires more effort for man to survive if he is totally independent. Even the American Civil War followed the principle of least effort. The issues were so complex and emotional that compromise was too difficult. The way of least effort was to get out on the battlefield and slug it out.

Not everybody would buy Zipf's contentions, but that's neither here nor there. What is of interest to us is some of the empirical observations he recorded on huge amounts of data, particularly the ones concerning the behavior of words in texts, which appear in a chapter of the book called "On the Economy of Words." As one might suspect, Zipf believed that language is governed by the principle of least effort, in the sense that over a period of time, language finds the least number of words that will convey the most information. Normal, everyday language uses relatively few of the total words available in the dictionary.

Zipf counted words in different texts and came up with this observation: If words of a given text are ordered so that the most frequently used word is first and has rank one, and the second most frequently used word comes second and has rank two, and so on, then we have:

$$\text{Rank x Frequency} = \text{Constant } (RF = C)$$

One of the first things that becomes obvious in studying the distributions is that the words with low frequency don't seem to follow the pattern as well. As we move further down in the rank, the constant becomes more variable. Consequently, Zipf also made some observations on the low-frequency words in texts. The low-frequency law was expressed as

$$I_1/I_n = (4n^2 - 1)/3$$

where I_1 is the total number of words having the frequency of one, and I_n is the total number of words having the frequency of n.

A. D. Booth (1967) found that the ratio as calculated by I_1/I_n is empirically lower than the prediction from the formula $(4n^2 - 1)/3$. He did some tests, extended the parameters, did some more tests, and proposed a modification of Zipf's second law, which states that

$$I_1/I_n = n(n + 1)/2$$

This modified law, which is a more general expression, seems to conform to the empirical observations very well. It is obvious that these two laws of Zipf are different, since they involve two different behavioral patterns.

From the law for the high-frequency words and Booth's revised law for low-frequency words, W. Goffman postulated that it is reasonable to suspect that there is a critical region where the behavior of high-frequency words conforming to Zipf's law transforms to the characteristics of low-frequency words as predicted by Booth. He hypothesized that this region may consist of one single word or a group of terms that are characterized by their high content-bearing nature in relation to the entire text. Goffman based his assumption on the fact that functional words always occupy the top positions of the frequency word list, which is presumably inherent in the structure of the language, and that low-frequency words reflect the style and the richness of vocabulary of individual authors. Therefore, the transition exhibits neither the basic language requirement nor the varying styles; it represents the semantic embodiment of the document. To arrive at this transition, it is known that the special feature of the low-frequency words is that there are many different words having the frequency of one, and that there are less different words having higher frequency of occurrence. In fact, generally some unique words have the higher frequencies. It is possible that the critical point of transition lies where the number of different words approaches one. That is to say, from Booth's equation:

$$I_1/I_n = n(n+1)/2$$

becomes

$$I_1/1 = n(n+1)/2 \text{ as } I_n \text{ approaches } 1$$

Then, solving for n from the quadratic equation:

$$n = \frac{-1 + \sqrt{1 + 8I_1}}{2}$$

Thus, the critical region can be identified at the point where the frequency of word occurrence is n.

The point of all of this is that Zipf's laws predict the behavior of words, and the most direct application is in the area of automatic indexing. What follows illustrates the fundamental attempts at using the computer to index documents.

Automatic indexing is the assignment of index terms on some quantitative basis. We feed the title, abstracts, or texts into a computer and the index terms are automatically generated.

Zipf's law, combined with Goffman's transition point, is one example of how this might be done.

The procedure would be:

1. Feed in the text of a document.

2. The computer counts and ranks the words according to Zipf's first law.

3. Goffman's transition point is calculated.

4. A stop-word list knocks out cement words—*the, and, but*, etc.

Since the transition region contains the content-bearing terms of the document, they are our automatic index terms.

Miranda Pao (1978) tabulated all the words in a paper of Booth's called "On the Geometry of Libraries." This article proposes that libraries be designed around frequency of use—that is, the closest access points should have the most frequently used materials. It deals with collection access, distances to the stacks, and so forth. Pao's analysis, using the proposed automatic indexing method, resulted in the following table:

Frequency	Word
33	book
26	access
23	frequency
22	library
19	collection
16	distance
16	most
15	shown
13	stack
13	analysis
12	can

A comparison of this table with the article indicates that the most frequently used terms reflect the content of the article. This method seems to work very well as a quantitative indexing procedure. In fact, it is doubtful that a manual indexing procedure would have assigned very different terms, except that obvious terms, like *can*, would be omitted.

Zipf's law has been discussed in some detail because it has been the basis of automatic indexing approaches that are based on word frequencies. For example, in the 1950s H. P. Luhn suggested that if we plot word frequencies against their rank of occurrence, we could get a Zipf's law curve such as the following:

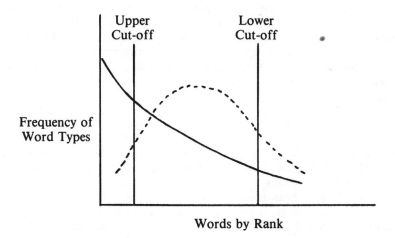

Words by Rank

Luhn believed that this frequency approach is sound because it reflects technical writing itself. That is, when an author writes a paper he chooses a relatively small set of words, but those words do not vary in meaning within that paper. He uses these same words over and over in proportion to the amount of space devoted to a notion. Thus, the words used the most will reflect the major ideas of the paper. Luhn used two methods for establishing cut-off points on the illustrated curve: (1) comparison of the words in the text against a table of common words stored in the computer, and (2) use of standard statistical techniques.

Over the years, considerable variations have been used to try to make word frequency techniques more sophisticated. For example, a thesaurus is stored in the computer and basic words derived by frequency techniques are checked automatically against the thesaurus to add synonyms and related terms. Another technique is to weight terms, that is, increase their relative importance by taking account of their position in the document. For example, the words in the results section of the document may have high importance to a reader. Another approach is to use association measures. Statistical techniques can be used to discover how words appear in pairs, either next to each other or in the same sentence. These words are then synchronized in the resulting index.

In summary, word frequency techniques use the computer to count the words in a text and then select significant words on the basis of their frequency. These significant words become the descriptors. And this, with a number of variations, has been the main thrust of automatic indexing.

Other Approaches

On the semantic level, two approaches have been most often used. First, the use of a stored dictionary or thesaurus involves letting the computer reduce words to their stems and then working from the thesaurus to construct proper indexing terms. The burden here, of course, rests on the quality of the thesaurus. There have also been attempts to automatically develop classification groups from the text and then use these related words in the indexing process. Second, syntactical analysis attempts to apply ideas and techniques developed by linguists. Paralleling the research in information retrieval throughout the 1960s was extensive work in automatic translation, which explored the structure of language and tried to reduce language to a quantitative basis. Interesting work was done, but, unfortunately, the indexing world has not been able to apply much of it to its own problems.

COMPUTER-ASSISTED INDEXING

Computer-assisted indexing, as differentiated from automatic indexing, is the use of computers to do the mundane work while a human still does the intellectual task of indexing.

Computers have been used successfully as *aids* to human indexing. For a long time they have been taking in manual indexing, processing it, and then producing lists for index publications and the like. A three-step procedure might be suggested for a system of computer-assisted indexing:

1. Have a human handler scan a document and select portions for indexing — for example, the title; section headings; sentences covering purposes, methods, and results; first and last sentences in paragraphs; and so forth. A clerk can be trained to do this with a reasonably high degree of skill.

2. Input this material into the computer and let the machine use one of the standard automatic indexing techniques (such as the one derived from Zipf's Law) to produce index terms.

3. Edit the results, making whatever changes are judged necessary; this is a job for an experienced indexer.

This approach is an economic balance between unskilled labor, skilled labor, and a computer. An example of successful semiautomatic methods is the PRECIS system, discussed in an earlier chapter. In this system, the intellectual work is done by human indexers, while the tedious manipulations necessary to complete the indexing process are done by the computer.

Microcomputers have put a new wrinkle into the indexing task. Early on, people put the microcomputer to work to aid in indexing. They did this by using a word processor or a database management program, or by writing a program to do it. Indexing software for microcomputers began to hit the market in the early 1980s, and since that time many new programs have appeared to replace those that have quietly passed away. And slowly, the quality of the programs has improved.

This software can vary from simple word processing-type programs to complex aids for producing sophisticated back-of-the-book indexes. But, like all software, it must be evaluated carefully.

In 1985, Linda K. Fetters (1987) outlined some useful guidelines for evaluating indexing software:

1. Formatting

    a. Automatic formatting of the final index in a commonly recognized style, i.e., run-in or indented

    b. Automatic creation of an acceptable number of subentries (3-7)

    c. Suppression of repeated main entries

    d. Automatic combining of page references for identical entries

2. Entering and Editing Entries

    a. A reasonable length for each entry

    b. Easy recall of previously entered data and on-screen editing

    c. Method for displaying and printing entries at any point in the indexing process

    d. Method for storing or copying previously used headings or subheadings

    e. Capability of storing the final index as a word processable disk file while preserving the original records for future use

3. Sorting

   a. A sort order that treats upper and lower case letters the same

   b. Method for marking characters or words that are not a part of the sort order, such as articles and prepositions

   c. Capability to sort letter-by-letter or word-by-word

   d. Capability to sort by main entry and each level of subentries

4. Printing Effects

   a. Provision for underlining, bolding, subscripts and superscripts

   b. Provision for changing or inserting the codes for printing or type-setting as needed for each publisher

5. Cumulation or Merging of Indexes

   a. Capability to handle enough entries for large or multivolume projects

   b. Capability of cumulating or merging separately created indexes into one large index

Following are some examples of software that has indexing capability. Each example lists the operating environment required and shows some of the program's primary functional characteristics.

AUTHEX
Contact: Reference Press
      Box 1141, Station F
      Toronto, Ontario M4Y 2TB, Canada
Functions: This program is designed for periodical indexing and has an online authority file and automatic generation of cross-references. It will support up to four levels of subheadings and has flexible output formats. The program is menu-driven and easy to use. It can also be used for vertical file indexes, current awareness reports, catalogs, bibliographies, and subject lists. There is a maximum of sixteen fields of 2,048 bytes each, a maximum record length of 4,096 bytes, a maximum of 32,000 records per file, and a maximum file size of 14MB.
Hardware: IBM PC, XT, AT, PS2, or compatibles; 256K memory, and a minimum of one disk drive.

CINDEX
Contact: Indexing Research
      P.O. Box 27687, River Station
      New York, NY 14627-7687
Functions: This is a very useful indexing program that offers most of the functions necessary to produce an index online. The absence of a menu allows the program to work fast. Commands are two-letter abbreviations or function keys, and once users master these function keys they can move immediately through the program. An index can contain up to 65,534 records, and entries may go up to 2,000, which, of course, is not needed for most index entries. Fourteen levels of

subheadings are available, and it is easy to invert headings and subheadings. Sorting can be done letter-by-letter or word-by-word, or by page number, and it ignores articles and most prepositions. It has the usual word processing formatting capabilities.

Hardware: IBM PC or compatible with at least 128K memory and a minimum of one disk drive.

DATA RETRIEVAL SYSTEM
Contact: Dynacomp, Inc.
        1427 Monroe Avenue
        Rochester, NY 14618

Functions: This is primarily a database management program, designed as a cross-indexing system, which may be used to store and retrieve by keywords. It was primarily constructed to aid in indexing journal articles, but it can be used for other types of indexes.

Hardware: Z80, 8080, 8085, or 6502 CPU, with 32K memory and one disk drive. This is a CP/M-based program.

INDEX AID 2
Contact: Santa Barbara Software Products
        1400 Dover Road
        Santa Barbara, CA 93013

Functions: The program is menu-driven and aids in entry creation, error checking and correction, sorting, and formatting of the final printout. Entries for the index can be created by using either a word processor or the built-in text editor. Entries are checked for correct syntax and sorted either letter-by-letter or word-by-word.

Hardware: IBM PC and compatibles.

INDEX EDITOR
Contact: Harley M. Templeton
        7807 Lazy Lane
        Austin, TX 78757

Functions: Sorting routine is automatic and ignores capital letters. Entries are limited to seventy-nine characters and duplicate entries are automatically eliminated. Printer control characters must be entered with a word processor.

Hardware: IBM PC and compatibles with two disk drives. A minimum of 128K memory is required.

INDEX PLUS
Contact: Personal Bibliographic Software, Inc.
        P.O. Box 4250
        Ann Arbor, MI 48106

Functions: This program has four supporting sections: Index, Merge, Delete, and Balance. These are not used alone, but work on a previously created database.

Hardware: IBM PC, XT, AT, with at least 128K memory and one disk drive. There is also a version for the Macintosh.

INDEX PREPARATION SYSTEM
Contact: Foxon-Maddocks Associates
10807 Oldfield Drive
Reston, VA 22091
Functions: It can create up to six heading levels. It has a capacity for up to 1,500 characters in an entry, with multiple run-on lines and cross-references; will hold up to 2,500 records.
Hardware: IBM PC, XT, AT compatibles with at least 128K memory and two disk drives or a hard disk.

INDEXER
Contact: Abacus Computing
271 Vose Avenue
South Orange, NJ 07079
Functions: The program scans through a document and selects words for a word list. Then it reads the list and produces an index based on either line or page number reference. The program lets the user eliminate redundant words by word length, word frequency, or through a stop-list of words.
Hardware: IBM PC and compatibles, 128K memory minimum, and one disk drive.

INDEXER'S ASSISTANT
Contact: Omega Electronics
P.O. Box 294
Oswego, NY 13126
Functions: This is a menu-driven program with help screens at every point. There are five levels of headings and each can have sixty-four characters. Final production is done with a word processor. It has letter-by-letter sorting and provides both indented and run-in style formatting.
Hardware: IBM PC, XT, AT, and compatibles. PC DOS or MS DOS, 384K memory, and at least two floppy disks are required. The program is also available for CP/M.

INDEXIT
Contact: Graham-Conley Press
P.O. Box 2968
New Haven, CT 06515
Functions: This program can handle 4,000-5,000 entries in a single index. It keeps all the entries in order, ready for display or printing. It can interfile upper and lower case and ignore punctuation marks in alphabetization if the user wishes.
Hardware: IBM PC, XT, and compatibles with two disk drives or a hard disk, and 128K memory.

ININDEX
Contact: Schwager-Holt Indexing Systems
130 West Mount Airy Avenue
Philadelphia, PA 19119
Functions: This program allows 128 characters per each entry level with up to six subheadings under the main heading. It will hold up to 1,420 entries under each

alphabetical subfile, with a maximum index size of 36,920 entries. It automatically presorts as data is concerned, and the index preview is available at any time.
Hardware: TRS-80 Model IV with two disk drives and 64K memory.

INMAGIC
Contact: Inmagic, Inc.
          238 Broadway
          Cambridge, MA 02139
Functions: This is an information management-text retrieval package with a Boolean query language and a report generator. This program can be used in libraries for cataloging, circulation, indexing, serials control, and information retrieval. It has no limits on field sizes.
Hardware: IBM PC, XT, AT, and compatibles, DEC Pro 350 and Rainbow, Wang PC.

IN>SORT
Contact: Kensa Software
          P.O. Box 49, Cathedral Station
          New York, NY 10025
Functions: This is a menu-driven program that allows up to 395 characters per record and up to 1,400 records per index; it can cumulate indexes of up to 36,000 entries with the alphabetizing module. It will create a main heading with up to three levels of subheadings and has both indented and run-in style formatting.
Hardware: IBM PC, XT, AT, or compatibles, with at least one disk drive. It will run on MS DOS, PC DOS and CP/M.

KWICINDX
Contact: Miracle Computing
          313 Clayton Court
          Lawrence, KS 66044
Functions: This is KWIC indexer with a stop-list for words usually removed from a KWIC index.
Hardware: IBM PC, 64K memory, one disk drive, printer.

MICREX and MACREX
Contact: Drusilla and Hilary Calvert
          38 Rochester Road
          London, England NW1 9JJ
Functions: This program features run-in or indented subheadings and user-determined spaces for subheadings and sub-subheadings. Identical entries are combined into one, and abbreviations can be defined at any time.
Hardware: IBM PC and compatibles with at least one disk drive and 56K memory.

MICRO INDEXING SYSTEM
Contact: Compugramma Inc.
          P.O. Box 60
          Cranbury, NJ 08512

Functions: This system is based on *The Chicago Manual of Style* (indexing guidelines). The program allows alphabetization either letter-by-letter or word-by-word and operates up to the first punctuation mark encountered in an entry level. The program ignores prepositions, articles, and conjunctions. The format may be either indented or run-in. Of special interest are the very good tutorials with the program.

Hardware: IBM PC or XT, with 128K minimum memory and one disk drive.

PRO-CITE

Contact: Personal Bibliographic Software, Inc.
             P.O. Box 4250
             Ann Arbor, MI 48106

Functions: The purpose of this software is to aid in the development and management of bibliographic databases. It allows the user to create and maintain formatted bibliographies or reading lists. It identifies the major parts of a citation (author, title, publisher, etc.) for twenty different types of materials. Each of these types has a work form associated with it and the form presents the user with a list of fields relevant to the types of material. The user then "fills in the blanks." The program will format the citations into a bibliography. The program includes both word processing and a database function and allows indexing for later retrieval.

Hardware: IBM Personal Computer (PC, XT, AT) or compatibles and 256K memory.

PROFESSIONAL BIBLIOGRAPHIC SYSTEM

Contact: Personal Bibliographic Software, Inc.
             P.O. Box 4250
             Ann Arbor, MI 48106

Functions: This is a menu-driven program with variable length fields. It will hold abstracts or annotations of any length and has a flexible formatting capability. Retrieval is based on the index term field, and any term is searchable once it has been keyed into the index term field.

Hardware: IBM (PC, XT, AT), with 128K minimum memory and one double-sided disk drive. There is also a Macintosh version.

SEARCHLIT

Contact: Citadel Software
             1595 Soquel Drive, Suite 350
             Santa Cruz, CA 95065

Functions: 32,000 references can be entered on each disk directory. The program provides publication-quality bibliography output and includes sorting, underlining, superscripts, and subscripts. Since there is no limit to the size of the abstract, full text could be input. All text is searchable.

Hardware: IBM and most compatibles, 256K memory, two disk drives.

WORD.EX

Contact: Supplemental Software
             1825 Westcliff Drive, Suite 116
             Newport Beach, CA 92660

Functions: This program creates an alphabetical index of any memo, letter, report, thesis, periodical, or book. It generates an index reference containing all words in the file and their associated page numbers, and uses exclusion and inclusion words from separate files created by a word processor.

Hardware: IBM PC, XT, and PCjr, with 128K memory and one disk drive.

CHANGES IN INDEXING

The last two decades have brought on huge collections of online databases, and the trend points to even greater collections. What impact will this have on indexing? The most obvious impact will be an increase in indexing depth because of the computer's ability to quick process large amounts of information. In many of the situations now existing where there is both a printed and an online version, the online version contains a deeper range of descriptors. The physical constraints on the printed indexes often limit deeper coverage.

Also, with the improving technology there is a renewed interest in making the computer a more useful tool. The use of artificial intelligence, for example, will be discussed in a later section of this chapter.

AUTOMATIC ABSTRACTING

Just as manual abstracting is functionally related to manual indexing, so is automatic abstracting related to automatic indexing. For example, Luhn carried over his word frequency ideas from indexing to abstracting. He developed a technique for giving a priority rating to each sentence in the text based on the frequency of occurrence of the words, and observed how many of the words occurred not more than four words from each other in a sentence. Sentences loaded down with highly significant words, one next to the other, would be selected by the computer as part of the automatic abstract.

Luhn's rule for assigning priority was based not merely on the words' presence in the sentence, but on the relationship of keywords within the sentence. The method involved an overall look at the sentence to break it down into phrases set off by significant words. These segments were then candidates for processing if there were no more than five nonsignificant words between the significant words. Next, the priority calculation for the sentence was made by tabulating the significant words in each isolated phrase, squaring that value, and then dividing by the total number of words in the phrase. For example:

> The history of Siamese cats in Texas is written in long, rambling sentences but is of interest to the field of cat biology and its history.

Suppose that the significant words in this sentence, derived by a frequency technique, are the following:

Biology	History
Cat	Siamese
Cats	Texas

The sentence would be broken down:

The [history of Siamese cats in Texas] is written in long, rambling sentences but is of interest to the field of [cat biology and its history].

The first cluster has four keywords and a total of six words in all, so:

$$4^2/6 = 16/6 = 2.66$$

The second phrase has three significant words and five total words, so:

$$3^2/5 = 1.8$$

The highest value is assigned to the sentence as its priority rating, so the sentence has a score of 2.7. After all sentences in the paper have been rated, the highest ones are lifted verbatim from the text (or *extracted*) and are printed out in sequence. The results of this technique have been mixed, with some abstracts reading very well and others producing nonsense that gives the user a laugh and little else.

Another approach is to concentrate on certain stylistic aspects of the document. For example, the computer might be programmed to hunt for topical sentences, such as the first and last in the paragraph. Also it has been observed that prepositional phrases tend to carry more significant words than other sentence construction parts. The computer can be easily instructed to find these phrases by using a stored list of prepositions in its memory. Such sentences are prime candidates for the extracted sentences.

Some attempts have been made to construct a thesaurus that could be stored in the computer to help identify words. The thesaurus would be a subject-oriented one, not a general type, that recognizes content-bearing words in a subject field. With the help of the thesaurus, significant words and sentences could be identified for extracting. The problem, of course, is that a thesaurus is expensive to construct and maintain, and it increases the use of memory space and processing time.

Up to this time, automatic abstracting has had only partial success. In some cases it supplies concise, understandable information. Too often, however, the abstracts read like strings of disconnected sentences, which indeed they are.

EXPERT SYSTEMS

In the last few years widespread attention has been given to the possibilities of applying expert systems to the traditional bibliothecal processes in libraries. This accelerating interest in the application of such systems in libraries parallels recent advances and a renewed interest in the field of artificial intelligence. Seminal work is already underway and it can be briefly summarized as follows:

Online database searching. It is not surprising that this would be one of the first areas of inquiry, since a "good" online searcher is considered to be a special expert. The work in this area has concentrated primarily on gateways and front-end systems, which appear to have the goal of allowing end-users to do their own searching.

One of the problems in online database searching is that the various systems have developed independently and even though they have many similarities, they have many differences in file structures, command languages, and access protocols. Only an expert intermediary is able to master the complexities across these various systems. The results of this has been an intense interest in interface systems, and this joins quite nicely with the concepts of an expert system. The early gateway software has allowed automatic dialing and log-on, offline search formulation, downloading, and other such amenities, but they were not truly expert systems. However, researchers have seen the obvious possibilities and work is well underway in this area.

Indexing. In the last two or three years several projects have been initiated to study the use of expert systems in indexing, including the construction and maintenance of thesauri. This is a very complex area which involves the most fundamental intellectual aspects of library and information science. The MedIndEx System at the National Library of Medicine is probably the best example of the recent work in expert indexing systems. The system uses a frame-based experimental version of the LISP programming language and is run on a Sun Workstation. The expertise for the system is captured by having medical indexers supply index terms to documents in order to construct knowledge-based frames. This system is a true expert system, and its general approach is probably the most logical one for future work, not only in indexing, but also in abstracting.

General reference services. A few research projects have addressed general reference services. Most of the systems are standard IF-THEN types, which lead the user through an elimination sequence until the appropriate reference tool is found. An example of this type of work is ANSWERMAN, an experimental microcomputer-based expert system at the National Agricultural Library. The system allows library users to perform their own reference work by moving through a question/answer session until they find the right book. One of the problems with most of these systems is that they are highly subject-specific and are built around actual reference tools. Since a general applications system will require a very large knowledge-base, other approaches should be sought.

Cataloging and classification. Work is being done to apply expert systems to cataloging and classification. This seems natural, since expert systems and cataloging both function on the basis of knowledge expressed as a set of rules. For example, Davies and James (1984), working at the University of Exeter in England, used the PROLOG programming language in an attempt to build the use of the AACR1 rules into an expert system. The problems they encountered are typical of the ones researchers are having in the cataloging area, including the identification of a proper programming language. It might be suggested that the bibliographic utilities in the private sector should be more vigorous in supporting research in this area.

Other areas. Other areas include natural language information retrieval, graphic representation of information, and abstracting. Most of the ideas in these areas are not much beyond the speculation stage.

The bottom line is that rule-based tasks are inherent to the bibliothecal processes and are prime targets for the use of expert systems. Wide-scale implementation is years away, but the needed basic research is now under way.

Although it is not possible to explain here in detail how expert systems are designed, it might be useful to give a brief example of how such a system might be designed. The example we will use is abstracting, for which an expert system might be useful for the following reasons:

1. *Quality abstracts are essential.* The need of the scientific community to have timely, well-constructed abstracts, digests, and reviews of the literature remains a critical concern. Although online searching has revolutionized reference service, it should be remembered that finding a list of computer records in nanoseconds is not the key point. What *is* important is the information in those computer records. More and more, the user is giving first priority to obtaining succinct and readable abstracts. Productive scientists and other scholars have come to value abstracts in their work, but abstracts, like all devices for bibliographic control, are imperfect. Computer-based expert systems may be useful for creating effective abstracts.

2. *Expert systems offer certain advantages.*

   (a) Financial—Once operational, an expert system can be run on a computer at far less expense than would be required for a high-priced expert.

   (b) Productivity—An expert system might be thought of as a clone of an expert and, as such, productivity can be increased.

   (c) Transportability—The "expert" can be in many different geographical locations at the same time.

3. *Innovative approaches are needed.* The National Library of Medicine (and others) have repeatedly pointed out the need to improve abstracting services and to develop innovative methods. It has been suggested that the use of expert systems might be one such innovative method.

There is nothing mystical about the concept of an *expert system*. It simply means the designing and programming of computers to accomplish tasks that experts accomplish using their intelligence and experience. Broadly speaking, such systems have three major components. First, they have a knowledge base that captures expertise in terms of procedural knowledge. The system relies on this "knowledge" to work itself through a current problem. Second, expert systems have an inference engine that controls the process by making decisions about how to use the system's knowledge. It organizes and controls the steps needed to solve the current problem. And third, an expert system has input data about the current problem it is being asked to solve. There are a number of computer software programs designed to create expert systems, ranging from relatively easy-to-use "shells" to complex programming languages.

It should be made clear that an expert system is *not* the same thing as automatic abstracting in the traditional sense of that term, although the two could be related. Automatic abstracting is the generation of abstracts by the computer directly from the text of the documents, using strict, predetermined algorithms. Most automatic abstracting systems rely on statistical patterns of words in documents and are actually automatic extractions of sentences directly out of the text. Despite many years of experimental work in automatic indexing and abstracting, the writing of abstracts remains primarily a manual activity.

The objective of an expert system for abstracting would be to capture expertise and then lead a human processor, regardless of level of experience, through the process of writing an abstract. The objective is to create a human-machine interface where the intellectual and mechanical effort in writing an abstract is divided between the human intermediary and a computer-based support system.

The first step would be to design an initial script for the expert system. The expert would use the script to build and alter the knowledge base. Also, the interactive probing during the development of the knowledge base would cause the script itself to change. The following is an example of what an initial script might look like at this state. The script is based on the general abstracting steps that were outlined in chapter IX.

SCRIPT
System request: *Publication source?*
(e.g., should this document be rejected for abstracting because it is from a disreputable publisher? How does an expert abstractor decide? Does the abstractor have a list of "disreputable" publishers? Should the computer have such a list in its knowledge base?)

System request: *Of subject interest to the users?*
(e.g., some things will clearly be of interest, others clearly not, and some items will be of marginal interest. Who is our user? The item itself may be of value, possibly earning the author a Nobel Prize, but it may be of no interest whatsoever to the users of this abstracting service. Again, what does an expert abstractor do?)

System request: *Bibliographic reference?*
(e.g., incorrect reference entry is an unpardonable sin, since the purpose of the entry is to give exact steerage to the original paper from the abstract. How is the information verified? Is there a "standard" way to enter the reference?)

System request: *Title?*
(e.g., if titles are vague or misleading, does the abstractor take corrective action, like adding modifying words in brackets? How does the abstractor decide what is "vague" or "misleading"?)

System request: *Author?*

System request: *Subject indicators?*
(e.g., determination of subject, objectives, scope, methodology used, results, and conclusions.)

System request: *Begin writing?*
(e.g., the results of the analysis must be expressed in natural language. How? How long? Key sentences down first? What type of abstract is to be written? How did the expert decide? How is the structure of the abstract unified and logically developed?)

System request: *Edit*?
    (e.g., How? On what basis are decisions made?)

System request: *Final form of the abstract*?
    (e.g., What is the format? If not "standard," why a different form?)

The second step in the design of the expert system would be to begin the construction of the computer programs using artificial intelligence software such as LISP or PROLOG.

Step three would be to call upon abstracting experts to slowly build their abstracting expertise into the framework constructed by a beginning script similar to the one illustrated above. Following a standard expert system developmental approach, the program would create an internal representation of the abstractors' value judgments, and the general rules captured by the original script would evolve into less general, more microlevel rules.

One of the things learned about expert systems is that often relatively few and relatively simple decision devices will work as long as there is a rich, complex knowledge base to drive the program. Consequently, a great deal of care and time must be expended at this step in the procedure.

Step four would be a run-time implementation. Now that the system has been developed, someone who is not an expert abstractor should be able to use the system and write an abstract of a quality near or at the level of an expert abstractor.

PROBLEMS WITH AUTOMATIC METHODS

A number of studies, particularly by Gerard Salton (1969, 1970, 1971), indicate that automatic systems do at least as well as manual indexers. These carefully controlled experiments are hard to argue with and are more convincing than the counterarguments that say such inane things as "a computer can index only words, not concepts." Concepts can be represented only with words. What this quote implies, of course, is that assigned indexing is better than derived indexing, but a growing body of research is seriously challenging this belief. Are the indexer's words really "better" than those of the author, who supposedly knows more about the topic than the indexer? An indexer seeing the word *cats* in the text may feel that the "concept" is best represented by the term *felines*, when in fact the author meant *cats*, pure and simple. And, as mentioned above, the work of Salton and others seems to show that authors' words convey as much "concept" as manually assigned terms.

However, this does not mean that automatic indexing presents no problems or that universal application is upon us. For one thing, most automatic indexing is still in the laboratory, and we simply do not know how well these techniques will hold up in a large, real-world system. The information retrieval field is strewn with schemes that looked good in the wind tunnel but simply would not fly.

A number of studies have been made to see if less than full text could be used for automatic techniques. For example, what are the comparative results of using titles as the basis for indexing rather than the full text? What about using abstracts? Titles and abstracts together? The point of this is that in automatic systems it is faster and more economical to not use the full text even if it does exist in machine-readable form. But does it work better? There is not a consensus on this question.

People often are opposed to the computer because they consciously (or unconsciously) feel that a machine will somehow diminish their importance. That's why some sturdy indexers will stand up and say, "The computer can manipulate only *words* and not concepts." In fact, it would be to our benefit to have machines that can perform routine activities so that we can spend our time exploring the unknown and inventing the future.

To close out this discussion let us tell a little story that can be explored in detail in the historical literature of librarianship. Once upon a time there was a great debate in the library world over the introduction of a machine into the daily operations. The liberal, left-wing dreamers believed it would speed things up, increase accuracy, and, after a time, save money. The conservatives stood their ground. The machine cost too much money, it required specially trained people, it was in no way cost-effective, and there was no *proof* that it could do bibliothecal functions. Letters were published in the library literature. At meetings people argued violently. The decade was the 1880s and the machine they were talking about was the typewriter.

Automatic indexing and abstracting have not quite arrived yet, but there are very strong indications that computerized processes will be refined and widely used in the not-too-distant future. In the beginning, computer-aided indexing primarily mimicked manual indexing, or was limited to the printing operation of the indexes. But slowly and surely the situation changed, and as the software becomes more sophisticated, the computer is allowing us to go far beyond merely replicating the 3x5 card technique on the computer screen. Exciting possibilities are now upon us.

SUGGESTED READINGS

Booth, A. D. "A 'Law' of Occurrences for Words of Low Frequency." *Information and Control* 10 (April 1967): 386-93.

Davies, Roy, and Brian James. "Towards an Expert System for Cataloguing: Some Experiments Based on AACR2." *Program* 18 (1984): 283-97.

Earl, L. L. *Automatic Informative Abstracting and Indexing. Part I.* Palo Alto, Calif.: Lockheed Missile and Space Company, 1973. (LMSC-35014. AD 762 456)

Fetters, Linda K. *A Guide to Indexing Software.* 2nd ed. Washington, D.C.: American Society of Indexers, 1987.

_____. "A Guide to Seven Indexing Programs ... Plus a Review of the 'Professional Bibliographic System.' " *Database* 8 (December 1985): 31-38.

Hodgson, Elizabeth. "Microcomputer Software for Indexing." *Library Software Review* 6 (March-April 1987): 74-79.

Humphrey, Susanne M., and Nancy E. Miller. "Knowledge-based Indexing of the Medical Literature: The Indexing Aid Project." *Journal of the American Society for Information Science* 38 (March 1987): 184-96.

Jonassen, David. "Producing an Index with Your Microcomputer Database Manager." *Collegiate Microcomputer* 3 (November 1985): 375-81.

Luhn, H. P. "The Automatic Creation of Literature Abstracts." *IBM Journal of Research and Development* 2 (April 1958): 159-65.

Maeda, T., Yoshio Momouchi, and Hajime Sawamura. "Automatic Method for Extracting Significant Phrases in Scientific or Technical Documents." *Information Processing and Management* 16 (1980): 119-27.

Paice, Chris. "Expert Systems for Information Retrieval?" *AsLib Proceedings* 38 (October 1986): 343-435.

Pao, Miranda L. "Automatic Text Analysis Based on Transition Phenomena of Word Occurrences." *Journal of the American Society for Information Science* 29 (1978): 121-24.

Pollard, Richard. "Microcomputer Database Management Systems for Bibliographic Data." *The Electronic Library* 4 (August 1986): 230-41.

Salton, Gerard. "Automatic Indexing Using Bibliographic Citation." *Journal of Documentation* 27 (June 1971): 98-110.

_____. "Automatic Text Analysis." *Science* (April 17, 1970): 168.

_____. "A Comparison between Manual and Automatic Indexing Methods." *American Documentation* 20 (January 1969): 61-71.

Waters, Samuel. "Answerman, the Expert Information Specialist: An Expert System for Retrieval of Information from Library Reference Books." *Information Technology and Libraries* 7 (September 1986): 205-11.

XII
Indexing and Abstracting Services

INTRODUCTION

With the exception of the public catalog, the most used devices for bibliographic control in the library are the indexing and abstracting services. Although these services are usually in printed form, access to them by online computer is growing by leaps and bounds. Both the traditional aspects and online access to indexing and abstracting services will be surveyed in this chapter.

Most of these services are aimed at the journal literature, which is the most extensive source of information. Coverage ranges from broad and general areas to highly specialized topics. However, much more than journals is covered. The services also index and abstract books, reports, pamphlets, newspapers, government documents, and even materials in collections such as plays and poems. Although, as was pointed out earlier, much of the world's information is lost, the indexing and abstracting services in this country and around the world are an outstanding tribute to the information profession.

DEVELOPMENT AND GROWTH

In the beginning, indexing and abstracting were done by individuals on their own; then, individual libraries and other local institutions took on the job. Libraries were self-sufficient, acquiring what they thought their own clientele wanted and handling whatever bibliographic control they needed themselves.

The major impetus for change in this stance was the rapid growth of the journal literature in the nineteenth century. Here was a medium for spreading information throughout the scientific and scholarly world, allowing members to keep up with new developments and also providing a backup reservoir of retrospective information, all in a very handy form. With time this type of publication, along with other materials, came to be called the "primary" literature. The popularity and growth of the journal introduced a new problem, however. All journals published could not be acquired by any one library, and the libraries were no longer able to index and abstract adequately all they received. Before the middle of the nineteenth century, indexing and abstracting journals were being published. A number of German journals had begun a century earlier, and in England there had been *Universal Magazine of Knowledge and Pleasure* and the *Monthly Review*, which ran for almost a hundred years (1749-1844). By the middle of the nineteenth century there were indexing and abstracting journals covering most fields of knowledge. For example, the *Annales de Chimie et de Physique* ran from 1816 to 1913. The *New York Times Index* began in 1851. Many medical services began in the nineteenth century, such as the *Medical News and Library*, running from 1845 to 1879.

The turn of the new century brought a continuation of growth of these services, with the broad, overall scope giving way to more and more specialized services. Also, government began to get into the act, seeing the need for abstracts and indexes and perhaps realizing that the government itself is one of the main information creators. For example, *Statistical Abstracts of the United States* had been started in 1878, and throughout the first half of this century numerous government information services were made available.

By the end of World War II, abstracting and indexing services had grown in every technologically advanced country. In fact, they had grown to the extent that no one could say for sure how many there were. In the last few decades a number of directories to these services have been published. A good current one is *Abstracts and Indexes in Science and Technology: A Descriptive Guide* by Dolores B. Owen and Marguerite Hanchey. Other sources are to be found in such standard references as *American Reference Books Annual* and *Ulrich's International Directory of Periodicals*.

The number of abstracting and indexing services is one indicator of growth, but the primary indicator is the number of abstracts and indexes being produced. In our time this number measures in the millions per year and represents one of the most costly and extensive activities in the information handling profession.

Of particular note in the past few years have been the use of computers and the development of new kinds of services. For example, the citation indexes and other services from the *Institute for Scientific Information* have brought a whole new dimension to indexing and abstracting.

TYPES OF DATABASES

The standard types of groupings for online databases are *bibliographic* and *nonbibliographic*. As the terms indicate, the first type deals with citations to periodical articles, books, government documents, conference papers, company research reports, directories, names, and so forth. Bibliographic databases can be citations to a document, an abstract or summary of the document, or a full text of the document. A full-text database contains the complete text of each document, rather than just a reference or a reference and an abstract. Full-text searching means that every word in the text is an index term. This has advantages and disadvantages, but certainly the computer makes such an approach entirely feasible.

Nonbibliographic databases consist of thousands of numeric data points from science, business, government, and society in general. These types of databases contain graphics of all kinds.

As indexers, we have an obvious concern about bibliographic databases, but as information professionals in general we have an equal concern about both kinds of databases. Our major concern with bibliographic databases is the validity of our indexing, and our major concern with numeric databases is the validity of the numbers.

OPERATIONS

Types of Operations

Indexing and abstracting services are known as "secondary" services, since their product is not new knowledge in a subject area, but a guide to the basic, or "primary" sources. These operations originate from five general segments of society: (1) business and industry, (2) learned societies and professional organizations, (3) institutional establishments, (4) government, and (5) for-profit commercial organizations.

The primary interest of business and industry is to create and market products. The indexes and abstracts produced in this field are a part of the internal informational support activity; in daily operation, technical reports are generated that need bibliographic control, and material is acquired from other business and industrial research and development departments. This vital material can be utilized effectively only if it can be indexed or abstracted. The concern of business and industry is not for information distribution to the general public, but for their own business activities.

The goal of learned societies and professional organizations is to give service to their members and to promote knowledge advancement in their areas. These societies and organizations often issue a substantial number of primary publications, and many also offer indexing and abstracting services, both to their own publications and to the general literature in the field. In fact, they account for a large portion of indexing and abstracting services – over half.

Institutional establishments include such organizations as museums, private nonprofit research groups, and universities. Their overall portion of indexes and abstracts is relatively small, but by no means unimportant.

Government agencies contribute considerably more, producing indexes and abstracts to a myriad of subject areas. The U.S. Federal Government is the world's largest publisher, and its informational output is both formidable and complex. Much of the information is neither indexed nor abstracted and is often hopelessly buried from everyone except the most determined investigator.

Commercial organizations have as their objective to make a profit by creating indexes and abstracts. Contrary to what might be presumed, commercial operators produce a relatively small portion of the total output, somewhat over 10 percent.

Policies and Procedures

An abstracting operation has five basic steps: (1) the acquisition of the documents to be abstracted, (2) the assignment of the documents to the appropriate abstractor, (3) the abstracting process, (4) the editing and publication of the abstracts, and (5) the distribution of the abstracts.

Each one of the steps is complex and often expensive. For example, most of the documents are received in printed form and therefore a processing stage is necessary to convert information about the document (and sometimes the full text) into machine-processable form for the computer. In a large indexing and abstracting operation this is a time-consuming activity involving a large amount of keyboarding. As time goes by, scanning machines and the trend for material to be originated in computer-processable form should reduce or even eliminate the keyboarding step in the process.

Operating policies and procedures vary considerably according to the type of organization, its affiliation, and its objectives, but some general comments can be made. First, policies must be established for what is to be indexed and abstracted. These policies are conceptually similar to the policies librarians write concerning the acquisition of library materials. The services usually have a list of the journal publications in the fields covered by the operation. The basic questions to be asked are: What journals would be of important to the users? Are the articles original research? Are the articles usually significant?

Policy is usually established concerning whether the entire journal is to be indexed and abstracted, including communications, editorials, and the like. Some journals are merely scanned, with only certain papers selected. Papers may be rejected because they are of little or no interest to the users, because they are unoriginal, and because they simply are of no importance.

Incoming material is judged by an assignment editor, who then fans the items out to the appropriate indexer or abstractor. This assignment is based on a number of factors, including subject competence, interest, foreign language ability, and availability.

Most workers will tackle papers not in their area of expertise, but a good assignment editor will try not to assign papers totally outside the worker's field, and clearly avoids giving foreign language papers to someone who has absolutely no knowledge of that language. Smart assignment editors detect weaknesses in the indexers and abstractors and avoid sending them papers that have aspects they cannot handle well. For example, mathematically oriented papers would not be sent to workers who obviously do not know a logarithm from a toad, even though they may know the *subject* of the paper. An expert on the practical aspects of pig farming might be sent a scientific study of pig genetics that contains advanced mathematical explanations. While the pig farmer knows pigs, he cannot handle this paper because he does not understand the math.

In a previous chapter it was pointed out that abstracts are written by three groups of people: the author, subject experts, and professional indexers/abstractors. A service must establish a policy concerning who is to do the abstracting. There is a trend toward publishing author abstracts with papers, an arrangement that is fast and cost-effective for abstracting services. But, as was pointed out, these abstracts can vary in quality and may require editing. Many of these, especially the bad ones, cannot be edited without using the paper, so author abstracting may turn out to be more costly than was expected.

The use of volunteer subject experts can be cost-effective, but again it is not "free." True, the volunteers take their reward in performing a service to their professional area and in being given public credit, but someone has to oversee the operation—writing letters, keeping track, and finally checking the work. And the use of volunteers can cause a time lag, since a free laborer tends to be less prompt than a hired hand.

Most indexing and abstracting services have established guidelines that spell out policies and procedures to be followed. These guidelines are essential for consistency and are needed for the training of new workers. Some of these are quite detailed, but they vary according to the type of operation. For example, the following information could be suggested for a guideline handbook for abstracting:

- Objectives of the service

- User profile

- Content of the abstract

- Types of material

- Writing the first sentence

- Writing the rest

- Coverage

- Writing style suggestions

- Grammar and punctuation

- Handling nomenclature

- Abbreviations and symbols

- Foreign language material

- Worksheets and formats

- Examples

Dissemination

The different types of services have different procedures for disseminating their indexes and abstracts. First, the form may be a journal, a book, microform, cards, or magnetic tapes; or the material might be on random access machine-readable devices for online searching.

Distribution may be directly to user or it may be through an intermediary broker, such as an online database organization, who repackages the information and delivers it in a different form. Delivery varies according to individual philosophies of operation, size of the organization, and financial constraints.

Coverage

In selecting an indexing and abstracting service, a primary concern is its coverage. You turn to a particular service because you know it covers the material you need in the daily operation of your library or information center. You may want to know if all of the journal is included, not just major articles. Does the service cover pamphlets and books, patents, dissertations, reports, and government documents? Does it cover only original research or more? How much overlap is there between this particular service and other services? What are the exhaustivity and specificity of its indexing? Is the service mission-oriented or discipline-oriented?

ONLINE SERVICES

Development

One of the most profound developments in the 1970s and 1980s was the move to online access to indexing and abstracting services. The 1950s had brought the first computer retrieval systems, and the 1960s brought experimental work in online information retrieval followed by rapid developments. The 1970s gave us widespread conversion to online operations. A Senate committee report in 1960 describes in detail the status of processing systems for scientific information, with special emphasis on the economical utilization of electronic machines or equipment then available or being designed to speed up the retrieval process. Three National Science Foundation grants had been made to Chemical Abstracts Services for projects leaning toward mechanical processing and searching of chemical information. The Air Force had contracted with Lockheed Aircraft Corporation to develop a form of English amenable to machine manipulation using an algebraic representation of syntax in English sentences. Functioning automated processing of information in 1960 included three services provided to government agencies by Documentation, Incorporated, and the preparation by the National Library of Medicine of *Index Medicus*.

As bibliographic data were routinely added to the automated files for processing *Index Medicus*, the value of the retrospective database increased. In 1965 a few search analysts on the staff of the National Library of Medicine conducted about 3,000 retrospective, offline literature searches. The volume of offline searches increased with the implementation of the MEDLARS network, and by 1969 several dozen people were conducting approximately 20,000 searches per year.

In 1964 at MIT, M. M. Kessler began the first important experiments using online systems for information retrieval, in a project called INTREX. About the same time, from 1965 to 1969, Lockheed designed and ran an experimental system for NASA called RECON. In 1969 it became operational, and a commercial version, called DIALOG, was put on the market.

Also in the late sixties, System Development Corporation issued a service called ORBIT, which originally had been developed for the Air Force Foreign Technology Division as an intelligence retrieval system. It provided a number of databases and became a major competitor of DIALOG. ELHILL, another system developed during this period, was basically the ORBIT system changed to meet the needs of MEDLARS from the National Library of Medicine.

In 1977 another major service was started. Bibliographic Retrieval Services (BRS) was originally designed to be cheaper than either ORBIT or DIALOG. BRS came on fast with a widespread user training program in which 600 people participated within the first six months. They also decided to limit themselves to a smaller number of carefully selected databases. One of the important services they carried early on was the database of the National Library of Medicine.

For a discussion of these early online systems, see:

Lancaster, F. W., and Fayen, E. G. *Information Retrieval On-Line.* Los Angeles: Melville, 1973.

INTREX, pp. 88-91

RECON, pp. 103-9

DIALOG, pp. 78-81

ORBIT, pp. 101-2

ELHILL, p. 82.

The Industry

The online database industry has three distinct aspects: communications, database distributors, and database producers.

The remarkable success of online services could not have been possible without the development of certain communications technology. One development was the adaptation of telephone systems for the transmission of digital information. Specialized equipment, with interference-resistant lines, were integrated within existing telephone systems to form networks specifically for transmission of digital information. Two well-known companies are Telenet and Tymnet.

These types of services generally rent telephone lines and use packet-switching techniques. Digital information is packed into concentrated blocks and is sent together, supposedly to reduce transmission error. Access to the network is by telephone to the nearest node. A computer at the node connects users with whatever database service they want that is a part of the network.

The second major aspect of the online indexing services revolution is the people who put together and market the databases. The basic procedure is to collect machine-processable information from the indexing and abstracting services, write software to manipulate the data, reformat it, and then sell it as a service. Generally, a rate is based on time, and since different databases cost the vendor different amounts, the user is charged different rates. If users don't access the system, they usually do not pay anything.

BRS took a different approach. They charged a use fee, but also gave discounts for volume use. Users paid a fee, if they searched or not, but received discounted rates for special situations. The other two major services had to make adjustments, and at present the price structure is a complex mixture of hourly rates, group and volume discounts, precommitted charges, and so on. Charging systems are a long way from being totally standardized.

The last segment of the industry is the indexing and abstracting services themselves, those who supply the basic information. Some familiar examples are ERIC (education), MEDLINE (medicine), NTIS (government research reports), *Chemical Abstracts* (chemistry), COMPENDEX (engineering), and *The New York Times* (newspapers and current news magazines).

At this point it might be well to select one of the database vendors (DIALOG) and briefly describe the service as an example. It is essential for a beginner in indexing and abstracting to be keenly aware of online services.

DIALOG was designed by the Lockheed Palo Alto Research Laboratory and went into operational status with some 300,000 citations from a NASA collection. Since that time DIALOG has grown into the most comprehensive service of all, with over 200 databases in all fields of knowledge. Databases are available to book reviews and biographies; directories of companies, people and associations; and articles from newspapers, journals, and other sources.

DIALOG allows sorting of output information, either alphabetically or numerically, by certain fields, such as author or title or report number. It also has a selective dissemination of information (SDI) feature. An SDI system is an "alerting" service that allows users to create a *profile* of interest and store it in the computer. The profile is like a "standing order" or permanent query to the system (although it can be changed). When new material is acquired by the system, the profile is run against the new material and the system alerts users to what may be of interst to them. SDI systems have been around for a number of years and have been generally successful. Ideally, a user's profile is processed each time a file of interest is updated, and the user is notified of the new material available.

A typical search on DIALOG will run from $5.00 to $16.50, including telecommunication costs. Offline print charges are extra.

DIALOG's command language is flexible and easy to learn and is constantly being enhanced. DIALOG is available twenty-four hours a day on weekdays and for most of the weekend hours and can be accessed through DIALNET, TELENET, TYMNET, and INWATS.

Searching

Users often make the mistake of assuming that an online search will always give better results than a manual search because a computer is more adroit than a traditional reference librarian. The truth is that the computer is far from being as smart as a good reference librarian. The computer is electronically faster, but not intellectually faster. Of course, the ideal situation is when a first-class reference librarian uses a well-programmed computer.

We keep hearing reports that printed indexes and abstracts will soon be a thing of the past, and then we hear others argue that there will always be a demand for hard copy. We are reminded of Jesse Shera's comment that "the paperless society is about as likely as a paperless bathroom." Jesse was probably right for our generation and maybe the next two or three. But it isn't just a matter of society finally running out of trees to make paper. We still seem to like paper. For example, people can use printed indexes when library staff are not available. The printed forms are still far less intimidating than glowing computer screens with no instructions. But the time will come when computer literacy will be a basic educational skill and people will know what to do with a glowing computer screen.

Users can use printed indexes with a slow serendipity, with no sense of a ticking clock. As of yet, there is no convincing evidence that the results of a computer search is superior to a slow, thoughtful, manual search. However, we must not forget that this is the same comment that was made when John Henry challenged the rail-driving machine.

The online search is faster, so it gives users time to undertake speculative searches that they might not have tried with a printed index. Also, the online index is probably more up-to-date than the printed index. But the point that must be made here is that the retrieval results with either a printed index or an online system will depend primarily on the quality of the indexing and searching methodology used.

Of course, people must be trained to use these systems. The basic problem is that the online systems are generally postcoordinated systems, whereas most of the users are acquainted with precoordinated printed indexes. In addition, they must learn a computer searching language.

It turns out that learning the computer language is relatively simple, usually the easiest part, because most searching languages have few instructions and are simple in concept. The skill comes in learning to analyze the searching problem and to select the optimal Boolean combinations. The actual commands differ from service to service, but they are fundamentally similar.

The first step is usually a logging-on procedure. This is a password exchange that allows authorized users into the system. The second step is to select a database from the numerous ones available. The third step is to enter one or more possible index terms. The response is a tabulation of the number of documents with that index term attached. For example:

CATS (9023)

means that there are 9,023 documents in the file that have been indexed with the term "Cats."

Another command may allow a display of words in the neighborhood of the used term. For example:

CAT
CATS
CATALOGUE
CATS-AND-DOGS

Now the user may ask for the documents on "Cat" and "Cats" and, perhaps, "Cats-and-dogs," but not "Catalogue." Then the system may allow the user to ask for related terms, which would be:

FELINES (100)
ANIMALS, DOMESTICATED (9017)

Suppose the user is interested in diseases and uses the same procedure to get the following:

DISEASES (4063)
INFECTIOUSNESS (917)

The next move is to use Boolean operations to combine these terms, resulting in the following:

(Cat *or* Cats *or* Felines) *and* (Diseases *or* Infectiousness)

The response might indicate that these combinations narrow the number of documents to 1,509. At this point the user realizes that all kinds of cats in the animal world are included, although he is interested only in house cats. So the Boolean query might be reformed as follows:

(Animals, Domesticated) *and* (Cats *or* Cat) *and* (Diseases *or* Infectiousness)

The user, who is told there are 203 such documents, can at this point ask for an online printout of some or all of the bibliographic references or, more economically, can ask for an offline printout by overnight mail.

Some Related Problems

Cost and fee structuring remains a problem. As technology changes and people's searching habits change, the industry continues to change and experiment with different modes of pricing and fees.

In addition to cost and fee structuring, there are some other problems, such as document delivery. It is senseless for a librarian to provide a user with a computer list of wonderful bibliographic citations when the librarian knows that the user has no way of obtaining most of the papers on the list. Clearly, online searching will affect both acquisition policies and interlibrary loan activity. A study by Lockheed showed, for example, that people were using the online services in a public library and then going to an academic library to get the actual documents. Of course, the advent of full text online will certainly help to ease some of the problems of document delivery.

Many people believe that online indexing service is going to change the basic concept of the librarian's role, that online services of the future will use natural language to search documents themselves, and that there will be no indexing or abstracting between the users and the documents. At the present time the librarian stands between the user and the library sources. The user tells the librarian what is needed, and the librarian interprets this information for the system.

However, people like Lancaster look toward the convenience and ease that future computerized service will bring. Lancaster talks of a communication system in which we will have full-text databases accessible through a communication network. The system will have an easily used command language, and users will sit down at their own terminals, scan the index, pull up an abstract, and if they want to read the document, it, too, can be flashed on the terminal. These types of databases are being built, users are already learning to use the databases themselves, and the librarian of the future will be freed to perform higher-level intellectual tasks.

Copyright is another problem that simply will not go away. As we move into the future modes of online services, the way will be open for more abuse of copyright laws. At present the major concern is with downloading, especially of a large number of records that are then used in violation of copyright law. As of yet, no definitive rulings have been made by the courts.

INDEXING FOR ONLINE DATABASE RETRIEVAL

An online system can be no better than the databases the indexing services provide. Indexing errors that cause misdirection will not vanish simply because the index is made available on a computer terminal.

From time to time it is claimed that databases can be created without the use of indexers and that searchers can ignore thesauri and other indexing devices because of the refinement of free-text searching. On the other hand, another group continues to argue that free-text searching simply cannot give the same satisfactory results that a controlled vocabulary can. Conflicting studies support both viewpoints.

In the meantime, there is no convincing evidence that retrieval systems of the future will not have a need for indexing. But the nature of the indexing may change.

Online bibliographic database searching puts a heavy burden on the quality of the indexing in the system. Psychologically, a user might be more comfortable flipping slowly through a printed index than engaging in the mechanical interaction required in using an online searching system. The computer is cynically in control, and the machine depends entirely on the indexing vocabulary that drives its decisions. Thus, it is clear that, as indexers, we must have the last word.

There is a challenge to professional indexers to help pull together the diversities of indexing and searching approaches in online systems. The lack of standardization in the various systems and in individual data files leads to inconsistent search commands and different display conventions, which confuse the user. Unfortunately, a computer cannot use serendipity. If an exact match is not made, the computer says, rather emphatically, that the information is not in the system. Indexers should take the initiative to find solutions to this problem.

Indexing systems and procedures must change as new technology becomes operational. For example, online access to databases allows us to have many more access points than are available or are practical in printed indexes. This permits greater flexibility, complexity, and speed in the searching process. Indexing language and procedures must permit the index to offer this type of access. The advancing technology, including compact disk developments, allows indexers the chance to redefine their task in innovative ways.

Online postcoordinating systems opened up new searching possibilities for the traditional Boolean operators (AND, OR, NOT). The computer allows complex combinations and instant alteration of the search query, which was impractical with notch-card systems and nearly impossible with precoordinated systems, such as printed indexes.

The construction of the index is a major factor in the successful searching of an online database. A well-constructed index enhances the user's potential to choose subject terms and all the variants and to interpret the retrieval results. For example, some systems will give a user results of only exact hits, but others will automatically show related results and, in a sense, will suggest alternative strategies for the searcher. But if the indexing system fully supports the searching activity, it is an expensive part of the information retrieval system.

Martin Kesselman and I. Perry (1984) have discussed some of the key points about what searchers and indexers should know about each other. This paper is well worth reading.

Searchers need to know how exhaustive the indexing is. Determining how many index terms are usually used in an index will give the searcher a clue as to whether a broad search or narrow search is needed. If the index has very detailed indexing, the searcher will need to narrow the search with Boolean AND operations.

Related to this, the searcher needs to know how specific the indexing is and to what extent hierarchical indexing is involved. In some online indexes the documents are indexed very specifically, with little posting-up to more generic terms, while in other indexes, posting-up is very extensive. The searcher should be able to obtain this information in the documentation to the particular database.

The searcher might also want to know if the index uses weighting or terms designated as major or minor descriptors for a particular document.

Also, is the controlled vocabulary completely controlled or does the index have a provision for adding noncontrolled terms and tagging them as such? Can parts of compound terms be searched as single term units? And, finally, the searcher should be aware of any indexing differences between the online index and printed index.

Indexers, also, should understand certain things about online searching. First, indexers should know if the users will be general users or will be looking for highly specific information. General users will need extensive cross-references and scope notes and other such structured guides. General users will also need extensive documentation and user aids.

In addition, indexers should understand that different subject areas have different literature structures, and indexing decisions should be made on the nature of both the subject and the user. For example, the mathematics literature seldom has joint authors and usually has a short reference list, whereas the medical literature often has multiple authors and an extensive reference list. The differences in the nature of the literature will make a difference in how the document is indexed. Another example is the nature of the *language* of the subject area. In subject literatures with a high number of synonyms, a controlled vocabulary is probably preferred, whereas in a new field in which new terms are constantly being added, a controlled vocabulary may quickly be obsolete, and free-text searching is the best option.

The indexer should also remember that indexing for online systems should be highly exhaustive and very specific, for the simple reason that the computer wastes very little time and the searcher can change the general approach many times. Inappropriate retrieval results will flash on the screen, but with a computer this is a minor problem. The search can be quickly modified and reentered and the process can be repeated as long as the user's money lasts.

One problem that is concerning more and more people is the incompatibility among databases and the duplication of information in them. Indexing is one of the major stumbling blocks to compatibility among many online databases. Each database is built with its own vocabulary control devices, which makes cross-searching difficult. (Cross-searching, or cross-file searching, allows more than one file to be searched at one time.)

For example, the online services have started offering the capability to search many databases simultaneously. Users welcome this addition, but indexers see problems to be solved. The primary one is vocabulary control across the many databases produced by different indexing and abstracting services; this is a domain of professional concern to the indexer.

An example of the multidatabase approach is DIALOG's *OneSearch*. This software allows the user to search up to twenty files at once. The user can compare results across files, can modify search terms, combine search terms, and display results as though only one file is being searched. However, one of the problems is that the user must be aware of the differences among databases in order to ensure an optimal search. DIALOG cautions the user to identify differences among the databases before going online, because some indexing terms are unique to particular data files and specific index terms may not give a comprehensive return in all the databases. This is an indexing problem that should be addressed by research.

Multiple thesauri management in online systems is a growing concern of the profession. There is an increasing interest in creating computer software that will tie together the separate thesauri in the various databases. This in effect would standardize the indexing and searching as far as the user is concerned. Several approaches are being explored, such as integrating all the vocabularies into a master list, which would be carefully edited. Other suggestions include creating an intermediate switching language and technique for mapping vocabularies to each other.

There are, of course, problems involved. For example, a term in one language may be an index term, and the same term in other vocabularies may be a nonpostable term that refers to another term.

The services offered by online vendors continue to grow rapidly, and a lot of work and thought is needed to meet these services' needs for adequate indexing.

ONLINE THESAURI

In recent years there has been a rapid growth in the number of online thesauri. In the near future it is probable that most online databases will have an accompanying online thesaurus. In fact, the integration and control of these thesauri is of great interest to the profession.

It might be useful at this point to list a few of the better known online thesauri as examples of this current trend. It should be noted that not all of the examples on the following pages are described in the text. Examples 52-56 are additional examples of previously described types of thesauri.

A-V Online Search Guide
    Contact: National Information Center for Educational Media
               P.O. Box 40130
               Albuquerque, NM 87196
    This covers school curriculum materials, media, nonprint materials, and audiovisual materials. The arrangement is categorical.

Alphabetical and Hierarchical Listing of CANCERPROJ Index Terms
    Contact: International Cancer Research Data Bank
               National Cancer Institute, Bldg. 82
               Bethesda, MD 20892
    Used by CANCERPROJ, this thesaurus covers cancer and oncology. The arrangement is alphabetical and hierarchical.

American Petroleum Institute Thesaurus (See example 42.)
    Contact: American Petroleum Institute
               156 William Street
               New York, NY 10038
    This is used with the index to API Abstract/Literature, and it covers petroleum and energy.

Child Abuse and Neglect Thesaurus (See examples 43-46.)
    Contact: National Center on Child Abuse and Neglect
               U.S. Department of Health and Human Services
               P.O. Box 1182
               Washington, DC 20013
    This covers child abuse and family life and law and is used by the Child Abuse and Neglect database.

Computer Sciences Microthesaurus: A Hierarchical List of Indexing Terms Used by NTIS
    Contact: National Technical Information Service
               U.S. Department of Commerce
               5285 Port Royal Road
               Springfield, VA 22161
    This covers computer science and electronics and is used by the National Technical Information Service.

Harvard Business Review/Online
    Contact: John Wiley & Sons, Inc.
               Electronic Publishing Division
               605 Third Avenue
               New York, NY 10158
    This covers business, accounting, finance, marketing management, and economics.

(Text continues on page 262.)

ACCIDENT

ABSORBER *(cont'd)*
stead.
BT: SEPARATION EQUIPMENT
NT: ABSORPTION TOWER
SA: ABSORBENT
    SCRUBBER
    SHOCK ABSORBER
    TREATING UNIT
UF: Absorption Tube
    plus TUBE

ABSORPTANCE
see: ABSORPTION
    OPTICAL DENSITY

ABSORPTIOMETRY
use: ABSORPTION SPECTROSCOPY

ABSORPTION*(1506)*
Phenomenon. Includes absorption of electromag-
netic radiation as well as materials. For absorp-
tion (separation process) use ABSORPTION
PROCESS. For absorption (optical density) use
OPTICAL DENSITY.
BT: SORPTION
SA: ABSORBENT
    ABSORBER
    ABSORPTION PROCESS
    ABSORPTION SPECTROSCOPY
    ADSORPTION
    DESORPTION
    OPTICAL DENSITY
UF: Absorptiveness
    Imbibition
    Radiation Absorption 72
    plus RADIATION

ABSORPTION (OPTICAL DENSITY) 77
use: OPTICAL DENSITY

ABSORPTION OIL*(1507)*
Material by function.
BT: ABSORBENT
    SORBENT
NT: FAT OIL
    LEAN OIL
UF: Menstruum 70
    Scrubbing Oil
    Wash Oil

ABSORPTION SPECTROSCOPY *(cont'd)*
    Moessbauer Spectroscopy 77
      plus GAMMA RAY
    Mossbauer Spectroscopy 77
      plus GAMMA RAY

ABSORPTION TOWER*(1510)*
BT: ABSORBER
    SEPARATION EQUIPMENT
    COLUMN
SA: SCRUBBER
    TREATING UNIT

ABSORPTION TUBE
use: ABSORBER
    plus TUBE

ABSORPTIVENESS
use: ABSORPTION

ABSTRACT*(1511)*
Index term for a document. Use only when the
source document abstracted is an abstract.
Index also the form of the source of the abstract.
E.g., use ABSTRACT plus MEETING PAPER to in-
dex an abstract of a meeting paper.
SA: ABSTRACTING
    CONDENSATION OF A DOCUMENT
UF: Summary

ABSTRACTING*(1512)*
BT: INFORMATION SERVICE
SA: ABSTRACT

ABSTRACTION REACTION*(1513)*
Use only when specified. For more complete
search, search reactants and products. Added in
1967.
SA: TRANSFER REACTION

ABU DHABI*(1514)*
Added in 1966.
Broader term ARAB EMIRATES added in 1979.
BT: ARAB EMIRATES
    MIDDLE EAST

ACADEMIC*(1515)*
UF: College
    University

Example 42. *American Petroleum Institute Thesaurus* (main entry). (Reproduced with permission of the American Petroleum Institute.)

DESCRIPTOR GROUPS

0010 Abuse and Neglect

Concepts generic to child abuse and neglect, including specifically named types of abuse and neglect. Examples of descriptors in this group include CHILD ABUSE, DEPRIVATION, EMOTIONAL NEGLECT, ETIOLOGY, IDENTIFICATION, SEQUELAE, and SEXUAL ABUSE. For physical injuries not specific to abuse and neglect, *see* Medicine. For abnormal psychological conditions not specific to child abuse and neglect, *see* Psychological Disorders.

0020 Agencies and Organizations

Types of public and private institutions involved in child abuse and neglect, including specifically named organizations. Examples of descriptors in this group include FEDERAL GOVERNMENT, HUMANE SOCIETIES, STATE AGENCIES, and WELFARE AGENCIES.

0030 Behavior

Types of normal human behavior and related concepts. Examples of descriptors assigned to this group include CHILD BEHAVIOR, CRYING, EMOTIONAL DEVELOPMENT, and INTERPERSONAL RELATIONS. For mental or psychological processes and theories, *see* Psychology.

Example 43. *Child Abuse and Neglect Thesaurus* (descriptor groups). (Reproduced with permission of National Center on Child Abuse and Neglect [DHHS], Washington, D.C.)

```
ABANDONED
  ABANDONED CHILDREN

ABANDONMENT

ABDOMINAL
  ABDOMINAL INJURIES
   UF   VISCERAL INJURIES

ABILITY
  ABILITY TO COPE
  ACADEMIC ABILITY
  VERBAL ABILITY

ABNORMAL
  ABNORMAL PSYCHOLOGY
   USE   PSYCHOPATHOLOGY

ABNORMALITIES
   UF   CONGENITAL DEFECTS

ABORTION

ABRASIONS

ABSENT
  ABSENT PARENTS

ABUSE
   USE   CHILD ABUSE
  ADOLESCENT ABUSE
  CAUSES OF CHILD ABUSE OR NEGLECT
   USE   ETIOLOGY
  CHILD ABUSE
   UF    ABUSE
         ILL TREATMENT
         MALTREATMENT
         MISTREATMENT
  CHILD ABUSE HISTORY
   UF   HISTORY OF CHILD ABUSE
  CHILD ABUSE LAWS
   UF   BATTERED CHILD LAWS
```

Example 44. *Child Abuse and Neglect Thesaurus* (permuted display). (Reproduced with permission of National Center on Child Abuse and Neglect [DHHS], Washington, D.C.)

VERBAL ABUSE
WHIPPINGS

0020 AGENCIES AND ORGANIZATIONS
ADVISORY COMMITTEES
AGENCIES
AGENCY RESPONSIBILITY
AGENCY ROLE
CENTRAL REGISTRIES
CHILD PROTECTION ORGANIZATIONS
CHILD WELFARE AGENCIES
CHURCHES ROLE
CITIZEN ADVISORY COMMITTEES
CITY AGENCIES
CITY CHILD WELFARE AGENCIES
CITY HEALTH AGENCIES
CITY SOCIAL SERVICE AGENCIES
CITY WELFARE AGENCIES
CITY YOUTH AGENCIES
COMMITTEES
COMMUNITY AGENCIES
COMMUNITY ORGANIZATIONS
COUNTY AGENCIES
COUNTY CHILD CARE AGENCIES
COUNTY CHILD PROTECTION AGENCIES
COUNTY CHILD WELFARE AGENCIES
COUNTY HEALTH AGENCIES
COUNTY SOCIAL SERVICE AGENCIES
COUNTY WELFARE AGENCIES
COUNTY YOUTH AGENCIES
FCIU
FEDERAL GOVERNMENT
FOUNDATIONS
GOVERNMENT
GOVERNMENT ROLE
HUMANE SOCIETIES
INSTITUTIONS
INTERAGENCY COOPERATION
INTERAGENCY PLANNING
INTERNATIONAL ORGANIZATIONS
LOCAL GOVERNMENT
MEDICAL SOCIETIES

Example 45. *Child Abuse and Neglect Thesaurus* (descriptor group display). (Reproduced with permission of National Center on Child Abuse and Neglect [DHHS], Washington, D.C.)

ALPHABETIC DISPLAY

ABANDONED CHILDREN
  0090
    BT   CHILDREN
    RT   ABUSED CHILDREN
          NEGLECTED CHILDREN

ABANDONMENT
  0010
    RT   CHILD ABUSE
          CHILD NEGLECT

ABDOMINAL INJURIES
  0130
    UF   VISCERAL INJURIES
    BT   INJURIES

ABILITY TO COPE
  0030
    RT   ADJUSTMENT PROBLEMS
          PSYCHOLOGICAL
            CHARACTERISTICS
          SOCIAL ADJUSTMENT

ABNORMAL PSYCHOLOGY
  USE   PSYCHOPATHOLOGY

ABNORMALITIES
  0130
    UF   CONGENITAL DEFECTS
    NT   HYDROCEPHALUS
    RT   GENETIC COUNSELING

ABORTION
  0130
    RT   BIRTH CONTROL
          ILLEGITIMACY
          PREGNANCY

Example 46. *Child Abuse and Neglect Thesaurus* (alphabetic display). (Reproduced with permission of National Center on Child Abuse and Neglect [DHHS], Washington, D.C.)

Inspec Thesaurus (See example 47.)

  Contact: INSPEC Department
             IEEE Service Center
             445 Hoes Lane
             Piscataway, NJ 08854

  The major subjects covered include engineering, physics, and technology.

Medical Subject Headings (See examples 48 and 49.)

  Contact: National Library of Medicine
             8600 Rockville Pike
             Bethesda, MD 20894

  This thesaurus (also known as MeSH) covers medicine, biomedicine, diseases, biological sciences, etc., and is used by the various online systems from the National Library of Medicine.

NASA Thesaurus (See example 50.)

  Contact: National Technical Information Service
             U.S. Department of Commerce
             5285 Port Royal Road
             Springfield, VA 22161

  Subjects covered include aerospace, aeronautics, and astronautics. It is used by the various online services from NTIS.

Thesaurus of ERIC Descriptors (See example 51.)

  Contact: Oryx Press
             2214 North Central at Encanto
             Phoenix, AZ 85004

  This is used by a number of online databases that cover educational topics.

(Text continues on page 276.)

```
┌─────────────────────────────────────────────┐
│                                             │
│     Please consult page v and the           │
│     INSPEC Classification before            │
│     using classification codes              │
│                                             │
└─────────────────────────────────────────────┘
```

1/f noise
    USE random noise

2-6 semiconductors
    Roman numerals are filed as capital roman alphabet equivalents
    USE II-VI semiconductors

3-5 semiconductors
    Roman numerals are filed as capital roman alphabet equivalents
    USE III-V semiconductors

3-6 semiconductors
    Roman numerals are filed as capital roman alphabet equivalents
    USE III-VI semiconductors

4-6 semiconductors
    Roman numerals are filed as capital roman alphabet equivalents
    USE IV-VI semiconductors

28 CMa stars
    USE variable stars

aberrations cont.
       spherical aberration
  RT aspherical lenses
       lenses
       optical images
       optical instrument testing
       optics
       particle optics
  CC A4230F A4278 A4180
  DI January 1973

aberrations (visual)
    USE vision defects

abrasion
  UF abrasive wear
       rubbing (abrasion)
       scrubbing (abrasion)
       scuffing
       wear, abrasive
  RT diamond
       friction
       grinding
       hardness
       polishing
       wear
  CC A4630P A6220P A8140P
  DI January 1973

abrasive wear
    USE abrasion

absolute gravity
    USE gravity

Example 47. *INSPEC Thesaurus.* (Reproduced with permission from INSPEC, Institution of Electrical Engineers, London, England.)

BODY REGIONS (NON MESH)	A1	
ABDOMEN	A1.47	
GROIN	A1.47.365	
INGUINAL CANAL	A1.47.412	
PERITONEUM	A1.47.596	A10.615.789.
DOUGLAS' POUCH	A1.47.596.225	
MESENTERY	A1.47.596.451	
MESOCOLON	A1.47.596.451.535	
OMENTUM	A1.47.596.573	
PERITONEAL CAVITY	A1.47.596.678	
RETROPERITONEAL SPACE	A1.47.681	
UMBILICUS	A1.47.849	
AXILLA	A1.133	
BACK	A1.176	
LUMBOSACRAL REGION	A1.176.519	
SACROCOCCYGEAL REGION	A1.176.780	
BREAST	A1.236	A10.336.153
NIPPLES ·	A1.236.500	A10.336.153.
BUTTOCKS	A1.258	
EXTREMITIES	A1.378	
ARM	A1.378.209	
ELBOW	A1.378.209.235	
FOREARM	A1.378.209.350	
HAND	A1.378.209.455	
FINGERS	A1.378.209.455.430	
THUMB	A1.378.209.455.430.705	
SHOULDER	A1.378.209.749	
WRIST	A1.378.209.906	
LEG	A1.378.592	
ANKLE	A1.378.592.116	
FOOT	A1.378.592.350	
FOREFOOT, HUMAN	A1.378.592.350.300	
METATARSUS	A1.378.592.350.300.480	
TOES	A1.378.592.350.300.792	
HALLUX	A1.378.592.350.300.792.380	
HEEL	A1.378.592.350.510	
TARSUS	A1.378.592.350.510.800	
HIP	A1.378.592.467	
KNEE	A1.378.592.586	
THIGH	A1.378.592.867	

Example 48. *Medical Subject Headings* (tree structures). (Reprinted with permission of Executive Editor, *IndexMedicus*.)

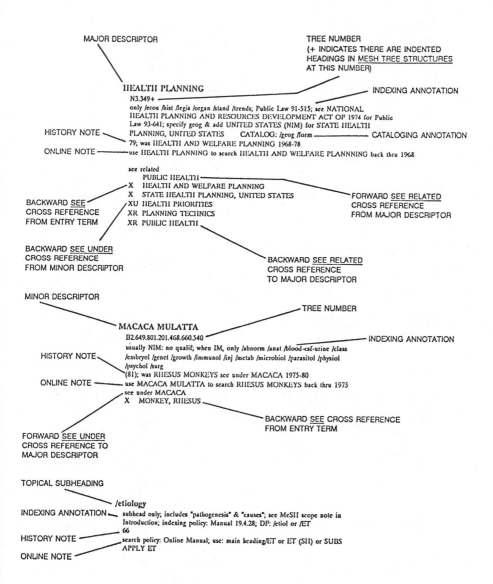

Example 49. *Medical Subject Headings* (subject index terms). (Reprinted with permission.)

A

A, Air Density Explorer
/ EXPLORER 19 SATELLITE

A, Anik
/ ANIK A

A, Atmosphere Explorer
/ EXPLORER 17 SATELLITE

A, BE
/ BEACON EXPLORER A

A, Beacon Explorer
/ BEACON EXPLORER A

A, Cassiopeia
/ CASSIOPEIA A

A, Compound
/ COMPOUND A

A Computer, CDC 160-
/ CDC 160-A COMPUTER

A, Energetic Particle Explorer
/ EXPLORER 12 SATELLITE

A, EOS-
/ LANDSAT E

A, EPE-
/ EXPLORER 12 SATELLITE

A, ERTS-
/ LANDSAT 1

A, Helios
/ HELIOS A

A, IMP-
/ EXPLORER 18 SATELLITE

A, Ionosphere Explorer
/ EXPLORER 20 SATELLITE

A, ISIS-
/ ISIS-A

A, Lunar Orbiter
/ LUNAR ORBITER 1

A Missile, Bomarc
/ BOMARC A MISSILE

A, OAO-
/ OAO 1

A, OGO-
/ OGO-A

A, OSO-
/ OSO-1

A Reactor, Tory 2-
/ TORY 2-A REACTOR

A Rocket Vehicle, Agena
/ AGENA A ROCKET VEHICLE

A, SAS-
/ SAS-A

A Satellite, AD-
/ EXPLORER 19 SATELLITE

A Satellite, AE-
/ EXPLORER 17 SATELLITE

A Satellite, DME-
/ EXPLORER 31 SATELLITE

A Satellite, HEOS
/ HEOS A SATELLITE

A Satellite, SEASAT-
/ SEASAT-A SATELLITE

A, SE-
/ EXPLORER 30 SATELLITE

A STARS

A, TELESAT Canada
/ ANIK A

A, TOS-
/ ESSA 3 SATELLITE

A, Vitamin
/ RETINENE

A-1 AIRCRAFT

A-1 Engine, RL-10-
/ RL-10-A-1 ENGINE

A-2 AIRCRAFT

A-3 AIRCRAFT

A-3 Engine, RL-10-
/ RL-10-A-3 ENGINE

A-4 AIRCRAFT

A-5 AIRCRAFT

A-6 AIRCRAFT

A-7 AIRCRAFT

Example 50. *NASA Thesaurus* (access vocabulary). (Reprinted with permission of the National Aeronautics and Space Administration.)

ALPHABETICAL DESCRIPTOR DISPLAY

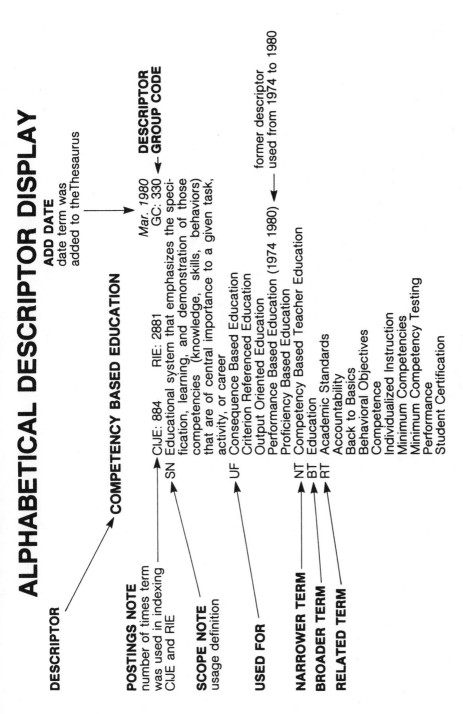

DESCRIPTOR

ADD DATE
date term was
added to the Thesaurus

**DESCRIPTOR
GROUP CODE**

COMPETENCY BASED EDUCATION
Mar. 1980
GC: 330

POSTINGS NOTE
number of times term
was used in indexing
CIJE and RIE

CIJE: 884   RIE: 2881

SCOPE NOTE
usage definition

SN Educational system that emphasizes the speci-
fication, learning, and demonstration of those
competencies (knowledge, skills, behaviors)
that are of central importance to a given task,
activity, or career

USED FOR

UF Consequence Based Education
Criterion Referenced Education
Output Oriented Education
Performance Based Education (1974 1980)
Proficiency Based Education

former descriptor
used from 1974 to 1980

NARROWER TERM

NT Competency Based Teacher Education

BROADER TERM

BT Education

RELATED TERM

RT Academic Standards
Accountability
Back to Basics
Behavioral Objectives
Competence
Individualized Instruction
Minimum Competencies
Minimum Competency Testing
Performance
Student Certification

Example 51. *Thesaurus of ERIC Descriptors, 11th Edition* (basic format). (Copyright © 1986 by the Oryx Press. Used by permission.)

Descriptor————————→ **VOCATIONAL TRAINING**
Language equivalents——→ **FORMATION PROFESSIONNELLE/**
                          FORMACION PROFESIONAL–06.03.07 ←————————————Facet
Scope note——————————→ *ACTIVITIES AIMED AT PROVIDING THE*
                        SKILLS, KNOWLEDGE AND ATTITUDES
                        REQUIRED FOR EMPLOYMENT IN A
                        PARTICULAR OCCUPATION (OR A GROUP OF
                        RELATED OCCUPATIONS).
Synonym (used for)———→ *UF:* *OCCUPATIONAL TRAINING*
                        TT: TRAINING ←————————————————————————Top term
Broader term—————————→ *BT:* TRAINING
                        NT: AGRICULTURAL TRAINING ←—————————Narrower terms
                             APPRENTICESHIP
                             BASIC TRAINING
                             FURTHER TRAINING
                             IN-SERVICE TRAINING
                             INDUSTRIAL TRAINING
                             MODULAR TRAINING
                             PERSONNEL TRAINING
                             PREVOCATIONAL TRAINING
                             RETRAINING
                             SANDWICH TRAINING
Related terms————————→ *RT:* APPRENTICES
                             OCCUPATIONS
                             TRAINEES
                             TRAINING ALLOWANCES
                             TRAINING CENTRES
                             VOCATIONAL EDUCATION

Synonym————————————→ *OCCUPATIONAL TRAINING*
Descriptor——————————→   USE: VOCATIONAL TRAINING—06.03.07 ←————————Facet

Example 52. *Macrothesaurus for Information Processing in the Field of Economics and Social Development, 1985* (alphabetical thesaurus). (A United Nations publication, New York, 1985. Used by permission.)

01. INTERNATIONAL COOPERATION. INTERNATIONAL RELATIONS.

01.01 INTERNATIONAL COOPERATION.
01.02 INTERNATIONAL RELATIONS.
01.03 INTERNATIONAL ORGANIZATIONS.
01.04 COUNTRIES AND REGIONS.

02. ECONOMIC POLICY. SOCIAL POLICY. PLANNING.

02.01 ECONOMIC POLICY. PLANNING.
02.02 SOCIAL POLICY.
02.03 SOCIAL SECURITY.
02.04 SOCIAL PROBLEMS.
02.05 SOCIAL SERVICES.

03. ECONOMIC CONDITIONS. ECONOMIC RESEARCH. ECONOMIC SYSTEMS.

03.01 ECONOMIC RESEARCH. ECONOMICS.
03.02 ECONOMIC CONDITIONS.
03.03 ECONOMIC SYSTEMS.

04. INSTITUTIONAL FRAMEWORK.

04.01 LAW. LEGISLATION.
04.02 HUMAN RIGHTS.
04.03 GOVERNMENT. PUBLIC ADMINISTRATION.
04.04 POLITICS.

Example 53. *Macrothesaurus for Information Processing in the Field of Economics and Social Development* (subject category fields). (A United Nations publication, New York, 1985. Used by permission.)

Sample of MathSci Record

```
AN 931868001.    8903.
SF SUBFILE: MR (Mathematical Reviews) AMS.
RN CMP 931 868.
MR NUMBER: 89c:46045.
CM CMP VOL/IS: 20/09.
AU AUTHOR/EDITOR: Muller-Paul-F-X (A-LINZ).
TA TeX AUTHOR:
   M\"uller, Paul F. X.
IN INSTITUTION: (A-LINZ) Mathematisches Institut, Johannes Kepler
   Universitat Linz, 4040 Linz, Austria.
TS TeX INSTITUTION:
   Mathematisches Institut, Johannes Kepler Universit\"at Linz.
TI TITLE:
   On the span of some three valued martingale difference sequences in
   $L\sp p$ $(1<p<\infty)$ and $H\sp 1$.
TT TeX TITLE:
   On the span of some three valued martingale difference sequences in
   $L\sp p$ $(1<p<\infty)$ and $H\sp 1$.
LG LANGUAGE: English (EN).
SO SOURCE:  Israel Journal of Mathematics  (Israel-J-Math).    60:    no.
   1,  pp:  39--53.    (1987).
YR YEAR: 1987.
IS ISSN/ISBN: 0021-2172.
CD CODEN: ISJMAP.
PT PUBLICATION TYPE: Journal (J).
RL REVIEW LENGTH: MEDIUM (15 lines).
RT REVIEW TYPE: Signed review.
AB REVIEW/ABSTRACT:
   A martingale difference sequence $(U\sb n)\sb {n\geq 0}$ is said to
   be nested if $\roman{supp}\,U\sb k\cap\roman{supp}\,U\sb
   j\neq\varnothing$ implies that either $\roman{supp}\,U\sb
   k\subset\roman{supp}\,U\sb j$ or $\roman{supp}\,U\sb
   j\subset\roman{supp}\,U\sb k$.

   The author considers subspaces of the martingale $H\sb 1$ space
   $H\sb 1(D\sb n)$ spanned by $\{-1,1,0\}$-valued nested martingale
   difference sequences.  He shows that such a subspace has to be
   isomorphic to one of the ten natural spaces he lists.  By
   interpolation he obtains that in $L\sb p$, $\infty>p>1$, $p\neq 2$,
   such a subspace has to be isomorphic to one of the five natural
   spaces.  It is known (cf.  J. Bourgain, H. P. Rosenthal and G.
   Schechtman, Ann.  of Math.  (2) 114 (1981), no.  2, 193--228; MR
   83j:46031) that there are uncountably many nonisomorphic subspaces
   of $L\sb p$ spanned by $\{-1,1,0\}$-valued martingale difference
   sequences.
RE REVIEWER: Wojtaszczyk-P.  (1-TXAM).
CC CLASSIFICATION CODES: 46E30.    46B25.    60G42.
```

Example 54. *MathSci User Guide*, Second Edition, 1990, p. 2-VI-3 (entry for journal article). (Reprinted with permission of the American Mathematical Society.)

Word	Code	Description
A-proper	47H09	Nonexpansive mappings, ultimately compact mappings, A-proper mappings, K-set contractions, etc.
Abel	40G10	Abel, Borel and power series methods
Abel	45E10	Integral equations of the convolution type (Abel, Picard, Toeplitz and Wiener-Hopf type) [See also 47B35.]
abelian	06F20	Ordered abelian groups, ordered linear spaces [See also 46A40.]
abelian	12A35	Abelian and metabelian extensions (including cyclotomic, Kummer, cyclic)
abelian	14Kxx	Abelian varieties and schemes
abelian	14K20	Analytic theory; abelian integrals and differentials
abelian	18Exx	Abelian categories
abelian	18E10	Exact categories, abelian categories
abelian	20Kxx	Abelian groups
abelian	20K01	Finite abelian groups
abelian	22Bxx	Locally compact abelian (LCA) groups
abelian	43A25	Fourier and Fourier-Stieltjes transforms on locally compact abelian groups
abelian	43A70	Analysis on specific locally compact abelian groups [See also 12A85.]
absolute	40F05	Absolute and strong summability
absolute	42A28	Absolute convergence, absolute summability
absolute	51F05	Absolute planes
absolute	51F10	Absolute spaces
absolute	54C55	Absolute neighborhood extensor, absolute extensor, absolute neighborhood retract (ANR), absolute retract spaces (general properties) [See also 54F40, 55M15.]
absolute	54F40	Compact (locally compact) absolute neighborhood retracts
absolute	55M15	Absolute neighborhood retracts [See also 54C55, 54F40.]

Word	Code	Description
abstract	28A15	Abstract differentiation theory, differentiation of set functions [See also 26A24.]
abstract	28Bxx	Measures and integrals with values in abstract spaces
abstract	34Gxx	Differential equations in abstract spaces [See also 58D25.]
abstract	34K30	Equations in abstract spaces
abstract	39B70	Functional equations on abstract spaces or structures
abstract	40J05	Summability in abstract structures [See also 43A55, 46A35, 46B15.]
abstract	41A65	Abstract approximation theory (approximation in normed linear spaces and other abstract spaces)
abstract	43-XX	ABSTRACT HARMONIC ANALYSIS {For other analysis on topological and Lie groups, see 22Exx.}
abstract	45N05	Abstract integral equations, integral equations in abstract spaces
abstract	46G12	Measures and integration on abstract linear spaces [See also 28Cxx.]
abstract	46M35	Abstract interpolation of topological vector spaces
abstract	49A27	Problems in abstract spaces
abstract	49B27	Problems in abstract spaces
abstract	49C15	Problems in abstract spaces or involving functional relations other than differential equations
abstract	51D05	Abstract (Maeda) geometries
abstract	51D10	Abstract geometries with exchange axiom
abstract	51D15	Abstract geometries with parallelism
abstract	55U05	Abstract complexes
abstract	55U05	Abstract homotopy theory
abstract	58E05	Abstract critical point theory (Morse

Example 55. *MathSci User Guide*, Second Edition, 1990, p. 5A-1 (subject classification words). (Reprinted with permission of the American Mathematical Society.)

Descriptor ——→ conflict

Descriptor Code ——→ DC D164400

Scope Note ——→ SN A context-dependent term for strife, mental or physical, among individuals or groups. Select a more specific entry or coordinate with other terms

    Former Descriptor Code

History Note ——→ HN Formerly (1963-1985) DC 111000, Conflict/Conflicts.

    Former Descriptor

Used For ——→ UF Confront/Confrontation (1969-1985)
    Contest/Contests/Contestation (1970-1985)
    Rivalry (1964-1985)

    Former Descriptors used in years indicated

Broader Term ——→ BT Interaction

Narrower Term ——→ NT Cultural Conflict
    NT Disputes
    NT Family Conflict
    NT Ideological Struggle
    NT International Conflict
    NT Interpersonal Conflict
    NT Role Conflict
    NT Social Conflict

Related Term ——→ RT Aggression
    RT Alliance
    RT Civil Disorders

Example 56. *Thesaurus of Sociological Indexing Terms*, Second Edition, 1989 (sample entry). (Reprinted with permission of sociological abstracts, inc. Copyright 1989. All rights reserved.)

A

General Section

A01/11

Languages
Linguistics X02/54

A02	International languages
A02.10	International auxiliary lingua
A02.20	Esperanto
A03	Indo-European languages
	UF European languages
A03.10	Indic languages
	Dravidian languages A07.10/30
	(ancient)
A03.10.10	Sanskrit
	(modern)
A03.10.25	Panjabi
A03.10.30	Sindhi
	UF Punjabi
A03.10.30/49	Hindustani
A03.10.35	Hindi
A03.10.40	Urdu
A03.10.45	Gujurati
A03.10.50	Bengali
A03.10.55	Oriya
A03.10.60	Assamese
A03.10.65/70	Dardic languages
A03.10.68	Kashmiri
A03.10.70	Romany language
A03.10.80	Nepali
A03.10.85	Marathi
A03.10.90	Sinhala
	UF Sinhalese
A03.15	Iranic languages

Example 57. *UNESCO Thesaurus* (classified list). (Extract from *UNESCO Thesaurus*, Vol. 1, © Unesco 1977. Reproduced with the permission of Unesco.)

Ability
. Reading ability

Absorption (wave)
. Light absorption

Achievement
. Academic achievement

Administrative sciences
. Administration
. . Archive administration
. . . Archive legislation
. . Church administration
. . Communication administration
. . . Communication legislation
. . . . Broadcasting legislation
. . . . Copyright
. . Cultural administration
. . . Museum administration
. . . . Museum reorganization
. . Educational administration
. . . Educational cooperation
. . . . University cooperation
. . . Educational coordination
. . . Educational legislation
. . . Educational supervision
. . . . Educational inspection
. . . . School supervision
. . . . Teacher supervision
. . Financial administration
. . . Accounting
. . . . Auditing
. . . . Cost accounting
. . . . Cultural accounting
. . . . . Cultural budgets

Administrative sciences (cont.)
. . . . . . Judgments
. . . . Acquittal
. . . . Conviction (legal)
. . . . . . Decrees
. . . . . Mediation
. . . . . . Arbitration
. . . . Industrial arbitration
. . . . . . Conciliation
. . . . Industrial conciliation
. . . . Industrial arbitration
. . . . . . Industrial conciliation
. . . . Industrial arbitration
. . . . . Pleadings
. . . . . Summons
. . . . . Trials
. . . . . . Political trials
. . . . . . Trial by jury
. . . . . . Trial in camera
. . . Economic administration
. . . Educational administration
. . . . Educational cooperation
. . . . . University cooperation
. . . . Educational coordination
. . . . Educational legislation
. . . . Educational supervision
. . . . . Educational inspection
. . . . . School supervision
. . . . . Teacher supervision
. . . Environmental planning administration
. . . Social welfare administration
. . Science administration
. . Social science administration
. Management
. . Business management
. . . Financial administration
. . . . Accounting
. . . . . Auditing
. . . . . Cost accounting

Example 58. *UNESCO Thesaurus* (hierarchical display of terms). (Extract from *UNESCO Thesaurus*, Vol. II, © Unesco 1977. Reproduced with the permission of Unesco.)

RELATIONSHIP SECTION

Abdomen

Abdomen 73   SC 00010
PN 41
R   Anatomy/ 67

Abdominal Wall 73   SC 00020
PN 3
B   Muscles 67
   Musculoskeletal System 73

Abducens Nerve 73   SC 00030
PN 12
UF   Nerve (Abducens)
B   Cranial Nerves 73
   Nervous System 67
   Peripheral Nerves 73

Ability Grouping 73   SC 00040
PN 195
SN   Grouping or selection of individuals for instructional or other purposes based on differences in ability or achievement.
R   Ability Level 78
   Ability/ 67
   Academic Aptitude 73
   Education/ 67
   Educational Placement 78
   Special Education 67

Ability Level 78   SC 00050
PN 354
SN   Demonstrated level of performance. Used in academic, cognitive, perceptual, or occupational contexts.
R   Ability Grouping 73
   Ability/ 67
   Adaptive Testing 85

Ability Tests
Use Aptitude Measures

Abortion (Spontaneous)
Use Spontaneous Abortion

Abortion Laws 73   SC 00110
PN 38
B   Government Policy Making 73
   Laws 67
R   Induced Abortion 71

Abreaction
Use Catharsis

Absenteeism (Employee)
Use Employee Absenteeism

Absorption (Physiological) 73   SC 00140
PN 35
R   Cells (Biology) 73
   Intestines 73
   Skin (Anatomy) 67

Abstinence (Sexual)
Use Sexual Abstinence

Abstraction 67   SC 00160
PN 588
SN   Process of selecting or isolating a certain aspect from a concrete whole, as a part of the process of evaluation or communication.
B   Cognitive Processes 67
   Thinking 67
N   Imagery 67
R   Divergent Thinking 73

Academic Achievement 67   SC 00190
PN 9262
UF   Gradepoint Average
   Scholastic Achievement
   School Achievement

Acceptance (Social)

Academic Aptitude — (cont'd)
R   Student Admission Criteria 73
   Verbal Ability 67

Academic Environment 73   SC 00230
PN 120
SN   Physical setting or emotional climate where formal instruction takes place.
B   Environment 67
   Social Environments 73
N   Classroom Environment 73
   College Environment 73
   School Environment 73

Academic Failure 78   SC 00233
PN 285
B   Failure 67
R   Academic Achievement 67
   Academic Underachievement 67

Academic Overachievement 67   SC 00240
PN 425
SN   Academic achievement greater than that anticipated on basis of one's scholastic aptitude score or individual intelligence.
UF   Overachievement (Academic)
B   Academic Achievement 67
   Achievement 67

Academic Records
Use Student Records

Academic Specialization 73   SC 00250
PN 1010
SN   Concentration of effort or interest in a special area of knowledge or discipline at an institution of learning.
UF   College Major
   Specialization (Academic)
R   Educational Aspirations 73

Example 59. *Thesaurus of Psychological Index Terms* (term relationships).

END-USER SEARCHING

As online searching continues to be a major aspect of the information retrieval world, there is a growing demand for the development of end-user searching systems. The most notable examples of the excellent progress that has been made in this direction are the BRS system *After Dark* and DIALOG's *Knowledge Index*. There are others, of course. Such future systems must offer easy access and simplified procedures for searching. In the future, indexing systems will be complex, but this complexity will be transparent to the user, and these end-user indexing and searching systems will have to be more sophisticated than those that support trained and experienced professional searchers.

The availability of computer-based indexing services is not something of the future. It is a real and functioning part of today's information services. However, we have many economical, political, and legal problems to work out. Technical problems are minor compared with some of these other matters.

The use of computers will increase the capacity for processing material and making it accessible. We can hope that, with the availability of terminals beyond libraries—in laboratories and offices—and with users directly involved, abstracts and indexes will become an acknowledged part of research and not just secondary devices that one might go to the library to use.

There is little doubt about the place of online computer systems in indexing and abstracting services. We are moving toward natural-language systems that will make automatic devices as common and easy to use as the family telephone.

SUGGESTED READINGS

Blair, David C. "Searching Biases in Large Interactive Document Retrieval Systems." *Journal of the American Society for Information Science* 31 (July 1980): 271-77.

Booth, Andrew D. "A 'Law' of Occurrences for Words of Low Frequency." *Information and Control* 10 (April 1967): 386-93.

East, H. *Designing and Marketing Databases*. London: British Library, 1986.

Huleatt, Richard S. "Online Use of Chemical Abstracts: A Primer for Beginning Chemical Searches." *Database* 2 (December 1979): 11-21.

Kesselman, Martin, and I. Perry. "What Online Searchers Should Know about Indexing and What Indexers Should Know about Online Searching." In *Proceedings of the Fifth National Online Meeting*. Medford, N.J.: Learned Information, 1984, 141-48.

Markey, Karen, Pauline Atherton, and Claudia Newton. "An Analysis of Controlled Vocabulary and Free-text Search Statements in Online Searches." *Online Review* 4 (September 1980): 225-36.

XIII
Some Additional Topics

In the preceding chapters we have tried to give an introductory overview of what indexing and abstracting is all about. The purpose of this concluding chapter is to briefly mention several additional topics that do not fit logically into the preceding sequence of development but that should be of interest to the newcomer to the field.

RESEARCH

What is research, and does it have a place in indexing and abstracting? If we realize that research begins with a problem and that its goal is explanation, understanding, and prediction, then clearly research is needed in the field.

Research is a way of minimizing the uncertainty of any future action; thus, it provides the basis for rational decisions. Medical research helps us make decisions about health. Agricultural research helps us grow more food on less land. Indexing research can help us design better indexes and develop better indexing procedures.

What is research? First, we might ask what is *not* research? For one thing it is not an infallible way of knowing the universe and should not be thought of as being unquestionable, although we sometimes get that impression in our society. The TV ad tells us that seven out of ten New York doctors who *tested* Ajax stomach pills recommended them. The implication behind this is that a "scientific test" has been run and if I don't use Ajax stomach pills then I am an idiot. Three New York doctors and I are going contrary to "research."

A student in high school may be required to write an essay, so he goes to the encyclopedia and copies 1,500 words. He says he has completed his research on the topic. A woman with a white apron spends year after year running thousands of white mice through a maze and recording volume after volume of paths chosen by the animals. She tells her friends that she has plenty of research results. A librarian sends out questionnaires asking users which indexes they prefer, and then tabulates the figures backwards, crosswise, upside down, and from every possible viewpoint. The resulting tables are published in a leading library journal.

Which of these examples represents research? *None*. Not one of these is research, although all may conceivably be a part of a data-gathering activity within the framework of a research project. Isolated exercises do not constitute research.

Research is not the random collecting of facts or data. It is not experiment just for the sake of experiment. It is not haphazard trial and error, although *directed* trial and error is a research technique. Research is not digging up forgotten or little-known facts. That's reference work.

Research involves speculation, empirical observation, and deductive reasoning. Speculation comes both at the beginning and at the end of the process. Its driving force is the desire to understand why, although we often have to settle for understanding *what* is happening, given a set of circumstances. However, true scientists are never content until they can convincingly speculate about the *why*.

Although research involves moments of enlightenment and satisfaction, it almost always involves error, and error management is a major aspect of the scientific method. Methodological tools, such as statistics, make a serious issue out of the margin of error. Two major sources of error are uncertainty and self-deception, and examples of these two sources of error are obvious in countless research efforts in indexing.

The ideal research pattern is that:

1. We acknowledge that something is uncertain, but we're not sure exactly what the situation is. For example, is free-text indexing better than controlled-vocabulary indexing, is the reverse true, or is there no difference?

2. We become familiar with the facts of the situation. We run tests on both types of indexing until we have credible data.

3. We attempt to explain the facts. Why did we reach our conclusion? Thus, we end, as we began, with speculation.

Although research may not always answer the question of *why*, it must answer the question of prediction. If no prediction is involved, the research has failed to gain its critical objective. If outcomes cannot be predicted within acceptable ranges of probability, of what use is the research?

Another way to define research is as reflective inquiry. It is any systematic attempt to investigate problems and arrive at solutions. The purpose of research is to find out why things are as they are now and to predict what things will be like, given the same conditions, at some time in the future.

What characterizes research?

1. *It is problem-centered.* Within the framework of some human activity, something is not quite in order. The activity can range from intellectual abstraction to simple physical situations. Something is wrong.

2. *It is based on previous knowledge.* The fact that there is a problem means something is known, some framework of inquiry exists. What is known may be largely false, but there is some sort of previous knowledge.

3. *Logic alone is not enough.* If logic alone were adequate, we would, for example, never have to test new drugs before putting them on the market. Why isn't logic alone adequate? Because we do not have enough facts to depend solely on logic.

Observation is the starting point of research, since it is through observation that we realize that a problem is present. Of course, observation alone is not research. What is necessary is controlled, systematic observation. We step into a normal flow of events and deliberately change things; the resulting events tell us something about the nature of what we are studying.

We run experiments to explore phenomena we know little about, to double-check unusual or unexpected occurrences, to test theory or accepted laws, and to discover why things are as they are and how situations could be improved.

Certainly, indexing and abstracting activities are ripe for both pure and applied research. The objective of applied research is to improve the service we give our index users, and the purpose of pure research is to "understand" our processes.

We need to enlarge the scope of the research effort in indexing and abstracting. That is, most work is done on small databases under laboratory conditions, and this certainly is not to be faulted, except that we have very few, if any, application theorems. We know very little about how some of our conjectures will work in real situations.

Finally, it might be useful to list some of the broad areas that need to be researched:

How people use information

How people search for information

Content analysis

Vocabulary control

Use of uncontrolled vocabularies

Indexing and abstracting procedures

Coding

Economics of indexing and abstracting

Evaluation

Manual vs. machine methods

Development of a general theory

Indexing for online searching

Multiple thesauri management

Expert systems in indexing and abstracting

INDEXING ALTERNATIVES

It should be mentioned that there are alternatives to traditional indexing for establishing subject content of documents. One has already been discussed — citation indexing. This is a technique that identifies documents on a topic by tracing down references *to* a given paper. Another well-known technique, bibliographic coupling, also is based on reference linking. A brief look at this technique will show that there are valid alternatives to assigning descriptors to documents to identify groups of papers on a particular subject.

Most of the primary work on bibliographic coupling was done by M. M. Kessler in the 1960s at MIT. He described the grouping of papers on the basis of bibliographic coupling units. Based on this unit, two criteria of coupling were defined. The idea is that articles are grouped or linked together by the references that the authors include in papers. We develop networks of papers on a topic. We do not retrieve papers by index terms but by groups based on common citations. Clearly, when we use index terms we also group papers. We collect a group of papers that all include the term *cats*, for example. Bibliographic coupling would also create a group of cat papers, but on the basis of their related references. The premise is, of course, that a paper about cats will also have references related to cats.

Here are the two criteria Kessler proposed:

CRITERION A: A number of papers constitute a related group G_a if each member of the group has at least one coupling unit to a given test paper P_0. The coupling strength between P_0 and any member of G_a is measured by the number of coupling units (n) between them. G_a^n is that portion of G_a that is linked to P_0 through n coupling units.

CRITERION B: A number of papers constitute a related group G_b if each member of the group has at least one coupling unit to every other member of the group.

In the following example, the test paper P_0 has four references: a, b, c, and d. Document 1 has two common citations (a, b); thus its coupling strength is 2. Document 2 has three common citations to the test paper (a, b, c); thus its coupling strength is 3. Document 3 has two common citations to the test paper (a, b), so its coupling strength is 2. Document 4 has no common citations; therefore it is not coupled in this test.

Since documents 1 and 3 have the *same* coupling strength to the test paper, they form a "group" with a strength of 2. Document 2 is another "group" with a strength of 3.

Examples of Criterion A:

DOC. 1

> Ref.
> a
> b

DOC. 2

> Ref.
> a
> b
> c

DOC. 3

> Ref.
> a
> b

DOC. 4

> Ref.
> e
> f

DOC. P_0

> Ref.
> a
> b
> c
> d

Kessler's basic experiment centered on thirty-six volumes of *Physical Review*, volumes 77-112. He used a computer program to process this huge database. The computer sorted the articles into groups, based on criterion A, resulting in:

8,521 articles
137,000 references to 795 separate papers

From the 8,521 articles he gathered:

1. Volume and page number

2. Title

3. Authors

4. All bibliographic data in the form of:

   a. Title of journal or other source

   b. Volume number

   c. Page number

It should be pointed out that several possibilities exist for selection of a test paper P_O:

1. One or more papers outside of the database may serve as P_O, and all or part of the remaining papers may be processed. For example, search *Physical Review*, 1958, for papers that match a given paper.

2. Part of the database may constitute P_O's, and all or part of the remaining database may be searched. For example, search the past five years of *Physical Review* for papers that match certain papers in the latest numbers.

3. All or part of the database may be arranged into related groups, each item of the database serving in turn as P_O for all the others. For example, arrange a given volume of *Physical Review* into related groups.

Obviously, the processing result of the entire set of 8,521 papers is quite a mess of data. Kessler, in his report, picked out one volume, number 97 with 265 articles, as an example of the results. This is what he got:

The volume contained 265 articles. Each article in the volume was treated as P_O, and the remaining 264 as a database. Thus, 265 G_a's were generated. The number of articles in each G_a varied from zero (not coupled to any other paper in volume 97) to twenty-seven. The number of coupling units observed varied from one, the weakest coupling, to eleven. The results of this work shows the existence of the G_a phenomenon.

Kessler observed that this technique is independent of words and language, since all the processing is done by a quantitative method. We thus avoid all the difficulties of language, syntax, and word habits involved in human indexing. No one reads the papers or makes intellectual decisions. As a matter of fact, the text of the paper does not even have to be present. Also, the method does not produce a static classification or permanent index number for a given paper. The groupings will undergo changes that reflect the current usages and interests of the users.

Of the other studies Kessler made, one is of particular importance. He compared groups generated by bibliographic coupling with "groups" of papers generated by using the manually prepared analytical subject index used by the editors of the *Physical Review* and found a high correlation.

With the continuing development of computer technology, this kind of approach may have a lot to offer to the indexing field.

PROFESSIONAL SOCIETIES

There are several professional indexing and abstracting organizations. For example, in Great Britain in 1957 the Society of Indexers was formed under the instigation of G. Norman Knight. The society has had a viable agenda of activities, including the improvement of standards for indexing and indexers, training courses, and the selection of the most outstanding index of the year for the Wheatley Medal, which is awarded by the Library Association. One of the society's primary contributions is the publication of the journal *The Indexer*, which is the official journal of the society and of other indexing societies in several countries. In addition to its goal of improving standards and uniformity, the society seeks to establish communication lines to editors and publishers concerning qualification and pay of indexers.

In 1968 the American Society of Indexers (ASI) was formed with the goal of promoting "indexing as a professional calling." Like the Society of Indexers, the ASI acts as an intermediary for advice between publishers and qualified indexers. It has a number of publications, including the useful directory of available indexers called the *Register of Indexers*.

Another example is the National Federation of Abstracting and Information Services, which is a collective organization of individual indexing and abstracting services.

The Association of Records Managers and Administrators is of interest to indexers and abstractors because one of the fundamental activities of a record manager is the classification and indexing of records.

In Canada the primary organization is the Indexing and Abstracting Society of Canada.

Many indexers and abstractors, of course, belong to the American Society for Information Science.

CAREERS

There are several avenues open for those who want to work in indexing and abstracting. Many people are saying that the 1990s will be the decade of "information." By that they mean that information handling is going to come to the forefront as the most important activity of society. With the successful move to technology in all aspects of information handling, from fifth generation computers to new laser devices to satellites to sophisticated transmission devices, information science concepts are being applied. Already job notices are appearing all over the country for "information scientists," "information specialists," and particularly for "information managers." These positions are characterized by a need for personnel whose expertise goes beyond what is generally taught in library schools or computing science departments. A careful analysis of the stated requirements usually reveals that this information scientist needs to have some of the skills of library science, plus a theoretical understanding of the basic phenomena of information (which comes from the study of information science), computer training and familiarity with other technologies, and systems analysis and management. More and more there is a need for indexing and abstracting expertise, since this is a growing concern. Good abstractors and indexers are now in demand and will continue to be in demand as we move into a new information age.

These positions are opening up in publishing, data processing, research project management, museums, information broker organizations, market research areas, information centers, and special libraries of all kinds. It appears that the information field will continue to be the fastest growing job area well into the next century.

For the indexer and abstractor, career opportunities can take several tacks: indexing and abstracting work in a library or information center, indexing and abstracting in a nonlibrary organization, full-time professional work for a commercial abstracting and indexing service, or part-time freelance work.

In the past decade or so there have been many publications dealing with "alternative" careers for librarians, and indexing (outside of a library environment) is almost always mentioned. In the various options listed, such as information broker, designer of information systems, information searcher, and so forth, indexing is usually involved. The opportunities are exciting, and the profession should solidly support these enterprising individuals. But as a caution to students, we must not forget that it takes more than a business card to make it as an information entrepreneur. It takes special dedication and a good bit of luck.

Successful entrepreneur and freelance indexers usually are well-prepared individuals. Catherine Fay (1984) gave a profile of a group of "at home" part-time indexers and abstractors who work for an information services company. According to her survey, the average indexer/abstractor for the business database is a very well-educated woman in her mid-thirties and has two children at home. She has a masters degree, usually in accounting, marketing, or finance, and often has an MLS as well. On the other hand, the typical indexer/abstractor for the computer database is a man in his late or early thirties. He usually holds another job in systems, retailing, or education, and he is highly technical.

Within a service organization there are several kinds of positions. First, there are the indexers and abstractors themselves. Generally, these persons must be college graduates and are often expected to have studied in the subject area in which they will index and abstract. Second, there are editors, often promoted from the indexing ranks to the editorial position. It is the editor's job to see that policies are carried out and to edit the results that come from the indexing and abstracting corps. Third, there are checkers, whose responsibility is to proofread the indexes and abstracts, looking for inconsistencies and errors. These are the three groups of professionals. In libraries, information centers, research organizations, and other settings, the indexing and abstracting may turn out to be a one-person job, with the worker doing everything from indexing and abstracting to publishing the final product.

How does a person become an indexer or abstractor? It is by formal education, by self-education, or by training on the job. Formal education can be courses on the topic offered at universities, generally in library science departments, or it can be short courses offered by professional associations. Self-education is accomplished by studying books and instructional manuals in the area. On-the-job training is a popular way to learn, since very few people start college planning to be indexers and abstractors. Generally, the student earns a subject degree and then is trained while working. Indexing and abstracting can be a satisfying career, allowing its practitioners to develop unique skills and to work in an intellectually challenging environment.

What kind of education or training is needed? Educational preparation for an indexer or an abstractor can vary, but there are some general directions a student can take. Although an MLS is not always a requirement, it certainly can be useful, especially if the course of study is slanted toward an indexing and abstracting career specialization, which is possible at a number of library schools. Generally, the course of study will include courses in cataloging, reference, indexing, abstracting, advanced theory of classification and indexing, online searching, information storage and retrieval, and technical writing.

Short courses, continuing education courses, and workshops give a quick introduction to the fundamentals of indexing and abstracting. Also, some employers give on-the-job training, although the larger organization expect employees to be experienced when they are hired.

REFERENCE TOOLS FOR INDEXING

Indexers can hardly survive without reference tools to support their activity. Certainly, the task would be difficult without the tools. K. G. B. Bakewell (1987) published an excellent list of reference books for indexers. Although he says that the list "is essentially a personal one and that omissions are inevitable," it is a good working list for any indexer, either student or professional. The list is a good, comprehensive guide.

These reference tools answer such questions as:

- How do I find reference books in the subject I'm dealing with?

- What subject thesauri exist in the subject I'm dealing with?

- Where can I learn about the techniques of indexing?

- How can I use computers in my work?

- What are the general reference questions related to my work?

The following list of tools is not as definitive as Bakewell's list, but it is intended to give the reader a short, beginning list and to suggest the *types* of reference tools that might be useful.

Abstracting and Indexing Services Directory. Detroit: Gale Research, 1982.

Aitchison, Jean, and Alan Gilchrist. *Thesaurus Construction*. 2nd ed. London: AsLib, 1986.

Akire, Leland G., ed. *Periodical Title Abbreviations*. 4th ed. Detroit: Gale Research, 1983.

American Men and Women of Science. New York: Bowker. (Triennial)

Anderson, M. D. *Book Indexing*. New York: Cambridge University Press, 1971.

Anglo-American Cataloguing Rules. 2nd ed. London: Library Association, 1978.

Annual Review of Information Science and Technology. White Plains, NY: Knowledge Industry Publications, Inc. (Annual)

Art Index. New York: H. W. Wilson. (Quarterly)

Austin, Derek. *PRECIS: A Manual of Concept Analysis and Subject Indexing*. 2nd ed. London: British Library Bibliographic Services Division, 1984.

Basic Criteria for Indexes. Rev. ed. New York: American National Standards Institute, 1984. (ANSI standard Z39.4:1984)

Biography Index. New York: H. W. Wilson. (Quarterly)

Bulletin of the American Society for Information Science. Washington, D.C.: ASIS. (Monthly)

Burton, Paul, and Howard Petrie. *The Librarian's Guide to Microcomputers for Information Management*. London: Van Nostrand Reinhold, 1986.

Business Periodicals Index. New York: H. W. Wilson. (Monthly)

Carey, G. V. *Making an Index*. New York: Cambridge University Press, 1965.

Chambers Biographical Dictionary. Rev. ed. Edinburgh: Chambers, 1974.

Chambers Dictionary of Science and Technology. Edinburgh: Chambers, 1974.

The Chicago Manual of Style. 13th ed. Chicago: University of Chicago Press, 1982.

Collison, Robert L. *Indexing Books: A Manual of Basic Principles*. London: Benn, 1962.

Dictionary of American Biography. 17 vols. ed. by American Council of Learned Societies. New York: Scribner, 1970. (Set includes supplements 1-7.)

Dictionary of Scientific Biography. 16 vols. New York: Scribner, 1970-1980.

Directory of Online Databases. Los Angeles, Calif.: Cuadra Associates, Inc. (Issued quarterly. 1979- .)

Education Index. New York: H. W. Wilson. (Monthly)

Encyclopedia of Associations. Detroit: Gale Research. (Annual)

Encyclopedia of Business Information Sources. 6th ed. Edited by James Woy. Detroit: Gale Research, 1986.

Encyclopedia of Information Systems and Services. Detroit: Gale Research, 1989.

Facts on File: World News Digest with Index. New York: Facts on File. (Loose-leaf service)

Fowler, H. W. *A Dictionary of Modern English Usage.* 2nd ed. Oxford: Clarendon Press, 1965.

Gazetteer of the British Isles. Edinburgh: Bartholomew, 1970.

Guide to Reference Books. 10th ed. Edited by Eugene Sheehy. Chicago: American Library Association, 1986.

Harling, Bruce S. C. "Indexers' Reference Books." *The Indexer* 7, no. 4 (Autumn 1971): 151-55.

Hipgrave, Richard. *Computing Terms and Acronyms Dictionary.* London: Library Association, 1985.

Hunnisett, R. R. *Indexing for Editors.* London: British Records Association, 1972.

Information Hotline. New York: Science Associates/International. (Monthly)

Knight, G. Norman. *Indexing, the Art of: A Guide to the Indexing of Books and Periodicals.* London: Allen & Unwin, 1979.

McGraw-Hill Encyclopedia of Science and Technology. 5th ed. New York: McGraw-Hill, 1982.

The New Encyclopaedia Britannica. 15th ed. Chicago: Encyclopaedia Britannica Educational Corporation, 1974.

The New York Times Index. New York: New York Times Company. (Semimonthly)

Orna, Elizabeth. *Build Yourself a Thesaurus: A Step by Step Guide.* Norwich, U.K.: Running Angel, 1983.

Recommendations for Alphabetical Arrangement and Filing Order of Numbers and Symbols. Rev. ed. London: British Standards Institution, 1985. (BS 1749:1985)

Recommendations for Bibliographical References. London: British Standards Institution, 1976. (BS 1629:1976)

Recommendations for Examining Documents, Determining Their Subjects and Selecting Indexing Terms. London: British Standards Institution, 1984. (BS 6529:1984)

Recommendations: The Preparation of Indexes to Books, Periodicals and Other Publications. Rev. ed. London: British Standards Institution, 1976. (BS 3700:1976)

Seltzer, L. E., ed. *Columbia Lippincott Gazetteer of the World.* New York: Columbia University Press, 1962.

Towell, Julie, and Helen E. Sheppard, eds. *Acronyms, Initialisms and Abbreviations Dictionary.* 11th ed. Detroit: Gale Research, 1988.

Webb, William H. *Sources of Information in the Social Sciences.* 3rd ed. Chicago: American Library Association, 1986.

Webster's Biographical Dictionary. Rev. ed. Springfield, Mass.: Merriam, 1980.

Webster's New Collegiate Dictionary. 9th ed. Springfield, Mass.: Merriam, 1983.

Webster's New Geographical Dictionary. Springfield, Mass.: Merriam, 1976.

Webster's New International Dictionary of the English Language. 3rd ed. Springfield, Mass.: Merriam, 1962.

Wellisch, Hans H. *Indexing and Abstracting: An International Bibliography.* Santa Barbara, Calif.: ABC-Clio, 1980.

Wellisch, Hans H. *Indexing and Abstracting, 1977-1981: An International Bibliography.* Santa Barbara, Calif.: ABC-Clio, 1984.

Who's Who in American Art. New York: Bowker. (Biennial)

The World Almanac and Book of Facts. New York: Newspaper Enterprise Association. (Annual)

The above list is by no means an ultimate list. Each indexer will develop a personal list of useful tools. And, of course, the nature of the indexing work will call for different types of tools.

SUGGESTED READINGS

Allen, G. G., and F. C. A. Exon, eds. *Research and the Practice of Librarianship: An International Symposium*. Perth: Western Australian Institute of Technology, 1986.

American Society of Indexers. *Proceedings of the Second Seminar on Freelance Indexing*. Washington, D.C.: American Society of Indexers, 1979.

Bakewell, K. G. B. "Reference Books for Indexers." *The Indexer* 15, no. 3 (April 1987): 131-40.

Borko, Harold, and Charles L. Bernier. *Indexing Concepts and Methods*. New York: Academic Press, 1978.

Cremmins, Edward T. *The Art of Abstracting*. Philadelphia: Institute for Scientific Information Press, 1982.

Directory of Fee-Based Information Services. Houston: Burwell Enterprises, 1985.

Fay, Catherine H. "Off-site Indexing: a Cottage Industry." *Information Services and Use* 4 (1984): 299-304.

Grieg, Peter, comp. *The Indexer as Entrepreneur: A Selective Guide for Freelance Indexing and Indexers*. Ottawa: Indexing and Abstracting Society of Canada, 1985.

Kessler, M. M. "Bibliographic Coupling between Scientific Papers." *American Documentation* 14 (1963): 10-25.

_____. "Comparison of the Results of Bibliographic Coupling and Analytic Subject Indexing." *American Documentation* 16 (1965): 223-33.

Linehan, C. D. "Amateur Indexer and the Local Historian." *The Indexer* 12 (April 1981): 145-54.

Neufeld, M. Lynne, Martha Cornog, and Inez L. Sperr, eds. *Abstracting and Indexing Services in Perspective: Miles Conrad Memorial Lectures, 1969-1983*. Arlington, Va.: Information Resources Press, 1983.

Schabas, Ann H. "Postcoordinate Retrieval: A Comparison of Two Indexing Languages." *Journal of the American Society for Information Science* 33 (January 1982): 32-43.

Smith, R. "Compensations of Indexing." *The Indexer* 12 (April 1981): 141.

"Society of Indexers' Conference: Indexers in a World of Change." *The Indexer* 12 (1980): 57-61.

Glossary

Abstract. A condensed, representative surrogate of a knowledge record. A narrative description of a document, which may include pertinent data and occasionally critical comments.

Abstractor. The person who creates an abstract. This may be the author of the original paper, a subject expert, or a full-time professional abstractor.

Access Point. An entry into an index where a user's chosen word matches a word in the index, thus giving the user a starting point in the search.

Acronym. An abbreviation that is often formed from letters within the word or phrase that is being abbreviated.

Added Entry. In a catalog, an entry that is in addition to the main entry. A secondary entry that allows the user to find the information with a different approach.

Alphabetic Subject Indexes. Indexes arranged in alphabetical order containing important words that reflect subjects of interest.

Alternative Title. The second part of a title that is joined by a connective word such as *or*, e.g., *Raising the Roof*, or, *How to Build Your Own House.*

Analytical Entry. An entry for a part of an item for which a comprehensive entry has already been made.

ANSI. The American National Standards Institute.

Artificial Intelligence. An area of study that attempts to program computers to emulate human reasoning.

ASI. American Society of Indexers.

Associative Retrieval Systems. Information retrieval systems whose indexing is based on the frequency of the co-occurrence of terms as a method of grouping.

Author Abstracts. Abstracts that are written by the authors of the original papers.

Author Indexes. Indexes arranged on the basis of the authors of the documents. Alphabetical lists of the authors of documents in a file.

Authority List. A formal list of terms to be used in cataloging or indexing. The use of terms not in the "authorized" list is prohibited.

Automatic Abstracting. Using a computer to construct abstracts.

Automatic Indexing. Using a computer to construct indexes.

Bibliographic Control. The intellectual access to public knowledge. More specifically, the processes necessary to generate and organize records of materials in libraries and other information systems for effective retrieval.

Book Indexes. Indexes to the content of individual monograph publications. These usually appear at the end of the book and are alphabetical, including subjects and name terms.

Boolean Searching. The procedure of identifying information on a yes or no binary basis. For a yes answer, a user's request term is the same as an index term on the individual document under consideration from the file of documents.

Bound Terms. Index terms that are joined together and treated as a single concept. For example, *artificial* and *intelligence* form the concept *artificial intelligence.*

Broader Term. In a hierarchical thesaurus, broader terms and narrower terms express relationships between class and subclass. A term in a subclass would refer to class by indicating a "broader term."

Chain Indexes. These are basically alphabetically arranged indexes with a separately provided entry for each term or a link for all the terms used in a classification or subject heading scheme.

Citation Indexes. A citation index leads users to papers by citations, rather than by index terms. The entries in a citation index are the names of authors of earlier works on a subject. The index is a list of publications that have been referred to in the sources covered by the index. Citations lead the user to desired information.

Classification. The process of bringing like things together on the basis of similarities and differences. A systematic arrangement in sets or categories according to established criteria.

Collective Title. A title proper that is an inclusive title for an item containing several works.

Colon Classification. An analytic-synthetic classification system developed in 1933 by S. R. Ranganathan. Facets are separated by colons.

Computer Program. A logical sequence of detailed instruction that directs a computer's operation.

Concept List. A list of words representing the ideas in a knowledge record not yet translated into the formal indexing vocabulary.

Concordance. An alphabetical index of the words appearing in a text with a pointer to the precise point at which each word occurs. The index shows every contextual occurrence of a word.

Content Analysis. An attempt to infer the meaning and intent of a knowledge record in the absence of the creator of the record. A subjective interpretation of what a record is about.

Controlled Vocabulary. A vocabulary in which only an approved list of words can be used as index terms; used to manage synonyms and near-synonyms and to bring together semantically related terms.

Coordinate Indexing. An indexing scheme that combines single index terms to create composite subject concepts (e.g., the terms *eye* and *surgery* are combined to create the concept *eye surgery*). The system allows the coordination of classes either before or during searching. In precoordination the combinations are made at the input stage, and in postcoordination the combinations are made at the output stage.

Corporate Body. A group of people or organizations that are considered as a single entity, e.g., the IBM Corporation.

Critical Abstract. An abstract that comments on the contents of the paper.

Cross-Reference. An entry in a work that points to another entry.

Discipline-oriented Abstract. An abstract aimed at an activity concerned with a specific area of knowledge.

Display. The final, usable form of the thesaurus or index.

Dissertation. A formal report on original research usually prepared by a graduate student at a university.

Documentation. An activity that concerns itself with the reproduction, distribution, and utilization of documents. The movement began in Europe, spread to the United States in the 1930s, and became one of the intellectual streams leading to the information science discipline.

Element. A word or phrase representing a distinct bibliographic unit of information.

Enumerative Classification. A system in which all the elements are named and placed in fixed relationships prior to use.

Entry. A point where users' request terms allow them into the vocabulary of the indexing language.

Entry Differentiation. The practice of breaking up long, solid blocks of entry components into several, more readable lines, sometimes with additional subheadings.

Entry Redundancy. The assignment of superfluous entries.

Entry Scattering. The undesirable practice of spreading closely related entries throughout the index.

Expert System. A computer system that is designed and programmed to accomplish tasks that experts accomplish using their intelligence and experience.

Extract. A form of abstract which is constructed by stringing together verbatim sentences from the original paper.

Faceted Indexes. Indexes based on any definable aspect that makes up a subject. Composite concepts are then created in such a way that access is possible for each facet, or notion, contained in the subject composite.

False Drops. Nonrelevant documents retrieved as a result of a semantic breakdown. For example, a request for "Venetian Blinds" might also result in information on "Blind Venetians."

Formula Indexes. Indexes in which the entries are listed in order by the symbol for the first element of a molecular formula.

Free-text Vocabulary. An uncontrolled vocabulary in which any word in the natural language is a permissible index term.

Generic Vocabulary. A vocabulary consisting of those words that represent the basic type of an entity, e.g., INSECTS (generic) for ants, bees, fleas, etc. Generic terms are generally cross-reference terms.

IASC/SCAD. Indexing and Abstracting Society of Canada/Society Canadienne Pour L'Analyse Documents.

Index. A guide to the contents of a knowledge record. A systematic analysis of such records, arranged in an organized way. A list of bibliographic information arranged in order according to some specified datum such as author, subject, or topic keyword.

Indexing Depth. The degree to which every facet and every aspect of the facets are covered. The number of headings or descriptors assigned per unit of text.

Indexing Rules. A set of guidelines used for indexing a document.

Indexing Syntax. The order and structural relationships of descriptors.

Indicative Abstract. An abstract that indicates the content of the original paper without data or comment.

Information. Facts told, read, or otherwise communicated, usually previously unknown to the recipient.

Information Retrieval. The techniques of storing and retrieving recorded knowledge. Specifically, it is the process of selecting bibliographic citations from databases, using a variety of access points, such as subjects or authors. The selected recall of recorded information.

Informative Abstract. An abstract that gives key data and procedures from the paper.

Knowledge Record. A physical object that conveys information over time by symbols, sounds, or sights. It may be printed on paper, digitalized on computer storage devices, imprinted on microforms, or chiseled on stone.

KWIC. Keyword in context. A type of automatic indexing in which the significant words in a string (usually a title) are rotated and displayed, surrounded by the other words in the string.

KWOC. Keyword out of context. A type of automatic indexing in which the significant words in a string (usually a title) are rotated and displayed in a column separate from the rest of the string.

Links. The tying together, at the indexing stage, of related descriptors in order to avoid syntactical error.

Machine-readable. Data that has been converted into a form that can be directly put into a computer.

Machine Translation. The conversion of text from one language into another language in a computer.

Mission-oriented Abstract. An abstract aimed at an activity concerned with an application assignment, not necessarily confined to any particular subject discipline.

Narrower term. In a hierarchical thesaurus, broader terms and narrower terms express relationships between class and subclass. A term in a class would refer to a subclass by indicating a "narrower term."

NFAIS. National Federation of Abstracting and Information Services.

Numeric Indexes. Indexes to numeric data, e.g., tables of statistics.

Online. Working directly with a computer through a terminal.

Postcoordinate Indexing. A type of indexing where searching terms are combined at the time of searching by the user.

PRECIS. Preserved Context Index System. An index created by human and computer. The content analysis is done by a human, while the index is generated by the computer from the string of index terms created. The index provides the user with the context of all major indexing words.

Precision. A quantitative ratio of the number of relevant documents retrieved to the total number of documents retrieved.

Precoordinate Indexing. A type of indexing where terms are combined prior to searching. The combinations are not under the control of the user.

Professional Abstractors. Individuals whose livelihood is full-time abstracting.

Recall. A quantitative ratio of the number of retrieved relevant documents to the total number of relevant documents in a collection.

Related Terms. Terms in a hierarchical thesaurus that are parallel to each other in meaning, not broader or narrower.

Relevance. The measure of the degree to which retrieved informational material satisfies the needs of the user.

Roles. The modification of descriptors at the indexing stage to show their meaning for that particular document in order to avoid syntactical errors.

Search Strategy. A plan or method for systematically identifying useful data or documents in an information storage file.

Slanted Abstract. An abstract that is aimed at a mission-oriented activity, emphasizing selected material from the original documents.

Society of Indexers. Professional indexing society of the United Kingdom.

Specificity in Indexing. The degree to which a descriptor matches the exact meaning of the subject concept.

Subject Specialist Abstractors. Abstractors whose primary livelihood is in a subject area, but who contribute time to abstracting.

Technical Reports. Monographs usually reporting on isolated research topics and not generally available elsewhere.

Thesaurofacet. A combined thesaurus and facet classification that is linked by notation and that shows the principal hierarchies in the thesaurus section.

Thesaurus. An authority file of terms that shows the full scope of each term along with its relationship to broader terms, narrower terms, and related terms.

Weighting. Assigning a value on some kind of scale to descriptors in order to show their relative importance for a particular document.

Bibliography

Adams, Scott, and Dale B. Baker. "Mission and Discipline Orientation in Scientific Abstracting and Indexing Services." *Library Trends* 16 (1968): 307-22.

Aitchison, Jean. "Thesaurofacet: A Multipurpose Retrieval Language Tool." *Journal of Documentation* 26 (1970): 187-203.

Aitchison, Jean, and Alan Gelchrist. *Thesaurus Construction: A Practical Manual.* 2nd ed. London: AsLib, 1987.

Ajiferuke, Isola, and Clara M. Chu. "Quality Indexing in Online Databases: An Alternative Measure for a Term Discriminating Index." *Information Processing and Management* 24 (1988): 599-601.

Allen, G. G., and F. C. A. Exon, eds. *Research and the Practice of Librarianship: An International Symposium.* Perth: Western Australian Institute of Technology, 1986.

American Documentation Institute. New York Chapter. *Tutorial Sessions on Indexing.* Philadelphia: Drexel Press, 1967.

American Library Association. *ALA Filing Rules.* Filing Committee, Resources and Technical Services Division, Chicago: ALA, 1980.

American National Standards Institute. *American National Standard for Library and Information Sciences and Related Publishing Practices: Basic Criteria for Indexes.* New York: American National Standards Institute, 1984.

_____. *American National Standard for Writing Abstracts.* New York: American National Standards Institute, 1987.

_____. *Basic Criteria for Indexes.* New York: American National Standards Institute, 1984.

_____. *American National Standard Guidelines for Thesaurus Structure, Construction, and Use.* New York: American National Standards Institute, 1980.

American Society of Indexers. *Indexing: The State of Our Knowledge and the State of Our Ignorance*. Edited by B. H. Weinberg. Medford, N.J.: Learned Information, Inc., 1989.

_____. *Proceedings of the Second Seminar on Freelance Indexing*. Washington, D.C.: American Society of Indexers, 1979.

Anderson, Charles. "<<Answers >>: An Off-the-Shelf Program for Computer-aided Indexing." *The Indexer* 13 (October 1983): 236-38.

Anderson, James D. "Indexing Systems: Extensions of the Mind's Organizing Power." *Information and Behavior* 1 (1986): 287-323.

_____. "Structure in Database Indexing." *The Indexer* 12 (April 1980): 3-13.

Anderson, James D., and Gary Radford. "Back-of-the-Book Indexing with the Nested Phrase Indexing System." *The Indexer* 16 (October 1988): 79-84.

Anderson, M. D. *Book Indexing*. New York: Cambridge University Press, 1971.

Andrews, Charles R. In "Current Issues in Reference and Adult Services." *RQ* 24 (Winter 1984): 155-61.

Ashworth, Wilfred. "Abstracting as a Fine Art." *The Information Scientist* 7 (June 1973): 45-53.

_____. "Abstracting." In *Handbook of Special Librarianship and Information Work*. 4th ed. Edited by W. E. Batten. London: AsLib, 1975, 124-52.

Askling, John. "What Is an Index?" *California Librarian* 12 (1951): 159-60.

Austin, Derek. *Guidelines for the Establishment and Development of Monolingual Thesauri*. Paris: UNESCO, 1981.

_____. "PRECIS: The Preserved Context Index System." *Library Resources and Technical Services* 21 (1977): 1-30.

_____. "Vocabulary Control and Information Technology." *AsLib Proceedings* 38 (January 1986): 1-15.

Austin, Derek, and M. Dykstra. *PRECIS: A Manual of Concept Analysis and Subject Indexing*. 2nd ed. London: The British Library, Bibliographic Services Division, 1984.

Bakewell, K. G. B. "How to Let Your Fingers Do the Walking and Not Lose the Way (Index Compilation)." *Times Higher Education Supplement* 412:12, September 26, 1980.

_____. "Indexer's Reactions to PRECIS." *Journal of Documentation* 35 (September 1979): 164-78.

_____. "Reference Books for Indexers." *The Indexer* 15, no. 3 (April 1987): 131-40.

_____. "Symposium: The Inadequacies of Book Indexes." *The Indexer* 9 (1974): 1-8.

Bakewell, K. G. B., and G. Rowland. "Indexing and Abstracting." In *British Librarianship and Information Work, 1981-1985, vol. 2.* London: Library Association, 1988.

Barber, John, Sheena Moffat, and Frances Wood. "Case Studies of the Indexing and Retrieval of Pharmacology Papers." *Information Processing and Management* 24 (1988): 141-50.

Barnett, Lynn. "Indexing and Retrieval in ERIC: The 20th Year." In *Thesaurus of ERIC Descriptors*, 11th ed. Washington, D.C.: Educational Research Information Center, Bureau of Research, 1987, x-xx.

Bates, Marcia J. "How to Use Controlled Vocabularies More Effectively in Online Searching." *Online* (November 1988): 45-56.

_____. "Locating Elusive Science Information." *Special Libraries* 75 (April 1984): 114-20.

_____. "Subject Access in Online Catalogs: A Design Model." *Journal of the American Society of Information Science* 37 (November 1986): 357-76.

Batty, C. David. "Chain Indexing." In *Encyclopedia of Library and Information Science*, vol. 4. New York: Marcel Dekker, 1970, 423-34.

Bawden, David. "Citation Indexing." In *Manual of Online Search Strategies.* Boston, Mass.: G. K. Hall, 1988, 44-83.

Bell, H. K. "Publishers and Indexers: A Colloquy." *The Indexer* 12 (April 1981): 141.

Bell, H. K., and K. Suggate. "Computer-assisted Indexes: Two Results Assessed." *The Indexer* 14 (1984): 95-98.

Bellingham, D., C. Annis, and C. Grande. "Computer Index to Slides Collections." *Humanities Communication Newsletter* 9 (1987): 26-29.

Bennion, B. C. "Performance Testing of a Book and Its Index as an Information Retrieval System." *American Society for Information Science* 31 (1980): 264-70.

Bernier, Charles L. "Alphabetic Indexes." In *Encyclopedia of Library and Information Science*, vol. 1. New York: Marcel Dekker, 1968, 196-201.

_____. "The End Users." In *Proceedings of the 25th Annual Conference of the National Federation of Abstracting and Information Services.* Arlington, Va.: 1983. Philadelphia: NFAIS, 1984, 48-51.

Besterman, Theodore. *The Beginnings of Systematic Bibliography.* 2nd ed. London: Oxford University Press, 1936.

Bingham, W. V. "How to Make a Useful Index." *American Psychologist* 6 (1951): 31-34.

Blair, David C. "Searching Biases in Large Interactive Document Retrieval Systems." *Journal of the American Society for Information Science* 31 (July 1980): 271-77.

Bliss, H. E. *The Organization of Knowledge and the System of the Sciences.* New York: Holt, 1929, chapters 1-4.

Bloomfield, Masse. "Evaluating Indexing." *Special Libraries* 61 (1970): 429-32, 501-7, 554-61.

_____. "Evaluating Indexing." *Special Libraries* 62 (1971): 24-31, 94-99.

Boll, John J. "From Subject Headings to Descriptors: The Hidden Trend in Library of Congress Subject Headings." *Cataloging and Classification Quarterly* 1 (1982): 3-28.

Booth, A. D. "A 'Law' of Occurrences for Words of Low Frequency." *Information and Control* 10 (April 1967): 386-93.

Borko, Harold. "Toward a Theory of Indexing." *Information Processing and Management* 13 (1977): 355-65.

Borko, Harold, ed. *Automated Language Processing.* New York: John Wiley, 1967.

Borko, Harold, and Charles L. Bernier. *Abstracting Concepts and Methods.* New York: Academic Press, 1975.

_____. *Indexing Concepts and Methods.* New York: Academic Press, 1978.

Borko, Harold, and S. Chatman. "Criteria for Acceptable Abstracts: A Survey of Abstracting Instructions." *American Documentation* 14 (1963): 149-60.

Borokhov, E. A. "Methods of Eliminating Textual Redundancy in Abstracts." *Scientific and Technical Information Processing* 14 (1987): 80-89.

Bose, Anindya. "Information Resources Management: A Glossary of Terms." In *Encyclopedia of Library and Information Science*, vol. 41. New York: Marcel Dekker, 1986, 92-161.

Bottoms, J. W. "Fulltext Indexed Retrieval Systems." In *The CD-ROM Handbook*. Anchorage: Intertext Publishers, 1988, 309-28.

Boyce, Bert R. "Computer-assisted Instruction of Online Searchers." *Bulletin of the American Society for Information Science* 13 (1987): 34.

Bradford, Samuel C. *Documentation.* 2nd ed. London: Lockwood, 1953.

Bramer, M. A. "A Survey and Critical Review of Expert Systems Research." In *Introductory Readings in Expert Systems.* New York: Gordon & Breach Science, 1982, 3-29.

Brenner, Everett H. "American Petroleum Institute's Machine-aided Indexing and Searching Project." *Science and Technology Libraries* 5 (Fall 1984): 49-62.

_____. "The End Users." In *Proceedings of the 25th Annual Conference of the National Federation of Abstracting and Information Services.* Arlington, Va.: February 2-March 11, 1983. Philadelphia: NFAIS, 1984, 48-51.

Brenner, Everett H., and Tefko Saracevic. *Indexing and Searching in Perspective.* 2nd ed. Philadelphia: National Federation of Abstracting and Information Services, 1985.

Breton, Ernest J. "Why Engineers Don't Use Databases." *ASIS Bulletin* 7 (August 1981): 20-23.

Brown, Alan George. *Introduction to Subject Indexing: A Programmed Text,* 2 vols. London: Clive Bingley, 1975, 1976.

Bryon, J. "Topographical Indexing." *Indexer* 15 (1987): 211-14.

Buchanan, B. *Glossary of Indexing Terms.* London: Clive Bingley, 1976.

Burwell, Helen P. "Inmagic in Practice—Version 7 in a Law Library." *Database* (December 1986): 31-34.

Calkins, Mary L. "Free-Text or Controlled Vocabulary? A Case History Step-by-Step Analysis ... Plus Other Aspects of Search Strategy." *Database* 3 (June 1980): 53-67.

Carothers, Diane Foxhill. *Self Instruction Manual for Filing Catalog Cards.* Chicago: American Library Association, 1981.

Chambers, John. "A Scientist's View of Print Versus Online." *AsLib Proceedings* 36 (1984): 309-16.

Chan, Lois Mai, and Richard Pollard. *Thesauri Used in Online Databases: An Analytical Guide.* New York: Greenwood Press, 1988.

Chan, Lois Mai, Phyllis A. Richmond, and Elaine F. Svenonius, eds. *Theory of Subject Analysis: A Source Book.* Littleton, Colo.: Libraries Unlimited, 1985.

Chan, P., and P. Harrison. *Automating Index Preparation.* Berkeley: University of California, Department of Computer Sciences, 1987. (AD--A179/2/WLI)

Chandler, J. "A Proposal to the ASTM Committee for Medical Informatics for Building a Scientific Thesaurus." *Journal of Clinical Computing* 15 (1986): 64-83.

Chandrasekharan, N., R. Sridher, and S. Iyengar. "On the Minimum Vocabulary Problem." *Journal of the American Society for Information Science* 38 (1987): 234-38.

Cleveland, Donald B. "An n-Dimensional Retrieval Model." *Journal of the American Society for Information Science* 27 (September-October 1976): 342-47.

Cleveland, Donald B., Ana D. Cleveland, and Olga Wise. "Less Than Full-text Indexing Using a Non-Boolean Searching Model." *Journal of the American Society for Information Science* 35 (1984): 19-20.

Cleverdon, C. W. "The Cranfield Tests on Index Language." *AsLib Proceedings* 19 (1967): 173-94.

Cleverdon, C. W., and J. Mills. "The Testing of Index Language Devices." *AsLib Proceedings* 15 (1963): 106-30.

Coates, E. J. "Scientific and Technical Indexing." *The Indexer* 5 (1966): 27-34.

_____. "Some Properties of Relationships in the Structure of Indexing Languages." *Journal of Documentation* 29 (1973): 390-404.

_____. "Switching Languages for Indexing." *Journal of Documentation* 26 (1970): 102-10.

Cochrane, Pauline A. *Redesign of Catalogs and Indexes for Improved Online Subject Access*. Phoenix, Ariz.: Oryx Press, 1985.

Cochrane, Pauline A., and Karen Markey. "Preparing for the Use of Classification in Online Cataloging Systems and in Online Catalogs." *Information Technology and Libraries* 4 (1985): 91-111.

Collison, Robert L. *Abstracts and Abstracting Services*. Santa Barbara, Calif.: Clio Press, 1971.

_____. "The Elements of Book Indexing, Part II." In Knight, G. Norma. *Training in Indexing*. Cambridge, Mass.: MIT Press, 1969, 2.

_____. *Indexes and Indexing*. 4th rev. ed. London: Ernest Benn; New York: J. DeGraff, 1972.

_____. *Indexing Books: A Manual of Basic Principles*. London: Ernest Benn; New York: J. DeGraff, 1962.

Compugramma. *Micro Indexing System for the IBM Personal Computer.* Northport, N.Y.: Compugramma, Inc., 1984.

Courtial, J. P., M. Callon, and M. Sigogneau. "Is Indexing Trustworthy? Classification of Articles through Co-word Analysis." *Journal of Information Science* 9 (1984): 47-56.

Couture, Carol, and Jean-Yves Rosseau. *The Life of a Document.* Montreal: Vehicule Press, 1987.

Craven, Timothy C. "Adapting of String Indexing Systems for Retrieval Using Proximity Operators." *Information Processing and Management* 24 (1988): 133-40.

_____. "Customized Extracts Based on Boolean Queries and Sentence Dependency Structures." *International Classification* 16 (1989): 11-14.

_____. *String Indexing.* Orlando, Fla.: Academic Press, 1986.

Cremmins, Edward T. *The Art of Abstracting.* Philadelphia: Institute for Scientific Information Press, 1982.

Cross, Ruth C. *Indexing Books.* Cambridge, Mass.: Word Guild, 1980.

Cruse, L. "MIMI, the Map and Graphic Information Index to Major Microform Sets." *Microform Review* 15 (1986): 224-27.

Cutler, A. G. *Indexing Methods and Theory.* Baltimore: Williams & Wilkins, 1970.

Cutter, Charles Ammi. *Rules for a Dictionary Catalog.* 4th edition. Washington, D.C.: Government Printing Office, 1904.

Daily, Jay E. "Classification and Categorization." In *Encyclopedia of Library and Information Science,* vol. 5. New York: Marcel Dekker, 1971, 43-66.

_____. "Filing." In *Encyclopedia of Library and Information Science,* vol. 8. New York: Marcel Dekker, 1972, 405-31.

Davidson, C., and S. Betrand-Gastaldy. "Improved Design of Graphic Displays in Thesauri through Technology and Ergonomics." *Journal of Documentation* 42 (1986): 225-51.

Davies, Roy, and Brian James. "Toward an Expert System for Cataloguing: Some Experiments Based on AACR2." *Program* 18 (1984): 283-97.

Debons, Anthony. "Concept Formation." In *Encyclopedia of Library and Information Science,* vol. 5. New York: Marcel Dekker, 1971, 586-92.

Defense Documentation Center. *Abstracting Scientific and Technical Reports of Defense-Sponsored RDT/E*. AD 667000. Alexandria, Va.: Defense Documentation Center, March 1968.

Dennis, G. W., and D. W. H. Sharp. *The Art of Summary*. London: Longmans, 1966.

Denno, D. "Indexing of Interdisciplinary Literature on Crime, Violence, and Mental Disorder." *Journal of Information Science* 13 (1987): 117-22.

Diodato, Virgil P. "Tables of Contents and Book Indexes: How Well Do They Match Readers' Descriptions of Books?" *Library Resources and Technical Services* 30 (1986): 402-12.

Diodato, Virgil P., and Karen Person. "Source Indexing in Science Journals and Indexing Services: A Survey of Current Practices." *Science and Technology Libraries* 6 (1985-86): 103-18.

Directory of Fee-Based Information Services. Houston: Burwell Enterprises, 1985.

Dobb, Sue A., and Ann M. Sandberg-Fox. *Cataloging Microcomputer Files*. Chicago: American Library Association, 1985.

Doszkoes, James E. "CITE: NLM: Natural-Language Searching in an Online Catalog." *Information Technology and Libraries* 2 (1983): 364-80.

Doyle, Lauren B. "Indexing and Abstracting by Association." *American Documentation* 13 (October 1962): 378-90.

Dronberger, G. B., and G. T. Kowitz. "Abstracting Readability as a Factor in Information Systems." *Journal of the American Society for Information Science* 26 (March 1975): 108-11.

Dubois, C. P. R. "Free Text vs. Controlled Vocabulary: A Reassessment." *Online Review* 11 (August 1987): 243-53.

Dykstra, Mary. *PRECIS: A Primer*. Metuchen, N.J.: Scarecrow Press, 1987.

Dym, Eleanor D., ed. *Subject and Information Analysis*. New York: Marcel Dekker, 1985.

Earl, L. L. *Automatic Informative Abstracting and Indexing, Part I*. Palo Alto, Calif.: Lockheed Missile and Space Company, 1973.

East, H. *Designing and Marketing Databases*. London: British Library, 1986.

Elliot, J. E. "Making and Evaluating an Index." *Subscription Books Bulletin* 4 (1933): 33-36.

Elvin, P. J. "Making Better KWOC Indexes Even Better." *The Electronic Library* 4 (1986): 282-89.

EMBASE plus: The Excerpta Medica Database. New York: Elsevier Science, 1988.

Enser, P. G. B. "Automatic Classification of Book Material Represented by Back-of-the-Book Index." *Journal of Documentation* 41 (September 1985): 135-55.

Fagan, Joel. "The Effectiveness of a Non-syntactic Approach to Automatic Phrase Indexing for Document Retrieval." *Journal of the American Society for Information Science* 50, no. 2 (1989): 115-32.

Fay, Catherine H. "Off-site Indexing: A Cottage Industry." *Information Services and Use* 4 (1984): 299-304.

Feinberg, Hilda, ed. *Indexing Specialized Formats and Subjects*. Metuchen, N.J.: Scarecrow Press, 1983.

Fetters, Linda K. *A Guide to Indexing Software*. 2nd ed. Washington, D.C.: American Society of Indexers, 1987.

_____. "A Guide to Seven Indexing Programs ... Plus a Review of the 'Professional Bibliographic System.' " *Database* 8 (December 1985): 31-38.

_____. "INDEXIT: An Economical but Limited Indexing Program." *Database* 9 (October 1986): 54-56.

_____. "Progress in Indexing Software." *Online* (1988): 116-23.

Fidel, Raya. "The Possible Affect of Abstracting Guidelines on Retrieval Performances of Free-text Searching." *Information Process Manager* 22 (1986): 309-16.

_____. "Writing Abstracts for Free-text Searching." *Journal of Documentation* 42 (March 1986): 11-21.

Foskett, Antony C. *The Subject Approach to Information*. 4th ed. London: Clive Bingley, 1982.

Foskett, Douglas J. *Classification and Indexing in the Social Sciences*. London: Butterworth, 1963.

_____. "Thesaurus." In *Encyclopedia of Library and Information Science*, vol. 30. New York: Marcel Dekker, 1980, 270-314.

Gardner, Richard K., ed. *Education of Library and Information Professionals: Present and Future Prospects*. Littleton, Colo.: Libraries Unlimited, 1987.

Garfield, Eugene. *Citation Indexing—Its Theory and Application in Science, Technology, and Humanities.* New York: Wiley, 1979.

Gaudreault, C. "Indexing Software versus General Database Management Systems for Vertical File Management and Access." *IASC/SCAD Bulletin* 9 (1987): 4-5.

Gibb, Forbes, ed. "Expert Systems in Libraries." In *Proceedings of a Conference of the Library Association Information Technology Group and the Library and Information Research Group.* November 1985. London: Taylor Graham, 1986.

Gibson, John. "When Is an Index Not an Index?" *Local Historian* 17 (1981): 281-84, 290-94.

_____. "The Indexing of Medical Books and Journals." *The Indexer* 13 (April 1983): 173-75.

Goffman, William. "An Indirect Method of Information Retrieval." *Information Storage and Retrieval* 4, no. 4 (December 1968): 361-73.

_____. "On Relevance as a Measure." *Information Storage and Retrieval* 2 (February 1964): 201.

Grieg, Peter, comp. *The Indexer as Entrepreneur: A Selective Guide for Freelance Indexing and Indexers.* Ottawa: Indexing and Abstracting Society of Canada, 1985.

Greiner, Gotz. "Some Reflections on Teaching Subject Analysis in the Field of Documentation." *International Classification* 11 (1984): 66-68.

Grodsky, Susan J. "Indexing Technical Communications: What, When, and How." *Technical Communication* 32 (Second Quarter 1985): 26, 28-30.

Grunberger, M. W. *Textual Analysis and the Assignment of Index Entries for Social Science and Humanities Monographs.* New Brunswick, N.J.: Rutgers University, 1985. (Ph.D. dissertation)

Grycz, Czeslaw Jan. "The Seven Steps to Desktop Publishing." *Scholarly Publishing* (July 1987): 254-62.

Gull, C. D. "Historical Note: Information Science and Technology: From Co-ordinate Indexing to the Global Brain." *Journal of the American Society for Information Science* 38 (1987): 338-66.

Guy, R. F., and T. P. Cairnes. "The Production of Printed Subject Indexes by Microcomputer." *Electronic Libraries* 3 (December 1985): 346-50.

Hall, Deanna Morrow. "Writing Abstracts: The American National Standard." *Bulletin of the American Society for Information Science* 13 (October-November 1986): 35.

Hall, J. L. "Abstracting, Indexing, and Online Services." In *Information Sources in Physics*, 2nd ed. London: Butterworth, 1985, 55-73.

Hardy, Paul. "Computer-aided Indexing of Technical Manuals." *The Indexer* 15 (1986): 22-24.

Harris, K. "Indexing a Special Visual Image Collection." *Catalogue and Index* 83 (1986): 6-8.

Harter, S. P. "Detrimental Effects of Searching with Pre-coordinated Terms." *Online Review* 12 (1988): 309-28.

Hartley, James, Lindsey Davies, and Peter Burnhill. "Alphabetization in Indexes: Experimental Studies." *The Indexer* 12 (April 1981): 149-53.

Hess, Dann. *Fast Facts on Online: Search Strategies for Finding Business Information.* Homewood, Ill.: Dow Jones-Irwin, 1986.

Hewison, Nancy. "Online Updates: A Column for Search Analysts." *Medical Reference Services Quarterly* 54 (1986): 47-59.

Hicks, Carol E., James E. Rush, and Suzanne M. Strong. "Content Analysis." In *Subject and Information Analysis*. New York: Marcel Dekker, 1985, 57-105.

Hines, Theodore C., and Lois Winkle. "Microcomputer-aided Production of Indexes." *Indexer* 11 (October 1979): 198-201.

――――. "The Use of Microcomputers in Indexing." In *Indexing Specialized Formats and Subjects*. Metuchen, N.J.: Scarecrow Press, 1983, 250-59.

Hodgson, Elizabeth. "Microcomputer Software for Indexing." *Library Software Review* 6 (March-April 1987): 74-79.

Huleatt, Richard S. "Online Use of Chemical Abstracts: A Primer for Beginning Chemical Searches." *Database* 2 (December 1979): 11-21.

Humphrey, Susanne M., and Nancy E. Miller. "Knowledge-based Indexing of the Medical Literature: The Indexing Aid Project." *Journal of the American Society for Information Science* 38 (March 1987): 184-96.

Humphrey, Susanne M., and Anil Kapoor. *The MedIndEx System: Research on Interactive Knowledge-based Indexing of the Medical Literature.* Washington, D.C.: National Library of Medicine, 1988.

Hurt, C. D. "Conceptual Citation Differences in Science, Technology, and Social Sciences Literature." *Information Processing and Management* 23 (1987): 1-6.

Intner, Sheila, and Richard Smiraglia, eds. *Policy and Practice in Bibliographic Control of Nonbook Media.* Chicago: American Library Association, 1987.

Ireland, Norma Olin. "Indexes and Indexing." In *The Encyclopedia of Education*, vol. 4. New York: Macmillan, 1971, 562-68.

Jackson, E. B. "Indexing: A Review Essay." *Journal of Library History* 15 (1980): 320-25.

James, Barbara. "Indexing *The Times.*" *The Indexer* 11 (October 1979): 209-11.

Janke, Richard V. "Systems and Databases for Office and Home Use." In *Manual of Online Search Strategies.* Boston: G. K. Hall, 1988, 679-715.

Jillson, Willard Rouse. "The Indexing of Historical Materials." *The American Archivist* 16 (1953): 251-57.

Johansen, T. "Elements of the Non-linguistic Approach to Subject Relationships." *International Classification* 14 (1987): 11-18.

Jonassen, David. "Producing an Index with Your Microcomputer Database Manager." *Collegiate Microcomputer* 3 (November 1985): 375-81.

Johnson, L. C. "Archive Indexing." *The Indexer* 4 (1965): 97-108.

Jones, K. P. "Getting Started in Computerized Indexing." *The Indexer* 15 (1986): 9-12.

Judge, Peter, and Brenda Gerrie, eds. *Small Scale Bibliographic Databases.* Orlando, Fla.: Academic Press, 1986.

Kaske, Neal K., and Nancy P. Sander. "Online Subject Access: The Human Side of the Problem." *RQ* 20 (Fall 1980): 52-58.

Kaula, P. "Chain Indexing." *Herald of Library Science* 9 (1970): 318-25.

Kazlauskas, E. J., and T. D. Holt. "The Application of the Minicomputer to Thesaurus Construction." *Journal of the American Society for Information Science* 31 (September 1980): 363-68.

Kesselman, M., and I. Perry. "What Online Searchers Should Know about Indexing and What Indexers Should Know about Online Searching." In *Proceedings of the Fifth National Online Meeting.* Medford, N.J.: Learned Information, 1984, 141-48.

Kessler, M. M. "Bibliographic Coupling between Scientific Papers." *American Documentation* 14 (1963): 10-25.

_____. "Comparison of the Results of Bibliographic Coupling and Analytic Subject Indexing." *American Documentation* 16 (1965): 222-33.

Kim, Chai. "Retrieval Language of Social Sciences and Natural Sciences: A Statistical Investigation." *Journal of the American Society for Information Science* 33 (1982): 3-7.

Kim, H. *An Investigation of Automatic Term Weighting Techniques.* Cleveland: Case Western Reserve University, 1985. (Ph.D. dissertation)

Kleinbart, Paul. "Prolegomenon to 'Intelligent' Thesaurus Software." *Journal of Information Science* (1985): 45-53.

Knight, G. Norman. *Indexing, the Art of: A Guide to the Indexing of Books and Periodicals.* London: George Allen & Unwin, 1979.

Koch, Jean E. "Newspaper Indexing: Planning and Options." *Special Libraries* 76 (1985): 271-81.

LaBorie, Tim, Michael Halperin, and Howard D. White. "Library and Information Science Abstracting and Indexing Services: Coverage, Overlap, and Content." *Library and Information Science Research* 7 (1985): 183-95.

Lancaster, F. W. "Pertinence and Relevance." In *Encyclopedia of Library and Information Science*, vol. 22. New York: Marcel Dekker, 1977, 70-86.

_____. *Vocabulary Control for Information Retrieval.* 2nd ed. Arlington, Va.: Information Resources Press, 1986.

Landry, Bertrand C., and James E. Rush. "Automatic Indexing: Progress and Prospects." In *Subject and Information Analysis.* New York: Marcel Dekker, 1985, 198-239.

Langridge, D. W. *Classification and Indexing in the Humanities.* London: Butterworths, 1976.

Lennie, P. "Choosing a Computer for Indexing." *ASI Newsletter* 79-80 (1986-1987): 10-12.

Levitain, Karen B. "Information Resources as 'Goods' in the Life Cycle of Information Production." *Journal of the American Society for Information Science* 33 (January 1982): 44-54.

Library of Congress. *Library of Congress Filing Rules.* Prepared by John C. Rather and Susan C. Biebel. Processing Services. Washington, D.C.: Library of Congress, 1980.

Liebesny, Felix. *A State of the Art Survey of Automatic Indexing*. Paris: UNESCO, 1974.

Line, M. B. "Secondary Services in the Social Sciences: The Need for Improvement and the Role of Librarians." *Behavioral and Social Science Librarian* 1 (Summer 1980): 263-73.

Linehan, C. D. "Amateur Indexer and the Local Historian." *The Indexer* 12 (April 1981): 145-54.

Lowe, H. J., and G. O. Barnett. "MicroMeSH: A Microcomputer System for Searching and Exploring the National Library of Medicine's Medical Subject Headings(MeSH) Vocabulary." *Proceedings of the Eleventh Annual Symposium on Computer Applications in Medical Care*. Boston, Mass.: 1988 (publisher not given), 717-20.

Luhn, H. P. "The Automatic Creation of Literature Abstracts." *IBM Journal of Research and Development* 2 (April 1958): 159-65.

Lundeen, Gerald, and Carol Tenopir. "Microcomputer Software for Inhouse Databases ... Four Top Packages under $2,000." *Online* 9 (1985): 30-38.

Machlup, Fritz, and Una Mansfield. *The Study of Information: Interdisciplinary Messages*. New York: John Wiley, 1983.

Maeda, T., Yoshio Momouchi, and Hajime Sawamura. "Automatic Method for Abstracting Significant Phrases in Scientific or Technical Documents." *Information Processing and Management* 16 (1980): 119-27.

Maizell, Robert E., and Julian F. Smith. *Abstracting Scientific and Technical Literature*. New York: Wiley-Interscience, 1971.

Mandel, Carol A. *Multiple Thesauri in Online Library Bibliographic Systems: A Report Prepared for Library of Congress Processing Services*. Washington, D.C.: Cataloging Distribution Service, Library of Congress, 1987.

Maniez, J. "Relationship in Thesauri: Some Critical Remarks." *International Classification* 15, no. 15 (1988): 133-38.

Manzer, Bruce M. *The Abstract Journal, 1979-1980: Origin, Development and Diffussion*. Metuchen, N.J.: Scarecrow Press, 1977.

Marcus, Richard S. "An Experimental Comparison of the Effectiveness of Computers and Humans as Search Intermediaries." *Journal of American Society for Information Science* 34 (November 1983): 381-404.

Markey, Karen, Pauline Atherton, and Claudia Newton. "An Analysis of Controlled Vocabulary and Free Text Search Statements in Online Searches." *Online Review* 4 (September 1980): 225-36.

Maron, M. E. "Depth of Indexing." *Journal of the American Society for Information Science* 30 (1979): 224-28.

———. "On Indexing, Retrieval and the Meaning of About." *Journal of the American Society for Information Science* 28 (1977): 38-43.

Mathis, Betty A., and James E. Rush. "Abstracting." In *Subject and Information Analysis*. New York: Marcel Dekker, 1985, 445-84.

Matthews, Joseph R., and Joan Frye Williams. "The User Friendly Index: A New Tool." *Online* 8 (May 1984): 31-34.

Matyn, J., and A. J. D. Flowerdew. *The Economics of Information*. London: British Library, 1983.

McTeigue, R. "Indexing Journal Articles Directly into the Classified Catalogue." *Library Association Record* 89 (1987): 402.

Metcalfe, John W. *Information Retrieval: British and American, 1876-1976*. Metuchen, N.J.: Scarecrow Press, 1976.

Meunier, J. G. S., S. Bertraud-Gastaldy, and H. Lebel. "A Call for Enhanced Representation of Content as a Means of Improving Online Full-text Retrieval." *International Classification* 14 (1987): 2-8.

Milstead, J. I. *Subject Access Systems: Alternatives in Design*. New York: Academic Press, 1984.

Mohlman, J. W. "Costs of an Abstraction Program." *Journal of Chemical Documentation* 1 (1961): 64-67.

Molesworth-Roberts, H. V. "Compiling a Book Index: Some Practical Hints." *Library World* 46 (1949): 103-5.

Moses, Paula B., and Lee E. Nelson. "Indexing and Abstracting Chemical Information: The View of Two Industrial Chemists." *Journal of Chemical Information and Computer Sciences* 24 (1984): 189-90.

Mutrux, Robin, and J. D. Anderson. "Contextual Indexing and Faceted Taxonomic Access System. *Drexel Library Quarterly* 19, no. 3 (1984): 91-109.

Naisbitt, John. *Megatrends*. New York: Warner Books, 1984.

National Academy of Sciences. Committee on Scientific and Technical Communication (SATCOM). *Scientific and Technical Communications: A Pressing National Problem and Recommendations for Its Solution*. Publication 1707. Washington, D.C.: National Academy of Sciences, 1969.

National Library of Medicine. "Online Indexing System." *NEWS* 43 (June-July 1988): 14.

Neufeld, M. Lynne. "Abstracting and Indexing Services." In *ALA Yearbook of Library and Information Services '85*, vol. 12. Chicago: American Library Association, 1985, 25-26.

Neufeld, M. Lynne, and Martha Cornog. "Abstracting and Indexing." In *New Options for Librarians: Finding a Job in a Related Field*. New York: Neal-Schuman, 1984, 204-26.

_____. *Abstracting and Indexing Career Guide*. 2nd ed. Philadelphia: NFAIS, 1986.

Neufeld, M. Lynne, Martha Cornog, and Inez L. Sperr, eds. *Abstracting and Indexing Services in Perspective: Miles Conrad Memorial Lectures, 1969-1983*. Arlington, Va.: Information Resources Press, 1983.

Nishida, F., S. Takamatsu, and Y. Fujita. "Semiautomatic Indexing of Structured Information of Text." *Journal of Chemical Information and Computer Sciences* 24 (1984): 15-20.

Norton, Tom. "Secondary Publications Have a Future in Libraries." *AsLib Proceedings* 36 (July-August 1984): 317-23.

Orna, Elizabeth. *Build Yourself a Thesaurus: A Step-by-Step Guide*. Norwich, U.K.: Running Angel, 1982.

Ornager, Susanne, and Johne Mogeni. "Changes in Thesaurus Construction Caused by the Use of Boolean Searching." In *Proceedings of the 7th International Online Information Meeting*. London, December 6-8, 1983. Medford, N.J.: Information Inc., 1983, 167-73.

Paice, Chris. "Expert Systems for Information Retrieval?" *AsLib Proceedings* 38 (October 1986): 343-435.

Pao, Miranda L. "Automatic Text Analysis Based on Transition Phenomena of Word Occurrences." *Journal of the American Society for Information Science* 29 (1978): 121-24.

_____. *Concepts of Information Retrieval*. Englewood, Colo.: Libraries Unlimited, 1989.

Pennix, G. B. "Indexing Concepts: An Overview for Record Managers." *Records Management Quarterly* 18 (April 1984): 5-9.

Perez, Ernest. "Text Enhancement: Controlled Vocabulary vs. Free Text." *Special Libraries* 73 (July 1982): 183-92.

Polisskaya, O. B. "Improving the Content Structure of Abstracts on the Basis of Queries from Workers in New Technology." *Scientific and Technical Information Processing* 12 (1985): 16-27.

Pollard, Richard. "Microcomputer Database Management Systems for Bibliographic Data." *The Electronic Library* 4 (August 1986): 230-41.

Pratt, Allan D. *INDEXIT: A Microcomputer Indexing Program and Manual.* New Haven, Conn.: Graham Conley Press, 1986.

Problems in Bibliographic Access to Non-print Materials: Final Report. Washington, D.C.: National Commission on Libraries and Information Science, 1979.

Pruett, Nancy Jones. *Scientific and Technical Libraries, Vol. 2: Special Formats and Subject Areas.* New York: Academic Press, 1986.

Qureshi, Naimuddin. "Standards for Libraries." In *Encyclopedia of Library and Information Science.* vol. 28. New York: Marcel Dekker, 1980, 470-99.

Rada, Roy. "Connecting and Evaluating Thesauri: Issues and Cases." *International Classification* 14 (1987): 63-68.

Rada, Roy, Hafedh Mili, Gary Letourneau, and Doug Johnston. "Creating and Evaluating Entry Terms." *Journal of Documentation* 44, no. 1. (March 1988): 19-41.

Radecki, Tadeusz. "Similarity Measures for Boolean Search Request Formulation." *Journal of the American Society for Information Science* 33 (January 1982): 8-17.

_____. "Trends in Research on Information Retrieval—the Potential for Improvements in Conventional Boolean Retrieval Systems." *Information Processing and Management* 24, no. 3 (1988): 219-27.

Rapp, B. *A Comparison of Document Clusters Derived from Co-cited Reference and Co-assigned Index Terms.* Philadelphia: Drexel University, 1985.

Ratteray, O. M. T. "Expanding Roles for Summarized Information." *Written Communication* 2 (1985): 457-72.

Regazzi, J. J. "Evaluating Indexing Systems: A Review after Cranfield." *The Indexer* 12 (1980): 14-21.

_____. "The Silver Disk WILSONDISC: WILSONLINE on CD-ROM." *Database* 9 (1986): 73-74.

Repo, Aatto J. "The Value of Information: Approaches in Economics, Accounting, and Management Science." *Journal of the American Society for Information Science* 40, no. 2 (1989): 68-85.

Richmond, Phyllis A. *Introduction to PRECIS for North American Usage.* Littleton, Colo.: Libraries Unlimited, 1981.

Roberts, N. "The Prehistory of the Information Retrieval Thesaurus." *Journal of Documentation* 40 (1984): 271-85.

Rowlett, Russell J. "Abstracts and Other Information Filters." *Journal of Chemical Information and Computer Sciences* 25 (1985): 159-63.

_____. "An Interpretation of Chemical Abstracts Service Indexing Policies." *Journal of Chemical Information and Computer Sciences* 24 (1984): 152-54.

_____. "Perspectives on Editorial Operations of Chemical Abstracts Service." *Journal of Chemical Information and Computer Sciences* 25 (1985): 61-64.

Rowley, Jennifer E. *Abstracting and Indexing.* 2nd ed. London: Bingley, 1988.

Salton, Gerard. "Automatic Indexing Using Bibliographic Citation." *Journal of Documentation* 27 (June 1971): 98-110.

_____. "Automatic Text Analysis." *Science* (April 17, 1970): 168.

_____. "A Comparison between Manual and Automatic Indexing Methods." *American Documentation* 20 (January 1969): 61-71.

_____. *Dynamic Information and Library Processing.* Englewood Cliffs, N.J.: Prentice-Hall, 1975.

_____. *A Theory of Indexing.* Philadelphia: Society for Industrial and Applied Mathematics, 1975.

Salton, Gerard, and Christopher Buckley. "Term-weighting Approaches in Automatic Text Retrieval." *Information Processing and Management* 24 (1988): 513-23.

Salton, Gerard, and M. J. Mcgill. *Introduction to Modern Information Retrieval.* New York: McGraw-Hill, 1983.

Schabas, Ann H. "Postcoordinate Retrieval: A Comparison of Two Indexing Languages." *Journal of the American Society for Information Science* 33 (January 1982): 32-43.

Schelling, H. "Patterns Indexing: An Attempt at Combining Standardized and Free Indexing." *International Classification* 11 (1984): 128-32.

Schultz, Claire K. *Thesaurus of Information Science Terminology.* Hamden, Conn.: Shoe String Press, 1978.

Schultz, Claire K., Wallace L. Schultz, and Richard H. Orr. "Comparative Indexing: Terms Supplied by Biomedical Authors and by Document Titles." *American Documentation* 16 (October 1965): 299-312.

Schwartz, C., and L. M. Eisenmann. "Subject Analysis." In *Annual Review of Information Science and Technology, vol. 21.* White Plains, N.Y.: Knowledge Industry Publications, 1986.

Shannon, Claude E., and Warren Weaver. *The Mathematical Theory of Communication.* Urbana: The University of Illinois, 1949.

Sholtys, Pauline M. "Adapting Library of Congress Subject Headings for Newspaper Indexing." *Cataloging and Classification Quarterly* 4 (Summer 1984): 99-102.

Simpkins, Jean. "Assessing Indexes." *The Indexer* 14 (1985): 179-80.

_____. "Indexing Loose-leaf Publications." *The Indexer* 14 (October 1985): 259-60.

Small, Henry. "Co-citation Context Analysis and the Structure of Paradigms." *Journal of Documentation* 36 (September 1980): 183-96.

Smith, Linda C. "Artificial Intelligence and Information Retrieval." In *Annual Review of Information Science and Technology,* vol. 22. New York: Elsevier Science Publishers, 1987, 41-73.

Smith, Linda C., and A. J. Warner. "A Taxonomy of Representations in Information Retrieval System Design." *Journal of Information Science* 8 (1984): 113-21.

Smith, R. "Compensations of Indexing." *The Indexer* 12 (April 1981): 141.

"Society of Indexers' Conference: Indexers in a World of Change." *The Indexer* 12 (1980): 57-61.

Soergel, D. *Indexing Languages and Thesauri: Construction and Maintenance.* Los Angeles: Melville Publishing, 1974.

_____. *Organizing Information: Principles of Data Base and Retrieval Systems.* Orlando, Fla.: Academic Press, 1988.

Sparck-Jones, Karen. "Some Thesauric History." *AsLib Proceedings* 24 (July 1972): 408-11.

Stephens, A. "Abstracting and Indexing Services Produced in the UK." *Journal of Information Science* 13 (1987): 317-19.

Stirk, Jean. "User Approaches to Indexes." *The Indexer* 16, no. 2 (1986): 75-78.

Stobaugh, Robert E., David W. Weisgerber, and Ronald L. Wigington. "Indexes and Abstracts—What Lies Ahead." In *Serials Management in an Automated Age: Proceedings of the First Annual Serials Conference.* Arlington, Va., October 30-31, 1981. Edited by N. J. Melin. Westport, Conn.: Meckler Publishing, 1982, 53-72.

Svenonius, Elaine F. "Directions for Research in Indexing, Classification, and Cataloging." *Library Resources and Technical Services* 25 (1981): 88-103.

_____. "The Effect of Indexing Specificity on Retrieval Performance." Ph.D. dissertation, University of Chicago, 1971. (ED 051 863)

_____. "Unanswered Questions in the Design of Controlled Vocabularies." *Journal of the American Society for Information Science* 37 (September 1986): 331-40.

_____. "Use of Classification in Online Retrieval." *Library Resources and Technical Services* 27 (January/March 1983): 76-80.

Swanson, D. R. "The Evidence Underlying the Cranfield Results." *The Library Quarterly* 35 (1965): 1-20.

_____. "Information Processing, Indexes and Indexing." In *Encyclopaedia Britannica Macropaedia*, vol. 9. Chicago: Encyclopaedia Britannica, 1978, 567-74.

Taylor, R. S. "Value-added Processes in Document-based Systems: Abstracting and Indexing Services." *Information Services and Use* 4 (1984): 127-46.

Tenopir, Carol. "Searching by Controlled Vocabulary or Free Text?" *Library Journal* (November 15, 1987): 58-59.

Thesaurus Guide: Analytical Directory of Selected Vocabularies for Information Retrieval. Amsterdam: North-Holland, 1985.

"Thesaurus Construction and Format." In *Thesaurus of ERIC Descriptors*, 11th ed. Edited by James Houston. Washington, D.C.: Educational Research Information Center, Bureau of Research, 1987, xxi-xxvi.

Tomaselli, Mary F. "Microcomputer-based Indexing and Abstracting." *The Indexer* 14 (April 1984): 30-34.

Tousignaut, D. "Indexing: Old Methods, New Concepts." *The Indexer* 15 (1987): 197-204.

Townley, Helen M. *Thesaurus-making: Grow Your Own Word-Stock.* London: Andre Deutsch, 1980.

Urquhart, D. J. "The Distribution and Use of Scientific and Technical Information." *The Royal Society Information Conference* (1948): 408-19.

U.S. Congress. Senate. Committee on Government Operations. *Documentation, Indexing, and Retrieval of Scientific Information.* Washington, D.C.: GPO, 1960.

U.S. President's Science Advisory Committee. *Science, Government, and Information: The Responsibilities of the Technical Community and the Government in the Transfer of Information.* Washington, D.C.: The White House, 1963.

Van Rijsbergen, C. J., D. J. Harper, and M. F. Porter. "Selection of Good Search Terms." *Information Processing and Management* 17 (1981): 77-91.

Vickery, B. C. "Analysis of Information." In *Encyclopedia of Library and Information Science,* vol. 1. New York: Marcel Dekker, 1968, 355-84.

_____. *Classification and Indexing in Science.* 3rd ed. London: Butterworths, 1975.

Vleduts-Stokolov, N. "Concept Recognition in an Automatic Text-processing System for the Life Sciences." *Journal of the American Society for Information Science* 38 (1987): 269-87.

Wall, R. A. "Intelligent Indexing and Retrieval: A Man-Machine Partnership." *Information Processing and Management* 16 (1980): 73-90.

Wallis, Elizabeth. "The Business Side of Indexing." *The Indexer* 15 (October 1987): 205-9.

Waters, Samuel. "Answerman, the Expert Information Specialist: An Expert System for Retrieval of Information from Library Reference Books." *Information Technology and Libraries* 7 (September 1986): 205-11.

Weber, A. C. *A Guide to Freelance Indexing.* American Society of Indexers, 1988.

Weil, B. A., I. Zarember, and H. Owen. "Technical Abstracting Fundamentals." *Journal of Chemical Documentation* 3 (1963): 86-89, 125-36.

Weinberg, Bella Hass. "Why Indexing Fails the Researcher." *The Indexer* 16 (April 1988): 3-5.

_____. *Word Frequency and Automatic Indexing.* New York: School of Library Service, Columbia University, 1981. (Ph.D. dissertation)

Wellisch, Hans H. "The ALA Filing Rules: Flowcharts, Illustrating Their Application, with a Critique and Suggestions for Improvement." *Journal of the American Society for Information Science* 34 (1983): 313-30.

_____. "Flow Chart for Indexing with a Thesaurus." *Journal of the American Society for Information Science* 23 (1972): 185-94.

_____. *Indexing: A Basic Reading List*. Washington, D.C.: American Society of Indexers, 1987.

_____. "Indexing and Abstracting: A Current-Awareness Bibliography." *The Indexer* 15 (April 1986): 29-36.

_____. "Indexing and Abstracting: A Current-Awareness Bibliography. Part 2." *The Indexer* 15 (October 1986): 95-98.

_____. "Indexing and Abstracting: A Current-Awareness Bibliography. Part 5." *The Indexer* 16 (April 1988): 33-39.

_____. *Indexing and Abstracting: A Guide to International Sources*. Santa Barbara, Calif.: Clio Press, 1980.

_____. *Indexing and Abstracting: An International Bibliography*. Santa Barbara, Calif.: ABC-Clio Information Services, 1984.

_____. "Some Vital Statistics in Abstracting and Indexing." *International Classification* 7 (November 1980): 135-39.

_____. "Vital Statistics on Abstracting and Indexing Revisited." *International Classification* 12 (1985): 11-16.

Wheatley, Henry. *What Is an Index? A Few Notes on Indexes and Indexers*. 2nd ed. London: Society of Indexers, 1879.

White, Howard D., and Belver C. Griffith. "Quality of Indexing in Online Databases." *Information Processing and Management* 13 (1987): 211-24.

Wiberley, Stephen. "Names in Space and Time: The Indexing Vocabulary of the Humanities." *The Library Quarterly* 58, no. 1 (1988): 1-29.

Witty, Francis J. "The Beginnings of Indexing and Abstracting: Some Notes toward a History of Indexing and Abstracting in Antiquity and the Middle Ages." *The Indexer* 8 (1973): 193-98.

_____. "Early Indexing Techniques: A Study of Several Book Indexes of the Fourteenth, Fifteenth, and Early Sixteenth Centuries." *The Library Quarterly* 35 (1966): 141-48.

Wood, James L. "The National Information Standards Organization." In *Encyclopedia of Library and Information Science*, vol. 39. New York: Marcel Dekker, 1985, 291-332.

Wood, N. W. "Abstracts and Their Indexes — Style, Presentation, and Uses." *AsLib Proceedings* 18 (1966): 160-66.

Wynar, Bohdan S. "Filling." In *Introduction to Cataloging and Classification*. 7th ed. By Arlene G. Taylor. Littleton, Colo.: Libraries Unlimited, 1985.

Yuexiao, Zhang. "Definitions and Sciences of Information." *Information Processing and Management* 24, no. 4 (1980): 479-91.

Index